What other readers have remarked...

"Your first book communicates with all senses..."
— *Pat Royce, Author,* Royce's Sailing Illustrated

"...an antidote to the Six O'clock News"
—*Andy H., Boston, MA*

"A truly great read. One of the best cruising tales I've come across."
—*Doug M., Santa Cruz, CA*

"Thanks ... for giving me something more than a 'nice house with a white fence and a lawn to mow once a week' to look forward to."
—*Jon H., DePere, WI*

"Never before has a book given me so many chills down my spine because I felt exactly what you were talking about."
—*Gretchen S., Meriden, CT*

"Your narative has given me an inspiration to pursue a life outside of modern day hustle and bustle... to really enjoy what life and nature has to offer."
—*Chad H., Farmville, VA*

"It has been an imaginary haven for me to come home and read a chapter after toiling at my daily job..."
—*Denny E., Phoenix, AZ*

"I started last evening and could not put it down."
—*Anthoy Y., Winston-Salem, NC*

"Reading your story was a great way to escape the rat race."
—*Hans M., University of Colorado*

"Thanks ... for sharing your extraordinary experience and your philosophy for living... I felt as if I was on board Querencia with you."
—*Bob H., Bowling Green State University*

"The power of the ocean, and our own timidity are clearly conveyed."
—*Marcos G., Argentina*

"What a wonderful book! I sat in the sun over the weekend and read the whole thing... your words give me new strength to continue my battle against the norm."
—*Pete E., Prague*

"...my husband drives and I read... We have long discussions about all sorts of things you talk about... we feel like we are there with you."
—*Melinda S., Crown Point, IN*

"...a very well written story... gave me that extra encouragement to say to myself, 'See? It is possible to live your dreams.'"
—*Dwight P, Atlanta, GA*

"Your chronicles have brought me to laughter and brought me to tears."
—*Wanda M., San Francisco, CA*

"...you express, ...very eloquently, the feeling of oneness with nature and the fragility of our lovely little planet."
—*Vasilis R., Greece*

SAILING
THE
DREAM

Library of Congress #TXu 775-043

Printed in the United States of America.
ISBN 1-929317-99-9

Mention of any third party is for informational purposes only, and
constitutes neither an endorsement nor a recommendation. For more
information contact Coconut Info, not a third party, regarding
this publication.

Portions of this book previously appeared on the World Wide Web.
Polynesian type set by Coconut Info.

Cover photo photographer: Gus Konchar

Published by
COCONUT INFO
P.O. Box 75460
Honolulu, HI 96836

SAILING
THE
DREAM

An Autobiographical Odyssey

The Querencia Chronicles

John F. McGrady

Dedication

To Kyle McGrady, my father's uncle. Kyle was known as the "Hell's Canyon Mailman" in the 1930s and 40s as skipper of the riverboat *Florence*. Before the damming of the Snake River in Idaho, residents up-river in Hell's Canyon depended on Kyle to deliver their families, their livestock, and their mail safely through the treacherous rapids. The *Florence* was their only link to the outside world. Kyle's spirit of adventure, his courage, and his resolve, even after great personal sacrifice, I found an inspiration.

Contents

Acknowledgments   ix
Prologue   xi
1. Born to Choose   1
2. Storm at Sea   31
3. Cruising   61
4. California Dreaming   87
5. The Crossing   111
6. South Pacific   143
7. Bora Bora   181
8. The Private Sea   247
9. Hawai'i   287
10. Letting Go   319

Glossary   355
Index   363

Acknowledgments

Not all of the people that helped make *Sailing the Dream* become a reality are named here, but I thank them:

— My father, Gale Charles (Mac) McGrady, for teaching me about the great outdoors, as well as determination and the rewards of developing mechanical skills.

— Ken Osborne for reading the original manuscript and for his suggestions.

— Jim Higman, for first teaching me how to sail, and more importantly, teaching me boating and the fine art of jury rigging.

— My wife Davey for her relief and our children, Paul, Caroline, and Rain for their patient understanding.

Prologue

Most people would not cruise on a thirty-foot boat. Probably the best reason "not to" is because you will be forced to face the unknown. You will meet challenges that you may not be able to solve with the skills you have already learned. You may only overcome some circumstances with ingenuity, perseverance, and luck.

There are other reasons I have heard to not go cruising: it is not practical, it seems like an ambiguous goal, your family would consider it frivolous, it is not the answer you're looking for, it is not logical.

All these reasons are subjective arguments that not only keep people from taking a risk and sailing around the world but also might keep them from having a creative life no matter what they might do! You don't have to be a radical to believe that some changes could be made in your schedule of events that would enrich your life; yet, many people abandon the responsibility to accomplish innovative and creative new concepts with their lives. Are they stuck?

You don't have to sail across an ocean to change your life. You might go on any adventure, even if the adventure is flying first-class to a palatial resort with room service. Treat your self. Unless the good Lord takes you quickly, someday you and your physicians will be trying to plot your escape from the unforeseen disease or accident that is inevitable for every corpus sanctum. As a mortal this is guaranteed. And at that moment all your opportunities will be behind you.

Cruising the ocean highways is a glorious, challenging adventure. It is an amazing thing that we now have thirty-foot boats circling the globe! Less than 500 years ago the European people trembled at the thought of going into the "great void." Even just a hundred years ago only a handful of sailing ships would sail the coasts, and they were huge clipper ships! Today, despite talk of coastal traffic and possible collisions at sea, the truth of the matter is that once you are even just five miles off the continental U.S.A., you are five miles from 300 million people and you are alone. If you are out fifty miles or so you might only see a few other boats in a week and they are likely to be freighters. At a distance of a thousand or more miles from land your perceptions of yourself and your journey become a very singular experience. You find yourself totally free of any social pretensions or calculations.

If I had my way these bold and courageous people who are called "cruisers" would get a parade at each port! A cruiser who sailed his Valiant 40, *Carina*, into San Francisco the night before we arrived with *Querencia* said to me, "You'd have thought we would get a medal when we finally passed under the Golden Gate bridge!" Both *Carina* and *Querencia* had experienced horrendous seas and odd weather coming down from Canada. It isn't always a luxurious picnic amongst the lily pads out there. But it is glorious! It is an exceptional mixture of discipline and high flying freedom, somewhat risky yet predictably divine.

The sea drowns all worry. You say things to each other like "Will I die?" and "When do we eat?" almost in the same breath.

Is it a curious blend of godliness and hedonism that keeps a sailor longing for the sea after he has gone back to life on land? Is it the smell of the ocean breeze? The sailor, after all, lives and breathes the weather. The weather is the topic of every prayer and every cocktail hour. The sailor stands in awe of the weather and respects its mystery for it determines many of his actions.

Pick a night, not just any night but one when you feel slightly insecure — one when you feel the lonely darkness of the soul. Now add twenty-five knots of wind and a bit of a nip in the air. Take away all your familiar surroundings including the ground you stand on and replace them with a wonderful boat about the size of a small room.

Now add motion, lots of it: up and down, left and right, pitch, yaw, and roll. Add one empty stomach. You appreciate your empty stomach because at times the waves seem as high as the mast.

In the pitch black night you can see the white froth curl around the rail of the boat. The roar of the ocean and the howl of the wind are all you can hear. You stand in your rain gear, hanging on to your flashlight. The sweat beads up on your forehead, and the heat being generated underneath your hat makes you uncomfortable.

You are thankful for your crew, your family, people you love and cherish that can keep you company. Only now they are not with you in the cockpit because it is your night-watch, not theirs. You hope that they are okay, that they are sleeping restfully and will be ready when they are called.

You only have a general feeling of knowing where you are — at least until daylight. Then you'll catch up on your navigational chores. You only hope that the those jet-black clouds on the horizon won't turn this sprinkle of rain into a downpour of hail and even more wind. You're not in the mood for things to start crashing around any more than they are.

Good sailors, however, rarely complain of the weather, at least not too loudly because they depend on the weather to get them where they're going. It's also true that more often than not the hail, the thunder, the crashing storm, never come. Instead, when the sun rises the ocean is peaceful, like a large lake with a gentle breeze blowing across it. The sailor may feel exhausted and aching from an uncomfortable eight hours, but that passes just as the blackness of the night does. His boat heads in towards shore — a tropical paradise where he finds freedom among giant palms, white sand, warm water, and balmy weather. The life of a sailor is a special life of rapture — one that is hard to explain.

When you live on the ocean you become the ocean. It will take you away from not only man's busy civilization, but from the solid ground on which you stand. Then it will consume you totally; so totally, that land will only be a memory. It is probably true to say that it is more than a little helpful if you truly do love the ocean before you begin your journey; for when you sail across Earth's huge waters you will be feeling out reality itself instead of ideas and opinions about it.

I do remember once at night in a bit of a blow going below decks and turning on the saloon lights and suddenly being struck by the absurdity of the motion of the saloon, tossing this way and that, every which way, like a living room thrown into a clothes dryer. It struck me, the uniqueness of that living room in which I was standing.

The profound sense of *now* creeps in along your watercourse way, everything that you hear, see, feel, and smell reminds you of the natural world outside you. There is no way of deviating or separating yourself from your experience. On land you may imagine that you are outside or separate from nature and the universe. At sea you recognize, rather, your explicit innate existence, and see your imagination as just another facet of your self. You learn that inside your self there is another universe as well. One that also has sequences and weather that seemingly vibrate of their own accord. You learn hope because it is the hope of seeing the sun rise that enables you to make it through the night. You learn faith because you witness yourself having faith that the guiding star will return when the clouds move away. You learn that hard work, creativity, and laughter make you happy. You learn to love life. You understand that your love of life is a very real thing. Just possibly most of all, you learn that the world is truly cyclic and that by seeing and choosing alternatives you are protected from a humdrum existence. I learned this at sea; I'm sure all adventurers feel it. Adventure delivers us from the tedious sameness that tends to trap modern man.

I must admit right here that I am by no means such a sailor as, Chichester, Slocum, Hiscock and very many other sailors who have spent their time on the rolling heap. But I do believe that I understand the basic principles of sailing as thoroughly as most sailors and that I understand some principles of science, medicine, and humanity that many do not. I must also confess I am a romantic.

Many of us view life as if from above through a big magnifying glass. This view misses everyday features of existence. It seems to me that it is the higher nature of man to see himself as an immortal who has control of everything that happens to him.

My hope is that this book will show that "getting back to reality" means what it must have meant originally, to get back to living in a world of mystery and surprise, rather than in the eternal boredom many of us would like to think we have successfully manipulated with our lives.

Sailing has taught me and my family wholeness for in itself sailing is a whole art. As often with life, it requires you to keep wind in your sails while moving in a different direction. Trusting your self is very similar to trusting your boat and your work and your community. Each of us is truly sailing across the universe. There is nowhere else to be.

There are two options in a person's life — reflection and action. One is an opportunity to think about it, the other an opportunity to live it.

What follows is just a wonderful true story about all this. The story wouldn't have been possible if it weren't for a thousand incarnate souls who shared their lives, and for those hundreds of authors who have left their indelible marks upon me.

Aloha kākou,

Dr. John F. McGrady

Part I
Born to Choose

1.

My stint as a young professional on Vashon Island was nearing its end. Our breaking-in years with *Querencia* were over. Davey and I had adjusted to living aboard and had stuffed our yar little ship to the gills with our most necessary possessions. Now as we awaited news of the sale of our businesses, a home, and our automobiles, we practiced our celestial navigation.

This time using our sextant I calculated our position to be in New Mexico. We were actually in La Jolla, California.

We both stared at the rows of figures scratched on worksheets in front of us. Then we switched our gaze to our German sextant gleaming in the sun. "I don't get it. We must be doing something wrong by not entering that first figure."

That first figure to be entered on the list was our current position, or where we believed we were, known in sailing as your D.R. (dead reckoning) position. We were supposed to calculate where we were exactly on the globe using this position as a baseline and attacking it with mathematical formulas derived from our sextant. And yet, wasn't our current position precisely what we were trying to figure out? It seemed like a "Catch-22." I kept applying the formulae but mistakenly ignored the nonsensical first figure, the request for our current position.

Finally Davey suggested we make-believe we were in Malibu and plug that latitude and longitude in for our DR. Suddenly it started to make sense! That was how we began to understand celestial navigation. The sextant and math enabled us to see that we weren't in Malibu. We were on a line 110 miles southeast of there.

There is a parallel between navigating through life and navigating a boat. This was one of the basic truths we would learn sailing the next ten-thousand miles. Knowing the inner-meaning of life and knowing where you are both depend on your belief system. It's a Zen trick. The answer lies hidden inside what you think you know rather than what you know. You can't begin to figure out who you are without first knowing the answer. It doesn't matter if you're right or wrong; what matters is that you have a belief system to work with, from which you can *deduce* your answers. That is how the universe works.

We enjoyed La Jolla. We had gotten into the habit of stealing away to California whenever we could, and La Jolla was our favorite spot. It was in California that we first really started dreaming of palm trees and far away beaches with white sand. California is a whole lot more "tropical" than the Pacific Northwest. It was in California that we had boarded a plane two years before for a vacation to Bora Bora; and that is when we made the decision to return in our 30-foot *Querencia*, the yacht that we kept in Puget Sound. We had even visualized where we might anchor her when we arrived after a 5,000 mile sail.

This trip to La Jolla was more than just another vacation. We spent our days driving to all the marinas — Oceanside, Shelter Island, Coronado, Mission Bay. We absorbed everything we could and pictured our arrival next year. We went to all the marine stores and feasted on the wide range of equipment for cruisers. We also adopted a parrot: a tame and beautiful Amazon named Coco. We decided to add her to our family on first sight.

With our charts and books and Coco in a mailbox under my airline seat, we flew back to Seattle. We had moved aboard *Querencia* the week before we left and we were very eager to get back on board and begin outfitting for the adventure of our lifetimes.

2.

Dad and I

Sailing away was actually not a new idea; adventure and exploration had been my daydreams since I was a child. I suppose in the back of my mind I had always planned to do something more with my life than strive for material wealth and excellence in career. These were important to me, though, and I had planned on attaining them first. Once I had, I realized it was time to do that "something more."

By my mid-thirties, I had started more than one family. I had two businesses, a wonderful home, cars, a motorcycle, a computer, a garden, and a yacht. I traveled two to four times a year and had enough friends and money. I survived divorce proceedings. Then my dad died. I watched my beloved father die an agonizing death as a young man of fifty-four. He was from Virginia and loved the great outdoors and taught me hunting and fishing and tromping in the woods. A well-loved man from a family of eight, (both parents died before he was sixteen), he had started with nothing and had become a success at home and at work. He anticipated retirement. He was perfect for it. Standing by his bedside at the moment of his death I re-evaluated my values in life. Maybe I should say "our" values. My dad said some pretty strange things while he suffered on to his final hour, delirious with pain. He wanted to give back or get rid of all the trophies he'd struggled to attain — the Cadillac, the ski-boat... if only he could live. He would apologize suddenly and ask me to forgive him, saying he didn't know what he was talking about, but he did! Striving to fill our lives with wealth, happiness, and security, we often find ourselves in a confusing mumbo jumbo. Nothing matters more than to realize and appreciate God's gift of a full life.

I remember one day going to visit my dad at the hospital. He was in the oncology ward on the eleventh floor of Sacred Heart hospital in Spokane. When the elevator doors finally opened I could hear a patient screaming in pain down the sterile hospital corridor. I thought to myself, "What a horrible place for my father to have to be!" When I got to his room my face was flushed. My thoughts were on fire. My dad was the patient I was hearing.

Meanwhile my life droned on. I'd had my own dental practice for eight years and the reasons for going to work became fewer and fewer. Finally there was only one reason. *I had to!* It was wretched. I had a terrific practice with satisfied patients and it provided me with a nice income. It was a country practice and I got to do a lot of specialty work — surgery, periodontics, orthodontics, and endodontics. I was good at all of it, but even that couldn't hold off the boredom. Vacations and more and more days off didn't help either. Searching, I developed an interest in personal computers and started my own software company, but even that didn't satisfy my desire to do something else. Soon I had burn-out to add to my problems.

Another thing happened about then.

I fell in love with Davey, an attractive and vivacious redhead with a round face, who had been my respected friend for years. She was indeed "animated, pretty, competent in manner, and warm," as another sailor came to describe her years later in his own book, *Sailing Through Paradise*. Davey came to me, or rather the universe had us come together, after a time when I had finally given up on the idea of finding yet still another perfect woman. In exchange for sleeping alone I found a fulfillment of self and a peace of mind that had been previously missing in my person. I'm convinced that this then freed me up to find a most compatible partner in every way Davey. We started doing everything together.

Almost on a whim, Davey and I bought a sailboat, not just a sailboat, but a beautiful BABA 30. I'd been sailing for about fifteen years, but it was a new thing for Davey. One evening Davey and I were driving home through Seattle after a beautiful cruise on a friend's boat in the San Juan Islands.

"Want to see my dream boat?"

"Sure!"

We followed the twisted road down to Lake Union and parked near some houseboats. The brokerage was closed, but a BABA 30 was at the dock. We stared at her with big, round eyes. She was beautiful. Twelve weeks later that boat was ours. We named her *Querencia*, a very old Spanish word I had met through poetry years before. It's difficult to pin it down to an exact English translation, but refers to a place of safety or refuge, or affection, or, in bullfighting, the bull's ring of power. All the definitions seemed to suit us. We knew a yacht like *Querencia* was not meant to sit in a slip or even in the Puget Sound for that once-a-year vacation; especially if we were her owners.

Like a chick developing in its shell, the idea of sailing away on *Querencia* slowly grew and took shape in our minds. The time was ripe. Davey was also having similar feelings about her own life and vocation. Our relationship was miraculously working. We started thinking we would sail away together. We were sailing every chance we got and *Querencia* became our hideaway. Our short sails became longer. We took our respective children for a two-week sail to the

San Juans that wound up lasting six weeks! On sunny days when working at the clinic I would steal away to the beach. While gobbling a sandwich I would gaze across the blue Puget Sound and let my mind drift. I had a dream again — sailing away.

Undoing your doings is much more difficult than the actual act of sailing away. Selling the practice proved to be a painful process, mostly because of psychological overtones. After four years of college, four years of dental school, and eight years of building up the practice, it was natural for parts of me to rebel in the confusion. I needed encouragement. Davey had enough enthusiasm for both of us and that was a good thing because most of our friends and co-workers didn't have any. It was as if we were embarking on something terribly illegal. If there had been a way they could have chained us to our jobs and mortgages, they would have.

At the time, we were both deeply hurt by our friends' abandonment. We thought almost everyone would want to do that something more with his life and we were surprised to see that in reality most people really didn't even appreciate the opportunity to try. Most of my friends and colleagues saw themselves working eight to sixteen hours a day in the hub of spokes and concrete for at least a few more decades. However, almost everyone said *"I envy you."* At the time I remember telling Davey that if I heard the word envy one more time I would go nuts. They also said they wanted to do that "something more" with their lives but "couldn't." It seemed to me that the only real reason they couldn't was because they didn't really want to. Somewhere in there exists a difficult choice for each of us. I had read something by Alan Watts years ago that made perfect sense to me. It read something like "It's better to be secure with your insecurities than insecure with your securities."

3.

I was nearing the end of William F. Buckley's book, *Atlantic High*, a new release, as the jetliner soared somewhere over San Francisco. Mr. Buckley was describing all the ways a writer and a linguist might spend a day at sea. He spends time answering his mail. "For instance," he wrote, "here is a fellow who wants to know the meaning of the word *querencia*."

I almost broke the upright when I jumped. I was reading a new book about sailing written by W.F. Buckley, Jr. describing a random event that happened to concern itself with the meaning of "*Querencia!*"

This reminded me of a favorite debate between Carl Jung and Sigmund Freud about such "happenstance" occurrences.

Jung would exclaim, "Synchronicity, Dr. Freud! Synchronicity!"

And Freud would reply "Bosh, Dr. Jung! Coincidence!"

When we got back to Seattle, I immediately typed a letter to Mr. Buckley, partially to tell him about the coincidence and also to see if he really did answer his mail.

Eight months later, tied up in Monterey, California, we received a forwarded letter dated February 22, 1983. It had been dictated in Switzerland and transcribed in New York .

It read :

```
Dear Dr. McGrady:
Best of luck on your three-year cruise! I envy you.
Cordially,
Wm.F.Buckley, Jr.
```

4.

"Freedom is the increased knowledge
of what you can do without."
— Henry David Thoreau

You can do without a whole lot more than you think when you go to sea and yet, you do need everything you might possibly ever need. Your vessel becomes a miniature, self contained world. It takes months and months of getting ready. Putting up everything that you will need for the next three years or ten thousand miles takes major planning and preparation. As I've said before, I remember this as being much more difficult than the actual trip!

Moving from 4000 sq. ft. of living space to 300 sq. ft. took up most of the fall season of 1982. We were either having a garage sale, or taking a load to the dump, or to our storage crate, or to the boat. *Querencia's* waterline sank lower and lower. We had to put her on a diet! Stuff we couldn't take care of right away went into footlockers that we kept in a storage area at the marina. It seemed like we would never get through sorting through all our "stuff." All this packing and unpacking and stowing and restowing, plus nagging responsibilities from our businesses, as well as going over every inch of *Querencia*, stem to stern, mechanics and hull, kept us exhausted. All the while miserably wet, filthy weather made us more than ready to get on with the next phase of cruising: going somewhere else. You don't appreciate the weather until you live in it. Coco, our parrot, agreed. She ate a settee cushion one frustrating afternoon.

New feelings of happiness and freedom came quickly, though. The cost of living dropped drastically. Our heat and electric bill alone dropped from $300 a month in my big old house to $12 a month on the boat. Our resources suddenly could be described as "abundant!" We slept the best we'd slept in months, curled up under a big comforter in *Querencia's* v-berth, surrounded by teak and holly, a sky hatch and bronze portholes. It was absolutely wonderful.

Friends of ours, Al and Ginny Van Buskirk, had a tackle business. They came down once or twice to rig *Querencia* with offshore fishing tackle. Lucky for us, they took an interest in showing us how to catch salmon. We found that we could take *Querencia* out on a little putt in Commencement Bay and catch a salmon dinner in the same amount of time it took us to go and find a parking place at the Proctor Safeway. We were already learning some of the best things about living the simple life.

Slowly everything came into shape. Living on a boat will force you to be organized. In the evenings we started finding more time to quiz each other on the constellations, study navigation, and read the great sailing tales.

We had read about heaving-to, but had never tried it; we had never had need, navigating in the tight quarters of Puget Sound. One stormy night we even went out into the middle of Commencement Bay and practiced heaving-to. It was wonderful to see that even when it was blowing really hard you could "park" the boat and she would just sort of sit there crabbing along at about one to two knots. Getting that experience proved later to be an excellent advantage.

The week-end after making arrangements to sell our last car we decided to take some time off. We took our final sail down through the Narrows and into the Southern Sound, anchoring off Steilacoom in front of my godparents' home. At the library, on another day in Steilacoom, I'd seen pictures of how the tall sailing ships of the late 1800's from the east coast of the United States would anchor off Steilacoom in exactly the same spot where *Querencia* was positioned this particular evening. Steilacoom, (the oldest town in Washington state) still looks a little like Cape Cod. We rowed ashore and followed a little trail over railroad tracks and through wet blackberry bushes up to Joe and Anita's home which sits on a grassy knoll overlooking the water. Looking out their bay window, we saw the grey sky breaking clear in the west as it usually does in the Northwest just before sunset. Caught in the light, *Querencia* beamed up from below, surrounded by dark blue water. Glory rays streamed over the skyline of Mt. Olympus at the end of Carr Inlet. The whole sky was aflame, Peter Max style. I thought of how southern Puget Sound had been as special a place for *Querencia* as it had been for the tall ships that came from the very different and far-away worlds that lay beyond Cape Flattery and the treacherous Washington coast.

5.

In February we said our good-byes and took *Querencia* north to Seattle. Davey wrote:

> 2/2/83 - We're off, our home now truly Querencia - we leave our slip behind. We motor out across Commencement Bay when suddenly a hoarse cough comes from the exhaust. Definitely not enough water coming out the exhaust. We nurse her past Brown's Point by popping the sails. A lot of wind, we sail a ways, checking the engine one last time dry as a bone! We tack (back to our slip if we

have to) returning to fix our engine. I unload
the quarter berth and John checks the hoses
- all okay. We unload the lazaret and John
climbs into the engine room to discover the
sea cock for the water intake had closed. We
open it and our engine is back in business. So
are we. I must mention the sun, the mountains - Cascades, Olympics, Mt. Rainier, Mt.
Baker - all visible and set off against dark blue
water - a beautiful send-off from the South
Sound.

We had been warned to expect difficulty in finding a place to tie
up in Seattle; there was a six year waiting list for slips. Rather than
worry about it we just sailed *Querencia* into Shilshole and asked the
Harbormaster where to park her. We were given guest moorage for
two months! We found this to be the rule and not the exception, that
accommodations would be made rather than denied. This was true
in nearly every port we were to enter in the next few years. If we had
taken seriously all the rumors we heard about tight moorage, we
would have missed about half of the experiences of our cruise, I
think!

It was wonderful being anonymous visitors in a big city. We were
close to all our needs. Here in Seattle we were to commission our
offshore equipment: a self-steering windvane custom bent for
Querencia in England, our satellite navigation from California, our
Telefunken solar panel from Germany, running backs, rigging, compass, DC-AC 110 power inverter, more radios, batteries, more sails,
lee cloths, an Avon life raft, windlass, more ground tackle, offshore
pedestal, five coats of bottom paint, a spare depth sounder, taffrail
log, kerosene running lights, and the list went on.

We also had some well-deserved nights on the town, dancing our
legs off on the dance floors in Shilshole until the wee hours of the
morning and then walking down the dock in the glistening harbor
lights to our little self-sufficiency capsule, our home, *Querencia*.
Harbors, even in the busiest of cities, are always so peaceful compared to the hustle and bustle of life on shore.

We continued to take advantage of every opportunity to become
familiar with our new boat in a stiff blow - sailing in and out of our

slip, reefing, learning to set the self-steering, and changing to a storm sail were just some of the routines we practiced.

We noticed however, that we had both come down with an obvious case of "marina-itis." This is a syndrome characterized by aimless wandering around in marinas and in marine stores, watching dollar bills go out with each tide, beset by indecision over what exactly it is you are searching or waiting for, whether it be parts or provisions, that keeps you from moving on.

We did all of our errands by metro bus. One day coming back from the machine shop with our custom made stainless steel pedestal railing, I climbed up and through the hydraulic doors of the bus and stood right at the front along with three or four senior citizens. They all had their walkers and were quite fascinated with mine; they thought I had a newly designed model! Boy, did I feel silly.

We watched the Queen of England's Royal Yacht, bagpipes and all, come and go. Neil Young's huge classic schooner, the *H.M.S. Raglund* also paid a short visit to Shilshole. As for *Querencia*, she was still stuck, waiting for the self-steering vane and windlass to arrive.

Finally, by the end of March, all of our offshore equipment had been installed and commissioned and we had made our last haul-out. Even though everything had taken more time and money than we had planned, we were proud that we had done it all ourselves and that it had all come together so well.

The first week in April we left for the San Juan Islands archipelago, a group of 301 islands that lie on the border between the United States and Canada, sixty miles to the north. There we planned to hang out and live the self-sufficient life until summer brought safer, happier weather to the upper latitudes of the North Pacific ocean. We would then begin our trip down the west coast of the North American continent.

6.

Davey's daughter, Caroline, our redhead, and son, Paul, met us on the docks at Shilshole Marina one Friday morning eager to help us with our final provisioning. At this time none of our children shared our eagerness to leave the protected waters of the Puget Sound and go to sea in our little family yacht; however, Caroline was committed to make this first leg of our journey up to the San Juans with us. Paul would return to his father's home. We only hoped to see Paul one more time this summer before our departure date.

Half-way to Kingston only a couple of sailing hours to the north, we had a man overboard drill. We needed the practice and we wanted to try the suggestion of only sailing a little way on the first night of a long passage. It's a tip that we grew to appreciate. It gives your body an extra opportunity to adjust, and the result is almost always a more relaxed, enjoyable beginning to your trip.

In Kingston's Apple Tree Cove the dock signs suggested that moorage was *absolutely* not available. We spoke with several fisherman, though, who encouraged us to tie up to some unused pilings that we had been eyeing. We threw out a few lines and *Querencia* was secure. Once again we were struck with how wonderful it was to take your home with you when you travel!

Early in the evening we heard quite a ruckus outside and the three of us went to investigate. We found the local fire department running long hoses down the wooden docks to pump out an unattended yacht that had been reported as sinking. Soon everything was back to normal. Well, almost...

Upon returning to *Querencia* we were shocked to see a large white tomcat spring out of the main hatch and escape into the darkness. Coco! We all scrambled below expecting to find a flurry of feathers. Instead, we discovered things to be quite calm. Coco sat on her perch with her head cocked to one side, grinding her beak and whistling, all the while scanning the cabin sole with her evil eye. We decided that the tomcat probably didn't know what to think of the bird! Nevertheless we checked ourselves not to make that mistake again; next time Coco might not be so lucky.

When we left at daybreak the next morning our plans were to go forty-five miles to the north and anchor at Hope Island. It was one of our favorite anchorages, just inside Deception Pass, the bottleneck through which the waters rush back and forth between the Strait of Juan de Fuca and Puget Sound.

We harnessed the self-steering vane for her first three-hour sail in brisk wind. The vane performed wonderfully, and we christened her "Nelley." It was entrancing to watch this mechanical marvel hanging off the stern steer *Querencia* with just two little lines that came forward and attached to the wheel. Nelley constantly adjusted for wind direction and heel. We all watched in amazement for hours.

Traversing Possession Sound we tacked around Whidbey Island and changed our heading to NNW. This was the narrow Saratoga Passage and we found the wind to be right on our nose. As often happens when the weather is good in the Pacific Northwest, a nor'wester blows incessantly.

Soon we were motoring hard in four foot chop and making about one and a half knots per hour of forward progress. The weather did not ease and with the last embers of the day we found ourselves finally pulling into Penn Cove on the northwest end of Whidbey to try and find what little refuge there might be. With only a mile wide isthmus separating us from the straits we found little relief from the weather. We went in as far as we could, and at the far end of the cove I went forward and quickly "dropped the hook" that had been resting on our sprit. I did this only to watch us drag our thirty-five pound CQR anchor for about a half mile. How discouraging this was after having spent three thousand dollars on our ground tackle, all that heavy chain rode and the Plath bronze windlass from Oregon. But the problem wasn't with the equipment, it was with our technique. Being quick learners, this was the last time we would drop the hook so fast, especially with all that chain behind it. Naturally, all the chain just falls on top of the anchor and fouls with its flukes.

By the next morning the weather had eased and the brightness of the day afforded excellent navigation around Strawberry Point and the shallow Skagit River flats. This part of Washington had always been one of our favorite places. Here the San Juan Islands, which lie in the shadow of the Olympic Mountains, run into the Cascades. There is a remarkable amount of sunshine here between the fat jeweled rain showers that spatter down intermittently. Locals refer to this area as the "banana belt." It's the home of haikus and American Zen, white snow geese and trumpeter swans, Tom Robbins and twisted juniper trees.

We left the Skagit Valley and La Conner behind us and went out with the tide, out through the bottle neck drain of Deception Pass and into the Strait of Juan de Fuca. It felt like the current flushed us well into the Rosario Strait before we were free and on our way to Friday Harbor, a small island community that would be our new home port for the next few weeks.

Far away from the hustle and bustle of civilization, the solitude that was suddenly ours permeated us. We learned how to relax. Yet, every day we awoke to an exciting newness. Soon the major part of our adventure was to begin. Our stout little boat was prepared. Now it was time to prepare ourselves and do our final provisioning.

7.

As I already suggested, preparing ourselves meant a lot of relaxing — relaxing into our new life style and preparing our minds and bodies for the challenges ahead. We could also now concentrate on providing our ship's library with good reading material for the months to come. We spent many hours gathering novels and trilogies and weather books and autobiographies (we would later enjoy those the most).

Caroline's spring vacation was soon over and she went back to Seattle. On her last night we had a pizza party and laughed our way through a memory drill of the alphabet code for radio transmission.

We made new friends, Jo and Eli. Out of California and just in from Alaska, they were living aboard their sailboat *Seashell* . Eli had a great way of giving paternal advice to an appreciative newcomer like me. Jo caught more salmon than anyone else in Friday Harbor and invited Davey to be her fishing partner. Davey, already a proven fisherwoman, needed very little encouragement, and the two of them were very accomplished at gathering food from the sea to put on the table. Secrets were shared, how to clean a crab the quick way and what to do with a slimy little edible squid. We had a lot of fun together.

How to Clean a Crab

Don't be afraid to whack the crab on the back of the shell several times to stun it if it's being obstinate. Grab the two halves of the shell (the back [or top] and the bottom) and tear it apart. Now with the 'hood up' so to speak you should be able to see what's going on. Somewhat carefully remove the gills (often a bluish green) and all material that is discolored. This should leave you with mostly just the legs and some white muscle which extends from the legs up into the body. Separate the legs a few times, leaving the part of the body attached that still has the white body muscle on it.

How to Clean a Squid

Grasp the squid and remove its head. Lay it on its back, fins against the counter, and cut it lengthwise. Open the incision and spread the mantle into a triangular shape. Remove cellophane skeleton and internal organs. Flip the mantle over, and grabbing the fins, use your fingers to pull the purple skin off, leaving only the edible white triangle of meat.

On weekends both *Seashell* and *Querencia* would spend their time away from the dock. The hordes of people on holiday, crowded docks and boats, and loud all-night parties were too much for us.

As the end of April came, so did other friends. Al and Virginia drove north to visit and say their good-byes. Of all our contemporaries, Al and Virginia had been the most, if not the only, really supportive friends we'd had. They were warm, and their visit was fun. We sailed to Stuart Island together where we showed them how, by setting out a pot, it was possible to feast continuously on crab! We fished and ate and talked and hiked. They enjoyed seeing all the work we had put into *Querencia* in the past few months to get her ready to go to sea. While on Stuart, Al took our newly purchased, handheld one watt VHF receiver/transmitter to the other side of Tiptop Hill for a radio check with *Querencia*. We didn't realize it at the time, but that little radio would later prove invaluable. When *Querencia's* main VHF radio would fail later off the Oregon coast, it would prove itself good for up to a distance of eighty miles offshore.

One morning hot chocolate and enough wind to blow us out of the country had us on our way to the city of Victoria on Vancouver Island. Al had been there before by boat and acted as our pilot in the harbor, navigating us to a very comfortable slip directly in front of the famous Empress Hotel. After checking in with customs, we toured the local pubs and explored this polite English city.

Al snaps a photo of us lounging in the cockpit with Virginia

Our plans to continue this sailing adventure together the next day were changed by a sudden digestive illness with Coco. Our first clue should have been the unusual behavior we'd been seeing the day before, when she sat with her back to us and refused to look in our direction.

Al and Virginia caught a ferry home and *Querencia* stayed at the dock. Davey and I tried in vain, along with the efforts of a veterinarian, to save Coco, but two days later she died. On our way back to San Juan Island and Friday Harbor we paused on the U.S.-Canadian border and gave Coco a proper burial at sea. There was no wind and the Haro Strait was like a huge bathtub, the surface reflecting the morning sun like a giant mirror. Except for the putt-putt of our twenty-three horsepower diesel engine there was a silence on board, neither of us being up for conversation. To ease the lonely solitude we set out our fishing rig and lo! We caught four beautiful salmon. It was as if Coco were sending us a sign from the other side.

That evening the sun hung low in the sky. It was still a cold winter sun, a pale orange disk buried in an opal haze. When we made our last turn into Friday Harbor we were glad to see Jo and Eli aboard *Seashell* at the dock. They had been expecting us and had managed to keep a slip open right next to theirs. As great as our outing had been, as sad as Coco's death had made us, it felt good to get back to familiar territory. Jo and Davey brought up the traps and started to clean crabs and sauté calamari while Eli and I swapped arguments for the proper adjustment of the shaft packing. In three days *Seashell* would leave for Alaska and Davey and I, aboard *Querencia*, would leave for three weeks of sailing the islands to the north and "living off our hook."

8.

On May 6, 1983 I wrote in the log:

> 10:30 - Motored into Roche Harbor on the west side of San Juan Island for diesel and provisions. Here we've found nice people and empty docks this time of year and decided it a good place to catch up on all our aging phone business and mail. Nice, domestic geese eat from your hand here on the docks. Today one gave Davey a black-eye for getting too cuddly. It struck her with its beak. Researched what's available at the hotel for Davey's folks when they arrive in a few weeks. The hotel has several rooms much as they were almost a hundred years ago, fur-

nished with antiques, including a room that
Teddy Roosevelt slept in on one of his trips
to the Great Northwest!

After a couple of days of chores we were ready to go back to having fun. A late afternoon sail around the bay turned into an excursion
to Prevost Bay about eight miles away on the northern side of Stuart
Island. We decided to sail out of Roche Harbor under full sail using
our large genoa with its striking "Croix de Rouge" emblem. We discovered half way across the harbor that we are towing our crab pot
at six knots. I hauled it in all askew to find it had our biggest crab yet
to date inside of it!

Once off the north shore of Stuart Island we fished around Turn
Point where small gusts pushed us through gurgling rips. The point
backdropped by the white and red lighthouse was very beautiful and
eerie at the same time. Once we entered the Prevost channel it took
a lot of tacking to have middle passage, something we decided we
wouldn't want to do at night! One more boat followed us in and
some kayakers were already there, but our only neighbors that night
were pulling oars. It was very quiet and beautiful when I rowed out
after dinner in the dinghy and set the crab trap. Then quite suddenly the air became very ionized and electrified. I barely made it back
to the boat before a tremendous cloudburst — our first since Seattle.
We were definitely into high energy at this point in our contrived
escape from the world.

The next morning we awoke to wet decks and gray ominous
clouds and little to no wind. Undaunted, we decided to charge on to
points further north so we started the trusty diesel, "the iron spinnaker", and motor-sailed out Prevost channel. We sailed past
Skipjack, Bare, Orcas, Waldron, Patos and Sucia islands and finally
into the little cove behind Eagle Point on Matias Island. There we
anchored for lunch amidst natural rock carvings at the tides edge. It
seemed to us to be the Great Northwest's answer to Easter Island
and we spent the afternoon rowing along shore in exploration, fishing, and then hiking to the other side of the island through an emerald rain forest. The sunlight had returned and the flora was fantastic. As the sun began to fall in earnest toward the horizon we did a
final putt across to Echo Bay on Sucia Island, about two miles away,

to take the safest overnight anchorage of our choice.

The previous summer we had anchored in Echo Bay. Then there had been over a hundred boats anchored in one huge vacationing flotilla. This time it was different. *Querencia* was the *only* boat in the bay. After a feast of steak and kidney pie, followed with time in the cockpit to reflect on the day's accomplishments, we crawled off to the forward part of the boat into our cozy teak and holly v-berth. There a glorious night of sleeping and dreaming awaited us.

We both slept for ten hours, and probably would have slept longer except for the wakening pitter-patter of rain on the topsides. We peeked out the hatch. We were still alone. Big billowing clouds flew across the sky. Between them the sun intermittently flashed down bright yellow glory rays that buried themselves in the green woods of Sucia Island. Moisture gathered skyward like steam, swirling and ghosting upward. We decided to crawl back into our berth and read for a few hours, waiting for the weather to clear. After a leisurely breakfast of bacon, eggs, and corn bread, we rowed ashore. With the island to ourselves we decided on a morning hike.

The walk through a moist pristine forest is wonderful. The little twisted trail through the woods reminded us of our many hikes in Mt. Rainier National Forest and the Cascades, and it was nice to experience that wet fir freshness again. There were several varieties of flowers. Some very small and star shaped; purple, bursting in little groups here and there among the moss. Another was very large and growing on a woody bush; four or five plummeting blossoms tumbled from its bloom. And of course Indian Paintbrush and a few other varieties we recognized from our mountain climbing days. Davey and I felt a certain innocence coming back to us.

Back on *Querencia* later that afternoon we pulled up the hook and tried our hand at some serious trolling in hopes of landing a salmon. Although fishing proved unproductive, it did get us underway again. As the shadows grew long we pulled into Fox Cove on the southwest side of Sucia, anchored, and rowed ashore.

The beach was made from bleached, crushed shell and stretched long, underneath hard-weathered juniper trees. I scrambled up a green, grassy bluff to gaze over *Querencia* anchored beautifully in this wonderful cove. Davey was giggling when she caught up with me; finding me prostrate in a clover patch, savoring the view and chewing a long stem of grass. The sunset was spectacular, confirming our belief that all sunsets are new and never a one is "average." Looking south, the panorama resembled an exquisite water color. The islands of Skipjack, Waldron, Bare, Pender, and Stuart stood behind the reefs of Sucia in the foreground, propped up like cardboard placards on a stage set; each shaded a different pastel and mounted afloat in a seemingly huge pond that stretched forever.

The sun didn't set until well after eight that night and when we finally rowed back to the boat we couldn't leave the cockpit until after ten. We were in love with life. Two seals joined us in Fox Cove that evening and performed, repeating what must have been a love ritual. Over and over they slapped their fins on the water's surface with such force that it sounded like gunshot. Davey and I clapped gleefully. This went on until well after we crawled into our v-berth. With the portholes open we could still hear them cracking loudly in the darkness. We were glad to know what the sound was it would have been a mystery otherwise!

The following day we perfected our technique for hunting abalone. Earlier in my life I had gathered lots of abalone by diving for them, but this was much easier and more productive. Here in these inland waters the tide is often extreme with a difference of ten feet in a day. By simply rowing our dinghy along the craggy rocks at the shore's edge when the tide was at its maximum ebb we could find abalone hanging above the waterline desperately trying to loosen their muscular clutch so that they might fall back into the receding water. Once we found the right spot, Davey would reach over the bow of the tender and pluck them like tomatoes. We became really good at it and given a proper tide could get our limit in about an hour. This impressed us, knowing that in the grocery store they were always nine dollars a pound, and although we had never tasted store-bought abalone, I'm sure they wouldn't have tasted as good. They were so tender that pounding the meat was not necessary. I sliced them thinly and Davey breaded them with egg, a hint of cornmeal, and whole wheat flour before lightly frying them. The meal was delicious.

The next morning we left Fox Cove after a breakfast of fried potatoes and onions, fresh cod, eggs sunny-side-up, and coffee. We waved a so long to three fellas on the boom tug *Favorite* which had come in and anchored next to us around midnight. While the morning haze was burning off we motored all the way past the NW point of Patos, through amazing rip currents. We finally tied up to a mooring around noon and immediately made ready for reconnaissance via inflatable.

Patos Island is about four miles from Sucia Island and the furthermost NW island of the San Juans near the extreme end of the boundary of the continental United States. Sixty feet high and covered with rocks and jagged trees, it is a rugged sight. Before going to shore, we took one of Big Al's cod jigs and jigged at the entrance to the cove. The hand-painted eyeball and leather skirt must have been irresistible because we snagged a three-pound lingcod and a twelve-ounce snapper almost immediately! We were enjoying the fish weighing scales we had put aboard.

Later we went for a wonderful hike. Now totally deserted, Patos had once been a Coast Guard station, complete with pier, buildings, and a thirty-eight-foot lighthouse on the west end of the island. The lighthouse was now alone and automated, showing its signal and sounding the fog horn up Boundary Passage. Blossoming blackberry vines covered all the buildings buried window-deep in tall green grass. Swallows darted around us in the warm spring sunshine, scooping up the small insects that set out startled from under our feet.

This sort of life continued throughout the month of May. Feeding ourselves was a joy, and we got into the practice of foraging everyday for two to four hours. Fishing was another huge success. And for entertainment we were never at a loss for having a new island or territory to explore. We went into port only to replenish provisions and check our mail.

9.

We were beginning to feel very anxious about our departure for California. The occasional sou'westers became even less frequent and a few of the other offshore boats we had met were already leaving to go down the coast. But we decided to stick with our plan of going down the coast in the flattest part of the summer, wanting to take advantage of the increased odds of having our first ocean passage be a comfortable one. Besides, we still had obligations to our children and parents to spend some time together before we left. We had made it clear that our good-byes might be for good. We weren't just on holiday, we were starting a new life in a new world.

We brought *Querencia* into Roche Harbor for our family good-byes. Its quaint luxuries were perfectly suited for both the land and water traveler. The first to arrive were Davey's parents, Ginny and Bob.

From the log on May 18:

> The four of us stood here in Roche Harbor on the dock in the fresh sea air. Behind us the green hillside ran down to the water, and in front of us the long mirror of the harbor glinted under the afternoon sun. We trekked up the hill and into the hotel where we dragged the luggage up crooked steps over pink carpeting until, at the end of a hallway, we finally found room 2B. Once inside that little room in the heat of the late afternoon, flies hummed, the springs in Teddy Roosevelt's bed squeaked, the couch coughed up old change, the pull-down window shade

spun a wild death, and, (because this part of
the building was settling so severely), Bob
and Ginny got to feel their first starboard list
of the trip. Ginny and I stole out the fire
escape and found some funky metal chairs to
sit on. Surrounded by clambering ivy we
enjoyed a short leisurely moment together to
marvel at the view while Davey and her Dad
checked at the desk for something more contemporary. The newer condo units proved a
better tack.

Next to arrive were my godparents, Joe and Anita. It was the first
time they had met Davey's parents. Both had been a strong source of
encouragement and support for us. Joe brought humor reminiscent
of "Norton" (Art Carney), but was much more handsome and elo-
quent in speech. Anita, an animal lover, had always been a mentor to
me. Davey's dad Bob was unwinding from a career in broadcasting
and Ginny brought with her the honesty and practicality learned
from growing up in the beautiful wilderness of northern Idaho.

One warm, sunshiny morning we all climbed aboard and sailed
down Mosquito Pass through beautiful Garrison Bay. Before noon
just as the early day mists were rising and disappearing into a vacu-
um of blue overhead we were out in Haro Strait. The winds were
light and easy; so was the conversation. We had a wonderful time
together. Davey and I proudly showed off all *Querencia's* new offshore equipment. On the return, around Henry and Battleship
Islands, a group of six large Dahl porpoises joined us, playfully
charging and racing *Querencia* in "Blue Angel" formation. I'm sure
we were all doing as much gleeful squeaking as they were.

An old salt once told me that dolphins can sense your thoughts.
He suggested that humans try "thinking at them." He said that
although dolphins and porpoises couldn't understand words they
"sensed feelings" easily. I wondered if those porpoises were sensing
my anxious anticipation about sailing the Pacific Ocean.

The following day Joe and Anita left us to return to their home
in the southern sound and we headed *Querencia* north for three days
in the upper San Juans with Bob and Ginny, determined to show
them a few of our favorite places. Our first night we rowed into the

deserted beach of Fox Cove. We barbecued steaks on a driftwood fire while the sun slowly lowered itself behind the pastel panorama that Davey and I had been so anxious to share with them. Everything was perfect. We even had Orcas sounding just outside the cove!

The next few days were just as joyous. We sailed and gunkholed here and there. Davey enjoyed pointing out goats and bald eagles and deer to her mom. Bob and I got to know each other better, and, exposed to the relaxing atmosphere provided by Mother Nature, talked out solutions to most of the world's problems. Seclusion has a liberating effect on people. One of my silliest fond memories was stepping off the boat one night with Bob at the dock on Matia Island to take a pee underneath the stars together! The jeweled stars in the clear black sky were reflected at the shore's edge, their twinkling mimicked by the phosphorescence of tiny plankton splashing against the pebble beach shore. On top of everything else, Bob had just won at penny ante poker below decks and we were laughing our heads off! Innocence and immortality ran through our veins. The world was right.

We returned to Roche Harbor for the departure of Davey's folks. The docks seemed noisy compared to the tranquility we had discovered in the past few days. As a result, as soon as *Querencia's* stores had been re-stocked we set sail down the west side of San Juan Island, to anchor the night on the protected side of Long Island.

Long Island is only about a half a mile long and lies right on the Strait of Juan de Fuca. Its west end is a two hundred yard mound of rock that separates from the rest of the island at high tide. It is scattered with grass and little cacti that pop up here and there. On this sunny afternoon we anchored in our usual spot and put ashore for a short tour as humble guests of the local flora and fauna. We loved Long Island. It is surrounded by lush kelp beds and always teeming with hundreds of ocean birds and several families of seals. The water rushes by, often at five knots, creating large swirling rips and eddies. Just before sunset, slack tide allowed for a row around the island in our inflatable dinghy. We were discussing how we were almost accustomed to being alone with such silence and splendor when *woosh*. It was the deep, heavy, hollow exhalation of a huge, black, glistening pilot whale surfacing less than twenty feet from us.

The next morning we barely had time to gather a few abalone when a weather change had us quickly pick up our hook and move. One always has to be ready to leave quickly at Long Island, since it is so exposed and hazardous in bad conditions. The escape route requires navigating around Whale and Mummy Rocks, black ominous dangers that stick up about five feet above the water's surface. At least it was daylight; once before we had to leave at midnight! Now confused seas turned the whole area into a washing machine tossing *Querencia* around while Davey struggled to get some sail up. Unable to leave the wheel, I looked down the companionway to see everything below decks being tossed every which way, including the log book which landed right in the abalone bucket! Yuk!

By the time we had dropped our anchor again in Griffin Bay on the lee side of San Juan Island the winds were really howling. By evening, thirty-knot gusts were whistling through the rigging and in the gray twilight of dusk we noticed other boats, who had like us sought refuge in Griffin Bay, dragging their anchors. After dinner Davey managed to light the kerosene anchor light and hang it off the Aladdin cleat on the backstay. After agreeing on a schedule during the night to intermittently check how our hook was holding, we crawled up into the forward v-berth and snuggled under our overstuffed comforter. It was a good time to appreciate our properly-set heavy-duty ground tackle.

10.

By Memorial Day we had *Querencia* back in Friday Harbor tied up along the main pier. There was a lot of holiday activity and we got into the spirit ourselves with Davey's birthday on June fourth. As badly as we wanted to get the trip underway, we still had our children coming and there wasn't much we could do to hasten their visit. We settled for the enjoyment of meeting new boats and new people. It seemed like every other person that walked by on the dock would strike up a conversation with us, asking about our offshore equipment and our sailing plans. We were both proud and embarrassed by the constant flood of admiration for *Querencia*.

We met the skipper off the fishing vessel *Marcele*, out of Seattle and bound for the Gulf of Alaska. Although he had been first mate on *Marcele* before, this was his first season as skipper. His name was Terry. He had sandy blond hair and was in his late thirties. In the off season he was a commercial abalone diver in Southern California. After his customary afternoon jaunt on his windsurfer I asked him for a tour of *Marcele*, which he readily agreed to. This was a real fishing boat; it had rolled three times and sunk once! Creature comforts were few and we couldn't help but feel a strong admiration for the hard work and dangerous conditions that commercial fishermen subject themselves to.

We also met Vern and Jo Alford and their canine crew member, Tuna, on their thirty-five foot sailboat, *Java*. In their fifties, Vern had retired as foreman for an electrical utilities company in Portland, Oregon. Up from Oregon, they were on their way to Alaska with plans to then head down to Mexico and then back up to Oregon! I can tell you now that they did it! Far from the predicament of seeing your dreams stay in your living room armchair, Vern and Jo were really doing something with their lives that reinforced us in our choices. One day we sailed *Querencia* twenty miles to Anacortes just to catch up with *Java* and its "electrifying resources." We'd developed a short between our 110 volt and twelve volt systems that totally baffled us. After exhausting our own efforts and trying all the other local talent, Vern was our only hope. Not only did Vern fix our electrical problem, but he and Jo taught us pinochle and we sat out a two day storm at the dock playing cards together.

After the arrival of my daughter Rain, then nine years old, the three of us looked north over the indigo waters towards a mighty western wall of mountains rising on the horizon beyond the San Juans. Capped with snow and ribbed with rock, it was easy to visualize their draining icy torrents contributing to the freshness and cleanliness of the great northwest. We decided to sail up into the backyards of British Columbia.

Although time did not permit us to travel as far up into Canada's magnificence as we would have wished, the Gulf Islands were relatively close and definitely worth the little effort expended to cross the border and explore them. After checking in with customs in

Bedwell on Pender Island we pushed on up Swanson Channel and immediately found a favorite place, little Diver's Cove on the east side of Prevost Island. Not mentioned in the cruising guides, it was a secluded haven for us. Reacting as usual when we find something good, we opted to not rush off seeking more gold and more rainbows. We stayed there for a week while we fished and hiked and foraged for oysters, clams, and mussels in the tide pools.

A family of four goats were particularly amusing. Every day they would come down from the craggy hillsides and go out on the end of a spit of rocks, Red Isles Reef, on the north side of the cove. It was very entertaining to sit in the cockpit and watch these characters scramble around and even more amazing to see them jumping from one rocky reef to another during the rushing incoming tide.

From Prevost we lollygagged farther northward. After stopping at Ganges for provisions, we explored Saltspring Island and then a resort at Telegraph Harbour on Thetis Island. There we finally took the opportunity to do our laundry. After it was all hung to dry, there wasn't one inch of available lifeline left! That evening, during a period of mutual introspection, Davey and I came upon an idea. We put in a call from the dock to her sister and brother-in-law, Dale and Ed in Utah. We invited them to join us for part of our sail down the coast.

From Thetis, going down the south side of Saltspring, we wound up in Burguyne Bay surrounded by a majestic steep forest. We shared the anchorage one evening with several log booms and the sailboat of a Canadian couple from Maple Bay on Vancouver Island. They fixed us up with a "buzz bomb" lure and on the second cast Davey landed a four pound rock cod.

The next morning we were on our way back to the U.S. down through the spectacular cut rock hillsides of Sansum narrows, down Satellite Channel and across the border to our familiar Roche Harbor on the northwest tip of San Juan Island. The wind blew a steady twenty-five knots the closer we got to Haro Strait, and Rain got her first experience at the helm in such conditions.

We were eager to get around to the other side of the island. We tied up at the dock and while Davey and Rain were off gathering goods ashore, I tended to engine maintenance and filling the water tanks with the dock hose. Anne, the young college girl tending the docks during the summer, approached to collect our moorage fee and ask about our recent adventures. She was starting to find *Querencia* a familiar scene and always welcomed us with her big brown eyes and her warm grin. I fumbled around on deck opening the deck plates and smiling at her while she stood in an engagingly provocative stance chatting to me from the dock. Suddenly I interjected. "Anne!" I gasped with embarrassment, "I can't talk to you anymore, I've just put water in the diesel tank!"

It was, indeed, one of my most embarrassing moments and I paid for it with a full day of hard, unpleasant labor, pumping out the black tank by hand into small containers and then carting all the bad fuel containers in several wheel barrow loads down the long wooden dock. Then I would wheel them down a dusty dirt road in the hot sun to an old oil truck where I'd made arrangements for dumping. It was a behemoth task. The resort was packed with boaters and tourists, and I must have been asked what I was doing at least twenty times. Davey was a good sport, though, and upon seeing my crestfallen ego encouraged me to recognize that it was an admirable chore to clean the sludge out of *Querencia's* fuel tank before our passage down the coast. What a gal.

Pulling into Friday Harbor for the Fourth of July holiday we were greeted by a boater's zoo and decided to anchor at the south end of the harbor away from most of the commotion. As fortune had it, we anchored over a wreck. The depth sounder jumped from thirty to seventy feet in one swing of the boat. The next morning we did some jigging off the deck with our "buzz bomb" and one of Big Al's squid jigs. Jigging is easy, you just let the heavily weighted lure drop almost to the bottom and then jerk it up a few feet with your rod and then let it sink again repeatedly. Before breakfast we had caught four nice rockcod, one lingcod, and a ten pound cabezon. We'd caught cabezon before and loved Rain catching this one. A large and ugly sculpin fish, the leathery skinned cabezon feeds on mostly shellfish and crab. It has bright bluish-green gills and flesh. Surprisingly, the meat resembles poultry in texture and turns white and firm when cooked. It is delicious!

On July 6 we were underway to Orcas Island to pick up Davey's children, Paul, fifteen, and Caroline, twelve, arriving by ferry from Seattle. For the next two weeks Davey and I enjoyed showing all three children our San Juans. After almost four months of living the San Juans we knew the angle of the dangle for almost every island, every cove. But *Querencia* was used to having us all aboard graciously. The summer before the five of us had spent six weeks together aboard *Querencia*. The kids loved her as much as we did, and we felt that by exposing them to life aboard *Querencia* in the great outdoors we were giving them something that would forever enrich their lives.

Life ashore indoors can be dull and unimaginative. Happiness seems more fleeting. Yet life aboard *Querencia* remained a warm infinity, a measureless peace in which each new day brought a spontaneity that wasn't necessarily predicted by yesterday's tabloids. It was impossible to lose interest. You lived a dream, your dream. If we have taught our children anything, it is that the most fulfilling thing that they can do is experience the mysteries of life.

Knowing this we asked again if they wanted to go offshore with us for at least part of the trip. The response was a resounding, "No way!"

On July 22nd we said goodbye to Rain, Caroline, and Paul. They were waving from the upper deck of the ferry as it pulled out of Friday Harbor. That same day our brave crew, Ed and Dale, arrived from Utah. They had ten days. We would sail to San Francisco together and we were to leave the following day.

Rain, Caroline, and Paul fishing in Snoring Bay

Part II
Storm at Sea

11.

After speaking with other sailors I have discovered two general truths:

1. Anyone who heads offshore on his sailboat for that first time worries what it will be like to weather that first storm at sea.

2. There is a very high likelihood that the worst weather cruising is apt to be almost immediately after leaving the safety and comfort of your home port.

Maybe that's due to *uncreative* visualization; you think so much about a fear that you actually make it happen. The phenomena is better explained by C.G. Jung in *Memories, Dreams, Reflections.* Jung reminds us that it is in our collective unconscious that the ground work is laid for symptoms to surface from our psychic disposition and manifest themselves into our reality. This gives us an explanation for UFOs and, in my mind, an argument against violence on TV.

Of course, maybe we just think we make it happen. Maybe it's all a matter of relativity.

The sailor that returns from the sea is often asked to describe his experiences, especially those nasty times when horrible weather consumed his existence. Like most intense experiences in life, it is hard to describe adequately.

Richard Dana, in his book *Two Years Before The Mast*, explained that in the days of clipper ships and sailing around the horn it was considered in bad taste for a sailor to complain of the weather. Maybe it was because without the wind and weather there would have been no such thing as a sailor!

Describing bad weather is a subjective thing to do, just as some people are terrified with heights while others are quite comfortable with them. Describing good weather seems fairly easy — a broad reach to fill the sail, fifteen knots of steady wind, gentle seas, and a blue sky.

From all the stories I've exchanged and read, it seems that most sailors have only about a one-in-ten chance of getting caught in a gale in a whole year of cruising. On Querencia we saw severe weather at the very beginning of our odyssey, off the Washington - Oregon coast, and then not again. After 15,000 miles and three years offshore, our worst weather was restricted to the first 300 miles and nine days! I attribute a lot of that to more than bad luck. Anyone who studies the pilot charts of the Pacific will see that monstrous wave heights, with or without gales, are born and bred there. The north Pacific Ocean, particularly in the upper latitudes, can be a whole different ball game for the unseasoned sailor.

I understand that there are a few sailors who don't pay much heed to bad weather warnings when they begin a passage. There is an old saying,

"Some are weather wise and some are otherwise."

These sailors plow forth into the sea meeting a challenge. Maybe they figure that once they get through that first few bad days everything else will then seem easier. Not us! Now, even more than before, we try to pick our departure times with patience. It seems apparent to me that the weather is the most important factor for a little boat in a big sea.

Yet, there are pressures to leave before your time. Friends will ask *why* you haven't left yet. Others remind you that you are *supposed* to be gone by now. We were sitting in a restaurant in Shilshole Bay, Seattle, when one of my patients came up to me and said, "Gee, are you back already?" After conversing with her I realized she actually thought you could sail from Seattle to San Francisco and back in three days!

I was very moved by the space shuttle disaster of 1986, as was the rest of the nation. Yet I had been irritated with the naivety of the news media. After more than one postponed launching, I have seen headlines in the newspaper day after day that moan, "Shuttle Delayed Again." I wonder what is causing this underlying rush in our world today. Why the pressure to hurry? It's taken thousands of years for man to get to the point where space travel is even possible and he can't even wait for the weather to clear up! That's either impatience or ignorance

Similar to astronauts, brave, heroic sailors start passages that cross oceans and hemispheres and time as well in their self-sufficient life support capsules. At no point before in history had such superbly built small private yachts existed, ready to take the individual who had the time, the money, and the conviction, to the far ends of the globe with the conveniences of electronics, auxiliary engine, and modern comforts.

Here we were, ready to do the most exciting thing we had ever done; about to change our lives forever; and people were razzing us, comparing our courageous adventure to a week-end jaunt to San Francisco on a jetliner.

The twenty-third of July was a very busy day for all of us. Besides everything else, the oil pressure sender on the engine failed making the warning light on the control panel glow a permanent orange. I had to replace it with a back-up out of *Querencia's* spare parts stores. Dale and Davey used a taxicab to make some last-minute hauls from the local marketplace — thirty-six bottles of wine, fifteen boxes of groceries, and eight blocks of ice. Ed and I used duct tape to bind the snap rings on the lifelines, seal the forward hatches, and for anything else that came to mind. We didn't get far that day, but we did leave.

Taking Lin Pardie's advice we sailed a bit and anchored that first night out giving the boat, and us and our crew a chance to get to know each other better. Davey wrote in the log:

> The time has come - with butterflies galore
> we cast off our lines and head for anchorage
> and a steak dinner at Griffin Bay.

First thing the following morning Ed used the windlass to winch up the hook and away we went, out through the San Juan Channel, where as usual the tide rips were ferocious. Dale and Ed remarked that they were beginning to see why respect for the sea is imperative.

With the wind out of the northwest, *Querencia* dug in on a long southwesterly tack across the Strait of Juan de Fuca where we found large swells and waves. We had all stuck scopolamine patches behind our ears and yet we all felt nauseous and disoriented. A decision was made to lower the dosage by cutting the patches in half. I threw mine away. How to get seasick using seasick medicine!

The day grew long as we beat west. The wind and seas were not in our favor, kicking up in the afternoon to double reef conditions and taking some of the fun out of it. The swells and the waves pounded on the bow of the hull of the boat as she pushed her way to windward. By evening we were unexpectedly exhausted and rather than stay out overnight we opted to ease up on the boat and ourselves. We pulled into Port Angeles to anchor. Ed pointed out that after all, Port Angeles must be there for just such a purpose! We dropped our hook near the port dock. Tired and sweaty we let our tense muscles relax over drinks and chicken. What would tomorrow bring? We decided to take it as it comes - and a good thing at that.

We left Port Angeles at 0600 the following morning somewhat rejuvenated. Although things started out well enough, soon similar wind and sea conditions buried *Querencia's* bow in the water even more than the day before. We decided to motor along the shore. The scenery was large and fantastic. Davey and I were relaxing over lunch in the cockpit enjoying Dale's sense of humor when Ed called to us from below with his Jack Nicholson drawl.

"Should the floorboards be floating?"

Davey wrote in the log:

> Calm panic takes over. Have we lost the fresh-
> water from one of our tanks? Has the head
> been taking in water? Or is it from the
> engine? Ed helps the electric bilge pump with
> its massive task with a manual bilge pump
> while John starts eliminating possible sources.
> It's definitely salt water but he can't find
> where it's coming from. We decide maybe
> water has been coming in from the chain
> locker or anchor well drains in the bow; the
> uphill climb through long rolling swells forc-
> ing the water from the bow down to the bilge.
> I climbed up to our berth and started unload-
> ing everything stowed there. I pull out the v-
> berth cushions and the boards and a sinking
> feeling overwhelms me; the entire bow from
> the bulkhead forward is *full* of water. No won-
> der *Querencia* was so sluggish.

All the things that we had carefully stowed there were water logged. All our important papers, our clothes, dental tools, electric calculator, mementos, all of it soaking and mostly ruined. Woodwork and mechanical tools stowed underneath the main cabin sole were also mostly ruined. Ed and I continued to bail and unloaded every-thing into the cockpit where Davey and Dale were still motoring *Querencia* west. We were half-way between Port Angeles and Neah Bay, a distance of 60 miles.

Once the bow was emptied, including all the chain in the chain locker, the problem showed itself; a split drain hose from the anchor well allowed almost a quart of water in with every wave that washed over the bow. I pondered some design changes and then proceeded to cut and re-fit a hose from the ship's stores. This required heating water to soften the stiff new hose. It was hot, cramped, and clammy in the bow, and by the time Ed and I had everything repaired and re-stowed, we found the fresh air in the cockpit very liberating. Over the next week we would dry out and save what we could that was flooded — tossing the rest overboard.

By the time we reached Neah Bay our dismay over the events of the past two days was being replaced with the intuitive confidence that we must now be through the worst of it. We undoubtedly had passed a certain test. The wind was easing as the sun lowered itself into the hazy horizon to the west. The wooded, jagged peaks of this continental corner popped up behind Neah Bay bounteously clothed in verdure. We motored back and forth outside Wa'adah Island focusing again on our goals, easing up, reflecting and relaxing with our fishing rod, hoping to snag a salmon for dinner. None of us expected it to be so tough or take so long to get out of the straits.

"Shit happens" is an old sailing edict. Live and learn. Learn and live.

No salmon. We went into the bay just before sunset and anchored between town and the log booms. We were too exhausted to inflate the dinghy to go ashore and instead lay on the deck resting our tired minds and muscles, watching the local Indians drive over the dusty little logging roads in huge cars. We took our weary reverie to early bunks, assuring each other that our wits would be more about us in the morning. Then we would decide whether or not to head out past Cape Flattery and take the big left, or to lay over for another day.

12.

The big day was here! We awoke early and listened to the marine weather over the VHF.

"Out sixty miles: southerly up to twenty-five knots."

It was certainly nothing too heavy, and we felt rested enough. The leak had been fixed, so that wasn't a factor. Ed offered the following insight in a jocular tone of voice.

"You have to bite it off sometime." As he spoke his blue eyes were open wide, the corners of his mouth turned upward. We would cast those words in bronze.

In fifteen knots of wind we headed out and around Cape Flattery; out past Tatoosh Island, over the ocean swells and into the widening waters. We were underway in a body of water that is sixty-four million square miles in size and covers over a third of the surface of the earth. We were at long last sailing our yar vessel on the Pacific! I busily plotted our course and honed in our Sat Nav. We all quickly adapted to the swells and waves, and even as they grew larger and the wind blew stronger, the four of us are having a blast!

Indeed, it was building into a good ride; a warm wind from the south pushing us westward. The clouds sunk from the heavens and turned into dark gray, ragged, nimbostratus clouds that hung above the water. By afternoon we were picking our way through low standing squalls. Fish were everywhere, just floating on the surface, as if the sea had rolled them up from the bottom — huge sunfish with their odd shapes, brown sharks, and all manner of weird sea creatures. And then there were birds; hundreds of little, fat, awkward pigeon types flitting from wave to wave. Were they Mother Carey's Chickens, the storm petrels you can read about in any offshore sailor's log, birds that always do *this ritual* before a storm?

It wouldn't be too long until dark. The sky and sea had grown darker and the wind had picked up. I steered a course through large lumpy waves, greenish-gray, white foam strewing the surface. Dale's lighthearted humor was on the wane. We had a reef in the main and began to consider shortening sail even more.

My white knuckles had been clutching the wheel most of the afternoon and now I felt weary. I couldn't expect to steer all night long, nor could I expect anyone else to take over the helm easily. We carefully rigged up Nelley, guiding the self steerage lines forward from the steering vane through their blocks and adjusting them to the wheel. Would she be able to self-steer the boat? Nelley's first ocean test. She had to steer through a confused sloppy sea; charging over this wave, easing up, then gliding down the other side, into and off the gusting wind. She worked!

Blackness came and we dropped the main sail. The wind kept *Querencia* on her side with just the staysail up. We kept our offshore tack, always moving away from the dangerous Washington coast. Intermittently, waves broke against the hull on our port side, sloshing us in the cockpit. Nasty, filthy weather! It was pouring rain and blowing like hell.

The four of us sat in our rain gear with our backs to the monstrous waves, clipped in with our safety harnesses. I encouraged the crew not to look at the waves. It had been hours, we all tried to relax. The waves were huge, rolling walls of water that hypnotized you in the dark with their crashing noise and phosphorescent foam. Amazingly, they always passed under the boat as you stared in disbelief.

"Sit tight," I said aloud.

No one wanted to go below because of sea sickness. The muggy air and vertigo drove each of us back up on deck as quickly as we would go down below Ed, however, suddenly felt an inspection of the thru-hulls and hoses mandatory. I felt confident about the repair, but encouraged Ed to check things out if he wished. He disappeared down the hatch. The weather, meanwhile, began to rage. Dale and Davey and I sit there, wedged in the cockpit not saying anything. You had to yell to talk anyway. Ed was gone for half an hour although it seemed like an eternity. Suddenly he flung the hatch open and out popped his green head. Thoughtfully remembering to face downwind with his projectile, he wretched one forceful, quick expellation quite violently, then clambered back to a spot near the upside rail with his report.

"Everything's fine!"

An hour before midnight we had the wheel over hard, hove to, still crabbing along at about two knots. The winds were now up to a solid Force 8 and gusting. The sea was rolling with dense streaks of foam streaming along the direction of the wind. We tied everything on deck down twice, the additional noise of anything banging or flapping being an added aggravation to the already deafening storm. Any ideas to do anything more creative were squelched by the rain turning to hail; large chunky pellets of ice beat down on us covering the decks. It was unbelievable. The visibility had deteriorated so badly that now we couldn't even see the running lights on the bow. Suddenly I thought I saw a light, then another, appearing, disappearing in the blackness. I *did* see lights! Probably some poor fishing boats out here as miserable as we were. Now we had to worry about running into them or vice versa. With slow, deliberate movements Ed made his way back down the hatch to the VHF radio. He couldn't raise them on the radio and we resorted to turning on our strobe lights. We would not risk a collision.

The fear of collision added unbearably to the tension we were under. We all peered silently into the surrounding blackness, but we could barely even see the bow. On top of that, we all thought we might be hallucinating from the mixture of scopolamine and strobe lights.

By three in the morning we were four cold, aching, exhausted human beings. The rains had stopped and the winds were easing a bit and daylight wasn't too far off. Finally, each of us took a turn going below decks long enough to get some dry, warm clothes and tend to our personal plumbing. I went below and shut the hatch behind me. I turned on the saloon lights and *Querencia's* warm teak interior greeted me, reminding me we were secure. She was going along much better now. On the gimbaled galley stove was a pot of spaghetti that had been lashed down with shock cords ever since yesterday afternoon.

When Ed had said "You have to bite it off sometime" I think he meant you can prepare and prepare and prepare, but you have to eat it to understand.

13.

"The future is made of the same stuff as the present."
— Simone Well

When daylight arrived we were bobbing around like mamma duck in a lumpy lake. It was a pleasure to free up *Querencia* and get going the right direction again. At ten that morning a fix had informed me that the storm had blown us backward eleven miles off course. Naps all around returned our spirits, and soon we were making it all up with great blue-water sailing under full sails.

We passed a massive sea turtle. Now *that* was unusual — a turtle off the Washington coast! We had noticed the temperature of the water to be very warm and the air had a tropical feeling to it. We were witnessing the effects of El Niño. As we know now, the disturbance of the earth's global ocean currents by an El Niño can cause unexpected temperatures, weather, and species migration.

At night, the tropical effect was most noticeable underneath the light of the moon. The water was thick with squids covering the surface.

The predator was there too — large killer whales [*Orcinus orca*]. Ten tons and thirty feet long, the most intelligent of all sea life, they pushed along beside us all night, respiring heavily, blowing their moist breath into the damp air. Humans have nothing to fear from killer whales in the wild. In general they have very peaceful attitudes towards us, tolerating our intrusions into their realm or avoiding us all together, which is not necessarily the case toward their prey. The sea which had been so black and furious the night before was now calm and mysterious. I found myself with more questions than.answers about the orcas' way of life. Standing watch was a fascinating experience for each of us.

At daybreak we decided that in order to make good any significant progress we would have to motor. In the process of starting the engines, I was surprised to discover that one of our two batteries had gone dead and would need recharging. The satellite navigation system had also quit as a result of our electrical system going down. We had excessively used the ship's lighting the night of the storm, and the Sat Nav, at six amps, had been drawing juice now for two days. It seemed apparent that we needed to trim our voracious electrical appetite. It might be better to get the schedule of satellites and then only turn on the Sat Nav just before they arrived.

By noon we had a near perfect sailing day; fifteen knots of wind filling our big genoa with its red cross, *Querencia* gliding over four-foot seas under blue skies. In the cockpit we listened to synthesized music and enjoyed the aroma of Davey's breaded chicken wafting up from the galley.

From the log:

> Called the Korean freighter *Acumen* for position check on VHF.46 deg. 46.35 min. North by 125 deg. 16.5 min. West which is exactly where we thought we were. About thirty-six miles offshore. Nice exchange. — DT

The sun went down and a beautiful egg-shaped moon slowly

came up to share the heavens with the stars. Life was glorious and on this particular night sailing was easy.

The next morning the sun found Ed and me eating pears and drinking hot chocolate in the cockpit. Big mellow swells were coming in from the north. The horizon stretched in a perfect circle completely surrounding *Querencia*. The ocean reminded us of a broad plain, remarkably vast, blue and undulating. We were stirred from our reverie by a blue shark suddenly tugging on the lure we had been trailing behind us. Davey and Dale clambered up the companionway to stare with their sleepy eyes as we struggled to get it alongside and get the hook out. His long slender iridescent head ended in a pointed snout full of curved, serrated teeth.

The morning excitement was signaling the beginning of a picked-up tempo. By afternoon the wind had come up to twenty-five knots and we had heavy following seas. We were seeing a lot of logs, "deadheads" as sailors call them in the Puget Sound. These were presumably being spewed out from the Columbia River, and the anticipation of more ahead concerned us enough to keep a sharp lookout. Screaming along, racing down waves, it seemed it would be easy for one to put a hole in your hull if you hit it. The wind and seas just kept building and soon it felt like we were on a wild downhill toboggan ride, slip-sliding down, down, down the face of the globe. By evening it was blowing thirty-five knots and we were down to just our staysail again. The sky was hazy, like ground glass, with bright orange streaks scratched across the western vista by a dry wind.

We refined our technique for pouring cocktails offshore. Put all the glasses in the bottom of the deep stainless galley sink. After then unscrewing the cap from the bottle, tilt it and try to hold it over the sink for a few seconds. With all the lurching about, the bartender tends to pour a very relaxed round with one hand while hanging on to the boat with the other!

At precisely the same time that the sun kissed the horizon multitudes of dolphins appeared out of nowhere. They filled the agitated waters as far as the eye could see, all the way to the horizon. It was a spectacular panorama that made the hair on the back of our necks stand up on end. Hundreds upon hundreds of these glorious creatures in every direction; diving, jumping, chattering, squeaking. It was a phenomenon that I have never seen again.

We all felt a certain loneliness as the dolphins vanished as mysteriously as they had appeared. The wind's noisy howling consumed us, and the descending darkness seemed to surround our very souls. Just after 2100 hours I scribbled into the log:

> Huge seas.Desperately tired and cranky. Seas aft, running.Trailing three 200 ft. lines (streaming warps) off our port aft quarter. This seems to have slowed us down a bit and seas are no longer breaking over the cockpit coaming.It also is keeping the stern into the wave as we surf down into the troughs, and I am not as worried now about broaching. Concerned about taking water in the exhaust though. Not much we can do about deadheads. Will put on some lights for freighter traffic to see.

It kept on blowing right into the next day. We hauled in our trailing warps and only flew a minimum of sail.

> We are starting to adjust to the sleigh ride.
> Down, down, down the face of the globe.

The day passed quickly, with only a fishing boat and a sperm whale (with her calf) to remember.

Soon it was nine at night again and the going was very rough. Even rougher than the night before. We all agreed that fatigue seemed to the biggest problem. Even adding one-digit numbers after no sleep and lots of weather can be quite difficult. Our skin was weathering into cracks, and Davey's and Ed's lower lips were split and bleeding. It was like we'd been up on Mt. Everest or something.

We were new at this and it was hard to rest with the incessant jerking motion. *Querencia* was like a roller coaster with one wheel off the track. Side to side motion whipped the hull back and forth as we raced down the steep waves. The whole boat would shudder, the blocks would crash around, and then a hard jolt, a snap of the sails, and we'd be off again down the next wave. That night, although we wished we didn't have to, we trailed our warps once more. It seemed that a high pressure system over the North Pacific Ocean and a low pressure on the North American continent were making for heap big northerly winds just offshore.

By daylight the following day the wind was still blowing hard and the sea was still roaring behind us, but at least we had the sun, some light and warmth. I got energized and made potatoes, onions, and eggs for everybody. Not only does this meal stick to your ribs, but it sticks to your plate as well, an attractive quality when everything is being thrown around like a sack of rice!

We were now off the California coast, and we could feel that the geography was changing. We were about fifty miles offshore and on this particular day the wind was easing up. We had the time to make some minor repairs and get several good navigational position fixes. The temperature became comfortably warm. The swells became longer, gentler heaves. We decided that the description *"mellow"* fit the swells perfectly and that this was conclusive proof that we were off of California.

By cocktail hour the weather eased enough for us to be sailing wing on wing, sipping wine and plucking smoked oysters out of a tin with toothpicks, all at the same time! All the indications were there that it was going to be a good night and we relaxed. We could have been at least slightly suspect when we saw those two Mother Carey's Chickens go by.

When Davey and I came on watch at midnight the last gleaming sliver of the waning moon was just starting to rise up past the eastern horizon. We continued to sail along under full sail, marveling at it all. We had been on deck for less than an hour when we saw our first really big meteor at sea. A ball of fire, a blazing light falling out of the heavens, so close you could see it burning, embers trailing behind. Sparking, burning, falling, and then, "Phhhhhht...", out. I am not sure that it wasn't the lingering imprint of that bright spectacle that bleached my eye ink white, but I swear I could see smoke.

A fresh breeze and a second set of swells asynchronous from the first, coming in from the west, were our first indication that things were about to change. By four in the morning it was blowing twenty-five knots and we were surfing down eight-foot waves again. With all of our sail up, the port rail was starting to bury itself in the white froth. Even from our position in the cockpit we could hear the roar inside the hull below decks. We wondered how Ed and Dale were able to sleep.

I opened the companionway doors and barked, "Say Ed, you want to come up and help Davey drop the jib?"

Naturally, by the time Ed was on deck, although he came immediately, it was gusting over thirty knots and we were really thrashing around. Another near gale was upon us. By 0500 we were hove to. The first light of day found the four of us huddled below decks, the wheel tied hard over. Occasionally one of the huge waves would come from the odd direction and completely wash over the boat. Our minds were drifting into their own reality now, any resiliency quickly fading away. Once again it seemed we were in the most wretched of circumstances and the fatigue was insufferable.

I threw up a quick vote, and the vote was unanimous. Now eighty-five miles off the coast of northern California, as soon as we could we would put in for the nearest port for some sorely needed rest and recuperation.

Around noon the winds had eased enough for us to raise some sail and get under way again, and we started a southeasterly tack. The waves, however, were still huge, twelve feet or more, and when they would break just aft of *Querencia* white water foamed and boiled right up to the edge of the cockpit coaming. It seemed *Querencia* was barely keeping in front of them, and we anticipated a monster wave breaking into the cockpit, flooding everything at any moment where the four of us sat. A couple of hours passed until finally we started to relax enough to appreciate an appetite.

Querencia was corkscrewing left and right, port and starboard. The ocean roared all around us. As Ed stood at the companionway pausing before going below for some refreshments, he turned and looked at me. His bearded face reminded me of some poor merchant who'd just stepped off his camel in the Sahara desert somewhere. His cracked lips parted under the now blistering sun. His clothes were a mess. Very dryly he spoke.

"We're locked out."

This was unbelievable. I started digging for the fire axe in the cockpit lazaret at once, sputtering and cursing obscenities. Now on top of everything else we were going to have to chop a hole through our beautiful teak doghouse in order to have food and shelter.

"Well, fine," I spit, "if that's what it takes, then we'll do it." At least we had an axe.

Dale and Davey urged me to pause and be sure there wasn't a better solution. Peering through the cracks in the cockpit doors, Ed could see what had happened. The sliding overhead hatch had a bolt latch at each side. As *Querencia* was thrown side to side the bolts had extended and nicely seated themselves tighter than ever. With the threat of getting pooped, we had put the slats in the companionway to prevent flooding below decks. Now with the hatch locked shut, we couldn't get those out either.

"Hey, wait up a minute," Ed opted. "I've got my pocket knife here. Maybe I can pick open the latches."

This bit of bad luck had been intolerable for me, and I found Ed's optimistic idea somewhat weak. Although I visualized a scene where I was triumphantly swinging the axe in furious, revengeful arcs with splinters flying in every direction, I resisted my vision and let Ed have his chance. Surprisingly, after only twenty minutes he had picked open both hatch latches.

Still blowing like hell, Nelley steered us under a headsail only. The four of us went below, out of the sun and wind, to share some vienna sausages and sodas. Davey and I had been up at this point for sixteen hours and longed for some sleep. It wasn't much better for Ed and Dale, but I talked them into taking a watch as we collapsed into the port bunk.

For some reason I said to Ed, "Let me know if you see any other boats." We hadn't seen any boats for days.

In slightly under five minutes, Ed spoke. "You might want to take a look out a starboard porthole," he offered in the most neutral of tones.

I fought back my sleep once again, got up and looked at the world one more time through what was now for me a rose colored porthole. There, right *there*, just beside us, like some extravagant exaggeration, was a huge gray and hulking United States Navy attack carrier. It's black hull numbers were big and bold. Gun mounts were everywhere. We were sloshing around, doing six knots and this huge mammoth *thing* was just setting there.

We flipped on the VHF radio and immediately received a call from the ship's commander, who wanted to know if we were okay or having trouble. Actually, it was one of the most charming conversations I've ever had with another vessel. We must have talked for ten minutes and about everything it seemed. About our trouble, we explained that we didn't have any, other than we were a bit fatigued from all the weather and rough seas. He was as genuinely fascinated, I think, with us as we were with him.

Eighty miles away, the Eureka Coast Guard was monitoring our conversation! Although they couldn't hear us talking to the carrier, they could hear the carrier talking to us. They must have sensed concern in the commander's voice, because they suddenly interrupted and requested a full description and report from the commander as to who and what this sailboat was all about out there anyway. We listened patiently for the reply as the carrier forwarded a meticulous verbal report explaining who we were and that we were okay. Just spelling *Querencia* can be a hassle. Eventually the Coast Guard was satisfied and cleared the VHF. The commander said "so long," and wished us a better day tomorrow. I thanked the Navy skipper and told him I hoped we hadn't created too much red tape for him.

We all looked out again and carrier was suddenly gone. To my amazement she had totally disappeared. Ed reminded us that attack carriers probably cruise at over forty knots.

On the morning of August 2, the following day, a fix put us thirty-four miles east of Crescent City Harbor. Midway between San Francisco Bay and the entrance to the Columbia River, it is used almost exclusively by commercial and sport fishing boats. *Querencia* carried charts for every port on the west coast of the North America it seemed, excepting, of course, Crescent City.

However, the conditions were very forgiving as it was a perfectly beautiful day with gentle seas and light winds. It seemed like the nicest day at sea we'd had yet, now that we were pulling into port. After we came over the horizon flying our big genoa, a breakwater slowly became visible, then the local buoys and Mussel Rock. We tried calling a harbormaster and then the Crescent City Coast Guard station for further sailing directions, but couldn't raise anyone on the

VHF until we were actually in the harbor.

Negotiating a course into Crescent City proved easy anyway, and at a little after three in the afternoon we were the only yacht in the harbor, tied up between two huge, very fishy, fishing boats.

> The fishing boat *CITY OF EUREKA* is dilap-
> idated but has a nice crew! They give us three
> pounds of halibut and we plan a huge feast of
> fish and chips. — DT

Before preparing dinner we seized the opportunity to get off the boat for the first time in nine days. We were all really pretty wobbly and more than a bit disoriented. Wandering up to Route 101, we thumbed a dusty ride into town for ice and something cool to drink. Already rather lawless from our experience at sea, the noise, pollution, traffic, crowdedness, and multitude of advertising everywhere to buy, buy, buy was more than a slight shock. Had our experience caused us to forget who we were *or* to remember? We felt like aliens, fish out of water, and I am sure we didn't exactly look like local folk, but soon a kind soul stopped and offered us a ride in the back of his rickety green pickup. The truck screeched back onto the black asphalt and rolled down the highway at an incredulous fifty miles per hour.

Unanimously we exclaimed, "Oh my God!"

The following day we immediately took advantage of being at port. Once we started on the long list of chores and minor repairs we realized how smart our decision had been to put-in. For starters we caulked the anchor locker and sprit, repaired the ignition cover hatch (Ed had stepped on it and broke it off in our last good blow), re-wired the VHF directly to batteries (it kept needlessly throwing the circuit breaker), repaired the sump pump, re-stitched the main sail and our shredded U.S. flag. Then we tightened the pedestal steering, emptied and cleaned the head, re-mounted the galley oven door, serviced all the thru-hulls, changed the engine oil, and replaced a leaky engine check valve. Finished with repairs, we then cleaned *Querencia* from stem to stern and oiled all her teak. Davey and Dale washed all our clothes and bedding on the dock by hand (including those still wet from the flood). It was then that I noticed Dale was so bruised from the passage she looked like she'd been in a car wreck!

Ed walked with me as I limped across town to the hospital. I had not taken the boot off my left foot in almost a week, having severely stubbed my big toe early in our trip. My foot had become so painful and inflamed that leaving the boot on it, somewhat protected, had seemed the best thing to do. Now, I finally felt relief as the boot came off and the doctor removed the toenail and dressed the wound.

For our way back to the harbor we decided that I could hobble back if we stopped in the city park for a rest. There we found long stretches of green grass where clusters of giggling children in bright swimming suits were running through sprinklers. The sun was lowering itself in the western sky and its diffused golden light covered everything. Ed and I said little. We were two sailors, home from the sea delighting in simple daydreaming ashore.

A few days later Davey and I were left to ourselves. Ed placed a call to his office only to discover that he needed to return as soon as possible. Ed and Dale flew out — away and inland. Davey and I turned our attention back to continuing our adventure. We no longer were thinking in terms of sailing nonstop to San Diego. Stopping more frequently seemed a much better idea than pushing so hard, especially now that it was just the two of us. We decided we probably didn't need to stay so far off shore anymore, either. Nevertheless, the four hundred miles of rugged coastline between Crescent City and San Francisco offered little protection or marina development. On to San Francisco!

14.

"Courage is fear holding on a minute longer."
— General George Patton

On August 7 we motored our way out of Crescent City through a light fog that we hoped would burn off by noon. We had butterflies in our stomachs as we motored past the last buoy which was clanging lazily with the motion of the swells. Despite our worries and the foggy haze, it turned out to be a nice day at sea, with gentle winds of ten to fifteen knots.

Evening came soon though. Just before daylight disappeared Davey made a wonderful stroganoff dinner to help our growling bellies make it through the night. There being just the two of us now, we started our respective three-hour watches. Except for the disappointment of a thickening cloud cover and the occasional lights or engine noise of a distant ship, it was a fairly easy night for us and *Querencia*, although a bit too roly-poly.

By morning we were pleased to discover that we had covered a lot of ground without having had to work very hard, suggesting that we were experiencing the south set of the current. We had come over fifty miles from Crescent City and were thirteen miles off Trinidad Head. Trinidad Head was the first of several points or capes that were strung along the California coast about every forty miles or so from here southward. Each one represented an accomplishment to us with new sailing territory on the other side of it. Each one also had its dangers and particular sea and weather characteristics and sea traffic. Boats would naturally converge at the points as they navigated north and south.

> 10:59 A tuna fishing boat passed us going north buzzing along at eight knots or so. It appeared to be a single handed operation and he had his hands full, frantically pulling in hand line after hand line with a big tunas on them flapping away, then running back to the helm, then back to his lines. Also saw three more fishing boats and two freighters. Got a bit nervous when the freighter *SUMBA* overtook us and roared past our starboard aft quarter going southwest.It must have been only 100 yards away or so. Had a call on the radio from *EMM TOO*, one of the fishing boats out of Crescent City; said he was about nine miles in front of us.

In the afternoon we decided to try our own luck at fishing. The wind had picked up to twenty knots. With the sun now bright and brilliant, the blue water seemed to come alive. Birds were everywhere.

16:08 Something big ran off with the lure Joe
and Eli gave us, half our line, and almost our
"meat hook" of a fishing pole. Probably a
large tuna. We will have to learn the proper
method of catching these things — maybe
using hand lines like the fishing boats we see.

We passed over a submarine valley name Eel canyon. Those submarine valleys as well as the seamounts seemed to encourage the
build-up of large swells and confused seas. By nightfall we were
abeam of Cape Mendocino, seventeen miles to the east of us and we
wrote in our log that it was blowing a steady thirty knots and gusting.

Cape Mendocino, a huge headland sticking out into the Pacific
Ocean from the coast of California, was famous in the days of old
Spanish navigators and the sailing galleons that came from the West
Indies. When coming from the north here the coast makes nearly a
forty-five degree turn to the southeast and boats are always anxious
to get south of the cape and more in the lee, slightly better protected from the strong winds of summer. The NW through N winds are
reinforced by the sea breeze, and even in the summer, gales often
occur ten percent of the time.

And this is how we found it ourselves shortly before midnight.
We were down to just our stay sail, again, and trailing three 100-foot
lines, making mad toboggan rides down steep waves that snuck up on
us from behind.

In the darkness I could just make out the outline of the huge
rollers as they would creep up on us, larger and larger, sometimes
curling up into a heap and then breaking in white water all around
Querencia's stern. Eating and sleeping both seemed out of the question. Even being in the cockpit seemed much to dangerous.
Querencia was tearing through the water, mad seas chasing her with
the occasional waves washing the cockpit. Nelley continued to steer
for us, but you could almost imagine her huffing and puffing as the
wheel spun one direction and then the other as she corrected for the
wild conditions.

It was difficult to decide if we were totally right in how we were
handling our predicament. The gravity of the situation was having

an unsure effect on us. It was hard to do much more than stand in the companionway and peer out the hatch to keep an eye on things. Going forward to adjust the sails, or changing course and heaving to, seemed like ridiculously dangerous ideas.

Another wave broke into the cockpit and washed away our cockpit bucket, snapping its lanyard like thread. Then *Querencia* leapt ahead again. I crawled out into the cockpit and carefully examined the Aries steering vane with a flashlight. Everything was fine. There was nothing to do tonight but let her go and stay safe.

At the first light of morning we stared out the aft galley porthole at the stupendous heaving mass of water behind the boat. At the bottom of the troughs the whine in the rigging from the howling of the wind would become more hollow sounding, like when one blows over a jug. The waves were as high as the spreaders, and that would make them twenty to twenty-two feet high.

It was in these early morning hours that Davey and I, both tired and exhausted and dispirited, looked each other closely in the eye. We had only been out of Crescent City two days and we were back into frightening weather and conditions. We weren't having fun anymore. We sat down together wedging ourselves in the port settee and shared a piece of beef jerky. Like children in a confessional we both pensively admitted to one another that we really thought that maybe *this* wasn't for us after all. If this is what sailing oceans is all about then maybe we weren't cut out for it like we thought. Despite all our experience and preparation we were afraid that this might be true. We were very depressed and almost defeated. We were also angry. This wasn't fair.

What we didn't yet realize was that this was the very worst of it, and, that for the remainder of our passage down the North American coast, across to the South Pacific, and back to Hawai'i, we would be blessed with mostly good conditions contrary to what our experience so far would have us believe.

Davey brought up our hero, Sir Francis Chichester, the great English sailor whose books, *Alone Across the Atlantic* and *Gipsy Moth Circles the Globe*, we had on board. We recalled his descriptions of how alone he fought fatigue and the weather in cruel storms. At times, having done all he could do with the boat he would then curse off the situation and go below and have a Guinness.

Along with the rising of the sun, remembering Chichester lifted our spirits a bit. We drank a Guinness ourselves while we chewed another piece of jerky and split a biscuit. We poured over the charts and looked for a place to put in. We were forty miles from shore, and the shoreline wasn't exactly dotted with ports of pleasure. If we hauled around to a close reach and went dead east we had a chance of making Mendocino Bay or Fort Bragg. Otherwise there wasn't much else all the way to San Francisco, over 120 miles away.

To haul around to a close reach and go east meant turning *Querencia* abeam of not only the wind but the seas as well. The wind had eased to about twenty-five knots since sun up, but the swells were still as big or bigger. We could do it. I climbed out into the cockpit and unhooked the lines from the wheel that ran forward from Nelley and stood at the wheel. I noticed that my knees were weak and almost knocking.

"Careful, timing is incredibly important. Now!" I instructed myself.

And as we sat in the trough, I turned *Querencia's* nose to the east. The next towering swell seemed to hover over our port rail, then miraculously lifted up the bow and passed harmlessly underneath and went on its way. Then *Querencia* climbed the next mountain of water and slid down it's back side. Then the next swell, and the next. We were going east!

By early afternoon we were in much calmer waters off the entrance to Mendocino Bay. The sun was shining bright and the waves and the running swell had all but dissipated, leaving us with four-foot waves. The entrance was narrow and irregular and the whole bay was surrounded by a precipitous irregular cliff over 100 feet high. It seemed rocks were awash all around us. There were no boats and no people, although in the distance on the north cliff we could see picturesque weathered homes of the famous little town of Mendocino. A whistle buoy at the narrow channel into the bay gave a lonely tremulous moan as it suddenly sprang up just off our starboard beam.

We desperately wanted to anchor and rest, but everything here seemed disordered and dangerous. It was obvious to us that in west weather it would be a perfect place to lose your boat. We did a u-turn and headed back out to sea. The log sports a brevity here:

Mendocino looked too tricky.

By now it was late in the afternoon and the sun was starting to climb off its perch in the western sky. Davey called on the VHF radio up to the Fort Bragg Coast Guard Station stationed on the Noyo River, eight miles to the north, and asked them if they thought it was worth the motor north against the weather.

"What will we find there?"

They were very friendly and helpful and assured us that we would find excellent refuge on the Noyo River. A few hours later, at the channel entrance we met and followed a Coast Guard inflatable up the channel past the narrow mouth of the Noyo.

We passed underneath the eighty-foot bridge that supports the ocean highway and continued around the first sharp bend in the river. The river wasn't any wider than a city street and fishing boats were tied up four deep on each side, all kinds of wonderful old fishing boats sitting in the protected green waters between the banks of the Noyo. The scene was filled with funky fish houses and historic wooden docks backdropped with the lush green foothills of California Redwood country. It was beautiful, but where were we going to park?

Once again we felt the breadth of civilization. *Querencia*, with all her brass and class and colors and clean lines, sorely needed a place to tie up. Around one more bend in the river we went. There, off our starboard bow, against the south bank of the river was an eighty-six foot fishing boat named *San Juan* sporting a spanking new jet-black paint job.

"Here mate! Here mate! Come alongside, you'll be fine here!" a voice sang out, uplifting the waning tempo of our moment.

A man of slight build with warm eyes and a straight smile lowered a bright orange bumper on the port side of the *San Juan* and gestured for us to come along side. Davey and I quickly agreed.

"We'll take it!" we sang back in unison.

15.

"Just being a part of it is wonderful."
— Ken Kesey

We tied up alongside the *San Juan* and were then asked by a young Coast Guard enlisted man to help fill out a government form concerning our sailing plans and safety equipment. After obliging him with the necessary aid in filling out his paper work, he sheepishly asked us if we'd like to come back to the station with him for a piping hot shower and a cold beer. Now that was government hospitality!

After our shower and beer they filled our arms with all the extra charts they could spare in hopes of helping us with ports of call further south. Very appreciative, we wobbled back to *Querencia* experiencing a sort of trance from being ashore again. Bob Rawn, the kind soul that had taken our lines and invited us alongside the tug, and his wife, Beverly, were waiting for us with an invitation for coffee aboard the *San Juan*.

An incredibly gracious couple from Canada, they had been living aboard and refurbishing the *San Juan* for a year, ever since they had lost their own sailboat south of Cape Mendocino! Coming down from the U.S.-Canadian border as we did, they also had wanted to come in for a respite, but instead ran aground in foggy conditions. They lost nearly everything except their lives and their terrific sense of humor.

As Bob related it, the only serious injury they sustained was his. Determined to get help, Bob and Bev jumped off the boat and half swam and were half washed ashore still wearing their safety harnesses. Intent on getting to the Noyo and finding a tug to pull their boat off, they struggled up to the highway and flagged down the first vehicle that came by, a pickup truck. Jumping into the front seat, the lanyard of Bob's safety harness trailed down between his legs, behind him, and out the passenger's door of the pickup. In this moment of high anxiety and chaos the truck screeched back onto the asphalt highway and the wayward line caught and wrapped around the wheel axle.

"Nearly lost the family jewels, right then and there," said Bob.

Bob and Beverly and the gracious *San Juan* made us seem at home and understood. We swapped sea stories while we sipped our coffees and gazed out the portholes. The sun was setting and all the light was golden, the tide was at maximum flood and the whole river seemed full and green. It was like some big magic movie where Davey was Katherine Hepburn and I was Spencer Tracy and we were on this wild adventure, and now tonight here we were, surrounded by so much character — fishing boats, docks, and real, wonderful people.

Our joy took us further. Determined to celebrate, Davey and I continued our evening by walking down the boardwalk and up a dusty road to the Noyo River Inn for dinner. There just in front of the restaurant was our first palm tree. Now that was something! I will never forget the tremendous symbolism of that palm tree silhouetted against the twilight sky, and how meaningful the sight of it was to each of us.

Early the following morning we had more conclusive proof that we were getting further south, into the heartland of California. Eager to post a couple of letters but needing some stamps, we made our way into the little office of a "natural foods" sort of coffee mill that operated out of a small warehouse on the docks next to the *San Juan*.

There were two robust, young, attractive women in earth sandals and embroidered light dresses. The coffee beans smelled wonderful. It must have been a Monday because we stood there a long time waiting for someone to take notice of us. Finally, one girl looked up from her desk and stared at us. I asked if they might have a couple of postage stamps we could buy.

There was a long pause and then she looked at her co-worker who agonizingly spoke for both of them.

"Oh God, we don't have the space to handle finding stamps this morning!"

"No problem." I replied.

Anxious to alleviate the job stress we were imposing, Davey and I quickly withdrew outside where we nearly split our sides open with laughter.

We finally got to meet the skipper, Don, of the fishing boat *Emm Two* with whom we had spoken with on the VHF radio several times. A man younger than myself, he invited us aboard where he told us stories of the local fishermen, hard labor and fortunes won and lost. We exchanged stories most of the afternoon. He carefully made us some tuna lines that he guaranteed would catch us a fish, and then showed us how to make them ourselves. Upon leaving *Emm Two* Don shared with us his secret recipe for cooking tuna in lemon juice and then jumped down into the refrigerated hold. It was full of fish from his catch and he threw us up a nice ten pound albacore to go with the recipe.

We really enjoyed taking a vacation from the pressures of whatever it was we thought we had to do, and soon we had forgotten the worst of our struggle at sea. We were having fun and we loved the Noyo River. And we had found good friends in Bob and Beverly. They lent us an old pickup truck to drive to Mendocino one day. It was like escaping to an east coast town. On another outing we went to the movie house and saw *Return of the Jedi*. There was an abundance of fresh seafood with all the hard working commercial fishermen, and what wasn't offered to you as a gift, you could purchase fresh and inexpensive.

I couldn't possibly remember all the fantastic stories that Bob told about his time in the Queen's Navy as a torpedo man, but I can remember which were my favorites. There was the one story he told where he and a Soviet sailor found each other at the same watering hole on shore liberty. After getting totally bombed, each agreed to switch uniforms and go back to the other's ship. Following exchanged instructions but remembering nothing of it later, Bob and his new comrade each somehow made it to his respective bunk that night before passing out. Upon being discovered the following morning, neither the Canadians nor the Soviets knew whether to throw them into the brig for their inexplicable behavior or court martial them as spies, and neither ship could leave port until the mess was straightened out!

Then there was the time he had shore leave in North Carolina along with a bunch of his Canadian sailor buddies and wound up going to a cat house. He was very young and not exactly sure *what* he was doing there. Eventually, the madam of the house noticed his retreat and took it upon herself to lessen his tensions. She was so kind and understanding that Bob was suddenly overcome by a certain tranquility and a newfound warmth and confidence delivered him from his virginity. During the relaxed conversation that followed, the madam revealed that some twenty years previous she had seduced another young sailor in the Queen's Navy with exactly the same name and innocent disposition. In fact it turned out that this man had been Bob's father!

In still yet another tale, Bob recalled a seaman in the Navy who always amazed him and everyone else on board with his ability to carry a cup of coffee on a rolling deck without spilling a drop. In even the worst of weather they had witnessed the captain on the bridge ask the seaman to go fetch a cup of coffee from the galley for him. Each time the seaman would leave the comfort of the bridge, and, exposed to the cold and wet conditions, climb down the ladder to the lower deck and the galley below. A few minutes later he always faithfully re-appeared on the bridge with a full cup of warm coffee. One day he revealed his secret to Bob. Before leaving the galley he would drink the coffee but not swallow it, then climb to the upper deck and before entering the bridge re-deposit the coffee into the captain's cup.

Bob taught me a whole catalog of useful sea knots and gave me 200 feet of manila line and a book to practice with. We further readied *Querencia* again — filling our propane tank, lubricating the windlass, oiling the teak, polishing the brass, topping the fuel, and charging the batteries. Once again we re-sewed our frayed American flag.

We also mounted a large bronze oarlock on the stern rail for our new sixteen-foot oar. I had been thinking of carrying one, mostly as an emergency rudder, and Bob had found one for me in a nearby barn where a bunch of life raft oars had been stored for decades. The oarlock was a gift from Bob and Beverly salvaged off of the hull of their lost boat with original compliments to the Queen's Navy.

So our Noyo River experience came to an end, and it is among the most precious two weeks we will ever remember. It had also been a time for revamping our gear, our technique, and our happiness. We also had a fantastic storm while we were there, complete with thunder and lightening and gale force winds, and, I must tell you, it felt good to be in port for a change. But, soon after, the sun came out again and we both were feeling the itch to continue our trek down the west American coast.

Davey wrote in the log:

> The odiferous blend of fish and roasting
> cooking coffee beans every day has surpris-
> ingly become a little old.

Part III
Cruising

16.

"A sea changes into something rich and strange."
— Shakespeare

Shortly after ten on the morning of August 21 in calm conditions *Querencia* departed the Noyo River. Out, out, out past the overhead bridge and through the narrow channel, out into the big blue sea. It was a beautiful day to be on the ocean. Gentle swells met us as we rode over the bar and the fresh ocean breeze filled our nostrils with oxygen. It seemed like every fishing boat around was waving good-bye to us. Davey, finding herself quite suddenly elated, scrambled below to the navigation station to write in the log:

> Despite the agony at sea one suffers, from time to time it seems, I would still rather be here than back in the city watching John go crazy at the clinic and breathing stale rancid air and vacuuming! As long as I can keep saying that - this is where I belong.

The weather kept getting clearer and hotter and more still, and soon there wasn't any wind whatsoever. We enjoyed the glassy character of the sea, a new experience for us, and enjoyed motoring. Soon we were seeing the occasional whale and dolphin, snacking and sunbathing as we putted south.

About four hours later suddenly the engine died. It became apparent that continued attempts to start it up again simply weren't going to work. And the continuous cranking of the starter motor was wearing the batteries down. I cursed and whimpered and moaned and stammered, but Davey's cool mannerism and soft spoken confidence convinced me that all that was necessary was to get *Querencia* going again and then track the problem systematically. We raised all the sails and headed dead west for a good offing.

By now about ten knots of wind had returned, and under gentle swells Davey took the watch on deck. while I went below decks and bled the fuel line for suspected air. But it didn't work, and I soon found myself disassembling the entire fuel line. Davey managed the helm and I grunted away bent over the little diesel engine.

The whole ordeal took two hours, mostly because every time I reached for my screwdriver it would roll away. I reminded myself of Ernest Borgnine in some old WWII movie — sweaty and greasy and determined. Finally I reassembled the fuel line from the tank to the injectors, replacing the filters and meticulously cleaning the fuel pump. Davey turned the ignition key and it worked! We felt relief upon hearing the engine putt-putting again, and I joked that the engine was only acting up in protest of the sixteen foot sculling oar aboard which would enable us to "row" the boat if necessary.

By 20:10, shortly after a dinner of chicken and noodles, the sun was setting in a spectacular display of red for us. A full moon was rising about the same time at the opposite end of the sky and we could already see the light of Point Arena flashing on shore just below it.

We decided to take the advice of Don, our fisherman friend at the Noyo, and follow the forty fathom line down the coast to San Francisco. With the light breeze pushing us along it was tranquilly quiet that night, and the moon seemed bigger and brighter to me than at any other time in my life. Once again the water seemed to be teeming with life, with splashes here and there and dolphins sputtering and all manner of strange sounds constantly surrounding us. I've never heard of seals barking at the moon before, but I would believe it now.

It was during Davey's watch around midnight, with me deep asleep in the sea bunk, that there was a most unusual happening. As mentioned, we were sailing along the forty fathom line (240 feet deep), which put us fairly close to shore with points to get around. As a safety precaution we had the depth sounder alarm set for thirty fathoms. Lights ashore could just barely be seen.

Suddenly the depth sounder was beeping like a smoke alarm in an ashtray. The digital display read six fathoms.

"Six fathoms, John! How can that be?" Davey yelled down the hatch.

I had jolted up and was leaning against a bulkhead in the sea berth blurting back dialog from a dream, rubbing my eyes and slapping my cheeks to wake up. The depth sounder kept repeating its alarm.

"Beep! Beep! Beep! Beep! Beep!"

We had to be nearly five miles offshore with no hazards anywhere in the vicinity. I made my way to the cockpit and joined Davey in peering over the side. I was expecting to see a school of fish, or maybe seaweed stuck against the hull, but all I could see was the swirling and gurgling black water.

All of a sudden I was startled by a loud sucking, splashing sound, and there, less than twenty feet away was the huge monolithic head of a monster rising up out of the depths.

"Whooooosh!"

It was a *huge* whale, maybe a gray, sticking his barnacled head out of the water as if to get a better look at us. I could see every crevice in his craggy skin. Then he backed, going below the surface again, leaving the air full of a heavy, malodorous, low tide type of smell.

This behemoth creature, easily as big and wide as the hull of *Querencia*, was diving all around us! Slowly the whale did a u-turn, breaking away from the boat and momentarily disappearing. Here he came again and he was awesome! He was coming full speed for us from astern. I stood up at the rear of the cockpit gripping the stern rail with blanched knuckles and watched him charge along the surface of the water. At the last minute he rolled over and glided upside down just beneath our rudder and self steering mechanism. I watched him pass lengthwise opposite us underwater, his white belly as wide as the *Querencia*, reflecting the moonlight and phosphorescence outlining its hulking sleekness like twinkling little stars. It was the same feeling you get when you stand at the end of an airport runway and a huge jumbo jetliner flies right over your head. I was speechless, but prayed silently that this whale would not bump our rudder or think that *Querencia* was its long lost mother and try grabbing onto a thru-hull thinking it a teat. In that scary moment fortunately neither happened.

Another whale joined us alongside, then another. After a short powwow we decided that there was a very good chance that the whales, now huffing and puffing all around us, weren't really anxious to leave us alone. We decided to start the engine but leave the transmission in neutral, just in hopes that the sound of the engine would dampen their interest. It worked, or seemed to at any rate, and after about twenty minutes they all had slowly disappeared.

The next day, feeling confident of our navigation and the weather, we ran even closer to shore. Now twenty miles south of Point Arena we were pointing even more to the southeast. The wind was a perfect twenty knots and the scenery was magnificent, the shoreline alternating between gulches with steep rock cliffs and bold wooded ridges pleated with sandy dunes running down to the water. Nelley seemed to be in her prime, and steered us effortlessly, allowing us to be free to rollick in the cockpit, even take air baths, just like Benjamin Franklin used to do! Nakedness could never be better anywhere than it is at sea.

Our first pelicans made their appearance, marvelous birds that made long sojourns out to sea from the refuge of rocks and kelp beds along the shoreline. We hooked up our tuna line, the bitter end being a rubber snubber which we hooked to a cleat. Then we ran the 150-pound test line up to the port backstay where we clipped it on with a clothespin. If we snagged a fish it would pull free from the backstay with a loud snapping noise.

"SNAP!" We had a fish on. Almost in disbelief I pulled the fish in hand over hand while Davey readied herself with the net. We soon had a beautiful ten pound Skipjack in the cockpit. We were both grinning ear to ear as we took turns posing for snapshots with our first tuna. Meanwhile Nelley had *Querencia* really smoking along.

The blue water was full of little white horses, and the bold shoreline stood out against the clear sky. I filleted the tuna and Davey "cooked" it by smothering it with onions and soaking it in lime juice. It made a delectable "poisson cru" for dinner.

Why does the sun have to set anyway? That was the question that Davey and I asked ourselves. We never looked forward to another 'dark night of the soul'. We loved light and the sun and had to acknowledge that the days were getting shorter and darkness would soon be upon us again. We listened to the radio and watched the sun set to the tune of the *Beverly Hillbillies* (I would not be able to get that tune out of my head until we got to San Francisco), then we quickly doused most of our sail and prepared for the next eleven hours of darkness. It was blowing a good twenty-five knots as we sailed past Bodega Bay.

At midnight, we were still barreling along. The wind was over thirty knots and we had a double reefed main accompanied only by the staysail. The current was fantastic causing rips and ten foot swells that occasionally spit up and spattered against the hull and into the cockpit. But we were pretty tough cookies at this point, and despite a very rolling ride and the regret of having consumed so much fish earlier in the day, we found the going easy enough compared to what we had experienced farther north. Besides, we were getting very excited now about rounding Point Reyes.

Point Reyes is a bold, dark, rocky headland over 600 feet high that sticks way out to sea. At the end of the point is a light that flashes every five seconds and can be seen from a great distance at sea. Once past the point, you enter the Gulf of the Farallones where you can follow the coastline almost directly east for twenty-five miles into San Francisco. I will never forget how Point Reyes looked that night to me, standing out in the moonlight like some warden, a Gibraltar of the Pacific. It reminded me of a scene from one of my favorite movies as a kid, *The Guns of Navarrone*.

Eager to get into the lee, I unhooked Nelley and turned the wheel, bringing us in close. With the boat surfing every other wave we rapidly made our way around the point. Here we found considerable protection from the seas and the wind too. A decision was made to kill some time so that our entrance into the main ship channel over the bar into San Francisco would be in daylight. We stuck our nose into Drakes Bay, a large bight on the north shore of the gulf named after the English explorer Sir Francis Drake who anchored there in 1579. We considered anchoring ourselves, but the anchorage seemed somewhat crowded and spooky with several poorly lit vessels becoming visible and then disappearing again. We decided that we would be just as happy taking almost all the sail down and tacking back and forth for a few hours. That we did.

Now on approach to the Golden Gate bridge, we had to be very cautious. We were tired, so tired in fact that neither of us trusted each other alone on watch. Our brains had gone soft, but somehow, together, we made it.

At 0551 the moon set and the sun rose exactly on cue with each other. Sipping our morning coffee now in calm seas, we bathed in the splendidness that surrounded us. The golden rose light of morning was unveiling a beautiful panorama all around. Marin Peninsula, on our port side, was bold and broken. We were only a few hundred yards off the shoreline and, besides the visual excitement, the smells of warm moist earth and eucalyptus swept down from the grassy knolls and scraggly trees. Our spirits soared.

Two hours later, after motoring through the "Potato Patch" and riding the swirling bottleneck currents, we were passing under the Golden Gate. In agreement that we were each as euphoric as we had ever been before, we saluted all the marine explorers before us.

17.

> *"Where we stand is not as important as
> what direction we're moving in."*
> — Oliver Wendell Holmes

Suddenly the engine tempo started to wane — slower, slower, slower, then dead! There we were, right underneath the Golden Gate bridge, with very little wind and a fair amount of sea traffic and our engine had died again.

Luckily the tide was on our side and we were able to ride in on the flood. We made our way to Sausalito, just a little over two miles away, and finally were able to drop our hook, along with eighty feet of chain, in twenty feet of water about 100 yards from shore. We were parked!

It was a wonderful feeling to be in San Francisco Bay and for the moment we forgot about our engine problems. Out our starboard portholes Sausalito reminded us a little of a Greek village with its white stucco structures and palm trees clambering up the hillside. Out the port side the city of San Francisco beamed like a picture postcard complete with the little island of Alcatraz in the foreground. We had sandwiches and wine after showering on deck and then climbed into the luxury of our forward v-berth for badly needed sleep. At sea the forward v-berth was always a bit too bumpy and too high above the boat's center of gravity, but we always loved rediscovering its comfort in the calm and safety of port.

We slept all afternoon. Five hours passed before we got up. The full moon rose right behind the city skyscrapers while the sunset still reflected in their windows. It was a spectacular sight and a huge reward. The bay was full of sailboats in this evening muse, the wind blowing a gusting but friendly twenty knots. A sixty-foot ketch tacked quite close to us. Three elderly ladies were sailing the ketch by themselves and in such a relaxed manner that it caught us by surprise. They raised their stemmed wine glasses to us as they cruised by traversing the bay. Yes, San Francisco does have hearty sailors!

After digging around in the icebox we found pork chops and boiled potatoes from which we fashioned a formal evening meal complete with cloth napkins and real china. Then we hooked up our five-inch color TV to ship's power and discovered we could receive twelve channels! Boy, were we reminded of the luxuries of civilization and our own good fortune.

Looking out our porthole to San Francisco
from Sausalito across the Bay

San Francisco was a happy time for us. We did a lot of back patting for the successful leg of our trip from the Noyo river. It had been the best part of our trip so far. We enjoyed being tourists in Sausalito and San Francisco and wandered around for hours at a time, drifting from shop to shop and browsing in all the marine stores. We went out for Indian food and saw Woody Allen's film, *Zelig*, at a local theater. We stopped at a kite store and bought Rain and Caroline and *Querencia* the most colorful, fun kites we could find.

I fixed *Querencia's* engine problem, or at least I thought I did. After gathering all the advice available, the general consensus was that dirt or air in the fuel line was the culprit. I replaced the fuel filters again as well as the fuel pump diaphragm and then bled the system. Everything was back to normal.

On August 25 we were surprised to wake up and see the 400-ton Greenpeace ship, *Rainbow Warrior*, anchored over a mile away on our port side between us and the Golden Gate. We had taken notice in the network news that *Rainbow Warrior* was fresh in from Dutch Harbor, Alaska, where she had been awaiting the return of her skipper after a rather harrowing Russian-Siberian adventure.

That afternoon we rowed our dinghy in to shore for an afternoon of celebration. At the end of the afternoon we decided to have dinner at the hippest, wildest restaurant we could find in Sausalito. The good vibes of the restaurant turned out to be a bit of a ruse, and even though we had been the first to be seated, problem after problem kept us from being served. First our original waiter got sick and went home; then our waitress got our order mixed up with someone else's. With each faux pas the management brought us another carafe of wine, compliments of the house, but what we really wanted was our meal, having planned our whole afternoon around this extravaganza.

Finally our meal arrived, delivered on the slippery fingers of our new waitress who unpredictably stumbled, launching our precious dinners across the room like flying saucers. The plates made a thunderous crash against a plate glass door and we joined the rest of the restaurant in looking at the pile of broken dishware and food on the floor. The management quickly arrived with brooms, mops, apologies, and another carafe of complimentary wine.

At this point Davey and I took our usual quick vote and agreed unanimously that our best bet was to leave the complimentary wine on the table and head for *Querencia* as quickly as possible. At least there we could depend on having a sandwich before we passed out.

Climbing into our little raft at the shoreline, and escaping the madness of the shore life, we unexpectedly discovered ourselves in splendid moods, duly attributed to having imbibed so much flagon of the grape.

Full of newfound enthusiasm we decided that rather than return to *Querencia* we would row to the *Rainbow Warrior*, Greenpeace's big mamma. It was dark, blowing about fifteen knots and there was a medium current. We had our float coats on and set out with a flashlight and big grins on our faces. We were having a blast; we could have rowed to San Jose.

Looking back on it now, we were wonderfully crazy at the time. We weren't sure what we were going to say when we got there or, more specifically, what *they* were going to say. But heck, we had been Greenpeace supporters for several years and we wanted to deliver another supporting contribution. Life is full of occasions to expand your horizons if only you take notice of the opportunities around you. Meanwhile, we kept rowing. It was a *long* row.

About three-fourths of the way there a Greenpeace motor powered inflatable approached us and a young man yelled in a concerned voice.

"That's an awfully little boat, where are you going?"

"Why we're rowing to the *Rainbow Warrior* to pay a visit and make a contribution," we gleefully responded.

His face lit up like a Christmas tree. He couldn't believe it and immediately started referring to us as "bold" and "courageous." Of course we loved that to the point of declining a tow. After a gracious invitation we told him we'd keep rowing and meet him at the *Rainbow Warrior*.

That was Daniel. He had been on *Rainbow Warrior* for several years and was the onboard illustrator.

This was a big ship! We tied the inflatable up to the last ring of a rope ladder lowered over the side and climbed up the two story tall hull and over the bulwark. I couldn't believe it — we were on deck. Daniel insisted that we come into the mess hall and take our wet things off. Several waves had washed over the dinghy in our heroic journey.

Inside the bowels of the ship Daniel led us down the main passageway. As we passed the galley I paused to look it over. It was a large galley with lots of character. There was a big black stove surrounded with oak counters and cupboards. There were lots of natural foods sitting around; yogurt, spices, soybeans, nuts. I remember being struck that these pacifists were for real!

We made it to the mess hall where two large, five-foot wood tables with cushioned seats were bolted down. Claude, a calico cat and the only pet onboard, occupied one cushion. A young lady named Nancy sat on another cushion, sorting slides of sea life and the activities of the *Rainbow Warrior*. In the background she had a black and white TV going and was catching up on the most recent episode of *Magnum P.I.* She asked for understanding, explaining in so many words that after being held in Siberia by the Russians for seven days she was very glad to be home in the U.S.A.; TV was her constitutional therapy. She poked about, passing an occasional picture to us. I was particularly impressed with a slide of the re-commissioned freighter coming down the coast using a spinnaker as auxiliary sail power. Daniel went to get some wine (oh, no). The night was moving on.

Along with the return of Daniel, other crew members appeared. Although there was now only a crew of six aboard, usually *Rainbow Warrior* had a crew of twelve to twenty. Dan, a big fellow from Detroit came in. His voice was deep and baritone. He was the engineer and had never even been on a boat before the *Rainbow Warrior*. Two more women appeared. Wearing sweat suits and appearing somewhat weary, they reminded me of ourselves after a long passage. The skipper, the youngest onboard at age thirty, was ashore with another man and woman getting vittles.

Soon the weariness of the crew vanished and we all were engrossed in about three conversations at once, sharing thoughts and history and opinions. Daniel was busy sketching every whale Davey asked him about — he was a very good artist. He loved whales and he loved to draw. After an engrossing description offered by Davey, he drew her an artist's conception of the whale that had joined *Querencia* that one night on the last leg of our passage.

We were very pleased to see that Greenpeace was a sincere organization. It certainly appeared so to us. All these people obviously worked very hard and they did not get much for it in return as far as money and material wealth. They all loved the sea and all were dedicated to their cause without being jaded. Davey was impressed with the women and enjoyed them a lot. Rap, rap, rap. It was fun. A guitar appeared and we traded a few songs.

These were good folks who weren't hesitant at all to discuss the Siberian incident. They regretted the incident with the Russians, but insisted they really hadn't done anything more than get inside their territorial waters to make a statement about the seal slaughter. Soon they were surrounded by gunboats shooting tracers over the deck and had planes buzzing them. It went on for hours. Cindy, the cook, said she had to prepare food as usual in the galley although it was as stressful as cooking in a storm. Then the two Greenpeace inflatables were flipped by the prop wash of Soviet helicopters and seven crew members found themselves in the frigid waters. Unable to get back to their rafts they were forced to take rescue lines lowered from a helicopter or freeze to death in the Arctic waters. As each was winched into the cabin of the helicopter he found a pistol pointed at his head. But they were dedicated pacifists who had trained themselves to remain calm under duress. And they had to chuckle over the reaction of the Russians to the all-American Greenpeace skipper who managed to maintain a big smile on his face. The Soviets took this as a sign that he wanted to defect. When he realized this he started laughing. Then they were *really* sure he wanted to defect. Of course they were wrong, but it took some time to straighten things out and get released.

Next came the tour of *Rainbow Warrior*, a grand ship, originally bought in England and restored in Europe. We were escorted from stem to stern. The engine room, thirty feet wide by fifty feet long with a ten-foot ceiling, was a massive display of spotless machinery. Then came the library full of hardbound books on every conceivable subject, the walls covered with wonderful pencil drawings of the ocean whales. Then we went to the bow, where a large movie theatre had been integrated into the infrastructure of the ship. There was a large permanent reflective screen and seating for twenty people. From here we went on to see the cabins of the crew. Kathy was a paleontologist and her cabin was full of evolutionary charts of early life forms. David, in addition to being an illustrator, was a mammologist and his cabin walls were lined with drawings of all manner of sea mammals.

It was time to go. We thanked our hosts and left a small contribution to their cause. Daniel offered to take us home to our *Querencia* in their big mamma raft, towing our little dinghy alongside. Climbing down the rope ladder in the windy darkness was a little frightening. We'd forgotten all about the weather for a few short hours.

At *Querencia* Daniel joined us for a huge bowl of popcorn and then he was off. Before he left he assured us that as soon as Greenpeace's public profile had been refurbished, the *Rainbow*

Warrior would be off again, on a new adventure, in the interest of our planet's greatest resource: the sea and its beings.

The Rainbow Warrior at anchor off Sausalito

18.

Almost three years later, near the end of our extended cruise and in the Hawaiian Islands, we were shocked to read in the newspaper that the *Rainbow Warrior* had been sunk with explosives in New Zealand's Auckland Harbour by agents of the French secret service to counter anti-nuclear protests. Two French frogmen were charged with manslaughter in the death of a Portugese born photographer, Fernando Pereira, who happened to be in the Rainbow Warrior's library at the time.

I was moved enough to write the following letter:

```
September 9th, 1985

His Excellency David Lange
Prime Minister
Auckland
New Zealand

Excellency:
The recent tragedy of the Greenpeace ship, Rainbow
Warrior, makes my heart sad.
```

My spouse and I have recently completed a three
year sailing passage including the South Pacific.
We are familiar with the unique gifts and propor-
tional problems of the South Pacific.

Shortly before leaving the port of San Francisco
aboard our sailing vessel Querencia we anchored
next to the *Rainbow Warrior* offshore of Sausalito.
At twilight we rowed over to see what this vessel
just in from Dutch Harbor was all about. Friendly,
courteous people welcomed us up the rope ladder
from our tiny dinghy. The *Rainbow Warrior* and her
crew expressed a wholesome sincerity of cause in a
dedicated spirit of intelligence, education, and
nonviolence.

It is my hope that the cause and hope of *Rainbow
Warrior* will be remembered including the eradica-
tion of nuclear pollutants in the Tuamotus, Society
Islands, and islands further westward.

I appreciate and urge your efforts to see justice
in this historical incident.

Yours very truly,
Dr. John F. McGrady

In two weeks I received the following reply from the Prime
Minister, signed by his own hand.

Prime Minister
Wellington
New Zealand

30 September 1985

Dr John F McGrady
PO Box 75453
Honolulu, HI 96836

Dear Dr McGrady,
Thank you for your words of support for the

Government's actions in response to the sinking of the *Rainbow Warrior*. Our first priority is still to ensure that those involved in this criminal act are brought to trial. The Government is continuing to seek the cooperation of the French authorities to achieve this end. You will understand that at this stage, particularly while a case is before the New Zealand Courts, it would not be appropriate for me to comment in more detail on the situation. I have, however, taken note of your views.

Yours sincerely,
David Lange

A diplomatic rift between Paris and Wellington developed. France made apologies, the French defense minister resigned after accepting responsibility in the affair, and the secret service underwent a major housecleaning. Further, France paid $7 million in damages.

But the days of Fernando Pereira and the *Rainbow Warrior* were over. The extent of the ship's damage prevented any thoughts of resurrecting her, no matter how noble the cause. For eight years the Rainbow Warrior was the flagship of a campaign for peace and respect for the environment.

Today it is an underwater shrine for anti-nuclear activists.

19.

On September 1 we left our anchorage at Sausalito. We felt good. We'd had a wonderful holiday and had once again reconditioned *Querencia*. Under a light wind we sailed out of San Francisco Bay. Half way to the bridge Daniel and company came by in a Greenpeace inflatable to say "so long." It was sunny and warm and beautiful and we were having our favorite California experience — sailing *Querencia!* We were also excited because we only had a short hop ahead of us. In less than a hundred miles we would be in Monterey Bay, and we were very much looking forward to that.

By the time we reached Half Moon Bay the wind was a perfect

steady twenty knots and we were enjoying taking our daily 'air bath' when the news came over the radio that the Soviets had shot down a Korean airliner, killing over 300 passengers as it plunged into the northwest Pacific Ocean. For some reason, there in the blue waters of that vast peaceful ocean, it struck us as being even more incredulous than normal, if indeed there can be any such thing as a normal reaction to such news. Maybe it seemed especially grave since my own daughter had herself flown the previous summer from her mother's in Korea to spend some time with us. It was a somber cocktail hour that evening as the sun went down and set in the West as usual. The seas were gentle and forgiving, allowing us to tinker with minor adjustments to the self-steering vane in preparation for yet another night of blackness.

The following morning the coastline was enshrouded in fog. We welcomed the sunrise but with such little wind calculated our Estimated Time of Arrival in Monterey to be in the afternoon. This was just as well, since this would be preferably after the haze had lifted. Monterey Bay is so vast, biting twelve miles into the continent and over twenty miles long. Such a bay! None other like it on the west coat. Certainly, San Francisco is the only reason that Monterey was never developed into a major marine port.

Just after we had our breakfast victuals, a small fishing boat came out of the fog and passed us going west. They waved cheerfully at us and we took this as a sign, correctly, that we were going to find Monterey to be very friendly.

By afternoon we were just making out the prominent features of the shoreline inside Point Pinos and the town of Monterey. Now anxious, we motored for a while, holding our breaths. Once your engine fails you in a small boat at sea, you try constantly not to rely on it. Our insecurities over the engine were eased by a fresh breeze that suddenly filled in. In no time at all we had a lively wind, and *Querencia* was pushing through the bay at over 6 knots, white horses all around.

Monterey is a colorful and picturesque city that Richard Dana had described as "the most pleasant place in California" over a century and a half ago. Then it had been the capital of California under Mexican rule and remained the capital for sometime even after it had become a state. Monterey has a rich sailing heritage with a history of famous explorers in their tall ships having anchored there for centuries. An old adobe custom house, The Presidio, had been the center of Mexican government and fortification in Dana's day, and the town of Monterey had been built around it. Now it is used as a historical museum down near the waterfront. The *Coastal Pilot* sailing directions still use the Presidio Monument as a distinguishing prominent feature for the coastal navigator.

Soon we had the breakwater just off our beam. Monterey Harbor looked small and crowded. All 1500 feet of the breakwater were covered with loud barking sea lions. Their noise was incessant, and along with their numbers and mass, the big furry mammals made quite a presence. It mattered not that there was a hub of activity and human endeavor around them. You had the feeling that they had reserved 'this spot' of theirs a long, long time ago.

It was already after three in the afternoon and we decided on dropping our hook on the lee side of the long pier that runs out from the beach toward the breakwater. The swells were terrible, contrary to the wind, and as a result we did a lot of rolling from side to side, much to our discontent. The next morning we inflated the dinghy and rowed to find the harbormaster's office in the harbor. He was a very nice man and offered *Querencia* temporary asylum inside the tiny harbor. There the protection from the sea walls would bring relaxation and relief.

This was the beginning of a six-week stay. It was a stop we had been planning while we came down the coast. Here, like La Jolla, Monterey and Carmel, was for us the best of California's magic. There was an abundance of flowers and palm trees. Adobe architecture, with its white washed walls and red tile roofs, was scattered everywhere. There were beautiful beaches and one romantic sunset after another.

We must have walked ten miles a day exploring the whole Pinos peninsula, and soon we had made several new friends. Rus and Kathy, avid local sailors, had just purchased *Lila Marguerite*, an Erickson 38, and were in the process of outfitting her for an extended cruise of their own. We took turns day sailing on *Lila Marguerite* and *Querencia*, having great fun catching tuna with the tackle from the *Emm Two* and observing the numerous mammals, seals, otters, whales and dolphins in the bay.

Two other cruising couple boats arrived from Washington; *Resonde II*, a thirty-eight-foot Ingrid with Harold and Edie Erickson aboard (on their second cruise!), and *Carina*, a thirty-six-foot Valiant, with Jim and Alice aboard. Both boats also had plans to be in Mexico, on route to Tahiti after the first of November, when hurricane season would be over. Since *Querencia* had been the first to arrive, Davey and I were up on all the necessary information a cruiser might need — where to do the laundry, where to shop for food, and where to catch the bus. Then there was the especially hot tip; the bus number to Carmel and the name of a little Greek restaurant where you could have the most wonderful lunch for under four dollars. In return, Harold and Edie gave us some pointers on the approach into San Diego and some navigation tricks. Those are the kind of secrets sailors swap.

So, we enjoyed our good fortune at Monterey. We appreciated having *Querencia* in a slip, which allowed us to not only take everything in, from cannery row to the organ-grinder and his monkey on the boardwalk, but also allowed us to continue to re-commission *Querencia*.

> *"It is said that a sailboat is a little like a lady's watch,*
> *She is always welcome to a little repair."*
> — Anonymous

Finally, now that we were far enough south that the monstrous seas we'd experienced off the northwest coast were no longer a day to day threat, we felt comfortable removing all the sealing tape from our hatches. We cleaned the hull and replaced our zincs. We tuned the rigging and cleaned, sanded, and oiled all the teak. We stripped and varnished our new sixteen foot oar and mended all our sails and their sail bags. Add to this the usual maintenance as well as all manner of odd chores that are necessary to keep a boat ready to go to sea including replenishing the ship's stores.

So when the first whiff of fall came on October 18 we were prepared to depart Monterey before the first gale. The nineteenth was a Friday and we took care of some finalities and relaxed. At sunrise on Saturday, October 20, we putted out of Monterey Harbor leaving fond memories behind us. We were headed for points further south.

20.

   It felt good to return to the fresh ocean smell and our odyssey down the coast, leaving once again the smoke and hustle and bustle of civilization behind us. Monterey and the hills of Carmel stood out beautifully behind our stern, and in front of us a calm sea once again reflected the rising sun like a huge mirror . The morning was as clear and bright as you could find anywhere.

   The wind remained a whisper for only the first half-hour; then a gentle ten to fifteen knots of breeze came across the bay and we hoisted full sail. *Querencia*, all clean and polished, was geared up and full of glory. We even hanked on the genny with it's big red cross. As we rounded Point Pinos at the southern tip of Monterey Bay and "turned left" again we were feeling so cheery that I struck up a little sailing tune on my harmonica and Davey and I exchanged kisses at the end of each stanza.

   By mid-afternoon we were off Point Sur. Although shore was five miles away, we could still hear the surf roaring and rolling in upon the beach. We weren't the only ones migrating south. Most of the female sea lions had left the bay and were also on their way south. Their destination would be the same as ours on this current leg of our journey, the Channel Islands.

   Now heading dead downwind in consistently friendly conditions, we decided to sail wing on wing. We raised the whisker pole to hold out the genoa sail and keep it full opposite the main sail. This was the first time we had set the whisker pole since we had left Washington state, the reason being simply that before now, juggling it on the fore deck had been too precarious a task for our disposition. In gentle winds and seas it is more easily managed by a crew of two and once it's up it is glorious, acting as a second boom for the forward sail. The extra sail area provides some real wind power. Although we didn't realize it at that particular moment, from now on, all the way to Guadalupe Island off of Mexico we would almost always have the pole up whenever the wind was abaft the beam. The disordered, agitated North Pacific ocean was over.

Time passes very quickly, almost always, onboard and soon we were having a wonderful dinner of fried chicken, biscuits, and French fries. We had made a conscious effort to have as many meals as possible be fresh. Davey had even baked six dozen biscuits for this leg of the trip before we left Monterey. The wind stayed consistently gentle and easy, and we sailed studded (wing on wing) well into the night. We commended ourselves for picking a full moon for this leg of the passage — it makes such a difference to have a moon during your night watches.

Quite suddenly, half past midnight the wind picked up and at the same time it became very foggy. I roused Davey and we dropped the whisker pole and secured it on deck and put a quick reef in the mainsail. Naturally, no sooner had we done this than the wind dropped. The fog went from thick to very thick. We were glad that we had made a good offing from shore and calculated that we were presumably out of the shipping lanes. Along with the fog it got very wet on the decks. I took this as a sign of settled weather, and this helped us relax, fairly confident that nothing too extraordinary was going to happen on this particular night. Davey crawled back into her bunk and I spent the remainder of my watch totally fascinated by the play of the moonlight on the fog.

That night on my watch I saw several luminescent fog globules each the size and shape of the Seattle Kingdome. An amazing phenomena, it was very mysterious to sail by them. I admit to being glad our course did not take us through one!

A predicted navigational satellite passing over the horizon coincided with sunrise, so one hour before daylight I turned on the Sat Nav in anticipation of the information we would be receiving. A fix shortly after the morning coffee put us ten miles off of Cape San Martin at a bearing of 250 degrees WSW. This was where we had figured we were by dead reckoning.

As the day filled in, so did the weather. It was almost a carbon copy of the previous day. As the sun rose the fog lifted, and as the fog lifted, the wind filled in, staying between ten and twenty knots. By afternoon we were pushing seven knots, flying wing on wing again under a clear and sunny sky. At the end of the afternoon two whales, probably pilot whales, came by for a visit. A unity and harmony with the wind and water ran through our veins once again. We were experiencing a blissful togetherness with the world.

For the first time in over a thousand miles at sea we had dinner in the salon seated at the fiddled teak dining table. We enjoyed delicious hamburger steaks while Nelley did the steering. We popped our heads out the hatch now and then to keep a watch for traffic, but as usual there was none. On the distant eastern horizon was the outline of the continental shore, lit up by the tangerine light of the setting sun, as conspicuous and isolated as a purple and orange water-colored stage prop.

For the first time we were now keeping a kerosene lantern lit, hanging below decks in a free swinging area beneath the hatch. We immediately noticed what a difference it made in our levity during the long dark hours of night. How much cozier it was for the person off-watch in the sea berth, and with the full moon it didn't interfere with our night vision.

This night was much like the last, but luckily a bit clearer. I was glad because, now closer to shore, I knew that we were entering a traffic zone where freighters were likely to converge. Off points near San Louis Obispo, like Pt. Buchon and Pt. San Louis, all boats are apt to cut kitty-corner to save distance, creating a maritime intersection.

Although it can happen, the odds of a happenstance collision at sea are slight compared to the odds of colliding with another car when driving on a freeway, for instance. Nevertheless, you are concerned about it.

At 2300 I started hearing a whistle off and on and for the next hour it kept sounding closer and closer, the source of the sound remaining invisible in light fog. It eventually showed itself to be a freighter coming upon us from our port aft quarter at a good clip. Its course seemed destined to cross ours. I could not establish radio contact so I lit up *Querencia* like a department store and, using our bright search light, also flashed the "D Signal" on the main sail. I maintained a steady course until our separate intentions seemed clear, then made a demonstrable course change to a safer heading.

I considered us to be all right since he was tooting his fog horn (whistle); he had to be conscientious. I was quite sure he saw us, as I saw him slow down and change course ever so slightly. In the darkness of night the monstrous hull passing with its huge moon shadow was an awesome sight. I think every old salt would agree with me that in the end, it is the boat of superior tonnage that always has the right of way.

By the time it was Davey's watch we were starting to see what she called "martian hotels." Actually, they were offshore oil platforms. They looked like little twinkling cities to me. A little after daybreak we were passing our third one, ten miles offshore. They really did look Martian and had a noise all their own, a sort of hum. They seemed such a contrast to everything we had previously experienced in the unadulterated ocean environment. During our morning coffee klatch Davey and I had a long discussion as to our feelings about the damned things. From all we had heard there weren't any offshore drilling rigs north of Point Conception until just six months previously. Now word had it that they were springing up like mushrooms everywhere. There are few things as nauseating as the smell of crude oil when you are at sea on a small boat. Now, well downwind of the three oil platforms, that was all we could smell, even though they were miles away.

"Good God, Davey," I squawked, "do you think the day will come when the whole coastline is as stinky and polluted as the Tacoma tide flats?"

We were both silent for a rather long time. Then, rather than answering, she shared a question of her own.

"I wonder how many people really know what is happening to our little planet."

The bad odor dissipated as we made our way further south, returning the great outdoors to how we liked it. It was going to be another great day. We both felt very rested and ready for some serious sailing. If things went well, we would negotiate our way past Point Conception and into the big bathtub of southern California, the Santa Barbara Channel, before sunset.

We were now skirting the deserted coastline fairly close in, and long, lonely, grassy plains stretched on forever. The wind swept down the hillsides and blew the tall blades in an undulating wave — like a dance it was fascinating to watch as we sailed along.

Then, suddenly, our eyes came upon a big monolithic black box, nestled in one of the folds of the hillside. It was like a skyscraper without windows. Of course. This was Vandenberg Air Force Base and this must be a missile silo. Then there was another, and another, and another. There were no other structures nor any other sign of man or civilization. It was weird. Treeless and austere, there was definitely a certain loneliness on these rolling hills. They were bare except for these black sentinels facing west now visible all the way down the coast. From sea we had a unique perspective, and we felt an ominous nuclear rapture that made the hair on the back of my neck stand straight up. We could only imagine that the east coast of Siberia looked similar.

We saw a major point of land which we at first mistook for Pt. Conception. A fix on the Sat Nav confirmed that it was Pt. Arguello instead which was ten miles north. We were really smoking along now, quickly going south, as the afternoon breeze filled in. This was not an area to be unsure of yourself.

Point Conception — actually the whole distance of ten miles between Point Arguello and Point Conception — is described in the *U.S. Coastal Pilot* as the Cape Horn of the Pacific. Waves of twelve feet accompanied by thirty-five knot winds are the rule rather than the exception. There are terrific weather vectors meeting here. The coastline shifts from North — South to East — West and the water temperature changes as much as 10° as northern currents driven south by the strong NW winds collide with warmer currents sweeping up from the south. The climatic change from north of Point Conception to south of Point Conception is so remarkable and well defined that it is as if a vessel crosses a magic line.

Soon it had us and we were surfing down ten foot waves still wing on wing with the whisker pole holding the jib consistently full. The amazing thing about this splendid sail was that Nelley was steering *Querencia* perfectly straight downwind and there seemed little to do except sit back and enjoy the ride. Davey seemed a bit more concerned than I, the wind getting a bit gusty now and then, but I was having a blast and couldn't help but grin ear to ear with glee as we slid down one wave after the other at full hull speed, perfectly balanced. All was well.

The waves were ribbed and streaked with white foam in a sea of bright blue. As the ocean roared around us, it was a tumultuous harmony where it seemed you could hear the deepest bass and the highest treble. It was very exciting.

Sudden gusts rattled the rigging and *Querencia* started getting a little squirrely. The winds were strong and obviously blowing down the canyons on their way well offshore. We found ourselves quickly bracing in the cockpit for yet another thirty knot gust, and our glee turned to worry. It was about then that I had the blinding flash that it was time to get the damned pole down and maybe shorten sail! Davey agreed. She'd thought I'd never ask.

Well, getting the pole down was fairly easy but shortening sail wasn't. In the process of getting things untangled Davey wound up with a sheet burn on her neck under her chin that she would wear proudly for the next six weeks. We eventually doused both forward sails and reefed the mainsail. Much better.

The breeze continued stiff and the seas a bit confused. I could well understand their confusion — the coastline had almost vanished going east; it was ten degrees hotter, the water even changing color from blue to turquoise.

After the sail change though, boat stability and our good ride returned powering us past Point Conception and into the Santa Barbara Channel. Everything then seemed to ease up, especially the size of the waves and swells. As we hedged our way into the channel we enjoyed a warmth and humidity that we had not experienced on

Querencia before. It was a high time for us. Our last major challenge had been met for awhile. Point Conception, now behind us and silhouetted by the setting sun, was a pinnacle in more than one way to us.

Things continued to calm down. Sunset found us enjoying a leisurely dinner in the cockpit surrounded by calm seas and warm air. While I was watching the last embers of the sky's light reflect upon the waters, a fixed star suddenly popped out from behind a purplish cloud in the east. A puff of a breeze came offshore from high up in the Santa Ynez mountains to our north. I watched it race across the water, a flickering shadow, like a covey of quail running out of a bush. And as it passed, for a moment, all I could smell was the fragrance of the wild Juniper bush.

> Course dead East. Our only concern tonight will be avoiding martian hotels until daylight and looking over *Querencia's* charts in order that we might better be able to pick our first anchorage in Southern California. — DT

Pt. Conception

Part IV
California Dreaming

21.

"There is only one success: to be able to live your life in your own way."
— Christopher Morley

I will always remember our first landing in Southern California. Having been at sea for three days and three nights we were more than a little excited at the prospect of relaxing at anchor for a few days. We were halfway between Point Conception and Santa Barbara when we chose Refugio State Beach. There we anchored offshore in hard sand with four fathoms of water beneath our keel fairly confident that we would have some NW protection when the afternoon winds picked up.

Eager to take a trip ashore, we pumped up the inflatable dinghy and filled it with all of our garbage. After grabbing a change of clothes and some change, we jumped into the tender and I started pulling on the oars, rowing us toward shore.

We hesitated just outside the surf line to watch the breakers and discuss how we were going to negotiate a way through the waves and make a safe beach landing. As we sat there, Davey suddenly pointed out a small boat that was circling *Querencia* suspiciously. It was just gawkers, but the distraction proved disastrous for us. Quite unexpectedly, in an instant, a wave caught us and threw us headlong up onto the beach flipping the dinghy and emptying it of all its storage in the process. It was a radical thrashing that left Davey and me rolling around on the beach spitting sand. Garbage and clothes were scattered and floating everywhere, and one of our oars had been broken in half like a toothpick.

Naturally the beach was packed with people, and once we had determined that neither of us were hurt, we turned our full attention to feeling like complete fools! I tried to look cool and casual as I chased a Hefty bag that was spewing tin cans as it rolled over and over in the surf. Davey was as busy as a sand piper running around at the water's edge gathering the rest of our belongings.

Finally a local native, a fit and tan octogenarian, emerged from the crowd and handed us the one missing piece of our oar. With order restored, Davey and I retreated to higher ground with our soaking mess. Neither of us had been so embarrassed since we were little kids. There, in the shadow of tall California palms, we threw ourselves on the green grass and burst into laughter.

We still had our change so, after rinsing off in a beach side shower, we walked to a little store alongside the road and each got an ice cream cone. We returned to our spot on the grassy knoll and framed by the palms, there offshore was *Querencia*, bobbing gently in the bright blue sea. Another picture postcard. We were meditative and thoughtful as we sat on terra firma, licking our ice cream, and gazing at our amazing little vessel.

So quickly we had forgotten the power of mother ocean and how quickly she had reminded us. You can never take her for granted, even if you've just sailed the length of the American continent!

We had to paddle back to *Querencia* canoe-style with the one good oar at the stern and Davey pulling from the bow with the fragmented blade of the other. But soon we were aboard again, fishing and enjoying some well deserved leisure time. After the sun went down we lit our trusty kerosene anchor light and hung it in the rigging. Except for when the odd ocean swell would heave our hull contrary to the wind gusts coming down the Canada del Refugio, we had a very peaceful night and we enjoyed not going anywhere for a change.

The following morning I opened my eyes to see the first red rays of daylight slatting their way through the portholes in brilliant patterns that danced on *Querencia's* white headliner. Slowly Davey followed me out of the bunk to enjoy fresh brewed coffee and a bowl of cereal. Then we started up the 110-volt Honda generator and commenced to doing a nifty repair of our broken oar with the power tools we had on board. By 0930 all of our chores had been completed, the anchor was up, and we and our little vessel of self-sufficiency were on our way to the Channel Island anchorages. We headed nearly dead south toward Santa Cruz Island.

The Santa Barbara Channel is twenty-two miles wide at this point, and after we were about one hour into it there wasn't enough breeze to keep our genoa full even with the pole set. It was hot as blazes despite the fact that it was the last week in October, and the water was just as calm and blue and clear as you could imagine.

I mounted our sixteen-foot lifeboat oar in the bronze oarlock on the stern rail and began moving *Querencia* slowly forward with long sweeping arcs of the oar. If I really worked at it I imagined us going about half a knot. We had read that this was what many other cruising boats before us had done when there was no wind and no engine. We had an engine but we were trying to learn not to depend on it, so this was a perfect opportunity to hone our sculling skills. Davey watched me running back and forth in the cockpit with the heavy end of this monstrous oar, jumping from one side to the other, pulling and pushing and cursing. This went on for about fifteen minutes before Davey finally spoke her mind.

"Thank God we've come up with alternatives like engines."

But on this particular day we were not even in the slightest bit of a hurry. We were very much at home and enjoying ourselves. We let ourselves drift along in the right direction, sunbathing, and studying numerous seals who were also sunbathing and studying us. Relaxing on their backs they would stick their flippers and tails and heads entirely out of the water. It was one of the most peculiar sights either of us had ever seen. From a distance this contorted shape looked something like a moose's head, but when we got closer the apparition would suddenly roll over and slip below the surface.

Unexpectedly we found ourselves in an oily slick. It was really making a black mess of our hull along the waterline. Yuk! At first I blamed it on a derelict derrick but then I realized that it was very likely from one of the natural underwater oil springs I had read about. This was a prehistoric area, an area that is very rich in black oil and has been for a very long time. It is known that 200 years ago the Indians of this area used the tar seepage from the channel waters to coat their pine canoes.

Not only is the area rich in prehistoric oil and the early history of man, but fossils as well. Although debated by some, evidence has been brought forward to show that man was here in the Channel Islands over 30,000 years ago. From diaries, mission records, and more recently, current archaeological and anthropological discoveries, it has definitely been proven that about 20,000 Indians, speaking mostly Chumash and Shoshone, lived on the eight Channel Islands when the early explorers first arrived and that they lived entirely off of the sea eating mostly fish and abalone. Unfortunately, but not surprisingly, they were almost entirely extinct by the mid 1800's due to smallpox, syphilis, diphtheria, scarlet fever, measles, and tuberculosis, all introduced via interactions with Aleutian Indians, Hawaiians, and the White Man, brought there by the tall ships. Today the islands are for the most part uninhabited.

> 1115 Just listened on the VHF radio to a conversation between the U.S. Coast Guard and the sailing vessel *Island Sea Shell*, reporting from south of Santa Barbara Island that a man fell overboard last night and is feared lost. Seems the skipper woke up to find his crew had evaporated, therefore likely to have been swept over the side. The position of *Island Sea Shell* is a day's sail away and, with contrary currents, we will be of little value in the search for the missing man. — JFM

Boy, hearing that put our hearts in our throats! Any sailor will tell you of the fear of falling overboard. For me it has always been not so much the fear of myself but of the other person falling overboard, particularly on my off watch. To wake up after a long nap and find the other gone would leave you alone and in horror.

We then switched to the AM radio and heard that 146 marines had just died a senseless death in Lebanon; that did nothing to lift our spirits. But soon the afternoon wind came rushing in, just as the California cruising guides had promised. We turned off the radios and the Sat Nav, put away the sextant, and the solar panel, and the lunch plates. Raising all the "canvas" we could carry, we concentrated on finding our own unique getaway once again — sailing our *Querencia* onward into our dream, temporarily escaping the inevitable problems of the world.

Two hours later the steep shores and rugged terrain of Santa Cruz Island became visible. The ride since midday had been magnificent and before we knew it we were delivered through the five mile wide channel separating Santa Cruz from Santa Rosa Island. We turned east into Christy Anchorage, a large bight on the west end of Santa Cruz Island. With our nose into the wind we dropped all the sail on the deck and managed to set our thirty-five pound CQR hook without starting the engine. It was half past six in the evening and we were in forty feet of water just beyond the surf. We were the lone boat in the bay and we were surrounded by beauty. Now the moon was waning and with the sun gone the pastel sky was already filling up with a number of twinkling, jeweled stars. It reminded me of that time of evening when as a child I used to eagerly search for the stars as they appeared. We had something to eat and then lay in the cockpit on our backs taking in as much of the rich sky, with its dazzling Milky Way, as we could. Suddenly we were two beginners again, gazing at the heavens in absolute innocent wonder. Hearing the soft full sound of the surf in the stillness of the night was like a narcotic. Soon I began snoring and it was necessary for Davey to rally and drag us off to our bunk. Another blessed night under star-filled skies.

22.

The winds started picking up shortly after midnight and the whistling in the rigging and the grating of the anchor chain as *Querencia* swung from port to starboard had me up and peering out the hatch every ten minutes. By sunrise it was blowing thirty-five knots with higher gusts. As the surf rushed toward shore the strong wind would blow the top of the waves high into the air as a fine mist. Davey wrote in the log:

> This is the powerful Santa Ana winds we have heard about. Now we are going to experience them. I am glad they caught us anchored in the lee, rather than on the windward side of the island. With not very much of a fetch (the distance along open water over which the wind blows) the waves aren't very large, and with the holding ground being good there isn't a big reason for us to go anywhere. We'd only blow out to sea anyway. John has let out all our chain, all 200 feet, all thousand dollars worth. "After all," he said "it isn't going to do any good in the chain locker." And we've hooked snubber lines on the chain at the bow and put extra chafing gear in the hawsers and on the bob stay. Now I think I'll do the wash.

It was an excellent day to do the wash. The humidity was only 18% and being in the wind was literally like standing in front of an open oven door. For intellectual stimulation I used my Casio watch to measure how much time it was going to require to dry the clothes that Davey was hanging on the lifelines. About forty-five seconds!

We weren't used to this kind of weather. For us, when it was blowing this hard it was usually forty degrees and raining. We liked the change. In no time at all we were accustomed to the sirens in the rigging. Enjoy! We caught up on chores, flew our dragon kite, and took an afternoon nap.

When we awoke, two other offshore boats, *Gypsy Spirit* and *Chai Ling*, had sought refuge and anchored in Christy but at some distance from us. Must be rough out there! Much to our amazement though, by evening things had died down enough that we took out a lazy fishing pole connected to an old, Canadian "buzz—bomb" lure. Down, down, down went the lure, sliding this way then that way, flashing, flickering, down, down, down, ...POW! I've never enjoyed catching a fish more, and on the first cast too! With the light tackle it took me ten minutes to land a three pound mackerel.

I landed the fish and handed the rod to Davey for a go at it. Another first cast and, ...POW! This time the reel was really smoking. The spool of line was down to a couple of wraps and the fish was still running away from us. Davey and I were both squealing and laughing with excitement. Finally, with only ten feet of monofilament left, the fish finally called a time out.

> *Out went the line,*
> *the reel squealing like a noise maker,*
> *then reeling in, and in, and in.*
> *Out went the line,*
> *the reel squealing like a noise maker*
> *then reeling in, and in, and in.*

Eventually we got it in, and this time it was a beautiful seven pound tuna. What fun, and we had been dying for fresh protein.

That evening I sat in the navigation station and wrote about our good fortune. With great fondness I watched Davey standing in the galley on the other side of the boat. She was carefully preparing our fresh food dinner. The tuna baked in the oven with a little lemon and butter and a dash of smoke and pepper, on the stove top were home fries and onions. After supping, we retired to our observatory on deck.

The following morning the wind was back but it wasn't blowing nearly as hard. Indeed, we realized there was a chance that before the end of the day there might not be any wind at all. We decided to haul anchor and bend a sail, making as best use of the prevailing breeze as possible. Continuing our discipline to improve our skills as self-sufficient sailors, we made ourselves bring up the anchor without using the engine tacking up to it with just our staysail. With Davey at the helm and me up front, when the bow would cross the wind I would wench the windlass like crazy, then patiently wait for the next pass. With the hook up we then turned south, around Santa Cruz, and headed east. With sea conditions less than perfect, we left behind us Santa Rosa and San Miguel. The two islands are the most northwest and robust of this southern California basin and we look forward to seeing them another day, both islands being rich in story, with tales of ice age mammals and Spanish treasure. Reading our *Chart Guide for Southern California* was as much fun as reading about lost worlds.

It is reported that Santa Rosa Island had human settlements as far back as the earth's glacial epoch. More definite are the remains of 200 villages that have been dated from 750 AD. Much of the game on the island was probably originally put ashore by tall ships, as a convenient food source. American ranchers bought this island and San Miguel in 1902.

San Miguel, farthest to the west, once had a king. Well, actually he was a Harvard man by the name of Lester who moved here with some sheep in 1928. A young lady from New York joined him, and she became known as the queen of San Miguel. Except for sheep shearing season and when the odd ship came by, they were totally alone. Despite their isolation they were remarkably happy. Then in WWII the U.S. government repossessed the island for bombing practice. Lester was so distraught that he shot himself and it was necessary for the "queen" and her sheep to be relocated on the mainland.

Today San Miguel is the home of some 10,000 to 20,000 sea lions and seals. Some 4,000 elephant seals seek refuge here and some 100 northern fur seals may have returned here despite the near annihilation of their species at this very spot over a century ago.

We were twenty miles east now sailing along the southern shore of Santa Cruz Island. The winds had eased and we were having a wonderfully comfortable sail complete with dolphins and Christopher Cross' new release, *Sailing*, on the radio.

> *Well it's not that far from paradise,*
> *that you can be sure,*
> *when you're sailing, ... sailing.*
> *Sailing*
> *takes me away ...*
> *to where I'm going.*

Deep water runs close to the steep rugged terrain for the length of the south shore. We took turns climbing down the rope ladder and cooling off in the blue water that gurgled along the hull. As we were passing little Gull Island we ate tuna fish sandwiches, studied the sea lions through our binoculars, and recited history.

"In 1754 the Spanish galleon *San Sebastian* sank here," read Davey.

By six that evening we were approaching the east end of the island and were looking for a place to park for the night. The anchorages looked untenable, but we finally settled on Blue Banks Anchorage. It was still dry NE wind conditions and gusting as we hardened up our sails, tacking inside the rocky bight.

Once in the entrance it was obvious that there was surge from a bigger than normal surf and that the anchorage was also crowded. Three or four commercial fishing boats were sitting it out within yards of each other. As Davey dropped the genny I started the diesel in preparation for the crowded maneuvering. We were in the process of dropping the mainsail when the engine slowed in revolutions and then died. A quick shrug and then we responded, raising the sails once again and wind powering ourselves back into helm control. We wouldn't be caught in such an anchorage or predicament without an engine. We turned the wheel hard over, tipped our hats and bid sad adieu to Santa Cruz, letting our genoa pull us out of the tiny bay. We had managed to sail out of peril back to the open sea where we would be safe. We were discouraged, though not surprised, that our engine was still failing, and it was disappointing to have to leave behind further exploration of Santa Cruz and picturesque Anacapa Island.

Instead of working on the engine immediately, we took advantage of the last light from the setting sun and made *Querencia* ready for another night at sea. There we were most likely to be safe. This meant stowing everything and checking all our operations from electronics to kerosene lanterns. Then we grabbed a bite to eat and picked a course to navigate till daylight.

Santa Nicholas Island was forty-five miles almost dead south but prohibited due to military maneuvers. Santa Barbara Island was forty miles to our southeast more in line with San Diego and not in anybody's gun sights. We started three-hour watches, and while Davey took the first watch I bled the fuel line and the engine was working again — for emergencies, maybe, we decided.

The wind had died to almost nothing and the sky as clear and the stars as pronounced as ever. The masthead pointed at the constellation Orion, The Hunter, and it was fun and beautiful to steer by it. Orion would become one of our closest and very best friends.

23.

Most of the following day we spent becalmed, and it was late afternoon before we reached Santa Barbara Island. A tiny island only one and a half miles long, it is a National Park. We had planned to go ashore and explore, the island having been a favorite of eighteenth century pirates, but it wasn't to be. The anchorage was not that secure and already *full* with three commercial boats. With a questionable weather forecast, we found ourselves going on for another night at sea.

It was a night of contrary currents and almost no wind. Yet because of our proximity to land and traffic we were down to two-hour watches. I was glad to see daybreak and when I went below to wake Davey for the second time since midnight I made a chart entry:

> I feel like I have an I.Q. of twelve or something like that. My brain may have turned to oatmeal. Long hard sleep is the only remedy. Both of us are now anxious to put in at Santa Catalina Island today.

"Oatmeal brains" is a phenomenon that occurs at sea when you have had much too little sleep and you have to haul yourself out of the bunk and stand your watch. Part of it must be the constant motion, but I swear your head feels like your brains are sloshing around inside your skull. As with a lobotomy, thinking may be quite labored; recovery is slow, maybe taking half an hour for a bad case. During your recovery period good performance is still possible, but you have to think about what you are doing, and thinking is extremely difficult.

At eleven-thirty in the morning we were two miles around the west end of Catalina Island, dropping our anchor in a bight near Black Point. The water was crystal clear up to the shoreline where it met a steep rock face. Bending your neck back you could see rolling green hills beyond the top of the cliff.

No sooner had we stopped than we decided it was time to get going again. The swell was far from comfortable and it was blowing again. With our engine being unreliable we left immediately, somewhat contumely. But we'd only gone a few more miles when we came upon Emerald Cove. We anchored in thirty feet of water behind Indian Rock, protected from the wind and swell and it was heaven once again. The whole cove was an iridescent bluish green, and very clear. How nice to be able to check your ground tackle by standing on the bow and looking down at your chain and anchor. With the colors and reflections both above and below the water it was as if we were anchoring in a prism of glass.

The first thing we did was grab our masks, fins, and snorkels and jump in. It was the first time we were able to free dive with little more than our wet suit jackets on. In these warm waters we saw all kinds of different life. Later that night we would have fun trying to identify the new fish using our field guide. There were Opal Eyes, Oscars, Butterfly fish, and the bright orange Giribaldi. Hand in hand Davey and I swam around Indian Rock. Then we saw a small octopus, then our first lobster — it was a spiny one with its head sticking out of a cave. I reached down to touch its antennae, and it quickly withdrew into its cave, emitting an alarming buzz. We came back to *Querencia* totally refreshed and happy. It had been a spectacular swim and we felt absolutely marvelous about our anchorage. That night it was perfectly calm and so temperate that we were able to leave all the hatches and portholes open without feeling the slightest chill, and here it was going to be November in three days.

We spent the better part of the next two days at Emerald Cove, relaxing, swimming, and doing chores. It took a whole afternoon just to get the tar off the waterline and wax the hull. We also went ashore for the first time in four days and took a hike in the hills down the next couple of points on the coast.

On Sunday I awoke in time to see a bright red 'sun pillar' form as the sun came up. We slowly got around to pulling up to our hook and moving *Querencia* down the coast.

Santa Catalina Island, was "discovered" by the Spanish explorer

Cabrillo in 1542 and named after the Catholic saint Catherine in 1602. From then until the mid-nineteenth century, when it was sold to a Santa Barbara couple for $1,000, it was used to cache everything from treasure to slaves. For the next seventy years it changed ownership several times and finally in 1919 was bought by the Wrigley family whose love for it is still visible today in their developments.

By mid-afternoon we were at the Isthmus, where Catalina narrows to less than half a mile in width as if some mythological god had put a line around the island and drawn it in tight, leaving only a narrow spit of land joining the east and west portions of the island. A squall was upon us just as we were ready to drop our anchor and it was necessary for us to wait, instead tacking back and forth for about twenty minutes until the squall passed. Then we positioned ourselves carefully in Little Fisherman Cove next to Isthmus Cove and set down our hook.

Eager to reprovision, we rowed ashore in hopes of finding a small grocery store. That we did, but on this day the Isthmus was tourist oriented and we had to pay $3 each as a landing fee after a very long row. Two bags of groceries came to a surprising $70.

An unexpected visitor

After returning to *Querencia* our spirits were soon lifted by a visitor who appeared just as we had tied up the dinghy and were climbing back aboard. It was a seal, just about the friendliest seal I had ever seen. Like a dog, he barked and splashed as he swam behind the boat in loops and circles. Next he tried to climb the Aries self steering paddle. At first we cheered for him being such a clown, but then our glee turned to concern as he splashed into the dinghy and then tried to jump aboard *Querencia*! I gently shooed him away with the end of an oar, not knowing exactly what we would do with a large ocean mammal with a sharp set of choppers suddenly flopping around in the cockpit. He stuck around for another twenty-five minutes before leaving just as mysteriously as he had appeared. It was a wondrous thing! Later it was explained to us that the government trains sea mammals in the area for secret duties. It was probably a Navy seal, absent without leave.

We wound up spending a few more days there. It was very pretty, I think in large part due to the island development. It was apparent to me that a lot of money had been spent here to create a geographical oasis of sorts. Isthmus had been a favorite of Hollywood movie-makers. *Mutiny on the Bounty* (the early version with Clark Gable), *The Ten Commandments*, *Sea Hawk*, *McHale's Navy*, and *Route 66* are just a few of the many movies that were filmed there.

With summer over we were mostly alone during the weekdays. We rowed to the little tourist center ashore several times to take care of our financial affairs. By this time we were becoming more adept at running our lives from a phone booth. We also hauled water, did our laundry, and mailed correspondence. Some people ashore, watching us come and go, had noticed as I had, that our repair job on the oar wasn't holding up too well, so they gave us another oar. It didn't fit exactly, but it worked a lot better than the broken one.

On Halloween Day we attempted to counter our homesickness for our kids by diving and trying to stick a fish for dinner. The fish were easily spooked, but nevertheless we managed to spear a three pound sheephead. They're odd-looking fish, all red and blue, with a large head. Despite it's goat-like head and protruding teeth it was delicious for lunch and was going to provide us with dinner too. This left the rest of the day for lying around and fiddling with little chores like fixing my Mitchell fishing reel. It poured two inches of rain in one hour, rinsing all our diving gear in the cockpit. We wrote letters and slept a lot.

On November 3 at eleven in the morning we pulled up our hook and sailed the rest of the length of the island arriving in the famous town of Avalon in late afternoon. Here we stayed for two weeks, and it was just about as wonderful a visit as you would have anywhere. The massive marine facilities in Avalon Bay (over 315 moorings), largely oriented towards the tourist season during most of the year and therefore usually crowded, were now comparatively empty. Our engine had lugged and died again coming in and we were very happy to have our tired little *Querencia* on a mooring in the shadow of the Casino. Of course we both loved the period of American history from the twentys to the forties anyway, and it was, in a way, like going back in time. The Casino's rich architecture was a treat to look at in itself. It was a fact that in 1939 over 300,000 people came across the Channel between Catalina and the continental coast to see and hear Benny Goodman and his orchestra pack them into the Casino's fantastic ballroom.

We were left with a wonderful life aboard with frequent explorations of the shoreline and colorful Avalon, actually a town with a permanent population of less than 2,000. The weather was still good for this time of year and we also used the time to give *Querencia*, and ourselves, some needed attention. We re-filled the water tanks and the propane, changed the zincs, tended our batteries, made a trip up the mast, and thought we repaired the engine problem. We also went out to dinner and the movies.

An old friend, Ken Osborne, the writer who first gave me the word *Querencia* through his poetry while I was in still in college, arrived for a visit. He came by ferry from Los Angeles. We took a vacation, the three of us swimming, eating, and playing a backgammon tournament of champions. It felt good to play with an old friend who knew us before 'when', and we spent an entire day just catching up on old times.

24.

We sailed on to San Diego on November 15. Once past the Avalon breakwater we raised all of our sail and turned our engine off. Even though there was barely any wind we would sail the entire way mostly with our whisker pole studding out the genoa sail. That night we had one of our favorite sea meals, ham with boiled potatoes and corn, and we sat underneath the moonlight as *Querencia* slowly crept across the Gulf of Santa Catalina. With the arrival of morning we were gently sailing over big blue swells directly into the sun, a round red orb hanging in an orange sky.

The sun moved slowly west as we moved slowly east and by afternoon we were pleasantly surprised to see La Jolla ahead in the hazy distance. As a matter of fact we could see our old hang-out, the Sea Lodge! We were living a dream come true!

Getting in to San Diego took longer than we expected, and we didn't round Point Loma until well after dark. It had been a long time since *Querencia* had been in a big city, and, as if the myriad of confusing lights weren't enough, a squadron of fighter jets, a tug pulling a barge, and a Navy submarine, all managed to share the entrance channel with us at one time or another as we sailed in.

We waited until the last possible moment, then fired up the engine and motored the last thirty-five minutes to the Harbor Police dock, where we tied up for the night in a slip for the first time again since Monterey. It felt great and there was more fun in store for us when we woke up the next day and discovered that the *Resonde II* and *Carina* and two Canadian boats we had met coming down the coast were sharing the dock with us.

We would spend over two months in San Diego before making our "big crossing" to the Marquesas. Actually we planned to go down to Cabo San Lucas and then stick our nose into the Sea of Cortez, but it didn't turn out that way.

We were allowed to spend three days at the Harbor Police dock, and the first thing I did was track down a Volvo-Penta dealership with a good mechanic. He listened to my long tale, asked a few questions, and sent me back to *Querencia* with rubber neoprene fuel hose to replace the copper fuel line from the diesel tank to the engine.

The copper line had acquired a tiny pinhole in it and over a period of time, depending on how hard the engine was running, air would be sucked into the fuel line and foul the fuel supply to the engine. With the replacement of the entire fuel line came the welcome and final end to our engine suddenly dying without notice.

Next I carried our thirty-five pound Bruce anchor on my shoulder for about a mile down to a marine distributor and traded it for another CQR anchor like our primary hook. It laid up in the bow pulpit much better than the broad unhinged Bruce whose clanking we had both grown tired of.

We enjoyed Thanksgiving at the dock, a meal complete with turkey, stuffing, cranberries, and mashed potatoes. With a light drizzle outside it was a perfectly lazy holiday, and we celebrated in the afternoon with other cruising couples.

After anchoring for a few days between the two yacht clubs in the Shelter Island yacht basin we pulled up and *Querencia* putted in the warm sunshine down through San Diego bay and into Glorietta Bay.

Glorietta Bay is separated from the Pacific Ocean by the Silver Strand beach on the peninsula of San Diego. With the charming community of Coronado on its northwest shore we had once again found a perfect place to spend a while for the holidays and in final preparation for our departure to foreign lands.

Davey's children, Paul and Caroline, joined us from Seattle and we had a wonderful Christmas season together. To our amazement we were even able to secure a slip at the Glorietta Bay Marina, right across the street from the beautiful Coronado Hotel.

On a day sail in San Diego Bay a Navy tug passed us much too close and going way too fast, seemingly on purpose. It managed to push our inflatable tender which we were towing behind us underneath our wind vane paddle shaft where its bow was repeatedly punctured, ripping it to shreds. We replaced it with a twelve-foot Metzler sailing dinghy. Paul and Caroline took turns in Glorietta Bay sailing it everyday of their short visit. Davey and I continued to hack away at final chores in preparation of our big trip.

> We need to concentrate on leaving! We are working towards it hard though! We have cleaned the bottom, fixed the engine, outfit-

ted a new dinghy, installed a new voltmeter,
replaced all our anti-chafe gear, tuned our
rigging, had a Coast Guard inspection, practiced with our Spanish, our shortwave receiver, our sextant, replaced the sump pump,
compensated the compass, and provisioned
Querencia to the point where her boot stripe
is now at the waterline. — DT

At the time we didn't realize that there was a political dispute occurring between U.S. fishing boats and the Mexican Government. On January 1 it resulted in some unannounced changes in Mexican policy towards U.S. cruising boats. All U.S. boats, if they so much as had a fish hook aboard, were required to have commercial fishing licenses whether or not they were commercial fishing. Most all the other cruising boats we knew of had gone into the Mexican consulate to get their cruising permits the end of December and had no problem, but suddenly in the first week of January it was a big problem for us.

Most all the other cruising boats departed and we were forced to stay behind for the moment. The Mexican consulate was sympathetic to us, but of course the best that he could do was recommend that we wait until the rules changed or strip the boat of all fishing gear. Did that mean even the hooks in our life raft?

"Si, señor."

Meanwhile we could re-apply each week. Any infraction of the law would be met by a stiff penalty, we were reminded. The consulate office was crowded and unhappy, full of long lines and long faces - just what we were trying to get away from!

Back at the boat Davey and I stripped *Querencia* of all her fishing tackle and set it on the dock and stared at it. We had an enormous amount of gear, well over a thousand dollars worth, excluding our emergency gear. Bummer.

I wandered up to the marina office later mumbling and complaining. A salty fellow with a Siberian husky on a rope leash had been standing off to the side scratching a three-day beard and listening to me grumble. He reminded me of a character out of one of Jack London's books that I had read as a kid.

"Why don't you forget about Mexico and sail straight to the Marquesas?"

His words sounded right-on.

Of course, he was right. The pilot charts would show it to be a fine time to make a crossing, though maybe a few weeks early. I raced back to the boat to tell Davey about the new idea. Our Spanish lessons weren't going so well anyway.

As we poured over the pilot charts we got more and more excited. We traced our projected course over each little square, stepping our way southwest across the ocean charts. Each wind rose showed only a slim chance of gale force winds (Force 8 or above), and this area could be avoided by heading more south than west for the first week or so. For the most part there it was in front of us — our destiny.

It was January 20. We re-packed the fishing gear aboard *Querencia*. We were ready to make sail. Well, almost. Paul suddenly called from Seattle and said he wanted to come with us. We were thrilled. The next few days we worked hard on getting an extension course for his sophomore year in high school through UCLA and succeeded.

The Santa Ana winds picked up for a few days and it really blew. A trimaran in Glorietta also going south decided to leave anyway and we heard on the news that one day out the boat had capsized. Luckily they were picked up and rescued by the *Love Boat* cruise ship. They were in good shape, and as far as I know they went on to Acapulco.

Every morning I turned on our little five-inch TV and watched the pilots' weather on the local public television network. It was half an hour in length, and the satellite pictures of exactly where we wanted to go the next few weeks were superb. Paul arrived all supercharged, he even shinnied up the mast for one last check, and the weather cleared beautifully and everything looked stable. We would leave the next day.

We decided it would take three weeks, and we would provision for six. I keyed the coordinates into the Sat Nav.

> Bora Bora
> 16° 30' S
> 151° 45' W
> Distance: 4,143 statute miles

Of course the actual distance would be greater since we would not travel in a perfect straight line. We probably would stop at the Marquesas.

Nuka Hiva, Marquesas
8° 50' S
140° 05' W
Distance: 3,314 statute miles.

Just for fun I pretended that instead of sailing to the South Pacific we were driving to New York.

Albany, New York
43° 22' N
73° 04' W
Distance: 2,497 statute miles.

It was a little more than half the distance we would be sailing to Bora Bora. Whew! This was going to be some trip in our little yar ship!

Paul makes a final check up the mast

25.

"The great ocean of truth still lies before me."
— Sir Isaac Newton

We had made several friends and spent our early morning time saying our good-byes and accepting gifts of wine and champagne. It was 0920 when we finally slipped away from the dock. We spent another fifteen minutes in Glorietta Bay putt-putting around in circles checking and resetting our compass deviation with known landmarks. It was January 31, 1984 and it was very calm and a bit foggy in San Diego Bay. Despite the haze we were sure it would all burn off and it would be a great day. The mariner's radio message reported eight knots of wind outside, perfect for our taste. We would motor over the horizon and make a good offing.

Just as we were settling into our plans, lo and behold the orange amperage light started flashing and then burned a permanent orange glow in the control panel.

"No major problem," we sang in unison. It had to be a minor repair. We would take it in stride.

At eleven in the morning we pulled up to the Harbor Police dock and asked to make emergency repairs. We quickly replaced the voltage regulator with a spare we had in ship's stores and that was the end of the amperage problem. Then we ran down to the Volvo dealer, walking the one mile distance from the Harbor Police dock one more time to purchase another spare voltage regulator. Before you knew it we were back underway, going out the ship's channel entrance, rounding Point Loma at 1650 hrs.

1900 hrs. Good motor sailing in calm conditions. Plan to clear north point of Coronado Islands. Course Magnetic 210°. There is barely enough wind to sail, but we would have to take an inside course on the Coronado Islands. Prefer to stay outside of them. Wind NW, then SW, then NW again. We are anxious to be well west of where we are. A full moon would be nice, but it will be nice later on in our trip. All the chicken we fried up at the dock along with the biscuits we baked were easy and delicious. — DT

During the night the wind filled in enough for us to sail. Davey and I each stood a three-hour watch and Paul stood a two-hour watch. It seemed like before you knew it, it was daybreak.

> 0656 hrs. Sunrise shows we have made it through our first night. We are well south of Coronado Islands. The shifts worked well and we all feel rested. Already, Davey and I appreciate the extra watch. Whales last night were quite scary for me on my watch, but the dolphins this morning are great. — JFM

It turned into a perfect day of sailing with fifteen knots of wind. *We were underway.* The thought of it gave me butterflies. The plan was to head a bit south of a straight great circle course, running down the Baja coast until reaching Isla de Guadalupe, almost 200 miles from San Diego and a hundred and fifty miles off the coast of Mexico. I had decided to not cross 120° West until we got down to 10° North latitude. If we got out to 130° West too quickly there was a greater possibility of getting caught in a severe blow.

These first few days at sea our bodies and our minds worked at re-organizing themselves into accepting the physical reality that we were on the rolling sea and we were going to be on the rolling sea for weeks to come. We hooked up our Walker log meter off the stern of the boat. We watched the face of the odometer as the line twirled, round and round, logging off the miles. A full revolution of its hands would indicate a hundred mile day which turned out to be about average for *Querencia.*

The library was one of the first things we investigated for entertainment. A love affair with books at sea is easy. I got very "cerebral," and started reading *The Brendan Voyage* and re-reading Chichester's *Gipsy Moth Circles the Globe.* Chichester had become a role model for me. We also broke out the backgammon board and the Travel Scrabble a time or two in those first days, and we all studied the stars and participated in the navigation.

Unfortunately, with all the reading Paul fell seasick almost immediately. He wasn't throwing-up sick, but he really felt miserable

and seemed to spend more and more time each day sleeping or laying in his bunk. To top things off he smashed his finger in the main
hatch.

Davey was quiet. As a matter of fact she was the most quiet I ever
remember.

> 2/2/84
> 0121 John to bed. My watch is 0130 to 0430.
> Paul still snoring! Had his first solo watch
> from 1800 to 1900 last night. He did very
> well except he read some more and felt sick
> again. It sure is black out tonight. Unless it
> blows over there won't be much star-gazing
> for me. — DT
>
> 0230 Whales again. Turned engine on to
> scare them off and discovered key in the igni-
> tion was in the on position. — DT
>
> 2/3/84
> 0100 Sure do miss the moon. The stars shed
> a lot of light, but the clouds have been play-
> ing havoc with them. Mellow night at sea, so
> far; small seas, steady breeze, no shipping
> traffic, no whales. I feel spooked in the cock-
> pit alone tonight — I am sure the feeling will
> pass as the moon waxes. Whoops! I may have
> spoken too soon about a mellow night — a
> huge black cloud is hovering overhead and
> the wind and seas are picking up. Am going
> to try and make it through another hour.
> Three-hour watches and sleeps are best. Log
> reads 110 miles. Approx. 4.5 knots/hr. —DT

By the end of the following afternoon we were sailing with the
bold and rugged shores of Guadalupe Island on our starboard side at
a distance of about ten miles. A deserted island twenty miles long and
4,000 feet high, it was illuminated by the splintered wavelengths of
the setting sun. Life was abundant and birds were everywhere. It was
a spectacular sight. As we passed the two little islands off the south
tip of Guadalupe Island we came to the realization that the island was
our first sight of land since the night we pulled away from San Diego
three days previous. In the light air the strong smell of fertile valleys

and trees filled our senses. There was a longing to go and try to find an anchorage on the shore of this new land and fish and relax for just a few days.

The chart reported large concentrations of yellowfin, marlin, rockfish, abalone, and giant sea bass, as well as sea lions, fur seals, and elephant seals. Spanish galleons had landed here in the 1600s. Once heavy with vegetation, most of the island was now bare as a result of goats. Whalers had imported them for a food cache in the 1800s. What a wild and desolate place! We were enraptured by it all, but we concurred that there was really no safe refuge for *Querencia* and the three gringos aboard. Our judgment told us to pass it up and stick to our schedule. We all sat in the cockpit eating hamburger steaks with macaroni cheese and string beans that Davey had so lovingly prepared. I think we were all a bit wistful and pensive as we watched Guadalupe fade away behind us. We watched until the twilight was gone.

From here the coastline would cut east and pull away from us as we continued on our SSW course. There was only open water ahead of us with the exception of a dangerous group of rocks known as Rocos Alijos. Over 260 miles away and well off our course, they would not pose a hazard to us unless we got caught in a storm or made a major navigational error.

Surrounded by black-blue water, and with fifteen knots of wind returning to put the bone in her teeth, *Querencia* sailed on without hesitation. While Davey cleaned up the galley, Paul and I put a reef in the main and prepared for another night of sailing on the rolling heap.

Paul at the helm

Part V
The Crossing

26.

"Come, follow me, and leave the world to its babblings."
— Dante

And so *Querencia* truly became the only "island" the three of us would know for some time to come. Each of us, including *Querencia* was finding our niche, our daily routine, trying to find a groove. For some of us this was easier than for others. The same could be said of our onboard equipment. But together all of us, Paul and Davey and I and *Querencia* all learned together how to make our way across the deep blue sea as a team.

I noticed one day that the compass at the navigation station did not read the same as the pedestal compass. I couldn't figure out what had happened. And then I discovered that a spare Casio watch was laying next to the compass case. Moving it was all it took to put the nav station compass back in synch and eliminate the problem. The watch had caused an eight degree deflection of the compass needle!

The Sat Nav worked flawlessly. It is one of the most wonderful tools ever to fall into the hands of the adventuring yachtsman, a spin-off from space technology. By using the "next satellite" information provided from one satellite fix to another we were able to determine when the best satellite for the next fix would be available. We would then turn off the Sat Nav between fixes and turn it back on only about an hour before a satellite was expected to rise above the horizon. This system worked well and limited the electrical drain on the boat. We really didn't use the satellite navigation any more for navigation than we did our sextant and dead reckoning.

I spent about one or two hours a day "shooting" the sun and stars with our sextant and working up our estimated position. Harold, aboard *Resonde II* in San Diego, had given me the algorithm for programming the True Azimuth on an inexpensive programmable calculator we had aboard. It saved lots of time. Nevertheless, working up a sight was a long process, even when conditions were good. Quite often I would have to throw all my work out because it would be so obviously out of wack. It was easy to make errors, such as jiggling the sextant around too much when sighting through it, or accidentally jumping a column in the sight reduction tables. This necessitated checking all your work again and again and again. It was laborious. For the first couple of weeks my plotting sheets looked like a sketch of a web made by a spider on amphetamines. But each day it got easier and we got much better at it. Once in a while Paul and Davey worked up a sextant sighting from start to finish as well. Soon we had the whole process of guessing *where we were at* down quite well.

I remember a French sailor, a salty old dog who'd sailed the seven seas. We had met him in a mariner's shop when we were in Seattle outfitting for offshore. We had asked him about how one could be confident about knowing where he was at in the middle of the big ocean.

"But it is no problem, of course," he had said.

He held up his big, tanned, wrinkled thumb in the middle of a imaginary chart and continued, "If you say you are *here*, then you are *here!* There will be no expert around to argue with you!"

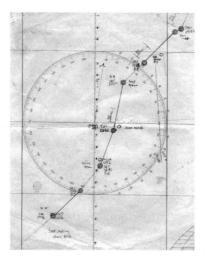

How true.

Within two weeks some chafe gear needed replacing. I went below one night during my watch after hearing a crash below. One of our hammocks full of fruit had chaffed completely through, spilling its contents, which were by then rolling all over the cabin sole. Upon examination I realized a second hammock of provisions was ready to do the same. This prompted me to make a daily check of all chafe above and below decks. With the constant motion, anything that could move would, and if it rubbed against something else it might just rub itself out over time! It really was amazing how things constantly "worked." We were really glad that we had put such good chafe gear on our running backs, shrouds, and boom hardware. We had a long way to go!

I think we fell in love with our kerosene lights right off the bat, especially with the lack of a moon. Once they were filled and secure and lit, the light they cast was a wonderful thing; putting a warmth and cheer below decks on the blackest of nights. I do remember one night springing from my bunk and hitting the cabin torch with my forehead so hard that I put it out. I almost put myself out as well I might add. But I was the cautious miser then and I especially appreciated the kerosene lights since I didn't have to worry about them draining our precious batteries. One filling seemed to last forever, actually about two or three days, and we had plenty of kerosene, or "paraffin" as Chichester referred to it.

Filling them was a trick though! We had learned off the Washington coast that spilling any on board was something you would regret, and regret, and regret. You had to live with the smell for days. And if the weather turned foul that wretched smell didn't make you feel any better. So we never filled them below decks and as a matter of fact we did it hiking out over the side! Davey would lean way out over the lee rail holding the lamp and I would lean way out holding the kerosene jug and fill it up. If we spilled a drop it wouldn't matter, and after awhile our sea legs got so good we didn't even spill. It was a ritual we probably did a hundred times in all kinds of weather. At times it reminded me of trying to pour refreshments on a roller coaster.

By the second week out we were realizing the reality of what we were doing and, with the weather picking up, we were starting to feel a little grungy and burned out. From the log:

> 0214 My watch. Feeling quite queasy, my stomach is. Couldn't sleep very well but did rest. Mostly just perspired, lying on my stomach..... visualizing a little marble rolling around in my stomach. We *do* need to go this fast and I'm sure that at daylight we can readjust things and get *Querencia* to not roll quite so much. Paul is now doing good two-hour watches in the middle of the night and that helps immensely. Found one rotten tangerine and one rotten lemon to put over the side — it was giving the whole boat a sickening sweet smell. — JFM

Davey turned the eggs every day or so to keep them from spoiling. She had made sure to stock our stores with unrefrigerated eggs. Then by "rolling the yoke" (turning the eggs) regularly it was possible to keep the egg shell from drying out. If you didn't turn them every day the top part of the shell would dry out leaving the yoke exposed to air and spoilage.

Davey measured our water consumption. She had allowed for 3.5 quarts per person per day for a one month passage, so we were all glad to hear that so far we were using only about 2.5 quarts each. One morning in the second week the large following sea had eased and we each jumped at the chance to take a turn on the foredeck in a blissful extended freshwater shower. It was luxurious. The origins of the phrase "Cleanliness is next to Godliness" had never been more clear to each of us. It is a feeling.

Next it was haircuts, at least for Paul and me. Our hair was driving us nuts. Styling was out of the question and the perspiration was enough for me to decide I wanted all my hair cut to the quick. At my request Davey cut all my hair off including my mustache. After seeing me Paul opted rather for a trim. But I felt great, almost reborn! I hadn't had hair that short since I was ten years old.

When we were in Monterey I had read about the origin of the old word "jack-tar." These were hearty sailors of the tall ships that sailed the Horn. They so hated the wet matting of their hair and the hygiene problems it created that they took to tarring their scalps. Tarring your hair not only slowed its growth and helped resist scalp infections, but it made haircuts easy too. Thick creosoted hair only needed to be chopped off when necessary. The only major drawback occasionally was that it could make a mess of the rest of you. The ship's officers wore large collars on their coats to protect the rest of their uniform. Later these large collars became stylish; even George Washington wore one.

In order to be sure we were well clear of rocks far off the Mexican shore we had gone west of south, putting the weather on our starboard side. With the seas running high accompanied with gusty winds, there was an occasional splash into the cockpit. The constant slapping against the hull was also disconcerting.

Listening to the Coast Guard shortwave radio broadcasts we

were able to determine that a large stationary gale was about ten degrees north of us. We surmised that it was generating the large swells and gusty winds we were experiencing. One morning sunrise following a particularly hellish night at sea, I made a decision to jibe and put the wind behind our aft port quarter. We had traveled south far enough to be out of coastal navigational dangers. With the waves stacking up as they were, I thought it would make for an easier ride to put them more behind us. In the processing of jibing, *Querencia* went hard over on her ear. Everything that was not secured below decks was dumped to the cabin sole. The navigation station was literally emptied of every chart, book, pencil, pen, compass, and watch.

It had been necessary for Davey to go to the foredeck and crew before the ordeal was over. She returned with a big grin on her face. She held up her prize: two squid that had washed up on the deck. By evening the boat had stabled out some and even though it was a bit rough Davey was able to fry up her catch of the day in a little garlic and butter as an appetizer. This was followed with a dinner of game hens cooked in the oven. It was an especially good meal. Paul laid down to catch some sleep before his watch started. Davey and I sat in the cockpit and talked.

We finally had relaxed enough that we felt the most focused we had felt in days. We talked openly about how things were going. We admitted to each other that it seemed awfully tough out on the big ocean in such a little boat. I confessed that up to tonight I had been for the most part completely exhausted and quite often seriously discouraged. Disheartened by the relentless rough motion, we both felt like the ocean had been beating on us. We wondered if we had done the right thing in starting our crossing so far north. Yes, maybe it would have been better to follow the more conventional "milk run" south hugging the Baja coast to its tip before turning west at all. We discussed the probability that the sea seemed extra rough and topsy-turvy because we were winding our way over some very big seamounts. It was a regular mountain range below us with one fracture zone after the other rupturing the earth's crust on the ocean floor. According to the bottom contours on our charts, seamounts were all around us rising up from 4,000 feet to within a few hundred feet below the surface!

Big, curious clouds of silence hung in the air while we spoke. For a second I believe we were both thinking of heading for Mexico and calling it quits.

"We should pick up better weather and things should get calmer a bit further south," I murmured to Davey. "We all seem resilient enough that we can dig in and keep going." There wasn't much tenacity in my voice.

"I agree," Davey said clearly, "but let's make it as comfortable as possible and lets have as much fun as possible. A lot of things on the boat, like the blocks for one thing, are still making too much noise banging around and Paul still doesn't feel very well."

I think we each said a silent prayer then that conditions would improve.

Hours later that night Davey wrote in the log:

> I'm going to have to wake Paul and ask him to relieve me for the last hour of my watch. Daybreak will be soon, but I just can't keep my eyes open. A couple hours more of sleep and I should be all caught up. —DT

27.

Inch by inch it's a cinch.
Go for a mile and it takes a while.

— Anonymous

I'm not sure whether it was coincidence or synchronicity or good old-fashioned prayer, but that very next day the sun came out, the seas and wind lessened, and everything seemed to get better.

We all showered again and sunbathed and even trailed our feet in the water over the rail as we continued our journey down the surface of our water planet. We were all once again infected with laughter about the silliest little things. Times seemed remarkably more easy going. Paul even took off his scopolamine patch. He announced that he felt immediately better.

It was a day that we were glad to make only seventy-five miles rather than our usual 100 or so. Today was a vacation, and the family yacht and the weather couldn't be better. We enjoyed futzing on the boat, fixing little things, and we decided to make a team effort at attacking every unwanted clink and clank. Silence *is* golden.

What we didn't realize was that the weather we were having this particular day was, for the most part, how the weather was to be for the remainder of our trip and we were just getting into our third week!

It was about now that Davey and I decided to firm up our decision to each do rotating three-hour watches at night. Every night the watches were split into three three-hour shifts; 2100-2400, 0000-0300, and 0300-0600 with a different person taking the first watch each night. This made sure that two out of the three of us could get six continuous hours of sleep each night. Every third night, at middle watch, you would get only three continuous hours of sleep.

	DAY 1	DAY 2	DAY 3
9-12	JOHN	DAVEY	PAUL
12-3	DAVEY	PAUL	JOHN
3-6	PAUL	JOHN	DAVEY

During the daylight hours at least two of us were always on deck so we didn't have to assign day watches. Dinner was always just before sunset to afford natural lighting; after our meal, we always gathered in the cockpit. Those social gatherings produced some of my fondest memories of the crossing.

The three of us would lean back against the coaming with our full bellies, Paul on one side of me and Davey on the other, as I dialed up the portable ham radio receiver. We especially enjoyed listening to the Pacific Maritime Net. All the boats would call in and talk about their days, how the weather was, and how life was going for them. We wished we had the capability to transmit, but just listening was very entertaining and comforting. It is amazing how stimulating just the sound of human conversation can be. Often after the sun went down AM radio stations from as far away as Nebraska would often come in extremely well, their signal bouncing off the atmosphere I suppose, and we enjoyed listening to them as well.

We would look up at the sky as we listened, and although we

never saw a plane, occasionally we could see a satellite. There wasn't a doubt in our minds as to what they were. Tumbling, rolling stainless steel marbles going from one horizon to the other. They were particularly visible just after sunset and we would have contests. First place went to whoever saw the first satellite and second place to whoever saw the most. It was a lot of fun.

Later, after dark, we had fun learning and memorizing the stars and constellations. The view of the heavens was really spectacular. Soon we could see the Southern Cross. We tried to learn all we could about this new world around us.

From the log:

> Constellations and Stars observed:
> Pollus and Castor in Gemini, Canis Minor
> with Procyon, Sirius in Canis Major, Auriga
> with Capella, Lepus the Hare, Regulus in
> Leo, Aldebaran in Taurus, Algol in Perseus,
> the Pleiades, Cassiopeia, Orion with
> Beletelgeuse and Rigel. — PTW

The sun was out in the day, and the moon and the stars were out at night. Despite *Querencia's* slow progress in the light air, every calendar day was exciting for all of us.

28.

When the sea settles down you can see forever. The horizon is a long way away. Like a coiled line it lies all around you. *Querencia* was in the middle, always, of a perfect circle.

More and more it seemed like we were sailing through a vast prairie. Instead of sagebrush and dust, it was water and salt! It reminded me of hiking in the potholes of eastern Washington state. The ocean prairie would change from time to time, just like terra firma does. When I say it changed I mean *it looked different.* Gentle, but big, fat, sine wave pulses of ocean would put you down in a valley or up on a plateau. And it went on forever, as far as the eye could see in every direction.

The weather became consistently light. We resumed a south-westerly course that kept the sails full and studded from dawn to dusk. We started appreciating a relaxed attitude, comfortably making about a hundred miles a day. We were spending our time resting and relaxing. If we weren't studying the wonderful world around us we were reading about it in the books we had brought. We scheduled games of backgammon and scrabble.

The warming waters seemed to be teeming with all sorts of critters big and small. The slight, but vast swells upon rising would now and then at their tops reveal glimpses of the strangest creatures. One day it was a large brown whale shark just lying there like a hulk, its huge brown tail fin flopping heavily back and forth at the surface. The fin was easily ten feet high.

Occasionally porpoise would come pay us a visit. I spent one whole morning trying to make a stereo recording of their squeaky conversations with one of our onboard cassette tape recorders. I hung microphones out the forward portholes just above the water's surface as they swam and squeaked in our bow wake. The recording turned out to be pretty poor, but I'll never forget the experience!

One especially still night Paul was on watch in the cockpit. Davey and I were each below in our port and starboard sea bunks snoozing. Totally naked with but a bed sheet we slept, the portholes were open to afford any air conditioning available as the days had gotten hotter and hotter.

Vaguely, waking me out of my slumber, I heard a "flap, flap, flap" and suddenly Davey was screaming. I sprang from my bunk. Paul came below turning on the cabin lights as he came down the companionway. The three of us stood in the middle of the cabin staring at a ten inch flying fish that was staring back at us, flapping and gasping, scales and all in the starboard bunk. Somehow it had flown in the porthole and joined Davey in her birthday suit. Wedging itself between Davey's back and a vinyl cushion it obviously had really stirred up her imagination for a minute, rudely awakening her. Paul was by this time bent over, laughing so hard I was worried he might fall over and break a rib on the galley bulkhead.

"Oh my god, Mom! I can't believe it! That is so funny!" he laughed.

"Oh! Please you guys. Get it out. *Please*," Davey pleaded.

As for myself, I didn't crack a rib, but I nearly laughed myself sick! I suggested saving the fish and cooking it up for breakfast in a few hours. But after thinking about it for a second or two even I had to join in a chorus of "Yuk!." Flying fish are just such scaly, boney looking creatures. I'll never know how Chichester took a liking to them.

We got serious about fishing during the day and it paid off. We started catching tuna… finally. Fish swam with the boat morning, noon, night, and day, but they were finicky, smart Dorado [*Mahi Mahi*] and would have little to do with us. The fish we caught were mostly delicious albacore tuna. Tuna swim in large schools that seem to migrate around oceans in a random nonstop fashion. We caught one every other day or so, and doing so always made for fun excitement and a scrumptious dinner. Davey usually served it with pasta and a canned vegetable, or cabbage dressed with mayonnaise and lemon — cabbages last forever. We garnished the pasta with parmesan cheese and were all set. It was a meal we easily learned to look forward to. As a matter of fact, when we didn't catch a tuna for more than a couple of days we got really anxious about it. At first I would even turn the engine on to try and motor over towards a swarm of feeding birds on the horizon. Usually where there were birds there were tuna. But it was hopeless to try and catch up with a school of tuna in a sailboat. Tuna go very fast (seventy miles an hour when they're in a hurry), and they seem to go where they want. In order for us to catch one they had to come to us on their own schedule. That seemed to be mostly up to chance.

Fresh food really was a blessing, even a privilege. It was the same with ice, which, unfortunately, we had run out of the day before Valentine's Day.

I ran out of Camels. Cigarettes that is. Not that I ever was a big smoker. To me it was a puff or two once a day and I was satisfied; the sacrament completed, I once again felt free to howl at the moon and braid my hair. A big fan of the American Indian, Humphrey Bogart, and Tom Robbins' *Still Life With Woodpecker*, a half a Camel a day kept me cool. Of course I had planned on quitting *(Right!)*, so I had only provisioned a minimum. Luckily Paul had managed to sneak a couple of packs of his own flavor aboard and was a big enough person to share, he had quit without even trying. *Anything* is better than nothing.

> *Expect nothing.*
> *Accept everything*
> *except nothing.*
> — J.K. Osborne

We noticed growth on the boat, mostly goose-neck barnacles. When I would hang over the side I could see huge clumps of shells and clutchy stuff growing on the hull. We also noticed quite remarkable changes in our bodies. We seemed to have stopped perspiring. Our skin definitely seemed more leathery, actually salty.

Vinegar tasted wonderful. Pouring it on our homegrown sprouts for our dinner salad every few days was a real treat. We watched funny old skin peel from our palms as our bodies continued to change and become accustomed to actually living on the watery heap.

One day during our third week the wind did pick up enough for us to put a reef in the main and strike the whisker pole. When bringing the jib across during a course adjustment one of the jib sheets fouled with a tie-down that had been temporarily hanked on to the pulpit. This happened just as a wave broke astern sending all seven tons of us surfing down a ten foot wave (surprise!) with the foresail backed.

"Damn!" I quickly tried to disconnect the self steering and free the backwashed rudder by unscrewing the threaded pin from the clutch wheel.

But I was one second too late. The pressure on the hardware was incredible. There was no way I could release the wheel clutch pin by hand, and the steering lines from the vane squeaked louder and louder as they continued to stretch and tighten. Then a long few seconds later, as I stood cursing, there was a loud "POP! PING!"

Luckily only one of the steering lines from the vane had broken where it attached to the wheel. If it had been the clutch or the wheel or the vane or the steering quadrant, we would have had big problems. I spent the next hour or so re-designing a quick release mechanism for the steering lines from the vane to the wheel so I would never have that helpless feeling again. Paul was steering by hand as we bore forward at hull speed. The sea was quite unexpectedly heaving and agitated. Big, black, ugly clouds were chasing us from over the horizon. It was impossible not to look back over your shoulder for more than a few minutes. This went on all day, and yet, those big black clouds just stayed there right on the horizon! Fish were everywhere, once again as if they were boiling up from the ocean, and yes, there were Mother Carey's chickens. It was hard not to worry.

Then much to our surprise, the wind died and it got very, very, humid. Big lightning bolts began displaying themselves, discharging from cloud to horizon over our right shoulders. The sails flapped around like they were confused as to where the wind was going to come from next. Then a hefty gust would hit and then more lightening.

I went below and quickly searched around in a big plastic box of stores we had labeled "Electric City" and found the copper wire I needed. Then I dug around in the fishing box and found some down rigging weights to tie on the end of the copper wire. I trailed these from the shrouds and the backstay well into the water. As I was tying them on I thought back to a conversation I had with Vern, the skipper of *Java* in the San Juans. Vern was the retired foreman for Portland Electric.

"Tell me Vern, what do you think would happen if lightening was to hit the mast of a sailboat?" I had asked, preparing myself to take mental notes.

"Well, I would imagine the charge would travel down the mast until it reached the shortest distance between the base of the mast and the water. Then it would blow a hole right through the hull to make the connection," he had said with a red, weathered grin.

Paul popped his head out the companionway holding the *Golden Guide of Weather* in his hands looking like a preacher who hadn't quite yet dried behind the ears.

"Oh my God, you guys, you don't want to hear what *this* book says!"

Then he proceeded to tell us anyway.

Bending the paperback wide apart at page 101 he read, "Lightning takes the path of least resistance. It tends to hit the highest places. Never stand under a lone tree in an open field during a thunderstorm. The mast of a sailboat may attract lightning. Stay away from boats and water during storms."

"Well at least we aren't under a tree," I grunted back.

Davey was silent and pensive.

We all knew the obvious — that *Querencia's* mast, although not a tree, was undoubtedly the tallest thing around. We were *seventeen hundred miles* from land.

A brilliant thought reminded me that we needed to immediately disconnect the antennas to the satellite navigator and the radio. Once again we were too busy to ponder for very long about all our possible problems.

Dinner was a brief affair. Later the only things audible from the radio receiver, especially the AM band, were loud cracks of electricity amplified more than any of us cared to listen to.

At 2130 Davey took time out from her watch to make the following entry into the log:

> No fix until tomorrow it seems. Miserably hot and humid below decks. Lightening totally illuminates the sky. So far lightening is the only thing except a hurricane that scares me to death.

With sleep impossible, we just sat there in the darkness, careful not to touch metal. Outside through the portholes we were witnessing the most incredible display of light and electricity any of us had ever seen.

This vast electrical storm continued throughout the night. Needless to say, after several hours of the same thing we were very unnerved. To keep our heads about us we found it necessary to unfocus, as it were, from a situation we could do nothing about.

As a therapy, I prescribed humorous distraction. I dug around in our cassette locker and came out with a nostalgic tape recording of a 1946 radio show featuring Abbot and Costello. I inserted it in our battery powered portable cassette player and we listened to the famous *Whose on First?* routine. It worked. A therapeutic distraction it was. As soon as that tape finished I started another.

Peering out the navigation station porthole occasionally, I was truly amazed. Sheets of rain, torrential rains, came and went. The rapid continuous bursts of flashing lights never stopped and once in a while were punctuated with the most fantastic cracks of thunder. The self-steerer, Nelley, continued us on our heading SSW.

It was still lightening at the first hint of daylight when I pulled out the log and wrote some verse:

> *Trailing wires and thoughts*
> *we ran before this deep black, flashing cloud;*
> *air thick, perspiration dripping,*
> *water going from blue to spray gray,*
> *the wind unsure as we were.*
> *The looming edge, closer, closer,*
> *and then the crack*
> *and all below*
> *inside this rolling hull,*
> *synapsed between the waves and God*
> *in blinding flashes.*
> *Ceaselessly they light the blackness of night,*
> *these rolling thunders.*
> *Below, below, all secure.*
> *Hot and sweaty.*
> *Don't touch metal.*
> *Peering out the portholes into the dazzling rage*
> *we see raindrops big as plums.*
> *Flashing, flashing, endlessly*
> *till daylight reconnects the soul to this body*
> *standing*
> *hot and wet and worried*
> *below the wave-washed deck.*

Daylight is such a wonderful phenomenon. We were immediately motivated and were out with our buckets and our sophisticated tarpaulins catching all the rain we could to replenish our water supply. We were so busy making our makeshift cisterns and carrying water and opening up the deck plates and filling our water tanks that we didn't notice exactly when it was that the storm stopped.

Few things are as bad as they seem. This day would be spent eating and sleeping and sailing. Davey even baked bread.

29.

I remember one day taking a three-way fix just after six in the morning. The Moon, Venus, and Jupiter hung in the early morning sky like escaped street lights. I worked up the fix and made a log entry.

> The conditions have moderated after a few days of big seas and everything is beautiful this morning. We're only about 8° above the equator now and well into the westerly current. The Marquesas are only 8° below the equator. We're entering the intertropical convergence zone. There has never been a severe storm recorded in this part of the world according to the pilot charts and all I've read. We're doing excellent as a boat. If anything, it would help for me to relax more, that's where the balance is. No more use for Captain Bligh.

Querencia slowed down to a snail's pace as she continued south, approaching the equator. The sun was traveling north as it does every year in it's migration from the Southern Hemisphere to the Northern Hemisphere. Before we reached land it's declination would be the same as our latitude; directly overhead. As a consequence of this convergence it would be a conservative statement to say it was getting quite a bit warmer onboard. As well as we had provisioned the boat we started wishing we had brought more drinks. I think each of us could have easily downed a six pack of soda a day given a choice to drink refreshments rather than eat solid food. During the day the sun beat down on us and the decks got hot as a firecracker. We took special caution not to get too sunburned or "fry your brains" as we called it. We wore all manner of imaginative hat ware and refereed bungie-wars during our repeated attempts to create "the great sun tarp contraption."

The occasional squall became something we would look forward to, a break in the day, a time to catch water or take a shower, a time to reef or not to reef.

We cherished our meals and our reading and ourselves. We made a reading library out of our forward v-berth, rearranging the sail bags between the two book cases in a way such that they reminded our tushes of a big comfortable sofa. One could be alone up there underneath the skylight, cushioned, gently rocking to and fro with the boat, reading or dreaming about what ever.

Paul made one of his best log entries after coming out of our "library":

> Things I've been dreaming of: dried fruit, liquids, bacon, water chestnuts, crab, tang, crackers, chips, squeeze cheese, pepperoni, beef jerky, potatoes, grapefruit, limes, Shed Spread, steak sauce, green beans, batteries, fishing equipment, fruit, grape jelly, mayonnaise, dry roasted peanuts, almonds, ice cream.

I couldn't believe it, the boy was even dreaming of green beans!

We were still catching fish, but we were running out of fishing tackle. We had broken our favorite reel, lost the tip of our best rod, and broken numerous hand lines. As Paul called them at the time, "mass hugo fish" more than once took our trailing fishing line away. One time the line had been left fouled with the starboard lifeline. It was easy to see upon discovery that the strike that broke the line had almost cut the white lifeline insulation down to the quick as well. Running out of 300 pound test brought our brains together. We decided to weave twine together in a sennit type fashion and make our own. It worked fine.

Who would think that you would run out of flashlight bulbs? Well, a good sailor could and we had, but who would think that a different bulb would fail every other day or so? That one really mystified us, and I was the busy Dr. Science for several days as I feverishly tested the resistance in one switch/bulb/battery after the other with my trusty voltmeter.

This part of the world *is* different somehow. There is a feeling that one gets when on the equator in a small boat, the celestial equator, that zone of intertropical convergence. You can tell you are sailing on the *fat part* of the world. Just as when you carefully examine the water in an undisturbed glass and see its convex surface; so it is on the surface of the globe between the poles. There is a meniscus. You can *see* it.

Not only does the watery horizon bulge, but the whole atmosphere seems to bulge. As a matter of fact, science tells us that even the earth's atmosphere is the widest here. The trade winds, blowing from the northeast in the northern hemisphere and from the southeast in the southern hemisphere, meet at the equator, poop out, and turn up rising upward to the limits of the atmosphere before turning north and south once again as the jet streams. All this air brings moisture and atmospheric particles to converge at this zero latitude. Dense masses of pastel colored cumulus obscured the low angled sun at sunrise and sunset. Light burst forth in bright psychedelic crepuscular rays between the towers of clouds. Being there really was just like being *in* a vivid painting. Even though Davey suffers the disadvantage of being partially color blind, she made the following entry. The log is full of similar entries by each of us, each noting the celestial beauty.

> 0700 Most spectacular sunrise — pinks and reds extending 90° on either side of the sun and reaching over *Querencia* in a tall arc. The sky at one point was a brightly buffed blue scattered with puffs of pink-orange coral clouds. The sun itself, upon rising was a huge clear yellow disk. — DT

Four degrees above the equator we ran out of wind entirely. At 1330 I decided to go for a swim. After unhooking the lifeline gate I stood on the rail staring down into the big blue sea. For a moment I was actually frightened, daydreaming about being in such deep water so far away from everything.

Davey came up from below decks and passed me my mask and snorkel from the cockpit, as I had asked for her help, but I wasn't paying attention to the hand-off. The snorkel fell into the water as a swell pitched us both off balance. Down, down, deeper it went, quickly.

I jumped in but couldn't catch up with the its descent. Once in the water I felt very vulnerable and exposed; a strange feeling for someone as experienced as myself. I had been SCUBA diving since I was fourteen years old, for twenty-two years. I looked up at Paul and Davey standing on the deck of *Querencia* slowly drifting away from me. The boat looked so different from my new perspective; the rolling was accentuated as was the height of the rail. It seemed ten feet above the water's surface instead of four. Along the waterline, and below, the hull was encrusted with goose-necked barnacles. I noticed all sorts of little critters darting here and there, hiding in the shadow of *Querencia*. Then out of the corner of my eye I saw this large object racing towards me. It came faster and faster, too fast to track with the human eye and got bigger and bigger. It only took a couple of seconds to arrive two feet from my face mask where it "screeched" to a halt. There it was. This huge five-foot, bull-headed dorado fish staring at me, face to face. His eyeballs were bigger than mine, and that was saying a lot for the moment. I wasn't sure if he meant to harm me, and I hadn't thought of the possibility before that very second. This beautifully luminous cold blooded creature was scaring the heck out of me. The hair on my neck was standing up as straight as a dorsal fin.

Paul and Davey had been watching this whole scenario from above, had clearly seen the dorado charge me, and were already yelling at me to get out of the water, which I did immediately.

Months later on Bora Bora I would meet a Tahitian fisherman who told me he had once been attacked by a mahi mahi, or dorado, although I know of no written record of such.

I really appreciated *Querencia* for what she was later that evening — the yar ship. Being on the boat is a lot different than being off the boat, I concluded. Davey's love insured a celebration of life when it was time for victuals; steak and kidney pie, corn, applesauce and, for dessert, oatmeal cookies.

I made a different sort of entry into the logbook on that particular evening.

> In the event that the wind remains as it has been the past few days I have calculated that it will take 919 hours, or thirty-eight days to reach Bora Bora. As the Beatles' song says, "We've got a ticket to ride, so we don't care!"

30.

Man must rise above the clouds and look back upon the earth.
Only then will he truly understand the nature of things.
— Socrates

I remember one night during my watch laying on my back in the cockpit staring up at *all of the stars and the Milky Way*. I was listening to synthesizer music on the Walkman headphones. It had been orchestrated by an old friend and myself and recorded with a small tape-recorder while we jammed away on the keyboards of "Prophet" and "Oberheim OBX" synthesizers. All of this going on at the same time in my head was very far-out. Suddenly, there *IT* all was, inside of me and outside of me, the whole universe.

"WOW!" I remember thinking in the middle of a fat portamento slide.

From horizon to horizon it was nothing but twinkling suns millions of light years away, some concentrated in our own spiral galaxy, one of its spiraling arms imprinted in the heavens above as a broad stripe I'd grown up learning to call the Milky Way. Our Milky Way galaxy is but an island of matter in the universe, a giant collection of gas and dust and billions of stars, our sun located approximately halfway out from the center of this galactic disk.

I was sailing across this Earth at this particular moment feeling very much by myself with Paul and Davey sleeping comfortably below. I felt alone and at peace, quietly ghosting along at three knots on our little ship at sea.

I visualized our earth hanging like a ball in space. I was one individual looking out into space from one unique position on that ball. As awesome as the view was, I realized that *I could only see one part of the view of the universe around our planet Earth*, just those stars and planets and galaxies that could be seen from my small observation platform floating somewhere south of the equator at precisely this hour.

Even before man could use a telescope, the vision of the sky at night must have filled him with awe and wonder at the immensity of the universe of which he was an insignificant part. The physical universe is unbelievably larger than what appears to the naked eye. Our Milky Way galaxy contains as many as 100 billion stars, some smaller than our sun and others very much bigger. It takes light 100,000 years just to travel from one side of our galaxy to the other, and light moves pretty fast!

And yet I knew, even from the books aboard in *Querencia's* little library, that our galaxy was only one of billions in the universe; thousands of other galaxies had already been photographed and cataloged.

Our own solar system around our one star, the sun, is insignificant by comparison. The maximum orbital diameter of the planets is seven billion miles. Our very own Earth has a diameter less than 8,000 miles compared with the 865,000 mile diameter of the sun, ninety-three million miles away.

A microbe, crawling over the surface of a school globe would be a formidable object compared to *Querencia*, sailing across the Pacific. What an illusion *Homo sapiens* may have made of his importance and his priorities, I thought. The synthesizer music only compounded my experience. Big tears filled my eyes, flooded, and then rolled down my cheeks.

"*My God, life is amazing!*" I said aloud.

I paused for a moment, took a big breath, and continued thinking and wondering what it was all about.

It takes light four years just to reach our planet from the nearest star which is beyond our sun. Time seemed to be nothing but an infinite succession of changes that seems to extend on both sides of us from the middle of *our* universe into the past and into the future. Despite this endless expanse of time, all that is reliably known to us is a few thousand years behind us with only vague and hazy conceptions of what is ahead in an uncertain future. Time devours everything including some pretty magnificent civilizations on our own earth of which only traces are left.

Today's man, how he "struts and frets his hour on the stage" with authority and glory in the few moments which are allotted to him. If only each modern man could isolate himself for a while as we were doing, away from his engrossing, all important, illusory, civilized environment and notice the mystery. If he could ponder over the truest facts of life. Maybe it would be a better world.

CLICK! The Walkman had stopped abruptly and I sat up and took the headphones off. I realized I had been sobbing.

Off to the south the Clouds of Magellan were visible now, enormous glowing clusters of stars, looking like mist, or clouds (*nebulae* in Latin), hanging in dark sections of the sky. Actually these "clouds" are separate spiral galaxies similar to our own but a very long ways away! It takes the light I was seeing from the Clouds of Magellan traveling nearly six trillion miles in one year, one hundred and eighty thousand years to get here! Undoubtedly they had been named by Magellan on his voyage around the world, charting them as his vessel sailed under the skies of the Southern Hemisphere.

What a profound experience to be alone in the middle of the Pacific Ocean with two friends, a boat, and a god.

31.

We were really creeping along now. We had been used to averaging better than 100 nautical miles a day and now we were lucky to do half of that. There just wasn't any wind to speak of. And it continued to get hotter every day. We accepted things as they were.

> *Querencia* glides along like a toy boat set upon
> the waters. It is mystical, magical, and even
> better, *real.* — DT

There was a good side to all the sun. Using a little transformer I hooked up the cassette player directly to our solar panel. We had guilt-free music all day long, as long as we wanted, without worrying about draining our batteries. Occasionally a cloud would pass over us and the music would stop for a moment, then continue on again as soon as the shadow moved along.

Naturally, noon and early afternoon were the hottest times of the day and we would all huddle for shade and read or take our quiet time.

It could be very silent.

"POW!" It was a very loud explosion.

I thought the propane tank had exploded and I was frozen in shock for at least a second.

"Oh my God, the bumper exploded," exclaimed Paul.

We had two big circular orange and blue bumpers a friend, John Coy, on Vashon Island had given us for our trip. They were too big to stow and we had hung them over the stern rail, one directly over the propane locker. Those big bumpers had come in handy more than once. You could tie along anything.

Davey joined me with weak knees as we inspected the bumper responsible for having nearly given us coronaries. It was now deflated with a hole in its side.

Ultimately the evening came that Davey and I had the last cocktails onboard. Paul joined us with a Diet Coke for which he had searched for ten minutes or so. We all sat in the cockpit and listened to Paul Horn's album *Inside*, which we had on tape. *Inside* had been originally recorded on location in the Taj Mahal in Agra, India in

1968. Listening to it conjures up images of an avatar playing an enchanting flute under a waterfall. The sounds bounce around and off of the circular solid marble walls and fill your head with a lingering ambient atmosphere that reminds one of an audio aurora borealis. Paul Horn describes it best.

> "I was using my alto flute and the low C just flew out and filled the entire room and just hung there. I couldn't believe it. It was the most beautiful thing I ever heard in my life."

We were enthralled with this music accompanying the sunset and said little as we gazed over the ocean prairie. Earlier we had smelled a strong low tide smell. We had started calling this smell "whale breath" since we had learned to associate the scent with whale sightings to windward. Even when the music had finished we just sat there sort of meditating and observing. The tape had clicked to a stop but the music had not. The music seemed somehow to have been caught up in the rigging. As *Querencia's* rig repeatedly tightened up and relaxed between the swells you could hear the sounds of Paul Horn's flute in the boom. The music having escaped from the speakers seemed to have been trapped in time and space along with *Querencia* in this remote environment. It was a lonely, sparkling phenomenon, with as much grace as a bird imitating a song.

Paul told me later that after thinking about it for a long time he had decided that there had been some sort of harmonic convergence between the shrouds and the gooseneck of the boom that was causing it all.

"You know Paul," I answered, "I think you're right."

Undoubtedly there had been a similar explanation for the sirens of Ulysses' odyssey. We would hear these mysterious sirens for days.

We crossed the equator on Tuesday, February 28, 1984, exactly on Paul's sixteenth birthday. It was a splendid celebration. Davey made a two layer chocolate cake complete with candles from special provisions. I contributed a large homemade pepperoni pizza from my secret recipe using cured pepperoni that we had been saving just for that moment.

We had devoured most of everything by the noon hour and were having a lot of fun together. A humorous note was entered by the skipper into the log:

> Floggings will be moved from Tuesday afternoons to Sunday mornings until further notice.— JFBligh

Paul opened up a little bag of presents sent along with him from his schoolmates complete with popcorn and batteries for his Walkman headphones, items that were now at a premium! We all seemed to gain more energy from having our social celebration and we spent the rest of the afternoon attacking chores. We serviced the engine, refastened the oven door, removed rust from the hardware, lubricated the blocks, polished the binnacle and changed our bedding. While we were airing our bedding we made elaborate tents over the cockpit for fun. We spent a half an hour pouring countless buckets of sea water down the galley sink in an attempt to determine whether or not water did actually drain *counterclockwise* in the Southern Hemisphere. It was a time of domestic frivolity.

Happy Sixteenth on the equator!

32.

The greatest prayer is patience.
— Anonymous

It seemed the best that we could do was sixty or seventy miles a day even after crossing the equator. At least there was *some* wind. We tried to remember the old saying: "A sailor doesn't mind as long as he's on his way."

But it was going to be a long crossing. No doubt about that. It was time to count what was left. We had run completely out of spirits. At least we still had a soda or fruit drink to look forward to at the end of the day.

Paul jumped at the job of counting all our beverages on board and mapping out our rations. He was soon scouring all the cupboards and underneath the floorboards taking inventory and making notes. After a couple of hours he surfaced on deck with his report.

"Well, I've got it all figured out," he said with a smirk on his face. "Presuming that the passage should stretch to another 3 weeks in length we could have the following ration:

Monday:	1 Coke
Tuesday:	1 orange juice, 1 beer
Wednesday:	1 Coke, 1 tomato juice
Thursday:	1 seltzer water, 1 beer
Friday:	1 Coke, 1 grapefruit juice
Saturday:	1 seltzer water, 1 beer
Sunday:	1 Coke, 1 orange juice."

He thumped his pencil on his notations as Davey and I pondered his observations.

"Well that doesn't seem too bad, not too bad at all," I remarked. "Can I switch my coke on Monday for a beer I'm supposed to have later in the week?" I asked.

"No. No. These aren't the rations for one person, they're the rations for *all of us*. In other words, on Monday we would split one Coke three ways." His head was bent down now and his eyes were looking up at me from below his eyebrows as if to peek at my reaction from a distance.

It wasn't really humorous, but I started chuckling as did Davey and finally Paul.

It wasn't really a disaster either, of course. Our water supply was in good shape. There had been plenty of rain to catch. The only concern with our freshwater was the amount of green algae that built up over a period of days. Davey, however, kept our water clear and healthy by adding one teaspoon of Chlorox for each five gallons of water. She also made the best sun tea for us each afternoon by setting a carafe of water with a couple of tea bags in it in the ever-present sun.

The mahi mahi fish that were still swimming along with us underneath the boat, however, drove us nuts as we tried to think of one way after another to catch them. Unfortunately I had the idea of using my spear gun to land one. Not only did I miss my mark, but the lanyard to the spear came off and I lost it forever to Davey Jones' locker. I felt like a fool, but I was also determined to make up for it and spent a whole morning making a flying fish lure complete with movable wings fashioned from a plastic bag. But the mahi were too smart. I could almost hear them chuckling as I lowered the lure below the surface.

There was a school of Oceanic Puffer fish, *[Lagocephalus lagocephalus]*, that were also following *Querencia*. We turned our attention to catching some of them. These unusual torpedo-shaped fish can carry a nerve toxin that is not destroyed by cooking and we knew it. But rather than eat them we decided we could use them as bait for the mahi mahi.

Catching a puffer fish was fairly easy. We just hid behind the coaming with the dip net until one swam up close enough in the wake. Then we would quickly net it and cut it into bait. The mahi mahi fish couldn't resist the tasty morsels we threw out on our small hooks, but still they continually broke our lines and tackle. We had better luck with tuna.

On March fifth the moon was coming back and we were very appreciative. In all of the past five days we had gone 5° south and 3.5° degrees west. Bora Bora at a distance of 1,166 nautical miles was still twelve to fifteen days away, and we would have to extend the possibility of it being twenty days away in case we ran into any bad luck.

Nuka Hiva, the principal island of the Marquesas, by contrast was only 285 nautical miles away. Only a slight course correction would put us there in less than a week even in light air. A decision was made.

> 0005 Decided to stop at Nuka Hiva for sure. We need to provision before continuing the passage to Bora Bora — it would be foolish to go right by Nuka Hiva and not stop. Everyone relieved by the decision. We celebrated by eating and drinking most of the day. Cereal and box milk for breakfast. In the afternoon we consumed a coke, cheese, breadsticks, vienna sausages, beef jerky, and sunflower seeds. With the pressure off rationing we could be little pigs for a day and we enjoyed every minute of it. We are planning a dinner of canned salmon and mayonnaise, complete with boiled potatoes, mixed vegetables, and the beverage of your choice. (We'll even use the whole jar of mayonnaise! It can't be kept once it's opened.) — DT

It was a good decision and we were rewarded the very next day with enough wind to accomplish a distance of 110 nautical miles towards Nuka Hiva. The sailing was glorious and we prepared for our landfall by getting everything ship shape including our crew lists which Paul offered to write in French for us. Large new fish appeared. During the day a huge brown shark swam behind us at a distance of about thirty yards. It was easy to see he had an interest in us, but he never came any closer. A striped marlin, which we estimated to be about ten feet in length, came within a few yards of *Querencia's* stern one evening at twilight.

Although it seemed we were constantly fatigued, our spirits stayed high. While Paul slept one afternoon I painted his toenails on his right foot with bright red nail polish we'd found on board. I'll never forget the look on his face when he discovered the prank, hours later while sitting on deck staring at his feet hanging in the cockpit well, as he tried to wake up.

33.

"John! John!" Davey was yelling.

I suddenly realized that I wasn't dreaming; Davey needed help.

I tried to focus my intentions so that the sleep and fog would pass from my mind as quickly as possible. I crawled out of the port bunk as quickly as possible and in the darkness I bumped smack into Paul who was scrambling out of the opposite bunk at the same time.

Querencia was well heeled over with her port rail buried under water. We were *really* racing along. The whistle of the wind in the rigging and water splashing along the hull accompanied my banging around as I managed to pull myself out the companionway and into the cockpit. Oh, how I wished we'd reefed as usual at sunset instead of leaving all our sail up!

Once into the cockpit I saw that Paul had already joined Davey at the steering pedestal. The boat was charging along, the stern yawing wildly side to side as she made her way through large waves in the blackness of night. Everything seemed to be noisily crashing around us. Large warm waves thrashed the boat and threw buckets of salt water into our faces. It had been necessary for Davey to disengage Nellie and she was steering by hand. The wind had changed directions coming all the way around the compass and now blowing freshly from the Northwest.

"What do you want to do? Do you want the wheel?" Davey quizzed.

Paul's big eyes joined his mom's as they stared at me briefly. I joined them in waiting for some sort of ancient mariner's wisdom to fall from my mouth.

Another wave sloshed the cockpit just as I eased the main sheet, luffing the main sail. It flapped noisily like some giant flag, but we were safe.

"Go find me my shorts and my tennis shoes, please somebody." I pleaded. I was naked as a jay bird, cold, and a little frightened, and at the very least my toes needed protection. Besides, we didn't need to rush.

I glanced at my watch. It was a little after two in the morning. I could see thunderstorms in the East and this northwest wind was building into stronger and stronger gusts. My brain was still very foggy and I continued to try and concentrate enough to bring myself back to an acceptable state of alertness.

Davey and Paul straightened up the deck lines and organized our life harnesses. Paul threw my shorts and tennis shoes up from below and flipped on the spreader lights at the navigation station. Then we all stood around the pedestal and discussed our plan for shortening sail. With the overhead "spot lights" from the spreaders it reminded me of a play, *Querencia* being a small stage where three very different characters were giving short soliloquies while being tossed about in an ocean of darkness.

But we came up with an unpanicked plan. I temporarily rounded *Querencia* up into the wind between swells while Davey and Paul went forward and lowered the jib.

> 0514 At about 2 AM we had a weather change. Unexpected blow put all hands on deck. Paul and Davey dropped jib while I pointed her up. Waves crashing over foredeck. Then reset main and boom to a more stable and safe position and, after raising the staysail, Davey took the wheel and rounded *Querencia* up while Paul and I dropped the main. Secured all, including both running backs. Still riding it out now, three hours later. Weird weather. Can see how cyclones get started. —JFM

But by sunrise the wind wasn't as strong or as gusty. Come nine in the morning we had all the sail up again headed towards a massive clump of rumbling clouds over the horizon. It seemed hazy and there was a large halo around the sun above the altostratus. I knew that those massive clouds over the horizon were in the direction of the Marquesas and I also knew that today, if all our calculations and numerical predictions were correct, there was a good chance we might see land before sunset.

We spent the day continuing to clean the boat; swabbing the decks, lubricating all the snaps and tracks, and doing some bright work. Davey also had to sew a batten tab back into the main sail from the night before. All our fixes seemed to indicate the same thing — the Marquesas were dead ahead!

On March 9 at 1756 hours I shouted, "Land Ho!" By sunset we had determined that what we were seeing directly ahead of us was the small island of Ua Huka. Not long after, west of it, on the horizon, the island of Nuka Hiva, six miles wide, fourteen miles long and three quarters of a mile high, was becoming visible through the haze as a large dim mass.

Part VI
South Pacific

34.

"For all that has been, thanks; for all that will be, Yes!"
— Doug Hammarskjold

The full moon, our second since leaving San Diego, was still a week away. It was a dark night. As we sailed in for our landing, we left the Sat Nav on full time in hopes of an extra fix to confirm our position. We reminded each other aloud that now on our approach we had to be especially careful. Yachts are like airplanes; they are most apt to have a problem when they are making for land. How often we hear the story of the sailor who sails his boat across a huge ocean, overcoming all kinds of dangers and challenges, only to lose the victory by running aground on some lonely reef awash between him and his goal.

But according to my calculations landfall would still be after sunrise, and as long as we were cautious we would do well to continue our approach. The channel between the island of Nuka Hiva and the island Ua Huka, twenty miles away, was twenty-four miles wide. That gave us a fairly big target to shoot for. We hardened down and focused meticulously on every last detail of navigation. We wrote lists of our data and checked it twice. Two of us stayed on watch at all times for the remainder of the night.

We had plenty of wind and even though we were reefed, *Querencia* charged along like a horse smelling the barn. We were smelling sweet land! Rich smells of plants and dirt came across the water. Smelling the flowers was like having a glass of fine wine.

Each hour the outline of the steep mountain island of Ua Huka forward of our port beam loomed bigger and bigger; *Querencia* charged forward all night long with the bone in her teeth. It was *very* exciting.

Cape Tikapo, Nuka Hiva

Eventually the sun rose on our port side behind Ua Huka and there before us on our starboard side stood the spectacular outline of Nuka Hiva, a volcanically formed island with steep, black cliffs and a huge green plateau forming the center of the island high above. The striking green colors of the dense foliage against the lonely black rocks, the smell of the good earth, and the beauty of numerous waterfalls literally took our breath away. Paul was so excited he started jumping up and down in the cockpit. His face was a grin ear to ear and it was flushed from stimulation.

As we passed Cape Tikapo on the southeast tip of the island the descriptive word that stuck in my mind was *prehistoric*. One expected to see a pterodactyl flying in big circles off the cliffs at any moment.

Instead several snow-white tropical birds with elongated tail streamers came out to see us. They were diving head first all about us. A small white cabin cruiser with a red smoke stack suddenly could be seen in the distance putting along out in the middle of the channel riding up and down with the swells. It was the first boat we had seen since we left the coastal waters of the American continent.

In no time at all we stood off Taiohae Bay, identified among other things by a large white crystalline cross embedded in the rock cliff to the east of the entrance. Here our sailing directions informed us we could make formal entry and tend to the local government's administrative details. We didn't look forward to making entry into French Polynesia at the Marquesas. We had heard and read rumors that the local gendarmes would be less than welcoming. The notion that they were going to say "Sorry, you'll have to leave immediately…" didn't seem like a strong possibility — but the thought *did* cross our minds.

At the entrance to Taiohae Bay two large bare black rocky islets stood like sentinels on each side of the channel looking to the South Pacific. We raised our yellow "Q" flag as is required when entering a foreign port and made our way into the bay. Taiohae Bay is large, a mile and a half deep and a mile wide with three lush valleys coming down from the plateau and meeting it at the innermost shoreline. The growth covering all sides of the bay was of the greenest green, like the kind of green you would remember from a dream. It was a beautiful sight, especially after being at sea for six weeks.

Eventually we dropped our sails and putted over to where eight yachts were swinging in anchorage between the middle and northwest end of the bay. It was a little disappointing to not find anybody up and about and to further discover that we were the only American vessel, but no matter. We turned *Querencia* in a long slow circle and anchored off to the east of the cluster of boats nearer to a group of buildings on the east shore where there was a concrete quay. I presumed that somewhere there amongst the buildings I would find the local gendarmes or they would find me. A group of about twelve children were jumping in and out of the water at the quay. You could hear their ceaseless giggling. Even from a distance you could see that they were extraordinarily pretty children, very Polynesian and very happy. Other people could be seen along shore and there was a small village along the east part of the bay.

It was noon and almost forty days exactly since we had left the Harbor Police dock in San Diego, California. I turned off the ignition and we all congratulated and hugged each other. We had made it without a hitch to the South Pacific!

How strange it was to all of a sudden *not* be going some place, leashed off our hook, bobbing in the gentle swells with only thirty feet of water beneath us. We still had chores to do. The first order of business was to put up our awning to protect us from the blazing sun. The second order of business was to hurry up and untie the two-man raft lashed on deck and inflate it so I could row ashore and gain clearance for entry. Not only did we wish permission for all of us to be legal visitors of this enchanting land, but we were more than a little anxious to find something to celebrate with like fresh food and cool drinks!

Davey emerged from the v-berth with three plastic bags. In them were neatly pressed clothes that we had saved packed especially for the occasion — white slacks, a collared shirt, a brand new pair of Topsiders and clean white socks.

Davey looked inquisitively at me as I stared through the zip-lock bags at my fresh "Sunday" garments.

"John, are you sure playing dress-up is necessary?" she asked.

"Yes, Davey! I'm not just playing dress-up for God's sake!" I sort of snapped back. "It's important to make a good impression with the local French gendarmes. After all, I'm supposed to be an American yachtsman."

After shaving I quickly dressed as Paul made the final strokes with the air pump filling the inflatable. No sooner had the raft been lowered into the water than I jumped aboard it taking the handheld VHF radio and paper work with me in one of the zip-lock plastic bags. They wished me luck, waving to me as I pulled hard on the oars moving myself away from *Querencia* slowly toward the quay about fifty yards away.

Half way there I realized I had a problem. A seam was quickly opening up on the raft. It was accompanied by the unmistakable hiss of escaping air. As the air rushed out of the inflatable I was struck with the knowledge that I could neither make it back to the boat nor to the quay. The better part of the raft was about to sink at least to the level of the water's surface. My best bet was to go directly towards the shore.

Unfortunately I did not make it to shore without having to "give up the ship" in about four feet of water. Equally unfortunate for me, both legs sunk up to the knees in mud as I struggled to reach higher and firmer ground. Repeatedly my leather Topsiders got sucked off my feet and I had to reach down with one hand to retrieve them from their muddy vestige. While one hand was busy digging in the murk the other was busy holding the VHF and *Querencia's* documents high above the mess I had gotten myself into. I managed to keep my nose just above the water's surface.

I found absolutely no humor in my predicament and once on firm ground I was madder than a wet hen, until I looked back toward *Querencia*. There I could see Paul and Davey taking turns peering at me with the ship's binoculars and laughing their heads off. I looked down at myself muddy and wet from head to toe. There was nothing to do but join them. If you can laugh at a problem you can live with it.

I dragged the deflated raft up on shore and promptly took off my shirt, socks, and shoes, and threw them all into the boat. It was now as flat as a pancake; it had gasped it last breath. I rolled up my trousers to my knees and rinsed off as much of the mud as I could. With a big grin on my face I looked up at the first stranger I had seen in a long time. A Polynesian woman stood along the road half-smiling at me.

"Bonjour!" I hailed.

"*I ora na!*" she said back in Polynesian.

It was my first opportunity to exercise my command of the French language. I'm not so sure practicing had helped much.

"Moi et mon famille arriver Marquises a la petite bateau quarante jours depuis California," I blurted out.

She turned and started to walk away rather abruptly.

"Pardon! Pardon!" I pleaded her further attention.

She stopped and once again turned to face "the creature from the dark lagoon."

I gestured and smiled and repeated "Où est la gendarme?"

The shy Polynesian lady finally pointed up a winding narrow road that cut its way up a hill beyond the buildings on the east side of the bay. Once released from my verbal grasp she disappeared like a bird released from a cage.

35.

As I walked up the hill in my "Sailor Jack" outfit I was struck by the charm of the little cottages on each side of the road. Carefully tended, each yard although very small was fenced. There were grapefruit (later I would discover the more familiar French word for this fruit; "pamplemousse," is the functional word of choice) and papaya trees and wonderfully fragrant flowers. I don't think I ever had appreciated land more for what it was than at that particular moment.

I was also struck with the absence of people. There were almost none, except for the children on the quay at the bottom of the hill, and the one woman that I had seen. Several blocks up the hill I came to a stone building with a red tiled roof and a government sign. It appeared to be the correct building although it too was deserted. Peering through the open blinds of the window I saw an old wooden desk decorated with an art nouveau cast iron typewriter and a temporarily abandoned revolving fan. I felt like I was sneaking a peek backward in time. It was more than that. Like a *déja vue*, everything in Nuka Hiva seemed just as author Hal Roth had described it in his book *Two on a Big Ocean* ten years earlier.

"This place has to be timeless," I murmured to myself as I backed up.

A light tap brushed my shoulder and I jumped about two feet off the ground turning around halfway expecting to find Paul Gaugin having risen from the dead, but it was just the blossoming branch of a Plumeria tree poking me in the back.

Wandering back into town I found one or two structures that

appeared to have commercial activity; I saw cash registers and Sprite soft drink posters hung in the windows. But, they too were closed.

"Of course!" I said to myself after I finally realized what was going on. "It's the middle of the day and everything is closed."

Such is the custom in many countries with tropical southern climates. After further exploration and more gesturing I surmised that everything would re-open at two o'clock in the afternoon, less than an hour away. I chatted with Paul and Davey on the VHF. As patient as they were, they were still understandably anxious to come ashore.

At two o'clock I was back at the gendarme's building where I found a young French man in flip-flops, red shorts, and a Cousteau Society T-shirt pacing back and forth between the antique desk and a counter of paper work.

"Bonjour! Moi et mon famille arriver Marquises a la petite bateau quarante jours depuis California." I blurted out again. Boy, was I glad that I had ruined my dress-up outfit.

"Oh, really!" he exclaimed in good English, looking up at me. "Welcome to Nuka Hiva and how was your trip?"

My French wasn't as good as his English but between the two of us we struck up a pretty good conversation. I made notice of his Cousteau Society T-shirt and told him what an avid fan of the sea I was. He said that he loved the Marquesas although most of the gendarmes didn't care for the assignment because of the isolation. He would be returning to France in the fall.

A co-worker was called in from the back room to meet me. They spoke to each other in French and then they both went over to a large shortwave radio and flipped it on. Listening to the squelches and buzz of the radio as he spun the analog dials, I surmised that they were tuning the radio in to headquarters probably located in Papeete.

The gendarme started going through the paper work — ship's documentation, crew list, insurance papers, birth certificates, passports, and the inevitable "etc." He pulled aside a letter of recommendation from Dr. Dennis Willows, a well recognized marine biologist. I had studied neurophysiology under Dr. Willows at Friday Harbor Laboratories when I was pursuing my degree in zoology at the University of Washington. I had written to Dr. Willows just before leaving Washington and he had sent a letter of recommendation, asking that I be given every privilege to study the flora and fauna of their unique locale. I'd forgotten about the letter being in with the paper work, but it seemed to most impress the head young gendarme who kept sending cryptic messages in French to his co-worker who in turn sent more cryptic messages over the radio to Papeete.

Then all that was needed was our sailing plans and every serial number of every piece of equipment on board over a hundred dollars.

"Every piece?" I asked.

"Oui, oui, monsieur. This will be necessary for every piece of equipment."

The hand held VHF paid for itself in the next few minutes. I was able to call Davey and Paul and they in turn were able to gather the serial numbers and transmit them back to me. Modern science can be wonderful sometimes. The gendarme was impressed with the quality of the miniature VHF himself and we both marveled over it together for a few minutes while the other officer transmitted the last of the serial numbers to Papeete including the one on the hand-held VHF.

Then, after a few minutes pause, the shortwave droned and crackled back more baffling French verbs and nouns.

"C'est bon. Dr. McGrady, entry into French Polynesia has been approved for your yacht and family!" The gendarme smiled at me.

If our total stay in French Polynesia exceeded thirty days each person aboard would require a visa to supplement our passports. It would not be necessary to post money for a bond at this time, but we could expect to post a bond in Bora Bora, our next scheduled stop.

I was thrilled! Still exuberant from making landfall alone I raced down the hillside eager to celebrate with my sailing comrades.

36.

"What is behind us and what is before us are small matters compared to what is within us."
— Anonymous

When I got back to the beach Paul had a "car," so to speak, waiting for me. He had inflated and assembled our other inflatable, the twelve-foot sailing dinghy, and sailed it to the beach to pick up the dead raft and me and take us back to *Querencia*. There I quickly stowed our important papers and together the three of us made our way back to town, now in a bit of a hurry to pick a few items up before the four-thirty closing time.

From what we had read we expected only to find one store named *Maurice's*, but instead of finding Maurice's (we would find it on another day) we found three other different places where you could buy cold beverages and tins of goods. I say *places* because in most instances they resembled houses more than stores — living rooms emptied of furniture and stocked with a few cans of vegetables and one freezer of delights. We managed to buy Sprite, Coke, Dr. Pepper, cheese, French bread, grapefruit, and of course beer, wine, and rum. These simple stores were wonderful. We even found a frozen chicken. As lonely as its carcass looked, we took it. It would be the beginning of the end of our taste for chicken in the South Pacific. I'm sure the poor scrawny feathered creatures down there would give anything to live in Nebraska.

We were no sooner back on *Querencia* when we were surprised by a small blue and white sailboat with a teeny American flag tacking its way up the bay. As it got closer I could see a little sailor somewhat my elder manning the tiller. He sported a full head of hair and a beard, all of it as white as snow. He reminded me of Santa Claus and we wound up calling him that amongst ourselves.

"Hi Yankees! I'm Dick, fifty-six days out of San Diego!" he barked up to us as he stalled off our port beam.

It was a little nineteen-foot sailing sloop. I imagined it was barely big enough to lay down in with all the provisions. Amazing. Fifty-six days. And I thought we had it bad. The name of the tiny fiberglass boat was *Vanity*.

"Named so because of my ego, of course," Dick clarified.

After a short discussion in the ebbing light of the setting sun, Dick asked to tie *Vanity* along side *Querencia* for the night. Just rearranging his gear to bring out all his ground tackle would have been a major ordeal, and it was easy to empathize with his obvious weariness.

"Sure!" I responded firmly as I put a few bumpers over the port side and cleared some cleats. I winked at Davey to assure her that it was an okay idea. Of course Dick was winking at her too by now with his twinkling eyes.

It was a fine idea. The bay was deep and calm and tonight there was no swell coming in. We had a wonderful cocktail hour taking turns spinning yarns. Dick told us his story. An aerospace engineer, he had been unhappily married for the better part of his life. When his two sons graduated from college he said he felt that he was finally free to do something for himself. He was a man that enjoyed being alone and enjoyed the self-sufficiency that cruising demands in a person. It was obvious right off that he had a good-enough sense of humor to live with himself; he rarely finished a sentence without punctuating it with a chuckle.

"But I don't know about these past fifty-six days. I think I was getting sort of crazy once in a while. Actually, I was loonier than a loon," he said.

"I bet! How did you keep it together, any ways, alone out there?" I asked.

"With plastic explosives. Somehow I wound up bringing some with me, left over from blowing up stumps from some property my son has been busy clearing back in northern California. I would make these little time bombs in Tupperware and then set them adrift in the wake. BOOM! Now *that* kept my interest up," Dick chortled, his eyes glimmering like birthday candles as they reflected the light from the kerosene lanterns.

As he finished his description he passed a little Tupperware contraption complete with springs and mousetrap and…

"Yikes!" I hollered. "What's going on here?"

"Oh don't worry, I ran out of explosives about two weeks ago. That's just to show you how I built 'em. Good God, I'm glad to be here. Sometimes out there, alone in those storms, I would just lie below feeling like I was already in my coffin," the funny little engineer said to us.

Dick on Vanity

Paul's eyes were the biggest I'd seen in a long while. So were Davey's. But we decided to let our fascination with Dick run unharnessed, it was the first social entertainment with another American (with anyone, actually) we'd had in a very long time.

We drank and talked until we were silly and then Davey served us a big meal of chicken and potatoes with cabbage. After dinner we all sat quietly in the yellow flickering light of our paraffin torches, too pensive to say much. In the distance you could hear the swells rumbling at the mouth of the bay. It was easy to feel that each of us was thinking how far we had come, how far from home we were, and how remote in time the Marquesas seemed.

Dick left after a bit deciding to take a row ashore in his dinghy for an evening stroll on *terra firma*. Davey and Paul made for a bunk. I looked up from my reclined position in the cockpit. Overhead the jeweled stars were still there as usual, but tonight they were swirling around. Around and around and around they went. The chicken and cheap wine (sold in plastic jugs) we'd purchased along with the strong smell of flowers now riding the breeze from shore all seemed too rich for me at the moment. I made my way to the foredeck and buried myself in the sail bags. Davey thoughtfully tossed me a blanket out the forward hatch in case I got a chill. The last thought I had was that *we had made it across*, and for the next few minutes nothing else mattered.

Zonk! I was out cold until daylight!

37.

*"Of course there is a great deal in the South Seas which appeals
to people tired of civilization. The climate is of mid-summer
warmth all the year round, and frozen travellers from northern
latitudes cannot help find it wonderful. The islands are as pretty
as a Hollywood film in Technicolor and the impression they make
is strengthened by the prevailing quiet and peace. The hope of a
comfortable lazy life with ripe bananas just round the corner and
lagoon fish jumping up into the outrigger canoe almost of their
own accord is also a factor in this free and merry life."*
— Bengt Danelsson, *Love in the South Seas*

Querencia did not bring the *first* visitors in search of paradise lost
and hoping to find it in the South Seas.

With the enthusiasm of anthropologists we had read the
accounts of explorers and sea captains, missionaries and merchants
who visited Polynesia at the end of the eighteenth and the beginning
of the nineteenth century before any great changes had been made
and information collected.

Tracing the ancestors of the Polynesian is like searching for hundreds of pieces of a puzzle scattered about over several continents.
Opinions vary from Margaret Mead's description of certain
Melanesian tribes migrating from west to east to Thor Heyerdahl's
first proven testimony with the *Kon Tiki* raft — that the Polynesian
most certainly could be a descendent of a certain Indian of the
Americas, possibly an pre-Incan Tucume, who arrived after traveling
east to west about the time of Christ or before.

The first Polynesian may have been man who before settling on
the American continent travelled out of Mesopotamia, the cradle of
civilization, and rode the consistent global winds that blow as a result
of the rotation of our planet. This was a man who belonged to an
ancient race of sailors and revered the sun. He followed the sun and
the world to the west. With the sea below him and the stars as his
guide, he more often than not had the weather at his back, at least in
the beginning of his migration.

The Tiki has been found all across the Pacific and was part of the

Polynesian culture. The multiple presence of Tikis from South America to New Zealand to Hawai'i — even with the Indians of the Northwest (totem poles) — helps support the theory that the Polynesian was an ocean voyager who followed the currents and trade winds that still exist in the Pacific today.

We know that these ocean voyagers were strong, muscular and athletic, and early sailors reported that when they were standing by Polynesian natives they were large, their well-developed muscles, erect carriage, and graceful walk giving them a very striking appearance.

Early accounts of the Polynesian people reported not only these remarkable physical features, but also that they had giving, gentle, and sensible dispositions. The Polynesians were very attractive and they were very engaging. The eyes of the true Polynesian are round and full of expression. The motions of the females are relaxed and graceful.

Polynesia means "the many islands," and it is a fairly apt name for there are about 350 of them. With the exception of Easter Island (Rapa Nui), which is quite isolated (the Spaniards only visited Easter Island as early as 1770) they form groups of different sizes, often a long way apart. For example, the distance from Hawai'i in the north to New Zealand in the south is 5,000 miles and from Tonga in the west to Easter Island in the east it is nearly 4,500 miles.

Perhaps all the wonder at the Polynesian's origin is best understood if one realizes that just the triangle formed by the Polynesian peoples, Hawai'i to New Zealand to Easter Island, is twice as large as the United States and four times as large as Europe. Yet it was only fully discovered by the "modern world," or modern man about two hundred years ago.

Here are the square mile dimensions of some of the main Polynesian islands:

Hawai'i (Hawai'i group)	4,030
Maui (Hawai'i group)	720
Savai'i (Samoa group)	700
O'ahu (Hawai'i group)	604
Tahiti (Society Islands)	600

Upolu (Samoa group)	430
Kaua'i (Hawai'i group)	555
Tongatabu (Tonga group)	100
Nuka Hiva (Marquesas group)	52
Easter Island (Rapa Nui)	50

Eliminating the area of the lagoons and the areas of the coral ring, or reefs, the land area is only 5% of the total area. More often than not, only half of that is habitable, the rest not permanently above the level of the water, not cultivable, or too fragmented into multiple small islets (called *motus*) to be of use.

What a challenge it was on the part of the Polynesians' ancestors to find all their common people on all these scattered islands out in the middle of the world's greatest ocean. Obviously their social order was more a horizontal organization in which their community 'glue' was very dependent on social communication, rather than the vertical organization which was the machine-like unity of the European white man that "discovered" them. The Polynesians were organized more as a result of being people with common interests than intellectual men in pursuit of a fraternity for government.

"The white man doesn't realize that his burden is the one he puts on his own back. Then he educates everyone and they put it on their backs, too." — Barry Stevens, *Don't Push the River*

You can be sure that to hoard for oneself was regarded as an unworthy vice and still is. On the contrary a Polynesian man gains great prestige if he gives away all that he owns. The Polynesian social economy was based on group solidarity and mutual help.

If the European explorers found the Polynesians were often astonishingly free in sexual matters I don't think it was because of a lack of rules of conduct. Rather, I believe their social, political, and religious culture had evolved far beyond what we understood. After all, these were a people simple in material wealth.

The Polynesians were called a Stone Age people, and this was true inasmuch as they originally had no metal tools. Nevertheless the number of objects and tools which were made of stone were few compared with those which were made of other materials such as bone, wood, turtle shell and mussels.

Without metal cooking utensils or earthenware pots and pans they could not boil or stew their food, but had to content themselves with roasting or baking it in an earth oven, a hole containing hot stones covered over with leaves and earth — an *imu*.

Their historical knowledge was profound, and on many of the islands interest in the past was so great that there were schools to which chiefs' sons were sent for courses which lasted for years. As the Polynesians had no written language it was necessary for them to learn everything by heart and to avoid mistakes. Polynesian historians used to recite all the traditions and genealogies rhythmically almost as if in a trance.

Public disapproval in Polynesia was simply intolerable, and there was as a rule no possibility of moving to another district or island because of the enmity between the different tribes. Good behavior was therefore a primary necessity.

These Marquesan Islands were originally inhabited by a population which Captain Cook himself estimated at 50,000 to 100,000 Polynesians during his voyage there in 1774. It is written that before him, 179 years earlier in 1595, a Spaniard had accidentally 'discovered' the Marquesas on a sailing voyage from Peru through the South Pacific.

The navigation in those days was so shaky that at first the Spaniards thought they had reached the Solomon Islands, an error in longitude of over 4,000 miles. Instead of being greeted by natives who were short and black, the people who came out to the ships were tall, fair, clear-skinned, and had long, loose hair. It is written that the regal women, graceful and nearly white, seemed more lovely than even the beautiful women of Lima, Peru.

The sexual conditions, naturally, were attacked here as elsewhere in Polynesia with particular violence by missionaries who did their work in the South Seas. More often than not, they considered everything Polynesian as brutal, sinful, and disgusting. As in the rest of Polynesia, of course, it was the white man who brought alcohol and disease as well as the missionaries to the Marquesas. By 1936 there were only 1,300 natives left in the Marquesas Islands. Today the total population of the Marquesas Islands is about 5,000.

So Paul, Davey, and I had come at last face to face with the disputed question of whether conditions in Polynesia really were and still are, paradisal. As so often happens, the question is wholly subjective in that the answer depends on one's idea of what a paradise ought to be like. You have to believe in paradise and *believe* you know *exactly* what it is (right or wrong), before you have any hope of knowing if you've found it or ever will find it.

Being the types to resist easy explanations or conclusions if we can find the answer through our own experience, upon arrival we immediately wanted to set out and discover for ourselves the truth about Polynesia. The next morning we would be sure to make it to town before the eleven o'clock shutdown. And we promised ourselves that we would check out the night life as well.

38.

When I arose the next morning after our arrival, Dick and his little boat *Vanity* had untied from *Querencia* and already anchored close-in. For us, one of the first orders of business the next day was to trudge up to the post office. It was very bare and informal looking. It reminded me of an abandoned train station in a small town nobody had ever heard of. If there hadn't been such a hub of activity from the other locals I might have guessed we were at the wrong location, since it was tardy in opening.

When it finally opened, a well-dressed Caucasian French madam smelling strongly of perfume emerged from the crowd. She spoke broken English well enough to inform us that yes, we could mail our parcels from here and, if we were lucky, place a call to the United States using the odd looking (and only) telephone hanging on the wall.

Suddenly she turned to the door and called, "Frank! Frank!"

At the door of the post office stood a tall unshaven fellow in a wrinkled white cotton shirt. About forty-five-years-old, he was tall and dark and smoking a cigar. He came over to the lady and after exchanging a few words with her they openly displayed their affection for each other with big, juicy kisses. She was speaking to him in English with a French accent and he was speaking to her in French like Humphrey Bogart in *Casablanca*. He had to be American!

And he was! A crusty, yet suave, expatriate, he soon was explaining to us in plain English how Nuka Hiva worked, which stores were where, what provisions were available and when, etcetera. Speaking French, he was able to arrange our phone call to the States with the clerk in the office. We gave the number to dial and were told to wait by the phone in the lobby. In a few minutes the phone rang and we picked up the heavy receiver to hear Davey's Dad, Bob, speaking to us from Utah. The connection wasn't the greatest, and, like radio transmitting, you had to say "over" after you were through talking a piece so the person on the other end could know when to start replying, but it was wonderful and exciting. Bob assured us he would contact our other loved ones and let them know we were alive and well in Nuka Hiva.

We posted a few envelopes and then made our way down the hill back to town. It was almost eleven so we had to hustle if we were going to buy a few items before the stores shut down. But we made it to *Maurice's* via Frank's directions and here we found the best canned goods in town. We also stocked up on a few loaves of warm baguettes before they disappeared along with the morning. Together with the cheese and tomatoes we had picked up they would make for a fine lunch. I looked forward to my first *Hinano* beer in accompaniment.

Back on *Querencia* we relaxed under our sun tarp in the cockpit after eating a most relaxing meal. We were surrounded by spectacular scenery and I couldn't possibly think of a better thing to do every day in a place like Nuka Hiva then take a two-hour lunch. We all laid around like bean bags, napping, and occasionally murmuring to each other about little wonders or nothings that came into our heads.

Sometime after two in the afternoon I jumped in the warm water with a diving mask on and worked for more than a couple of hours removing all the goose-necked barnacles and other crud that had grown on the hull the past six weeks and 4,000 miles. Some of the barnacles that had attached early in the trip were quite large now, approaching the two-inch size, and it was an amazing thing to witness. Davey meanwhile was doing some major housecleaning and wash on board. She was happy to use the old-fashioned washboard we'd carefully stowed. Paul brought seemingly limitless buckets of fresh water from shore for her in between helping me clean the bottom.

Paul ferries water across the anchorage

That evening as the sun was about to set we enjoyed fresh showers. Each of us put on some fresh clothes and sat in the cockpit relaxed and elated. The exercise here in the safety of port had been relaxing.

A few afternoon showers high up on the plateau had created waterfalls where the ragged green mountains ran into the steel-blue-pink clouds. It was a joyous thing just to sit there and look at them. Paul counted thirty-five waterfalls in all.

Paul was into "driving" which I guess is normal for most sixteen-year-olds. He offered to row us all to shore in the dinghy for a night on the town. He suggested we find the "Matai." That's what Frank had called it.

39.

Matai means "ocean" in the Polynesian language and was the name of a restaurant. Actually it was more a bar with tables, couches, and a grill. It was wonderfully warm and weird. I will always remember it as *The Matai Pub and Star Wars Bar*.

After successfully beaching the dingy and walking up the dark road between the jungle and the sea we found the small house that had to be the Matai. We were more than a little glad, once inside, when a yachtsman who looked exactly like an unshaven and perspiring George Hamilton interrupted a long drag from his cigarette to motion us to please come and sit down at the open couch and coffee table.

As we sat down I looked at George and recognized him to be the skipper of the large steel hulled ketch from France anchored between *Querencia's* port bow and the shore break. He had a cool drink in his hand and a calm, neutral smile. He seemed to understand English but he did not wish to speak it.

The proprietor presented himself. His looks startled the three of us so much that we were at first at a loss for words. His features belonged to a French revolutionary just back from storming the Bastille. He had a balding top, grey scraggly hair sticking out on each side of his temples, and a large hook nose, purple in hue. The corners of his mouth seemed to hang down. He wore flip-flops, a pareau wrap around his waist, and a white collared shirt.

It was my second opportunity to exercise my command of the French language. Practicing had not helped much.

"Moi et mon famille arriver Marquises a la petite bateau quarante jours depuis California. Je tres fatigue et beacoup faim.

Cheeseburgers s'il vouz plait. Merci," I blurted out.

Pierre, I learned later that was his name, stared at me incredulously. Surely I was as much an alien to him as he was to me. Then he spoke faster and faster and his hands went up and down and he shook his head.

"Impossiblé," he finished disappointingly.

George started speaking to him in French and they went back and forth for a few exchanges using the word "cheezaburger" [sic] a lot.

Pierre suddenly paused as if he understood something new and then turned to us and said, "Ah...bon... çava."

He then made a hasty return to his station behind the bar, and yelled something in French to the kitchen, where there was a whole lot of clanking of pots and pans going on. George explained to us in broken English that we would get our cheeseburgers. He also explained to us that Pierre had been upset because he had a big reserved dinner party arriving soon. Pierre had thought that we wanted a formal meal.

"Merci," I said emphatically and we leaned back into the couch, accepting our large ice-cold drinks that had just arrived. We were fascinated with all the people. It seemed we had been with just each other for so long. More and more people, either French or Polynesian, were arriving all the time. A couple of other young French gentlemen arrived and seated themselves next to us and started speaking with George. Soon the little place was packed. Then the world's best hamburgers arrived, complete with French fries, or "frites" as the locals called them. We were having a blast and the food was excellent. It was the first time I had taken Davey to dinner in six weeks!

Suddenly people's screams were heard over the music. People were jumping up on their chairs and even onto the tables.

"What is happening?" I anxiously asked. One of the French men, whose name was Jacques, told me in perfect English that I'd better join everybody else as quickly as possible and get my feet off the floor because a centipede was loose and about. In seconds we were all standing on our seats while Pierre yelled well-ordered instructions into the kitchen.

An enormous Polynesian woman, her hair in a bun, a pareau around her waist, and a Sears brazier for a top came flying out the kitchen door holding a broom high above her head.

There was the centipede, unbelievably big, a foot long, scratching and clawing its fossil-like plated body across the floor towards us like an electric train that had jumped the track.

"Whap. Whap. Whap. Whap. Whap. Whap. Whap!"

The large Polynesian woman, who turned out to be Pierre's wife, then scooped the creature up and took it outside. It most assuredly wasn't the first time that Pierre had called on her expertise.

"My God, that *was* big," I said to Jacques.

Jacques was Canadian and a medical doctor. Like myself he had a degree in zoology as well. Although he now lived in Quebec he had done his residency in Massachusetts. He loved the Marquesas. It was his second trip by plane. He said he liked the Marquesas because they were so primitive and isolated.

"I can assure you my friend," he said, "that was no garden variety centipede. If you get bit by a centipede that size in the Marquesas you will soon discover that you have had very unfortunate luck. You will be sick for over a week. There is no place in the world quite like the Marquesas with its insects."

After lots of talk I insisted on buying a round of drinks and went up to the bar counter which had been behind me. There were so many strange looking characters at the bar that I was totally engrossed for a few seconds. There was even one salty looking old devil with a black patch over one eye. Much to my surprise, when I finally did look for Pierre, he was no longer behind the bar. He was gone. A collegiate-looking fellow with slicked down black hair, ivy league shirt, and horned rimmed glasses had replaced him. In a very thick British accent he introduced himself as Harold, Pierre's nephew.

"I come here every year, you know," he told me. "With the exception of New York City, I simply can't think of a more exciting vacation."

I told him our story and he told me more of his. He had big ruby lips that curled up sort of funny-like when he spoke and his coke bottle lenses made his pupils so large it was hard to look at him for fear of falling in, but I liked Harold instantly.

"My uncle can be quite queer, but so is life, I think. Don't you?" he asked my opinion.

I invited Harold to join our table next time he had a break and took a tray of drinks back to Davey, Paul, Jacques, George, and the other fellows.

Jacques, Paul and Davey were busy entertaining each other with long stories. They were still on the subject of the wild kingdom and Jacques was speaking.

"The no-no bugs here will eat you alive if you are not careful. Tourists are hospitalized all the time for them. They don't realize that they are being eaten up and then suddenly 300 bites appear. Once they appear, scratching can not be resisted. The surface of the skin then breaks and next thing they know is that they have a terrible staph infection."

"Oui, oui!" chorused George.

"How is the diving?" I asked.

"The diving is beautiful, but you must be careful of all fish, not just the well known poisonous scorpionfish, lionfish, and stonefish. Are you planning on spear fishing?" he asked.

"Yes, we were thinking of snorkeling tomorrow at the mouth of Bay de Taiohae and seeing if we have any luck spear fishing."

"Do not eat any fish you spear!" Jacques and his friends exclaimed. "You will get ciguatera food poisoning here for sure. The Marquesas are really infected with it."

"Mal," chorused George.

So that was why we hadn't seen any fish for sale.

It wasn't the first time that we had heard of this type of fish poisoning that causes severe gastrointestinal and neurological symptoms. We had read about it in cruising guides more than once. Coral reefs become contaminated and the toxin is passed up the food chain as far as it can go. We were disappointed to hear that it was such a prevalent problem here at Nuka Hiva.

"Even the tuna will carry the toxin unless they are caught well off shore."

Jacques leaned forward to emphasize his point. He wanted to be certain that we understood the severity of the problem.

"Let's just try cruising the scene and bag sticking anything," Paul suggested as an alternative. His youthful American slang stopped the show.

"Qu'est-ce que c'est *'cruising the scene'* et *'bag sticking'*?" Jacques and George kept saying back and forth to each other.

"Well, Paul means we will just go swimming and forget about spear fishing," I clarified.

"Don't leave your spear behind. You might need it to protect yourself from a shark." I could tell that Jacques wasn't kidding.

Harold arrived from the bar with a round on the house and confirmed that the advice we had been given should be heeded. We would keep an eye out for sharks.

George tossed up the word "barracuda," but it was too late. By then the conversation had turned to medicine and dentistry and education and Polynesia and sailing and life.

Hours slipped by and I think it was well after midnight when the three of us made our way out the doors of the Matai. We fired up our trusty flashlights and made our way down the road toward the bay under the heavens. The stars lying beyond the shadow of the palm were nestled in the sky, a big black blanket embedded with those jewels. Each star shimmered hope and happiness.

Once in the raft Paul retold the story of the needlefish.

"Wait a minute," I interrupted, "what needlefish?"

Needlefish are silvery blue elongated fish whose maxilla and mandible (upper and lower jaws) are elongated to a spine. They swim in schools and leap and skitter about madly near the surface. We had begun seeing them once *Querencia* moved south of San Francisco.

"George said to keep our flashlights off because they are attracted to the light and will jump towards it. The needlefish down here are over three feet long. Two years ago a yachtsman was rowing back to his boat with a flashlight and one jumped across the gunnels and stabbed him in the heart."

"You're kidding!" I said to Paul. "George said that? I didn't even think he spoke English."

"Well, he can speak English and that is what he said," Davey testified.

We turned off our flashlights and Paul, happy to jump in the oarsman's seat, pulled us steadily back to *Querencia*, anchored serenely in the bay. Nobody said anything, but in the silence you could hear the needlefish ripping along the surface of the water and in the waning moonlight you could even see them.

40.

The next day Davey and I made our way to town early, going on a tip, while Paul enjoyed a leisurely morning by himself sailing the bay in the dinghy. We had been told that once a cow was slaughtered and brought down to the village where the butcher purchased the beef, then from his store he would prepare and sell various cuts for the villagers. Somehow we got across our request for steaks, "bifteck," and ground round. It wasn't the best beef in the world being grass fed, but we weren't too picky having arrived at that point of mind where "a steak is a steak is a steak." And the ground round enabled us to have our first homemade hamburger in paradise. We also bought lots of potatoes, which we would eventually decide were the worst in the world (spoiled and moldy), and long beans, or "Marquesan string beans" as we called them — long round green beans about a foot long and delicious. We were able to stock up with canned butter, eggs, crackers, bread and a small variety of canned goods — but really, the selection was so small one wondered how the local people got by. In retrospect, as I think about it, the answer is obvious — they were satisfied with what was at hand because that was for the most part all they knew.

Fish weren't available at market. This was due to the ciguatera poisoning which was rampant in the Marquesas at the time and even though Paul, Davey and I went diving one day as we had promised our French comrades, we just swam along the reefs that fringed the shores along the mouth of the bay. We found the presence of numerous small sharks too distracting to enjoy the other underwater wonders.

Paul got up before dawn one day and rowed ashore to meet Dick from *Vanity*. The two had determined to hike to the top of the plateau on Nuka Hiva. It was a formidable objective in such heat with so many insects and such dense growth. But they found themselves a trail and were up and back by sunset the same day, each carrying a long stalk of bananas on their return. I rowed ashore to get Paul and bring him back to the mother ship. We had been worried about him not only because it was getting late but because there had been some showers starting and we worried about him getting caught in a flood.

Back at *Querencia*, Paul was totally spent. I'd never seen him so exhausted and dehydrated. We hung the bananas from the boom, fed the young man, and watched him collapse!

The following morning he was much more animated and gave an exciting narrative about his adventures with Dick and the jungle hike over his breakfast of box milk and cereal. He discovered that despite his conscientious application of insect repellent he had really been eaten up by something. "No-nos" most probably, but we hoped not. At least they didn't itch, yet.

It was a lazy day and it really got very hot and humid with a large thunderstorm rolling through in the early afternoon. We were really glad not to be at sea. We mostly relaxed, napping. Occasionally we would peek out a porthole or out from underneath the tarp to stare at the waterfalls. All matter of jetsam came out with the flooding, including but not limited to litter, logs, mud, rats, and insects. Frank told us later that the local folk were very worried about the weather after the horrendous storms from the year before.

"As a matter of fact we had a bad one in March," he had said.

That evening Paul was up for going to shore with Davey and me before the sun set. We carefully filled the twelve-foot raft with all the garbage from the past few days which Davey had packed for haul-out and then climbed in for the row ashore. Paul pulled us toward shore but I insisted on taking over the helm once we got just outside the surf line. Big waves were breaking as a result of the now remnant storm and extra care was needed to bring us in for a safe landing. My back to the bow and rowing with both hands I carefully turned the raft around, putting the stern into the waves and watching for the right wave to catch a ride in on.

"Oh God, be careful," Davey said.

But it was too late. Or maybe IT was too early. The point is that my timing was off. Suddenly we were in the wrong place at the wrong time.

We weren't dressed for the occasion, but right after the raft flipped the three of us were half-swimming and half-running out of the surf, the raft upside down and all our garbage bags racing away from us in the torrent. Luckily the oars were tied in and we didn't break one this time.

We were right in the middle of picking up our garbage and emptying sand out of our pockets when we looked up to see that the dirt road that ran along the ocean front was now full of children staring at us. Well, Davey and I called them children. Actually they were teenagers and Paul's peers. Davey and I may have felt slightly chagrined, but Paul was mortified. How could we have done this in front of *them*?

We were continuing to gain appreciation for the power of the surf.

41.

> 0828 Hoisted our "P" flag and putted over to
> Dick on *Vanity* and gave him our address and
> a chart of Bora Bora hoping to see him again.
> [It would not be.] Last night I dreamt of Bora
> Bora; cool clear waters, bluish and dazzling.
> -JFM

Feeling sure enough that *Querencia* was once again well found, seaworthy, provisioned, and able, we set sail for Bora Bora in the Society Islands at 0940 on March 18, a Sunday. It was a distance away of only 950 miles as the crow flies and that seemed close compared to the miles we had put behind us coming from San Diego to Nuka Hiva. Actually, we would discover that we underestimated in planning what would be required of us in this part of the passage.

Although our cruising plans aimed only at sighting and passing the Tuamotu Archipelago, a low group of coral atolls that extend in a NW-SE direction between the Marquesas and Tahiti, their existence presented a new danger to be reckoned with. Their reefs cannot be seen until you are close-to, even in daylight, and in a storm it would be unlikely that you would be able to hear the breaking surf as a warning until too late. Added to this was the worry of a cyclone. The *Pacific Island Pilot*, which reported tropical storms to be quite rare in the Southern Hemisphere east of longitude 135° West, had proved to be wrong in recent years. Indeed, the year previous, 1983, the area west of 135°W had seen four tropical storms in March and April alone. Two had passed right over our charted sailing plans. The Polynesians were worried that 1984 might bring a repeat performance from Mother Nature, and we were worried, too.

We left Nuka Hiva on the day following the full moon and with very light wind we sailed that first night at sea under our big genoa and a full main along the east coast of the spectacular little island of Ua Pu. Its spiraled peaks and towers going up into the starry sky backdropped by a golden moon-obelisk haloed with misty clouds created a scene that was absolutely incredible. All of it was too much, unreal, like an illustration revived from a long-forgotten fairy tale of my childhood. As if that wasn't enough for one human soul to take in, all during the night every three or four hours a pod of dolphins would come and visit.

Ua Pu

At a color-splattered daybreak I was on watch when I heard the dolphins approaching again from the NW jumping, puffing, and squeaking. They came up to the boat and swam along with *Querencia* which was ghosting along at only two knots in the early morning stillness. There must have been twenty dolphins or so. I took off my

Casio diving watch and tied a small line to it, setting off its beeper and lowering it over the aft rail into the water to trail along behind us. The "mad scientist" in me had not drummed up a prize winning experiment but was just out to have a little fun with these marvelous mammals. They seemed to think I was fun, too. One or two bumped the watch with their noses while others did leaps and jumps previously only seen at Sea World.

In short time Paul and Davey were both on deck wiping the sleep from their eyes and joining me in amazement. I figured Paul and Davey probably were reminding the dolphins of seals the way they were clapping. The dolphins stayed with us and when the wind died altogether they just laid there on the surface resting and breathing. They were all around us, many laying right up against the hull. Paul and I each tried reaching down over the rail to just touch one lightly on the back, but when you got within an inch or two, they would gently move away from your hand as if they could see you with eyes in the backs of their head!

Dolphin Pod at Sunrise

Eventually they would leave us to continue our way alone across the South Pacific Ocean. Haze once again seemed to turn the sky into ground glass. The light wind and heavy humidity was interrupted by squalls. We took to catching fresh rainwater which we had decided was much better tasting than anything out of a hose or plumbing fixture. Paul noticed, as we confirmed with interest, that his skin was covered head to foot with insect bites. The culprit had to be the infamous no-no bug of course, finally rearing its ugly head as a result of successfully stalking Paul during his recent jungle expedition. I immediately reminded Paul if he scratched any of them we would have to risk a serious staph infection aboard; but he didn't need my reminder. He was seriously bummed-out by the "blooming" bites and well aware of their pestilential possibilities.

"Oh my God, mom, I'm history," he sadly reported to Davey.

We all sort of understood the possible seriousness of one or two hundred no-no bites, yet we could not formulate how it would exactly effect Paul in the next few days. We could only break out the calamine lotion from the ship's stores and hope for the best.

"Oh Paul!" Davey sympathized.

The next few days remained the same, except for Paul's bug bites which increased in itching intensity and added a special agitation to his disposition. The sky remained ominous and now there were reports over the radio that a certain cyclone named "Carol" or "Cyril" (the reception being what is was) was roaming around the South Pacific east of 180° W. It was not a present threat with coordinates well west of us but it was still nevertheless disconcerting.

Expecting to be in Bora Bora within the week, we enjoyed many of the stores we had hoarded in the North Pacific — canned salmon, ravioli, chicken a la king, potatoes, mixed vegetables — whatever sounded good that we could find aboard. We sided it mostly with pasta and or a few fresh vegetables such as cucumbers and potatoes we had picked up in the Marquesas. We came to a unanimous decision that Marquesan potatoes are the worst, tasting more like the good earth they came from than potatoes. The wine in the plastic jugs wasn't much better, tasting very green. It reminded us of pencil shavings.

On our third day the monotony was interrupted by a large whale breaking the surface ahead of *Querencia*. It seemed even larger than the dinosaurs that lived on the earth millions of years ago. But it soon disappeared and we were back to a very slow, hot, humid trip, often with our sails slatting.

It was 0245 and I came on deck fifteen minutes early to relieve

Paul at the helm. He was slumped over the pedestal wrapped in traditional rain garb . I looked at the compass face in the moonlight and it read a direction of 90° east!

"What the hell is going on here, Paul! Are you asleep?" I yelped.

"No! I'm not! What's wrong?" he quickly responded, managing to pull himself to an agonizingly erect position.

"Then why are we heading east?" I insisted.

"We're not!"

"The compass says we're heading east. *Damn* it. Paul, you've been sleeping!" I argued. I was getting rough now.

"Well, there must be something wrong with the *damn* compass because I have been steering by the stars mostly all night. Yea! Look! The compass is wrong! Compare it to the moon and stars, John!"

He was right! For a second I felt lost. Like a stranger in a strange land, with no familiar signs. A sort of vertigo descended on me. Then I realized that the stars didn't lie; we were heading SW, not E as the compass insisted. The compass at the navigation station also proved Paul right.

"What the hell is wrong with the pedestal compass?" we said in unison.

After closer inspection with a flashlight we could see that the compass card was so far tilted in its case that the edge of the circular card was hitting the compass's glass globe and hanging.

Later I would piece together a more complete explanation of the "dip" problem from the mariner's book we had on board.

When we had first fallen in love with the brass compass as it glistened underneath a showcase in Seattle, the compass card had been perfectly level. This was because it had been built, or adjusted, as it came out of the factory to be level despite the tilt of the Earth's magnetic field. If the compass had been unadjusted and the card at a substantial tilt, it is highly unlikely that the compass would have been very appealing or as useful to a yachtsman in the Northern Hemisphere.

But now the compass was no longer in the Northern Hemisphere and the card tilted so far that the edge of it hit the thick glass dome that covered it. For us their was no way to adjust the compass tilt, but if we thumped its case enough times the card would move around until it eventually pointed towards magnetic north. Although it was no longer free spinning we would live with this problem until returning to the Northern Hemisphere again. We were glad to have a backup — the high quality gimbaled compass in the navigation station. It remained unaffected.

We would run into numerous boats that had the same problem, and some makes of pedestal compass were worse than others. Indeed some skippers sent their compasses back to the manufacturer. Others bought compasses manufactured in the Southern Hemisphere.

At any rate, it was very much of a surprise to us and we were surprised that we hadn't heard of it before. Maybe they should make all world-class pedestal compasses on the equator and compromise the tilt.

42.

We were plagued by wind shifts and squalls. During the daylight hours it wasn't so bad because by now we had learned to 'read' the conditions and sailed a course between squalls. We even got to the point where we started to make the most of the squalls, having enough confidence to leave all our sails up and scream along with our rail in the water for a short burst of speed and distance before the wind again returned to being very light. At night it was a different story. We couldn't see the weather around us very well and had to pretty much take things as they came. Dark, ominous clouds hid our precious moon.

Occasionally we would get more of a squall than we bargained for in the middle of the night and it would put all of us on deck, performing our well rehearsed Chinese fire drill of shortening sail as the ocean threw buckets of sea water at us over the rail. An hour later the blocks would be banging and the sails would be hanging limp from their slats. It was very nerve racking and five days out it was evident that our morale was slipping. We weren't even catching any fish.

In an effort to do something besides worry and scratch the last of the no-no bites, I encouraged Paul to join me in carving a Tiki from a wooden dowel. We whittled away most of the day and in the end had a fairly handsome Tiki which we decided needed a name. After victuals that evening we were still working on a name and had made the process of selecting one into amusement. Paul was already in the sea bunk relaxing a bit before his first watch and Davey was in the galley serving us up some hot chocolate for desert. I was stretched out on the port side of the cockpit keeping an eye out.

"'Kowabunga!' How about the name 'Kowabunga'?" I yelled.

"Yeah," Paul yelled back from below. "Kowabunga's a good name!"

"Well, here's your hot chocolate, *Bwana*, to toast to your '*Kowabunga*,'" Davey said, passing me up a motion mug.

I sat up and leaned down the hatch to grab the cup from Davey.

"Twang! Crash! Thump!" There was a huge descending noise behind me in the cockpit. The boat seemed to shiver.

I turned around and *right where I had been lying* there was now a pile of wire and shackles and a block. I had narrowly escaped getting hit, possibly in the head, with several pounds of fallout. The topping-lift, a large wire and accompanying hardware used for adjusting the boom height, had parted from the very top of the mast. We all stared at the pile of rubble in disbelief.

"I don't know you guys. 'Kowabunga' sounds like a hexed word," Paul offered.

What a night. One good squall at the end of my watch. We dropped the main and were very glad we had already dropped the jib and raised the staysail. John cleated the spare halyard off on the Sampson post to make sure it would hold the now topping lift-less boom. Blow was over quickly but the rain and churned up seas were with us all night. One other strong blow on Paul's watch got us all up though we were all awake off and on most of the night due to the rolling motion. Took one large wave over the bow. John discovered bracket holding main sheet block on boom was coming loose. He tightened it in the dark right after we dropped the main. We all realized we have been ignoring the rigging on *Querencia* and vowed to go over her with a fine tooth comb tomorrow. This has been a

truly rough stretch of ocean weather-wise
and psychologically. It is a major passage, not
a Sunday sail, and we have a hard time keeping that in our heads. Hope we turn the
lethargy and waning morale into constructive
renewal of *Querencia* so she can make a grand
and proud arrival in Bora Bora — DT.

The following morning we carefully propped the Tiki up in the
navigation station so that it was nearly impossible for it to fall over,
and we remained very careful not to call it by name, again. It seemed
the logical thing to do. It wasn't the only icon we had aboard. A
rosary had been swinging in the forward berth since we left Friday
Harbor. (Today, years later they still both occupy their respective
spaces aboard *Querencia*.)

Once again it was obvious that there are numerous advantages to
having a sixteen-year-old aboard. After breakfast Paul quickly made
his way up to the top of the forty-two foot mast and reassembled the
topping lift. All that was required of Davey and me was to winch him
up, to try and keep the boat level and to send up tools on a halyard.
There was a certain amount of bravery involved. The air smelled
fresh and we were getting a brisk breeze filling in around us.
Querencia was doing a steady five knots and picking up speed. Paul
moved in a fairly large arc back and forth along the end of the mast
as the boat rode the rolling heap.

"Wow, you guys! You should see it from up here! I can see lightening and rain storms everywhere on the horizon!"

"Hurry up Paul. Just do your job and let's get you down," Davey
pleaded.

Paul had finished jury rigging the topping lift to the mast tang
and was just back down on deck when a really good squall caught up
with us reducing the visibility to zero and soaking us thoroughly. We
made our way below for a celebration of chili and wine and left
Nelley to do the steering.

Finally the southeast trades returned and we pulled ahead.
Querencia was once again accomplishing over 100 miles a day and the
anxiety we had felt over our weak forty to sixty mile-a-day accomplishments started to dissipate. The slow journey, however, had

eaten a major hole once again in our ship's stores and we were sorry that we weren't better provisioned. We did have plenty of bananas though, and Davey figured out a way to make a good banana split with boxed milk and syrup. They went nicely with some canned rum cakes we had purchased in Canada.

Our major next concern was to navigate either around or through the low-lying coral atolls that make up the northern Tuamotus. It would depend on the weather. The northernmost Tuamotu atoll was Mataiva and according to my calculations it was 116 nautical miles away at a course of 229°. After that we would make for Bora Bora, which was still 308 nautical miles, or about three more days, away, making our arrival time late the next Tuesday. Having crossed another time zone we set our clocks back another hour, the second time since leaving San Diego.

> 2208 A pod of six porpoises are chasing the boat. It's nice to have them once again visiting us. The anxiety of reaching Bora Bora grows, but we have returned to good sailing. You could make a book just about this last leg of our trip alone. I'll wait for the movie. Only three more days. I wish us luck! — PTW

43.

The following night Paul called us all up on deck to witness one of the most extraordinary curiosities any of us had ever seen. *Querencia* had come into an aggregation of jellyfish that stretched as far as our halogen torch would shine. Each *Cnidarian* was as big as 18 to 24 inches in diameter. They were packed as close as sardines in a can, with *Querencia* sort of plowing through the clumped-up invertebrate mass at four knots. The remarkable thing was that each jellyfish seemed to be equipped with a fifteen to twenty-five watt light bulb. Yes, that is very bright! I couldn't believe it. We'd all seen phosphorescence before, but nothing like this! It was incredible. From my studies I surmised that it was some sort of mating signal. We had arrived at *The Great Jellyfish Orgy*.

They would "turn-on" for a few seconds when the hull brushed against them or when the light of a flashlight fell on them. When I turned on the spreader lights to get a better look, the sea literally lit up all around us.

"Wow. Who turned on the pool lights?" Davey said as she came on deck.

By making a sweeping motion with our bright twelve volt torch along the horizon we could make the whole ocean incandesce. It was truly amazing. About an hour later we had passed through the last of the mysterious globs.

Once up, it was hard for those of us not on watch to go back to sleep. The weather was building and I calculated us to be within ten to twenty miles of the sunken reefs of Mataiva. Many cruising boats have run into these hidden reefs at night and sunk.

When the sun came up it was blowing strong trades, thirty to thirty-five knots, and the clouds were low and scuzzy. We were doing our hull speed, and we were very busy sweeping the decks, restowing below, and getting into being able heavy weather sailors again. At a little after six in the morning we all had the pleasant surprise of finding our reckoned position right-on. There on the horizon just a bit off of our port bow you could see foaming surf and the dense palm trees of Mataiva. With no visible land mass behind them it was as if the palms were growing right out of the ocean.

This atoll is the most westerly of the Tuamotu Archipelago. Actually it is a group of small reefs that together form an area that is five miles long and three miles wide. There is only one tiny passage through the reef into the lagoon. With the weather being what it was, for us the decision was easy. We would go on.

"We shouldn't mind saving the Tuamotus for next time. It's nice to have a reason to return some day," Davey reminded us.

Mataiva fell away from us quickly, and it felt very good to have nothing left between us and our goal of Bora Bora but 189 nautical miles across the South Pacific.

The day passed quickly and by nightfall the wind had eased enough to make sailing pleasant. The wave action seemed a bit more confused with swells coming in from the south, but the winds were light and consistent.

02:30 Strong odor of land, but I know we aren't near anything. The moon rose quickly tonight — at first it looked like a ship — then it looked like a giant UFO, the waning crescent being split into two giant headlights. The seas are different now that we are past the Tuamotu barrier. I definitely smell the civilization of the Society Islands we are nearing.— DT

We were finally on approach to the islands that come to mind when people mention the South Seas, the islands of Tahiti, the islands of every sailor's dream. Officially called the Society Islands, these islands extend over 400 miles in a WNW direction. All of the islands are fairly high and volcanically formed, giving them jagged towers that extend up from the coral barrier reefs that surround them. We would skip the usual port of entry and the large capital of Tahiti, Papeete, and make landfall at Bora Bora where we could continue our personal experiment in paradise. We had little interest in being in a big city. Spending half our time in a city and the rest island hopping was not why we came to the South Pacific.

By 1530 the next afternoon we were seeing what we thought was Bora Bora as well as some other large land masses in the distance, and it was a good thing. Our "Sunday sail" had seemed like a long bus ride at times. Quite possibly it was the longest ten days I have ever sailed! We were down to a few days of food. We hadn't even caught one fish.

That evening after a brilliant sunset, our Sat Nav put our position as somewhere in the mountains of Huahine, one of the Society Islands about fifty miles SE of Bora Bora. I threw out the fix since the satellite elevation was too low, and I knew we weren't in the mountains of Huahine. I pulled out the sextant and managed to secure several fixes by midnight using stars and planets for lines of position. They put us some seventy miles NE of Bora Bora. The wind was very light and the dangers would be few. There was no way *Querencia* could sail seventy miles by daybreak. I retired to the sea bunk leaving the last two watches to Paul and Davey.

0241 Port lantern just went out but no biggy.

Mom will help me re-light it when she comes
on at 0300. The only close call we've had
tonight of any kind was a near collision with
a small coconut that passed just to our starboard side. Strange to know the islands are
out there, but I can't see them. Partly cloudy.
— PTW

0345 Moonrise. I see the darkness of two
islands on the horizon. — DT

The following day there was next to no wind, but it didn't matter. Bora Bora stood out clear as a bell and was within easy reach. It
was very, very hot by late morning and we fired up the "iron spinnaker" eager to reach the pass through the coral reef. James
Michener once described Bora Bora as the most beautiful island in
the world, "The gem of the Pacific." I couldn't agree more, especially if you see Bora Bora from the sea with its thrusting peaks surrounded by gentle blue-turquoise waters.

We raised all our flags and did a quick spit-shine on the bright
work. There was only one pass through the reef into the lagoon, Pass
Teavanui. In the middle was a red buoy.

"Remember it is 'red-*left*-returning' now, we'll keep the buoy on
our port side! We are now using the international buoy system," I
reminded everyone.

As we sailed our way through the narrow entrance into the
lagoon that afternoon we saw the American we met two years earlier, Richard, taking a boat load of tourists for a sail aboard his graceful forty-foot catamaran. He was slowly making his way down the
lagoon.

"Home is the sailor. Home from the sea! Isn't it beautiful!" I
exclaimed jubilantly. Davey was as happy as a clam herself. Once
again we had done it.

"Hey, John," Paul suggested, "lets put up all our sails including
the big genny with the red cross and intercept Richard coming down
the lagoon. It'll blow his mind."

"Great idea Paul!"

Davey seconded the motion.

Part VII
Bora Bora

44.

It was a flood tide and we slipped through the narrow Teavanui pass and into the green lagoon of Bora Bora as easily as a leaf riding the downstream current of a gentle river, leaving the rolling waves of the open sea and the roar of the barrier reef behind us. Inside the lagoon it was blowing a gentle breeze of 12 knots and with all our sails up we were moving along at a good clip, sliding over the smooth protected waters like a skater over ice, on towards the catamaran loaded with tourists coming down the lagoon from the Hotel Bora Bora.

"I see Richard at the wheel," Paul reported with enthusiasm from the bow pulpit.

Although it might have first appeared as though we were on a collision course, I turned *Querencia's* wheel as we closed the final distance between boats; amid a flurry of clicking camera shutters we ran downwind along side Richard's large catamaran, *Vehia*.

"Ahoy, Richard!" we hailed. He was already eyeing us carefully. His young son, towheaded and brown as a berry, stood at his side. We had met Richard on our 1981 trip down to Bora Bora by plane. He was an American who had first sailed down to Tahiti from Hawai'i with some buddies. While in the Society Islands he met a beautiful French/Tahitian woman, Martine, and they married and soon had a son they named Maui. Richard quickly learned to speak Tahitian as well as French and reaped a lot of respect from the locals. Their tourism business had flourished as a result.

"Well, I can't believe it!" Richard whooped, looking us over as our two boats raced down the lagoon with just a few yards between us. His initial look of concern was changing to jubilation.

"Do you remember us?" Davey yelled across.

"Sure I do. You guys really did it! How the hell are you anyway?"

"Great!," the three of us chorused back, "It's good to be here!"

In a quick exchange we brought Richard up to date on our transit times. He had his first mate toss us a couple of cold canned Budweisers as he pointed out a safe anchorage for us. We would get together later. As I turned the wheel and *Querencia* pointed her bowsprit away from *Vehia*, the deck full of tourists were still taking pictures of our pretty *Querencia* as we waved them good-bye.

The anchorage was between the Yacht Club, identifiable by floating "fares" or huts, and an extension of land known as Point Pahua. There was only one other boat, a French steel hull and we anchored about thirty yards away from it in seventy feet of water. Despite our close proximity to shore it was very deep and to add to my surprise the anchor windlass had completely frozen up from salt deposits. We had to set our anchor twice by hand before we were satisfied and by then both Paul's arms and mine felt like wet spaghetti.

Our dream had come to reality. *Querencia* bobbed off her hook in crystal clear waters, once again in the center of a prism. Before us stood the magical mountain of Bora Bora, O'temanu, surrounded by lush tropical foliage, blushing faintly. I felt a certain harmony, or rhythm, to the this place, as if *Querencia* were inside a hologram.

Davey was quick to remind me to get a few chores done before sunset. It was already four in the afternoon. Davey was right — there were the sails and sheets to be put away, we had to pump up the raft, unstuff below decks, and rearrange our ocean-going, oversized "wind-surfer" into a floating home with accommodations for three.

By dark we had everything done that needed to be, including taking luxurious fresh-water showers and putting on fresh T-shirts and shorts. We all climbed into the raft and rowed to the Yacht Club with all the francs we could find. It was a long row but Paul had no problem in pulling us to the dock.

I carefully tied up the dinghy with a clove hitch and the three of us jumped up on the foreign dock which was dimly lit by lights from the bar and kitchen. I could see that under the opposite, lit-end of the dock people were sitting at small tables drinking and eating.

"Bonsoir!" rang a voice from a dark silhouette moving in the shadows next to us. Startled, we all jumped about three feet straight up.

"Bonsoir," I said. "Je suis Américan. Moi et mon famille arriver Bora Bora a la petite bateau cinquante jours depuis California."

"Fifty days from California?" he said in very good English but with a French accent.

"Well, actually we stopped in Nuka Hiva in the Marquesas for a few days."

"Ohhhhhhgh! Debbeeee. Debbeeee. Ohhhhhhgh! Oh my God! Welcome to Bora Bora! My name is Noel!" He yelled to the bar emphatically in French and you could hear the words "Americans cinquante jours California" echoing from one table to the next. Everyone was eager to see the Americans as Noel led us out of the shadows and onto the eating lanai at the head of the dock.

"Please join me and my fiancée, Debi, at our table as our guests," insisted Noel, "we are the new managers of the Yacht Club Bora Bora!"

Learning to grate coconut

Then it was cocktails followed by a huge feast accompanied with the finest of French wines. As soon as we finished one course Noel would order another. Debi and Noel spoke very good English. The food was excellent and the conversation delicious. It was wonderful to be truly wined and dined in the paradise of our choice, complete with the Southern Cross constellation overhead. At the end of the evening we rowed back to *Querencia* in the still waters of the protected lagoon. We looked forward to our coming days on Bora Bora, happy to be anchored to our dream.

45.

"Mysterious lost weekend in a land
where time stands still
Where people fall in love again
just for one more thrill"
— Jimmy Buffet
Hot Water

There are only be a few times in my life I can remember with such joy as rising to a new day on Bora Bora. I would go sit in the cockpit in the early morning sun and thoroughly enjoy that state in-between sleep and consciousness. Then the first thing I would do when I was well enough awake was jump off the rail into the water. The water was crystal clear and the same temperature as the air. It was absolute heaven. What a way to start the day. I would climb back into the cockpit and dry in the rays of the sun while, eyes closed, I brushed my teeth and organized my thoughts for the day.

In the past Davey and I had each divided our lives into different areas, like job, family, and spiritual practice and they all had become somewhat independent activities. This had worked to our advantage earlier in our lives because it had enabled each of us to go into greater detail in one area or another depending on our interests, concentration, and available time. It was the natural way "to be" since focusing our energy on one thing at a time was the only way it seemed we could fulfill our selves. But because of this division Davey and I had lost a sense of wholeness in our lives. Rediscovering that wholeness was our quest and we indeed re-discovered it in our five-month stay on Bora Bora.

It was a fulfillment of paradise. Can paradise be explained? For each of us life was now an inward experience, quiet and subtle, as compared to the overwhelming material and outward focus of daily activity in a metropolis. No longer did we view our existence as something that one has little control over, a victim of cause and effect. Moreover we had proved to ourselves that visualization, such as visualizing sailing *Querencia* to Bora Bora, was a very real and relevant act.

For me to have once upon a time pictured *Querencia* anchored in Bora Bora in my mind's eye while *being* in Seattle seemed crazy or like a dream. Yet, now we had actually done it and were in Bora Bora and there was a magical quality to *IT*. It was the magic of joining inner and outer worlds while at the same time achieving a major life goal. It was the magic of *believing*. Feeling accomplished, our minds were now free to re-examine the cause and effect of our very own life choices and those around us. With this image in our minds, feeling the water and hearing the surf and being surrounded by such stunning quintessence every single day profoundly relaxed all of us. Memory of the tension-filled situations of modern man in everyday life faded away. We remembered urban existence as a way of living that made life more tragic than magic.

After sailing so many thousands of miles across the open ocean following our dreams and our hearts we now knew that the order of nature goes along *without* consulting Carl Sagan, and that it is indeed possible that harmony can emerge of itself without any sort of external compulsion. Nature is only complex in its relation to man.

Bora Bora represents a poetic twist of this nature, where titanic forces transformed the molten furnace of a volcanic crater into the diaphanous waters of a lagoon and then inhabited it for the most part with a race of people whose way of life, temperament, and carefree existence became a legend throughout the world.

Geologists compute that Bora Bora is in actuality about seven million years old. The volcanic mountain gradually sank under its own weight and the caldera eroded and filled with water to leave a vast central lagoon partially fringed with remaining land. Here the coral barrier reef formed in a near perfect circle, making an offshore breakwater. The naturalist Charles Darwin when on his famous voyage aboard the *Beagle* studied the reef structure of Bora Bora closely and later used it to put forward his now accepted theory on the formation of coral atolls.

The island remained uninhabited until about 200 or 300 A.D. when the wave of Polynesian ocean migration reached the area. They found its waters provided sustenance and recreation and centered their life around the lagoon. Inland the remnants of the volcanic crater remained vertical monoliths, wild and unscalable, standing over 2,000 feet high. Belief in strong spiritual taboos of the past lurked there along with legends of the Polynesian gods and how they co-mingled with man and nature. The Polynesian people have their own belief in how Bora Bora came to be.

Since a written language did not exist until the arrival of the first Europeans, all history was dependant on the memory of story telling members of the society, *oripo*, and passed from one generation to the next. Versions varied depending on who was "talking story." One Polynesian version of the creation of Bora Bora credits the mating of a turtle stone, *'ōfa'i honu*, with a cliff on the mountain of Bora Bora. Turtles were thought to be shadows of the gods of the ocean and therefore sacred. This supernatural mating not only produced the island, but the ancestor of a royal family known as *Firiamata O Vavau*, and the island was originally named after him and known as *Vavau*. Vavau the chief was a great warrior and navigator and Polynesian tribes from the Marquesas, Tuamotus, Cook Islands, New Zealand and even the "islands with smoking mountains in the north," Hawai'i, trace ancestry and legends to the Vavau dynasty and its kings.

The warriors of Vavau were feared by all the neighboring islands which at one time or another had come to have differences with them. It was during this time that the island's name gradually changed from Vavau to Porapora which translated generally to "fleet of canoes with silent paddles." The Bora Bora warriors specialized in surprise attack, and accomplished this by muffling their paddles when they attacked other islands in their war canoes.

When Captain James Cook arrived on December 8, 1777, he recorded the name "BolaBola" in his log, the written English interpretation of Tahitian speech being what it was. This was the initial malapropism of *Porapora* that eventually led to its present name of Bora Bora.

46.

Often when walking to and from the only village on Bora Bora, Vaitape, the jagged peaks of the mountain of O'temanu would tear open the bottom of the skirting clouds that rode the trade winds. The torrential, tropical rains would then wash down, down, cooling and easing the thirst of the equatorial heat. We never minded being caught like this underneath a cloudburst but rather felt like we were witnessing a part of creation. We would stop and seek refuge under a tin roof that hung partially over the road and just enjoy the refreshment of the moment. In a few moments the sun would spring out again, the plumeria flowers would smell stronger than ever, white tropical birds fluttered about like butterflies, and we would continue our promenade through paradise.

> *As the wave breaks along the shore*
> *white albino birds*
> *and fish net hammocks*
> *swing across a pastel horizon*
> *above a turquoise sea.*

Besides the occasional pass of a scooter it was always a peaceful walk. And it was a walk we did everyday. Usually it was Davey that made the trip on her own while I puttered about with chores on the boat or went diving, but often I accompanied her.

"*Ia ora na,*" was the familiar greeting from the Tahitian women we met along the way and it meant "good morning." They didn't just say it, but sang it like a quiet, little song as if from a bird. The female Polynesian face was one that appeared in its modeless state as if something terribly sad was weighing heavily on its shoulders; the brow was wrinkled and the eyes dark and deep. Their shoulders bent inward as if they had been reflecting deep and long on a very sad subject. The most remarkable reverse was witnessed upon exchanging greetings; at least 100 watts of sheer elation poured out from their person and their eyes grew wide and joined a big new smile that affirmed their happiness with the world as it was.

Without ice available for our icebox, going to Vaitape was the only way to get fresh food which we enjoyed dearly. Even still, the supply boat from Papeete only arrived on Tuesdays and that was the only day you could find *exotic vegetables like lettuce*, or meat such as beef in the grocery stores. Fresh, long, green beans and poultry might manage to stay in the stores a bit longer, but if you wanted to score you had to be there Tuesday mornings after the ship arrived from Papeete. So we usually had a lot of motivation to schedule a trip to town on the second day of the week!

But in actuality we went anyway almost every day, just for the walk and to pick up some wine or beer, and bread, cheese, and tomatoes. These were our staples. The bread, or baguette loaves, were made fresh daily and smelled and tasted absolutely wonderful. It was even delivered daily to the little homes along the way. As we walked along the road each mailbox would have a baguette sticking out of it.

Usually back at *Querencia* by eleven-thirty in the morning we would have a typical lunch of a baguette loaf stuffed with slices of cheese and tomatoes garnished with Dijon mustard. Sometimes when Paul and I were really missing the good old U.S.A. we would fill a baguette with peanut butter. We were glad to have brought over a large supply of peanut butter with us in ship's stores, because here in Bora Bora it was nearly five dollars a jar when you could find it.

Paul as it turned out had some luck in making friends on Bora Bora. As a tall, good-looking, American lad with bright blond hair, he attracted a lot of attention especially with his island peers. He had met and made friends with Lauren (pronounced Lor-ohn). Lauren was France's answer to Eddie Haskell, Wally Cleaver's friend on TV's *Leave it to Beaver*. He was very polite and forced himself to speak English in the presence of Davey and me. When we reciprocated in attempt to speak better French, he helped by teaching us. He was also a bit of a rascal, an excellent shell diver, and very ebullient. It just so happened that his father was the Chief of Police on Bora Bora, an officer in the gendarme service on assignment from France. I do not know if this had anything to do with the courteous service we received from the gendarmes as we posted our security bonds and filled out the paper work for our visas, but it was obvious that it did not work against us.

Marcien, the cook at the Yacht Club, besides having a small son also had two daughters; one named Carole (pronounced "care-ol"), seventeen, and Michelle, thirteen. Carole was a big-boned happy girl. She acted as waitress at night for her dad and helped out in the kitchen too. She loved to listen to us speak English. She spoke

English very well as a result of her serious study of the language and was thrilled at the opportunity to "try it on" with us. She got the biggest kick out of my French, breaking out into tremendous laughter some evenings when she would take my order for dinner, which was "*bifteck avec frites*" or some of Marcien's bouillabaisse when it was available. We had a standing joke about me having to order a glass to get ice, which is "*glace*" in French. Carole also loved it when the three of us would teach her slang phrases like "skip the sauce" or "hold the mayo" or "let it slide." We taught her how to use these phrases in everyday conversation and she loved it.

Carole took her studying very seriously though, and Davey and I took this as a good influence on Paul. Often after school Lauren would come to the Yacht Club where he would try to study with Carole, Michelle and Paul. Paul was committed scholastically to those dreaded assignments he had to complete in order to pass his high school extension courses from U.C.L.A. Often the four of them abandoned their books and resorted to fishing off the dock or in the event of boredom, some sort of mischief.

One day when we returned to the Yacht Club from Vaitape we discovered that Lauren and Paul had split a Pinache (7-Up and beer were very popular with the European youngsters) and were taking turns riding a bicycle off the end of the dock, much to the amusement of some of the local Tahitians, including Gaston, a very handsome Tahitian student who started coming by on his scooter regularly to see Paul.

Noel and Debi it turned out were getting more than a little edgy about the Yacht Club being turned into a teen-town of sorts, so it was a very good idea when Lauren came up with the idea that Paul join him at school. Davey met with the high school principal to secure permission and soon Paul was getting up every morning before the sun rose and rowing to shore in one of our dinghies to join the French and Tahitians at their high school. He didn't have to walk through three feet of snow, but he did have to blow up his dinghy every morning because of a persistent leak. Lauren scored a school soccer shirt for Paul and he was all set. He loved the experience, sitting in with Lauren in all his classes, and then studying his U.C.L.A. courses in the school's study hall.

Some evenings Paul would go home with Lauren to spend the evening with his family. There he would help Lauren organize and polish his shell collection before dinner. Dinner at Lauren's was often Paul's favorite meal; swordfish cooked only in a way that Lauren's mother could cook it. Quite understandably it was expected that Paul would speak French when he visited Lauren's family, just as Lauren spoke English when he spent time on *Querencia*.

47.

> *"Our thoughts are our feelings gone to seed."*
> — John Burroughs

While we were in Bora Bora we became friends with a certain Polynesian man named *Metata*, or Meketa, depending on who was calling to him and who was listening. It is hard to differentiate between the consonants "k" and "t" in Tahitian. The top of the tongue meets the palate at precisely the same moment that the tip of the tongue strikes the backs of the front teeth. The similar difficulty is true for differentiating between an "r" and an "h" (or an "l") and a "p" and a "b." Since Polynesian was not a written language until European man decided to write it down, transferring the language to paper mostly depends on how the listener interprets the remarkable speech gymnastics of the Polynesian. Although the Polynesian language only consists of eight consonant sounds and the vowels, in some words the vowel sounds are held for a longer duration than others. Other words may be riddled with glottal stops, all sound breaking off for an instant, as when we say "oh-oh" in English. Anyway, when Metata said "Metata" it sounded like it could either be Metata or Meketa, and he was quick to inform us that either way was fine with him.

I am sure that Metata is some sort of saint, and most assuredly a mischievous one at that, a sorcerer defined by the society around him. If he had been an American Indian he might have been a shaman. If he had been an African native, a witch doctor. If he had been in India he might have been a yogi. Wherever he might be on this day, he may be only paddling his canoe and singing to a blue sky, or drinking beer and laughing heartily. But he is a sage and it is probably true, as the mystic poet Thomas Merton once said, that just eight such individuals in the world would be enough to keep our planet in an acceptable state of grace.

At fifty-five years of age, he had an aquiline nose and looked like a Tahitian version of Paul Newman. His hair was frosted gray of medium length. He had deep brown eyes delineated by thin fuzzy eyebrows and a playful, smirking smile with lips like rubber, often seeming to contort as much as Daffy Duck's. His skin olive and bronzed, he was of medium height and great physique. He was so solid it was hard to find any pudge on him whatsoever, although he told us that he was once fat.

"Like a pig!," he said emphatically.

In the five months he was our friend, I never saw him eat anything.

Metata was very animated, mostly due to his twinkling eyes and expressive face. When he spoke he repeatedly contracted his forehead muscles, using them like punctuation marks in a sentence, his eyebrows moving up and down in short, smooth movements.

Although we once saw Metata at a wedding wearing a white pareau with a flower neatly tucked behind his ear and playing his ʻukulele, he told us that pareaus mostly got in his way. He usually dressed in just a pair of tan cotton shorts, and he must have only had one or two pair. We never saw him in a pair of shoes or flip-flops. When the *maramu* (the winter wind) blew he would don a sweatshirt, or for evening attire he would wear an American T-shirt. His favorite was a red T-shirt with yellow lettering on it that read "Tuscon Fire Department". He got the T-shirt when he traveled to the U.S. as part of a Tahitian troupe that promoted tourism (from Arizona) for a large hotel chain. He laughed when he remembered the black pointed shoes that they wanted him to wear on that trip.

"Can you imagine," he said to us, "*me* in such funny shoes?"

In the evenings his hair was so well groomed he could have been a movie star. In the early morning hours though, if you caught him, you would see his stubbled grey beard. He would quite often be wearing a golfer's hat with the entire brim turned upwards and at such times he looked a little like a sprite. Other than his beard, his body was mostly hairless, warm and smooth, like a full-blooded Apache might be. But he would remind us, "I have white people's blood in me."

Metata was our guardian angel, our foster-parent, and became our dearest friend.

We were first introduced to Metata after paddling over to join Debi and Noel for lunch on their floating fare. These floating fares were basically A-frames on pontoons, complete with lanais, thatched roofs, sleeping lofts, and kitchens. With the exception of Debi and Noel's management unit, they were rented to tourists, along with boats to get back and forth from shore. Ground tackle tethered them to a two meter cube of concrete on the bottom of the lagoon and in the lee of Point Farepiti they bobbed around like lazy fishing floats. Atop each fare were two large solar panels that kept a twelve-volt battery system alive and well enough to supply electrical power for lights and refrigeration to the unit. Noel was happy to see us paddle over to their fare and join them for lunch. He had just finished showing Metata the solar panels. Following spectacular dives off the roof they both climbed back aboard and Noel introduced us to Metata. We had wondered who this fit Polynesian man was who had just dove from the roof singing out his loud call, laughing and giggling. He couldn't stay for lunch, but after acknowledging our brief meeting, he winked at us and said, "I like you guys." He then paddled off in his outrigger.

The next time we met Metata was soon afterwards, following a morning in which Davey and I had been both afflicted with "Polynesian paralysis." As *Querencia* twirled around on her mooring in the gentle southeast trades we alternated between lying below decks and in the cockpit, contemplating nothing and everything — a perfect picture of two daydreamers completely overcome by laziness. By the time noon had rolled around we were wise enough to recognize the wisdom of abandoning all ideas of doing anything of real value for the rest of the day. Instead we rowed *Querencia's* tender to the yacht club for a cool beer.

A few Tahitians were laughing and joking at the small bar inside the yacht club when we arrived. I could tell by Marcien's expression that everyone was having fun. With a little hesitation I went up to the bar and squeezed myself in with the announcement, "*Inu Pia,*" which I had learned in Tahitian means "Drink Beer!"

Metata was seated at the small bar, and Davey and I rounded out the attendance to an even six in number. Metata was hand rolling a cigarette from loose French tobacco called "*Bison*" but when I interrupted he sprang from his seat to produce two more bar stools for us to sit on and cheerfully insisted to his friends in melodic Tahitian that he be the one to order large Hinano beers for everyone. After he finished rolling his cigarette he slid the papers and tobacco pouch down the bar in front of me as if he knew I was dying for a smoke.

"Don't ask," he said. "What's mine is yours." He spoke in perfect English.

"Oh, really? Thank-you!," I replied.

Metata answered, "Yes, but what is yours is mine also. This is the Tahitian way."

His english voice was electrifying — full of spark and happiness. It was obvious that he liked to laugh and he liked to make other people laugh as well.

A nervous chuckle burst out of Davey and me as the rest of our new companions in the bar howled with amusement.

"But it's no problem. '*Aita pea pea!*," Metata reassured us. "I will take care of you guys and give you whatever you want. Please. Sit down, be happy!"

Davey and I were as game as anyone, but for a moment I was having second thoughts, even though I was laughing as I pulled up to chair.

"But I think maybe you worry too much." Metata said, looking me straight in the eyes, focusing my attention.

"Yes, I do." I couldn't believe I was talking this way all of a sudden. What was I talking about?

"And I think maybe you have a sad heart... from your family back in The States. Your father was very sick and died from the cancer. You were sick too. High blood pressure and your nerves," Metata quipped.

"Now this is strange," I remember thinking to myself. "How does this man know anything about *my personal history?*"

Davey and I had maintained our anonymity ever since we had left Seattle. All of us, including Paul, considered ourselves anonymous warriors without pasts. We kept to ourselves. We hadn't shared any secrets or personal history with any of our precipitated new friends, nor did we want to.

All of a sudden I felt as if I had been hit a sharp blow to my diaphragm and the wind had been knocked out of me. I wanted to cry. How did this man know anything about me? Davey grabbed my hand and leaned over in amazement herself, her eyes big, looking back at Metata.

Everyone else, including the bartender, were at a loss as to what exactly was going on; they didn't understand English.

"Your father was very, very sick... and you have a very sad heart. There were other problems too. You were both married before and you miss your two daughters."

"You mean Rain and Caroline?" I asked.

"Yea, I think that's right. You have a lot of pain from family and friends that have rejected you. *You guys, you make my heart sad!* I think maybe it was good you take a sailboat and come across the ocean to Bora Bora. That was very smart because I think maybe *that place* was horrible for you guys. Why would you ever go back to that horrible place? I think maybe you should stay in Tahiti." He was really chipping away at our reality now.

Metata had been so direct. He hadn't said much, but he had been precise in his facts and relentless in his approach. Here I was unexpectedly all choked up. What was going on? I stared out the thatched window at the palm trees gently swaying in the trade winds, the turquoise lagoon in the background. I felt a flood of tears ready to break the dam. It was true. I did carry a lot of pain around inside, but I thought I hid it well.

"No, wait a minute, I don't even think about hiding my pain, I just do it automatically, like everyone does," I thought to myself.

My attention snapped back to center and my eyes quickly looked to Metata when I heard him starting to chuckle. But it was easy to see he was really half-chuckling, half-crying; as if he could feel what I was feeling and hear what I was thinking. Abruptly he insisted that now it was time to laugh rather than feel sorry for one's self.

Instantly my heart felt lighter and I lifted my Hinano in a toast. I managed a smile and said rather incredulously, "How did you know all that?"

"Sometimes I dream. I believe it comes from the God. There must be something. *Something with you and with me.*," he said.

"You mean like the soul?"

"Uh-huh. Yea, I think so." He nodded his head and creased his forehead to emphasize his point.

And that was how we first came to know Metata. We spent the rest of the day with him and went back to *Querencia* that night feeling like we had spent the afternoon with Santa Claus. He never really demonstrated any "psychic" abilities much beyond what we witnessed that afternoon, and to tell you the truth that was not what impressed us about the man. It was the tremendous feeling of love that we had when we were around him.

48.

"Life is a foreign language. All men mispronounce it."
— Christopher Morley

We revered Metata. We tried to fight that feeling, it was embarrassing for us and I'm sure for him too. We were always dying to see him again, although we rarely went looking for him. When we did see him it was usually unexpected and always wonderful.

I can't count the number of times that we would row back to *Querencia* and find her cockpit full of papaya, limes, bananas, and grapefruit. Metata the mischievous guardian angel had been there again! One time he even left a brand new fifth of Johnny Walker Red Label for us. You couldn't find quality scotch like that just anywhere in the South Pacific, and even if you could it would cost at least forty dollars.

He was a well-traveled man and we discovered he had helped deliver yachts all over the South Pacific as well as Hawai'i and New Zealand.

"Ai yi yi yi yi!," he remarked speaking of his trip to New Zealand. "But all we had were small cans of green beans to eat and a big storm came and grabbed our boat. The white guy; he was sick the whole trip. But the storm was no problem, I just took all the sails down. But the beans… big problem."

He had even been sent by Club Med to work in Sicily for a period of time, but didn't care for it he said.

"I like Americans the best," he always assured us. Although he had always lived with one Tahitian woman with whom he had at least two daughters, he was not married he insisted.

"I think maybe it would be nice to have an American wife," he would remark, the corners of his mouth curling upwards in a smirk while his eyes sparkled at Davey.

One day I did pursue him. I had been reading the book *A World to The West* written in the early seventies by a young European cruising couple. It was a book loaned to us by a Dutch couple aboard a boat also anchored at the yacht club. Quite unexpectedly I came across a description of a benevolent Tahitian who had lived on the island of Raiatea and went by the name of *Meketa*. The description sounded perfect. All excited, I rowed to shore and went and woke Metata up from a nap at his home. He had never heard of the book, but remembered the couple and their boat anchoring near his home on Raiatea when he had lived there about ten years earlier. We sat on a bench in his garden at the front of his home, in the shadow of Mt. O'temanu, as I read the few pages to him. He listened to every word intently and patiently. In the end he said it was all true. I could tell it made him very happy to hear again about these cruisers he had befriended. I was amazed. Here it was almost a decade later and this man was treating us with the same generosity and care that he had shown them.

Although Metata did not read English, as I said, he spoke it very well. Some of his favorite sayings were:

"I go with you." (sounded like "which you")
"I think so."
"I know this."
"I noticed."

These last two phrases he would say so that it was difficult to tell the difference. And he would say this to us at the funniest of times, almost seemingly on purpose.

"I don't know what I will do with the rest of my life when my sailing days are over," I would say.

"I know (no) this (ticed)," Metata would invariably respond. Davey and I would have hysterics wondering what he had just said *exactly*, and he most definitely enjoyed seeing us think twice.

One day, insignificantly, I told Metata that "I was sorry."

He looked at me in the strangest way and said, "Forget about that! In the Polynesian people's language there is no such word as *sorry*".

I asked, and he said it was the same way with the word *guilt*. We were talking about more than language he assured me. We were talking about the way a person thinks of himself. But yes, there is a translation for the word *shame*.

The beautiful Polynesian people seemed to Davey and me to be easily shamed. Maybe that's why thieving was rare. You could leave your groceries on the curb and go into a store and not so much as worry.

> One day at the gendarme's office I tried to make light of the differences between me and the officer attending my visa with a small joke.
> I pointed at a map on the wall of Bora Bora with three colored thumbtacks stuck into it. "Are they the bad guys?" I jokingly asked him with a big American John Wayne sort of grin.
> "As a matter of fact, monsieur, they are!" he said to me in a perfect Inspector Jacques Clouseau (Peter Seller's) accent.

We were returning from Vaitape to *Querencia* one day when we saw Metata sitting with two other men near the entrance of a small, dimly lit hardware and grocery store. Our eyes met and he motioned for us to leave our groceries on the curb and meet his two old friends.

By the time we had set down our bags, taken off our back packs, and walked up to the entrance Metata and his friends had gathered several large, heavy rice bags and made a makeshift couch for Davey to sit on. At first I was concerned because it seemed we were partially blocking the threshold, but Metata insisted that I stop worrying and sit down. He had a fast round of Tahitian rap with the clerk running the cash register, mostly to assure us there was nothing to worry about. Davey plopped herself down on the rice bags but I balked. Finally I sat down on the dirty floor feeling somewhat inappropriate.

One man was quite aged. His name was Tetupa'a. For his small size he had a large warm smile and small dark eyes. His other friend was introduced as Perry.

They talked about the days when they had been little kids, recalling all the adventures they had experienced growing up together. Metata would translate for us, and after a bit Perry began having fun playing interpreter, too, although he spoke only broken English. All of them had fond memories of Americans in World War II. Perry told us his father had been an American soldier.

I told them a story about the first time Davey and I had been on

Bora Bora in 1982.

We had flown down on holiday with Davey's family. Davey and I had rented a small scooter to circumnavigate Bora Bora. Half way around the island we found a large Tahitian, easily weighing 300 pounds, husking coconuts along the road. He would sell the husks to the electrical generating plant for fifty francs a kilo. We approached him and were able to communicate a little with him; enough for him to tell us that he liked Americans and that his dad had been an American in WWII by the name of Joe.

"Your father then was one 'G.I. Joe' stationed here during the war?" I asked.

He quietly nodded in the affirmative then smiled and handed us some white meat freshly removed from a coconut.

"*Māururu!* [Thank-you]My name is John and this is Davey. What's your name?" I mumbled hoping to keep the conversation alive.

"Joe," he said matter of factly.

They liked that story and howled with laughter. In their unanimous decision our Hinano bottles were already showing the slightest sign of being warm and they insisted that they be replaced; Tetupa'a rattling off another round to the grocery clerk teller while Metata made a quick trip to the cooler, returning with fresh ice-cold full ones. While we were trying to figure out what we were going to do with all this beer, Perry continued story telling by announcing that his father's name had been Perry as well!

"And that my friends is the truth," Perry finished. I detected the slightest southern drawl in his English.

Both Perry and Tetupa'a had grown up learning and applying the skill of making large fish traps using intricate rock ponds. These fish ponds which are found throughout Polynesia are now important cultural and historical testimony of another civilization. Tetupa'a explained that we would have better appreciation for the benefits of a fishpond if we could have seen the lagoon twenty years ago, when it was teeming with *i'a* [fish] and people depended more on gathering their food from nature. Metata affirmed that both Perry and Tetupa'a were the best fishpond makers in both Raiatea and Bora Bora.

It was a rich experience listening to these older Tahitians recall their youth. Many things had changed, but not their friendship or their togetherness. After a while all the Hinano beer was having a warming effect on us and we all seemed to be bathing in a sort of reverie, or aura, together. Maybe it was the famous Hinano glow.

We had been talking for a long time. I was by now leaning way back on my right hand when all of a sudden a large, black, spiked high-heel came down between the knuckles of my outstretched fingers. Avoiding eye contact with any of us, Lauren's mother, the head gendarme's wife, squeaked her heel and literally stepped over me in her pleated white skirt and red lipstick to get into the store. She was an attractive woman of class and position; for a second Davey and I felt totally embarrassed. And then we couldn't help laughing and giggling like the Tahitian friends we were with. I'm sure we weren't invisible, but it felt like we were. Lauren's mother seemed not to see us.

It was a good cue however to consider picking ourselves up and meandering back to the boat.

"My God!" I said, looking at my watch. Three hours had passed. Both Perry and Tetupa'a said "Goodbye John! Goodbye Davey!" and suggested we give some serious thought to Metata's offer to grow watermelons on his land on the small island of Maupiti.

Back at the curb our two heavy sacks of groceries awaited us. Metata had his daughter's scooter and rather than let us walk the last mile to the yacht club he insisted on making two round trips to deliver us, one with Davey and one with me, each of us bulging with provisions. It seems we were always stocking up for the inevitable trip north.

49.

Lauren hand-rolled a cigarette for me from his Bison tobacco pouch with the buffalo logo on the front and said, "Is very good, Bora Bora, yes, John?"

I looked down at Lauren sitting on the teak deck. It was still wet from Lauren taking turns with Paul diving off the bow. They were having their own free-dive contests in the crystal clear waters. On Paul's final dive he was surprised to find a beautiful tiger shell cowrie just waiting for him on the bottom at seven meters. Together they had also just finished scrubbing *Querencia's* hull as a way of returning a favor to Davey and me for taking the boat to the south end of the lagoon for a few days play. It had been possible to anchor in a sand patch where the deep bottom of the lagoon ran up swiftly and left a white desert ledge at the edge of a coral forest. The diving was excellent and the boys were thrilled. It brought me much happiness to see the two of them enjoying diving as much as I did at their age.

Lauren and Paul

"Yes Lauren, Bora Bora is *very far-out,*" I answered.

He liked the word *"far-out"* He giggled and then suggested that he and Paul go get some ice for our cocktail hours. He was a bundle of energy.

"Ice! Did I hear someone say ice? I'll take some ice!" Davey quickly yelled up from the galley, where she was preparing another one of her many feasts.

"*Oú est la glace, Lauren?* Come'on now there's no ice around here."

"Ah. But there is, John! Paul and I will go get ice for you in this very far-out place called Bora Bora. And then you will have some ice for your wine tonight. That would be very far-out, no?" Lauren giggled.

"We'll take some *glace* for our *glasses*, won't we hon?" I answered.

"Sure!"

Everyone was still laughing, including Paul, when the two of them jumped back into the water and swam ashore to the Bora Bora Hotel. In a matter of minutes they returned with a zip-lock bag full of ice they had obviously withdrawn from a guest ice machine.

After a short stern lecture, in which I couldn't help but return Lauren's undeniable grin, Davey and I had a glass of wine complete with *glace*.

Then Lauren thanked Davey and me and jumped in to swim back to shore and go to his parents' home for the evening.

"Good night Paul. Good night Davey. Good night Dr. McGrady! I will see you tomorrow!" he yelled to us.

I pressed the illumination button on my Casio watch and it read one-thirty in the morning. The reef seemed to sound different to me as I half stumbled my way up through the companionway.

Boy, I was tired. I hooked one arm around the shrouds as a hedge against falling overboard while I took a pee into the phosphorescent ocean. It was a still night so far. I noticed that the lights of the Hotel Bora Bora were very far away.

"WHAT!" rang out in my head. "Oh no, we've slipped our hook," I mumbled to myself, biting my lower lip hard. Startled, I finished my business as quickly as possible and went forward to peer over the bow into the darkness. There was the anchor chain hanging rather limply, and yes, the lights of the Hotel Bora Bora, which earlier had been less than 100 yards off our port beam, were now maybe a mile and a half off the bow to windward. Behind us, the motu Topua was maybe a hundred yards away. My heart had picked up its tempo and the rushing blood was now warming me up from head to toe. I was almost nauseous.

I raced back to the navigation station and grabbed a flashlight. Back in the cockpit I peered over the side directing the beam below the water's surface. There was coral all around us just below the surface. I couldn't believe that we weren't hard aground. Looking forward over the bow I could see the water was deeper, maybe 10 feet. Some how we had drifted back into a trough and the hook had caught again, luckily just in time.

I went below and tried to wake Paul as quietly as possible.

"Paul... Paul... Please be quiet and come up on deck. Don't wake Davey just yet. I don't want to alarm her." I hadn't quite figured out the best way to get us out of this mess yet, and I was looking forward to having a powwow with Paul about it before waking up the prime minister. "Turn on the spreader lights on your way up." I whispered.

We were both shocked to see where *Querencia* had managed to drift to. There were so many coral heads around us and such little room to navigate. Negotiating any sort of turn, or swing, on *Querencia* would be impossible.

We went forward on deck and looked ahead. There was the channel. Straight ahead was clear. Well, sort of. It was pitch black. Nevertheless we surmised that we must have drifted straight back into a slot of deeper water amidst the coral heads.

Paul went and awoke Davey, breaking the news to her, and I started to slowly pull in on the anchor chain and pull us out the coral channel. The wind had started to blow a bit by now and I was more than a little glad to be working on the problem. Soon we were in twelve feet of water but the hook wouldn't come up any farther, even on the beefy bronze windlass. The hook was fouled. The three of us stood there on the bow looking down. You could hear little wind-driven waves now licking the hull. Huge coral heads reaching their way up from the bottom still surrounded us on all sides except dead ahead.

"Well Paul," I said, "it looks like you'll have to grab the diving light, your mask, and some fins and go down and unfoul the hook."

"What? Nah! Your kidding." Paul responded.

"John's right Paul, you could do it in a flash." Davey blurted, suddenly realizing that she was confident of her son, and happy that he was around to do the job. Me too.

After a brief discussion on the various types of dangerous marine life one is apt to find while holding his breath and diving below the surface of a tropical lagoon in the black of night, Paul, much to our amazement, like a good soldier jumped in! After a short dive, he surfaced to report that the anchor had caught on the overhanging roof of a cave of coral. Now, along with the chain rode, it had fouled. In two more dives he had it free, and while Paul hauled himself on board I hauled in the hook while Davey putt-putted us forward with the engine.

Once clear and after a short hero's welcome for Paul, we agreed that the best place to point *Querencia's* bow was directly upwind from where we came from, pointing towards the only two lights I knew for sure, the two up by the hotel. Then we would re-anchor using *all* 200 feet of chain rode.

Earlier the previous morning I had shortened our anchor scope to bring *Querencia* into shallow water while cleaning the hull. I didn't pay it out again before calling it a day. Obviously with a rising tide and a little surge we had pulled our anchor off the sand ledge near the hotel, and with it hanging straight down in deep water we had drifted across the lagoon while we slept. We were lucky enough for good weather and to have the hook catch again in a forgiving location across the bay.

By the time we had re-anchored in front of the hotel and found time to look at my wrist watch it was after four in the morning! The wind had really picked up by now and the dingy was thrashing around on its painter. Waves beat over the reef and slopped against the hull. It was starting to sprinkle rain too.

We had been very lucky. The three of us went below and back to our bunks. I etched the following afflatus in a corner of a page in *Querencia's* log book before nodding off.

> *Rushing water.*
> *Resting dangerously.*
> *Inside the reef,*
> *IT comes to us.*

50.

*"Without the human community
one single individual cannot exist."*
— The Dalai Lama

He was a good-looking young Frenchman, about twenty-six years of age, with an unusual name (at least in America), Igor. He was spending a day or two on Bora Bora with his friend Bernard and a string of mostly attractive young ladies. They wound up at the yacht club in the middle of the afternoon where they were joined by Noel, Debi, and Pascal for a *conférence du jour*. Pascal was a French photographer and musician that had the best looking motorcycle on the island and also liked to play guitars with me. Soon there was also Farawa, a large Polynesian man with a round belly, wild unmanageable hair, and a long scowl. Actually he was as light-hearted and easy going as a bird, and laughed easily. He kept an American cigarette behind his left ear that he would occasionally pull out and smell as if it was a good cigar. He had quit smoking about six month's previously and he claimed that was how he did it. I never saw him light up in five months. Accompanying Farawa was his Belgian wife Irené who was in the process of building a new restaurant between Vaitape and the Yacht Club.

We linked up with the French crowd although we never felt totally comfortable. Often we would feel like outsiders when we were with the French (never with the Tahitians) and would really miss just speaking with some Americans for a change. But we were entertained, and we understood more French than we spoke or that they thought we knew.

Soft-spoken Bernard held our fascination. He actually was very warm to us in comparison to the others and was quick to tell us that he considered himself more American than French. He had a recording studio in San Francisco that had brought him financial success and independence, having pressed labels that sold well globally.

"Please accept my apologies, the French can be so incredibly arrogant at times that it embarrasses me," Bernard said in perfect English but with a trace of accent. He admitted being slightly prejudice himself these days. His father had died in France recently and the French government would not allow the inheritance to be taken out of the country.

A small man in his thirties, his hair was worn long although he was slightly balding on the top of his crown. His relaxed demeanor and loose clothing were a perfect match to his calm mannerism. He told us that a few years back he had been an interpreter and friend of *the Dalai Lama* of Tibet, a position he acquired through his father, an influential man in France. For a number of years, as part of the exiled ruler's entourage, he had done an incredible amount of traveling, usually sitting at the left hand of *the Dalai Lama*, who was an incarnation of God according to Tibetan belief. About the Dalai Lama Bernard said, "The Dalai Lama is the most wise and non-violent human being I have ever known."

Davey and I asked Bernard what he thought about the state of the world. Beyond the environment, with him it seemed clear. Our two biggest human problems were described as a beast called greed and the entanglement of our lives in bad politics and/or bad drugs.

"Drug use directly reflects an aspect of the current human social and political weaknesses and strengths," he remarked. "This was true in the sixties with our fascination with the exploration of self."

I listened carefully.

"And you know of course that Hitler's whole Third Reich was on cocaine," he said matter-of-factly.

"What? Really?" It was the first time I had heard this.

"Yes it's true. As a matter of fact, Himmler was going through detoxification during the Nuremberg trials," he continued in his tranquil voice. "Cocaine is a drug reflective of a fascist social structure where activities such as hoarding profits and power are more important than humanitarian values."

We continued to talk about capitalism, socialism, fascism, communism, along with a dash of synthesizers, computers, medicine, and spirituality. To Bernard, clearly we were a pivotal generation with a need to re-examine our ethics, understand what we have inherited from the earth's bounty, nurture our knowledge and responsibility, and pass it on to future generations.

Davey and I were a bit bewildered from such unexpected discourse on this little island in the middle of the Pacific ocean with a man such as Bernard, and hoped to spend some more time talking to him again. But it was not to be. Bernard continued on his holiday and flew out of Bora Bora the next day.

Igor was a contrast. His father had started the black pearl farming business in the Tuamotus and had become a multimillionaire. Igor had rebelled against his father's wealth and withdrawn from the family business, choosing instead to seek adventure at a young age. Eventually he and a young friend joined three other men in an attempt to deliver a yacht to New Zealand from the Tuamotus. As Igor told the story to us, the skipper, in addition to his wealth of inexperience, wound up being totally seasick and disoriented. Igor and the other mate took over steering and navigating using nothing more than common sense.

They were lucky to wind up alive somehow in the islands of New Caledonia, although dangerously starved and exhausted. There Igor and his friend jumped ship and had to spend the night on a beach full of snakes and horrible insects. The serpents had been so bad that they had to sleep in a tree the first night. When they finally found civilization *and* a bar the next day, a surly bartender with a bone through his nose told them that if they knew anything about his stolen "Walkman" which had disappeared recently and didn't tell him they would be automatically *hexed*.

"But these people will kill you with their hexes in this part of the world! Do you understand?" Igor asked of Paul.

Images of voodoo and shrunken heads and a few die-hard cannibals filled my mind. It was a friendly reminder that some remote islands to the west of the Society Islands and the Cook Islands definitely have a different flavor than Bora Bora.

Igor's bright blue eyes accentuated his dark features, a blend of Burt Reynolds and John Travolta rolled into one. Being very confident and animated helped make him a fascinating story teller. His favorite stories were about sharks. He knew them all; the sharks you could swim with and the ones you didn't dare. Paul loved his stories, especially the one about how he had been chased out of the water by a tiger shark. Narrowly escaping from the snapping jaws of the beast, he scrambled up on a small clump of coral just barely above the water's surface. It scarcely accommodated him. The shark would not be denied however, and continually attacked the small coral islet itself, crunching and ripping big rocky chunks of it off in his powerful jaws. This went on for a quarter hour before *la tigre* finally gave up. Igor said they were absolutely the most terrifying moments of his life.

Paul in turn told Igor how there was a man hobbling around Vaitape with one leg and a crutch. Lauren had told Paul that it was the result of an attack by a shark in the Teavanui Pass into Bora Bora about ten years ago. I denied that such a story could likely be true, but Noel backed Paul up. Davey and I had been skin diving the day before in Teavanui Pass, and I realized that if we had had the knowledge yesterday that we had today we might not have been so adventuresome.

51.

"Beauty is its own excuse for being."
— Ralph Waldo Emerson

Davey and I had donned our masks and fins and went hand in hand for a swim through an underwater fantasia that special day. There we witnessed nature's complete improvisational talents. I'd left my goodie-bag behind and we agreed to go strictly sight-seeing for a change, toting a spear only for defense should the need arise. I was an experienced diver, having passed my scuba certification at the age of fourteen when I lived in Texas. I even still had the original galvanized tank, now twenty-three years old! It had so many hydro-tests stamped on it that it looked like a piece of art and I saved the tank now mostly for emergencies on *Querencia*, keeping it carefully stowed in the cockpit lazaret. Here in the astonishingly clear waters of Bora Bora a snorkeler could see for what seemed to be hundreds of feet in every direction. It was an absolute delight to just swim about unencumbered without any more equipment than a mask, snorkel, gloves, and fins.

Below the surface of the water was a composition of plant, fish, and coral creatures arranged in a rainbow of colored images beyond words. Swimming through the pass in the reef we were flanked by coral cliffs plunging down into deep water. Beautiful nooks and crannies provided homes for all manner of fish, many adorned with vivid "electric" pigment. We had become used to seeing the occasional and relatively shy sand shark, as well as moray eels and the venomous lionfish. We were, however, much more concerned with stonefish. One may lie motionless in shallow flats looking like a stone covered with debris. Put your hand or foot down on its dorsal spine and, similar to a snakebite, it unleashes a poison potent enough to kill a man. Everyone warned us of the stonefish. Luckily, they're for the most part rarely seen in Bora Bora despite their most assured existence there.

The sunlit coral garden was quite the haven for all forms of ocean life, and it was obvious that the great mysteries of this underwater wonderland held more living creatures numerically than any place on land I had ever been. Here the strange-looking octopus lived in his submarine cave. We found one venturing out in the open looking possibly for a Blue Spotted Reef Crab. Lucky for the octopus, today I would not pursue him as the predator I usually was. Davey, Paul, and I had brought our appetites for them from Puget Sound where they were quite a bit larger. There I had collected them using either scuba gear or the local fish market. While we were on Bora Bora we usually ate smaller octopus that we could gather diving once or twice a week. We were thankful for their bounty.

Huge schools of small silver fish swam this way and that as if they were dancing in a shimmering, emerald light. Now and then the fast and powerful jack tuna would rush by in a torpedo-like attack scattering a school like a shattered mirror. We saw two big, undulating reef sharks swim slowly in and out the pass, but they were shy and even the large shoals of needle fish seemed unimpressed. I was much more alarmed when I saw a flash of light zip up to me before making a screeching halt, turn quickly and disappear. It may have been a barracuda attracted to the metal on my wristwatch. But no matter, whatever it was it had made a hasty retreat once it had sized me up.

Davey squeezed my hand hard as we hung suspended just below the water's surface like Peter Pan and Mary Poppins, then she pointed suddenly with her free hand at two large manta rays swimming gracefully just twenty feet below us, their wing-like fins beating to a slow ancient rhythm. The manta rays were particularly abundant inside the lagoon and we had even seen one leaping six feet out of the water one morning. It was easy to understand how they had been tagged "devil-fish" by early sailors despite the now-known fact that the biggest thing they digest is plankton! The fins that look like horny protuberances actual roll down into two extensions of their gaping mouth when feeding.

Over the edge of the reef ledges moray eels were even more frequent, but for the most part they either retreated or eyed you without interest unless you provoked them. Interestingly enough, it seemed that the really big ones, the ones six feet long and armed with large sharp teeth, were less likely to be aggressive than the smaller, younger eels. Once in the lagoon, though, I had run into a large moray that absolutely refused to let me retrieve my spear after I missed a shot at a squirrel fish and the spear had stuck into the same coral head where the eel had his lair.

The squirrel fish, or *rouge* fish as the French called them, were relatively small red fish with big dark eyes. They hid in the shadows of coral heads during the daylight hours. They made for tasty safe eating, but we usually only collected them for food once a week because they were so bony and so much work to spear. I found myself getting metal rods at the hardware store in Vaitape and filing new spears to fit my spear gun almost on a weekly basis to replace the ones I bent or lost.

As we continued our swim we noticed a sea turtle lumbering along, surfacing every now and then to breathe, waving his flippers back and forth to propel himself through the water and moving his stubby, sharp beaked head from side to side. He caught a glimpse of us and was gone, expressing sheer fright! The turtle is still hunted in Bora Bora by the Tahitians, especially those living on the motus. As a matter of fact I was surprised one weekend when we went to Tiapai's for dinner. Tiapai was a very kind and gentle Tahitian about forty-five years of age. Unfortunately he spoke no English but spoke excellent French. He worked for the yacht club and owned his own motu near the airport end of the island. His family had befriended us much to our blessing. An avid fisherman, he was always giving us fresh tuna. As a small gift I had given him our crab trap that we still carried from our crustacean-harvesting days of the San Juans, hoping that he might find a way to use it for catching lobster on the reef. I was surprised and not too pleased to find he used it instead for a holding pen to keep captured turtles prior to eating them.

The tide was beginning to change in the pass and there was a fair amount of current going out to sea. Bucking a two-knot current is not something done with ease and I signaled to Davey that we should return to our raft before the return swim became a tough struggle. It was anchored inside the pass behind the motu Ahuna. As we swam back to the raft, all along the coral ledge and attached to the rocks were sea anemone and other polyps with their pretty fringed heads weaving in the constantly moving current, like flowers leaning in the wind. Pencil urchins and black urchins were scattered about in some secret order.

Before we untied the raft and headed back to *Querencia* we decided to collect *pāhua*, or giant clams, for dinner since they seemed abundant in the shallows beneath the raft. Indeed the pāhua were still a staple part of the diet for many who lived off the sea in Bora Bora. Also known as giant clams, or Tridacna, these large clams have been known to grow nearly four feet across and weigh over 500 pounds. Igor had told us a story about a free diver having to cut a finger off in order get free of one that had shut on his hand, nearly drowning him. Here in Bora Bora though, the average size was under a foot. Firmly anchored in the coral, they feed on algae and by filtering out plankton from sea water with their brilliantly colored mantles of blue, purple, yellow, and green. Locals taught us how to harvest them using a tire iron.

Paul and Davey and I went out many times to gather a gunnysack full of pāhua, which is what it would take to make a meal. It took a while before we learned how to pry them free without breaking the coral reef or the clam shell. Of course, as with most good tasting food, proper preparation is the key. Debi showed Davey how to include them in a special curry sauce that included the squeezed shredded white meat of a coconut for an excellent meal. Even today, these recipes along with Debi's Dijon vinaigrette salad dressing are still amongst our favorite. We found the meat of pāhua delicious, and

I'm confounded at the number of cruisers we've met that have never even tried them.

Maybe that's for the best. The sea, after all, has been able to balance itself and the life in it in a natural, normal way for a thousand million years without the need of man or a tire iron.

52.

I always enjoyed hiking and when I introduced Davey to it she liked it too. It was my Dad that had probably taught me hiking, although he didn't call it that. He didn't call it anything, it was just what you did when you walked in the country, usually from one fishing hole to the other. I grew up loving to scramble around outdoors and was always trying to find an excuse to go hiking. Of course the hiking had been spectacular in the Great Northwest. When I was in college I read Thoreau and was especially struck when he said something to the effect that a man doesn't even begin to think like a man until he has walked a couple of miles.

So it came to be that Davey and I wanted to get out and stretch our legs on O'temanu, that awesome *Close Encounters* type of rock that juts 2,379 feet high out of an island that is only six miles long and two and a half miles wide. From what we had surveyed of O'temanu in going around the island on a motor scooter, it appeared that the last quarter mile of it was unscalable, at least without technical equipment. Nevertheless, the big and tall Tahitian, *Taoto*, that we had talked to in Vaitape, had told us that you could get to the top, but only from one side.

"I have been up there many times!" he said to me when I had asked about O'temanu. He had caught up to us when we came out of the post-office one day, wanting to speak with us. He had noticed that we were Americans. He loved Americans and parties.

"Someday, maybe, I will take you to the top," Taoto had said.

He was a big, handsome Polynesian man. He was in his late twenties and nearly seven feet tall, towering above us as we spoke up to him. Atop his head he wore a crown of fragrant flowers and leaves, a *hei upo'o*, that partially blocked out the sun. He attracted a lot of attention, and many local people yelled their greetings to him.

"*My mother Bora Bora!*" Taoto had insisted to us, leaning heavily on my shoulder. He repeated himself a few times to me as if to make sure I understood. I assured him I understood, but it remained in my mind an odd thing to say. I had heard another Tahitian saying the same thing at a bar a few weeks earlier. That fellow had been quite drunk and sad and just kept repeating it over and over until finally somebody encouraged him to go home to his fare. He reminded me of a sad American Indian and it moved me, putting a lump in my throat.

Later that evening Metata said it was true that Taoto's mother *was* Bora Bora. His family's lineage *was* Bora Bora, and because of that Taoto held much prestige and honor in the Polynesian society, many considering him king of the lagoon, particularly Povai Bay. Metata said "maybe" though when we asked about the ease of getting up the mountain. He used to go up there and collect plants for medicinal purposes, but now-a-days there wasn't much need for him to go up the mountain because the plants had lost their powers. He said however that for the most part there was still much *tapu* about the mountain and people didn't do much on the mountain other than some people were trying to grow coffee high up on the slopes.

"How did the medicine plants lose their power?" I asked.

"Because of the balm." Metata seemed to answer.

I stared at Davey for an explanation or an interpretation but she had none. She returned a blank stare instead.

"Oh!" I said, turning back to Metata, not really understanding but pretending to, "You mean like today people have creams, or balms, for medicine?"

"What? No, no," Metata laughed. Then after a short pause to reflect he spoke seriously, emphasizing the English "b" consonant, "Not balm, but *bom-b!*" Indeed, he reminded me that the French nuclear testing that was active in the South Pacific was not appreciated by the plants, the fish, the Polynesian people, the medicine men, or the Earth.

"The bomb shakes the world and makes everything crazy," Metata elaborated.

He finished by saying if we wanted to go up the mountain for us just to go ahead and go up from a place along the road near his house. We could go up until we couldn't go any higher.

"*Aita pe'ape'a* (no problem)," he assured us, seeing a glint of worry in Davey's eyes.

We had gone up off the road where I figured we would find some sort of ridge line once we had gained a little elevation. Sure enough, we found the ridge and almost immediately came upon a couple of large guns located strategically, one pointed directly at the single pass through the barrier reef. The guns were left over from 1942 when the American military in World War II used Bora Bora as a fueling and staging area for ships and submarines.

The seven-inch guns were quite large, maybe twenty-two feet long, and were almost completely overgrown with jungle foliage. They seemed strange relics from the past, a testimony of Pearl Harbor in December 1941 and the subsequent rapid progress of the Japanese through the Philippines to Singapore. Bora Bora had become the necessary secret link through the South Pacific from the Panama Canal to Sydney. All other routes to Australia and New Zealand had been controlled by the Japanese. At one time there had been about 6,000 American servicemen on Bora Bora, yet, no enemy forces ever came to the island. Today the population rests at about 3,000 with most of the population being entirely Polynesian.

Higher up on the ridge we hiked into an area where the ridge itself became more defined and we took a short break. We could see both to the north and to the south from our vantage sight. We had left behind the coconut palms, pandanus, kapok, lime, and hibiscus, and tiare tahiti that grew along the lagoon. On the intermediate slopes to the north grew breadfruit, some mango, and great vistas of banana. The tops of Metata's papaya and grapefruit patches were visible, poking up from his yard. To the south we could look down through banyan, ironwood, and oleander onto the little village of Vaitape with its low-slung houses, spired church, little stores, and concrete dock. In the school playground far below children were playing Bora Bora's favorite sport of soccer in the green grass of the school yard. Dressed in their little colorful suits of mostly red and yellow they were running about like characters suddenly freed from an oil painting.

Farther up, perhaps an hour later, the ridge became steeper and steeper although it widened. Now the flora, mostly scrubby shrubs and ferns, were tall enough that they were well above our head. Still we went on, determined to reach the last pinnacle amidst the abundant volcanic debris and vegetation. The high mountainous interior had appeared more open and less overgrown from below; but having arrived, we instead found ourselves clawing our way through dense growth. It was hard going and we were dripping with sweat.

Eventually we came to the base of the last rock pinnacle. We were totally exhausted and stimulated at the same time. It was a magical place to be. We walked in the umbra along the whole west face of the pinnacle as best we could, the ferns damp and the rock wall face bleeding moisture here and there in eroded grottos. We both felt a manner of lonely presence, that, if you thought about it too much, made the hair on the back of your neck stand up, as if you could hear the distant hum of primordial people thinking. For the most part it was dark and eerie inside this canopy verdure and we couldn't help but feel fearful that we might stumble upon some sacred site of old, reserved for Polynesian gods or royal Tahitians. There were tiny caves and fractures in the rock face that suggested that one might be able to get higher without technical gear, but we chose instead to stop our vertical jungle pursuit and return to the day's full light. We climbed to a spot with a view we picked on the north edge of the face and sat there relaxing in the sunshine letting the trade breeze cool us down while we sipped water from a boda bag.

Far below us the cyan lagoon twinkled as if the sun's light was passing through a kaleidoscope. Around the periphery of the lagoon were numerous motus, or islands, that had grown from coconuts and debris that had washed onto the barrier reef over the centuries. The barrier reef, made of coral itself, was a great wall where waves from the azure blue of the South Pacific ocean crashed into it, making a white ring of surf around the entire island. Davey and I were impressed just thinking of the ancient Polynesian family that had settled here. The sound of their laughter seemed to rest on the sunbeams and it seemed to us that nothing could equal the serenity that they must have experienced during their lives on Bora Bora.

Below and away we could just make out *Querencia*. She looked a little like a toy from our perspective, but she wasn't. She was a tough little ship that had brought water warriors across thousands of miles of ocean prairie to climb a magic mountain in paradise.

53.

Several times I had asked Metata if the two of us could go fishing in his outrigger together. He said we could go out in his outrigger but he didn't know about my "fishing idea." We would need a motor to go outside the reef to get big fish now-a-days he said, unless I wanted to dive for lagoon fish.

"That would be fine with me," I said, eager to learn the edible lagoon fish and put some protein on the table.

Metata said, "Maybe, some day, I go with you."

I couldn't wait.

Several days later Metata rowed up to *Querencia* in his outrigger. He was ready to go stick some fish with me.

"You know how to paddle?" asked Metata.

"I think so Metata, but if I need to learn I would like you to teach me."

As we paddled across the turquoise lagoon with me in front and Metata in back, he hummed and sang Polynesian melodies. I turned around to talk to him.

It definitely was a relaxing day. Metata looked again like a little elf — the mischievous Metata. He had the old golfing cap with the brim turned up and he was wearing his favorite pair of beige shorts. His beard was stubbled and his eyelids blinked and his eyes twinkled as usual. He was taking big powerful strokes with his paddle that both moved the canoe forward and commanded our direction.

"But... " Metata blurted out, "you aren't paddling!"

"Oops! Sorry! Not paying attention!"

"Aita pe'ape'a".

I tried to pull us forward by leaning into my stroke with all my might in order to make up for sleeping on the job.

"But... " Metata started.

I looked back at him. He was smiling and had now quit rowing and was resting his paddle across the canoe.

I smiled.

He smiled even bigger, that great big Paul Newman smile of his, and then, at the precise moment that his eyes twinkled and his forehead formed a crease of concern, he spoke.

"I notice."

Or did he say "I know this," I wondered.

"I think maybe you try too hard. Don't care about that too much. But maybe you shouldn't fight my outrigger so much. Relax your shoulder, maybe. That's right. Mmmmmm. Mmmmmm."

Soon we were gliding across the lagoon as smoothly as an ice skater on Olympic ice. We passed Point Teahuatea and angled in towards the shore line of the motu on the south side of the pass.

"I think maybe here is good," Metata said. He took a large round rock out of the bottom of the canoe and tied a rope around it. He handed it to me to lower over the side in the shallow water as an anchor. We stowed our paddles, and I made a quick survey of the rest of the equipment for our expedition.

I had brought my jet fins, mask, a wet suit diving jacket, gloves and booties, my double arbalener five-foot spear gun, diving knife, and a goodie bag. Metata had nothing except a four-foot metal rod with one end sharpened to a point and a slingshot. Actually, it looked like a slingshot except that a one-inch steel nut had been meticulously tied with repeated wrappings [whipped] into the crotch of the "v." Metata demonstrated how he used it, passing the butt of the spear through the nut and pulling it back along with the surgical tubing, aiming at an imaginary fish. It was hard for me to see how he could spear anything with that homemade contraption.

"No wonder he's not too hot to go spear fishing," I thought to myself.

When we entered the water and stood up, waist-deep, I started to spit into my mask as I had always done before, to keep my face lens free from fogging.

"Why are you doing that?" Metata laughed, "I think maybe that's disgusting!"

I was wondering contentiously if he thought I should have

brought professional defogging liquid from a dive shop or some-thing! He motioned for me to follow him as he waded to the shore line to pluck a green leaf from a bush growing at the water's edge. "Use this instead," he said, demonstrating how to pinch the leaf and smear it around the glass on the inside of the face mask.

"This will keep your mask clear while you swim," said Metata.

"Really?" I wondered what kind of special plant it was.

"Sure. But it's not special." he said, reading my thoughts. "Any green plant that grows along the water's edge works just fine." He was already busy doing something else. He had selected a long palm reed and was busy attaching it around his waist.

To this day I have never spat in my mask again. I have always used a small green leaf or frond growing at the water's edge. It always works, just like Metata said it would!

Soon I was swimming around with my big professional spear gun focusing my attention on finding some fish. But there weren't very many, and my explorations were taking me further and further from the dugout where Metata was splashing around. He looked almost silly bent over with the white soles of his feet sticking out of the water periodically.

After thirty minutes I was really frustrated. I had swum over 200 yards in a widening circle away from the outrigger. I had only seen five fish close enough to spear. I had missed all of them in my anx-iousness and was frankly getting in a very sore mood with myself. Re-cocking the huge gun was getting to be monotonous and tiring. I was going to have to go back to the outrigger empty-handed. Fortunately, for my pride, I figured Metata was having similar luck. In the distance I could see him bobbing around in, what appeared to me, a half serious manner with the white soles of his naked feet still sticking now and then out of the water.

Swimming back over the little reef I suddenly came to a sandy spot that seemed to sink deep into the clear waters between brilliant coral heads. There on the bottom in about fifteen feet of water, par-tially sticking out of the white sand, were the largest mussels I had ever seen. Some nearly a foot in length, they were fairly well rooted in the sand. It took more than a little effort free diving to gather eight of them and stick them into my goodie bag. I was confident that Davey would save the day's catch with mussel chowder or some other creation.

By the time I got back to the canoe, Metata was already aboard sitting in the back seat singing one of his Tahitian melodies. In the bottom of the outrigger was the reed he had been wearing around his waist. It was completely strung with fish. To say that seeing the whole bottom full of fish was a surprise would be an understatement. I couldn't believe my eyes! I counted them — fifty-five fish! Unbelievable, and most of them were larger than the reef fish I had been chasing. How could he have done that? In less than an hour he had speared all those fish with the whittled crotch of a tree branch and a metal rod with a sharpened tip.

Metata was more interested in what I had in the bag and I was glad for that! I showed him the mussels. He said I had been very lucky because half of the mussels I had selected were hard to find. They were slightly rounder in shape than the others and when he carefully opened them with a knife it was easy to see why they were so special. Unlike the others, which were black on the inside, these were coated with Mother of Pearl. They just didn't look like Mother of Pearl, they were The Real McCoy!

"Imagine if we found a pearl!" I exclaimed.

"Now that would be something!" answered Metata with equal enthusiasm.

We pulled up our stone anchor and paddled back to *Querencia*. Davey couldn't believe her eyes when we came alongside.

54.

We had seen Metata standing on the weather station pier gazing towards the horizon one fair morning as we walked to Vaitape.

We stopped along the roadside by the concrete wharf and waved. We walked towards each other, meeting half way out the jetty, smiling at each other.

Suddenly I saw movement from the corner of my eye. We all saw it, although Metata seemed the least impressed. It was a very large octopus barely below the surface of the water. It was glistening from head to tip of tentacle, all shiny and undulating.

Of course I loved octopus and had learned to catch it whenever I could as it provided a good meal for my family. My first instinct was to capture it. My mind raced as I thought about how to handle the situation in front of Metata.

"'Aita pe'ape'a, John. Don't worry about the octopus. I think, maybe you think too much."

Metata's voice took command of the moment.

By that time we had all turned and we were standing there looking at this beautiful octopus in the morning light.

"The octopus will be there when you need him," Metata said casually. So casually, neither Davey or I gave it a second thought.

It must have been a month later and it was one of those Sundays when you just can't seem to get off your duff. We just laid there getting lazier and lazier. I remember when I was growing up the adults around me were always calling days like these the "dog days." I was thinking about that a lot, lying there, until I finally forced myself to get up and look up the meaning of "dog days" in the *Webster's Collegiate Dictionary* we had on board.

> **dog days** *n pl* [fr. their being reckoned from the heliacal rising of the Dog Star (Sirius)] (1538) 1: the period between early July and early September when the hot sultry weather of summer usually occurs in the northern hemisphere 2: a period of stagnation or inactivity.

Well, we weren't in the northern hemisphere but definition number two rang a bell! Polynesian paralysis had us again. We hadn't even bothered to row in to the yacht club.

Taking an expedition in the dictionary had been stimulating. Why not try and write some prose?

> The tropics, the craziness, the laziness, the sexiness, the mad longing delivered unto fullness of fulfillment, maxing out your dreams beneath the old volcano and wondering how long you can stand this heavy feeling called paradise, all friends, and family, and personal

history fading from your memory like invisible ink washed out by the sun.

After reading what I had just written, I called out to Davey and Paul, "I'm bored you guys," imploring them to toss me a cure.

"Dinner looks pretty bleak, too," Davey reminded me. It was late afternoon. We hadn't fished and the stores were always closed on Sunday. We were resigned to canned goods for our evening meal.

Paul was flat on his back alternating between reading a book and staring at the headliner. He was lost but I did manage to talk Davey into rowing the tender into the yacht club. From there we would take a walk along the shore and at least get some exercise.

We tied the dinghy to the wooden dock joining several other tenders. The dock had been busy all day with cruisers from French and German yachts. They were fishing with little bamboo poles. In the idle hours of the day back on *Querencia* I had spent several hours watching them through binoculars. They were catching tiny fish and putting them into plastic buckets. We stopped and chatted with them. They said they were catching the small fish with plans of using them for bait later that evening. They explained in broken English that with a little luck, they could catch something larger for dinner. We empathized with their predicament, then set off for our stroll.

We walked along the shore line and after about a block we came to the concrete meteorological dock. We jumped up on it and together were walking down the quay. There off to the side, much to our amazement, was the octopus that Metata had said would be there when we needed it. We had been on this same quay many times since that time with Metata and had never seen the octopus again. Actually we had not even thought about it. But, today, there he was. There was no hesitation this time.

Without fully sizing up the situation, I jumped off the dock, diving and grasping toward the octopus. He was below me in waist deep water and I grabbed him with my hands in each gill on either side of his mantle. I could see that he was larger than the average one- to three-foot octopus I was used to seeing in the lagoon, but I wasn't prepared to pull up a six-footer! I hadn't seen an octopus that large since Puget Sound.

I must say my sluggishness had totally evaporated. I was so fast that the octopus was on the dock in a second, all six feet and twenty pounds of him wrapping around me with the sticky grip of an Olympic wrestler. Its tentacles were lined with hundreds of sucking cups, each now trying to hold fast and control the intruder. I kept rolling his head away from me in an attempt to keep his parrot like beak, well concealed in its mouth which is buried between the trunks of his tentacles, off of my naked skin.

The octopus is actually a bivalve Cephalopod, a Mollusk along with the univalved Gastropods which make their lives in the ocean's seashells. Although usually timid, it is capable of using its well equipped venom apparatus that accompanies its beak to inflict a painful puncture wound in a human being. Although recovery is almost always guaranteed, I was to read later in a small caption on the back side of a pilot chart that there is a recorded fatality from the bite of an unknown variety in the South Pacific.

"Please grab the ends of those tentacles and pull them off of me," I blurted out, bringing Davey to action. With our bare hands, Davey continued peeling back the tips of the tentacles, releasing their grip on me while I constantly turned the octopus inside out. Eventually we had the octopus under control.

"Whew!" we chorused.

When we got back to the dock with our catch we had been gone less than ten minutes. As we clambered into our dinghy one of the French cruisers set his fishing pole down and said, "You Americans! You sure know how to go out and get dinner! Bon appetite!" I yelled back a thank-you as I started pulling us back towards *Querencia*.

Back onboard Paul sprang to life. And that was a good thing, because there is a lot of work involved in preparing octopus the way we like it best. Cleaning and pounding the tentacles were just the beginning. Then it was sliced and battered with egg, flour and oregano before being dropped into our favorite frying pan and cooked for twenty minutes over our gas-flamed stove.

That evening, just as we were cooking everything up, Tiapai came by in his fishing boat, speeding his way across the lagoon after having steered his way through Teavanui pass. He'd had a good day fishing and had come to share his catch with us, handing us two fresh

Bonito tuna.

"Māururu!" the three of us sang out. There was absolutely nothing better than fresh tuna, another favorite meal. We would not only eat well this day but for the next few days that followed.

We invited Tiapai to tie up along side *Querencia* and we had a little party. We were prepared to be the hosts this time! Davey passed Hinano beers to Tiapai and his two cousins. Happy all together, we ate octopus and repeatedly smiled at each other. Tiapai and his local buddies loved the octopus and indicated that they had never had it prepared that way before. The two boats bobbed around together bathed in colors; the clouds appearing like whorls crested with flame. All of us, including our Polynesian friends, were struck with the grandeur of the spectacle of sunset at Bora Bora.

The catch phrase would work. I turned to Davey and Paul and said, "This truly has been *just another day in paradise.*"

55.

One afternoon Tiapai brought his home made fishing boat alongside *Querencia* to ask me to join them in a fishing expedition outside the reef. Another Tahitian whose name might have been Peu was aboard, along with Noel, and they all encouraged me to jump aboard and go deep sea fishing. I needed little encouragement. Davey had gone to Vaitape and I had remained aboard, idly tackling odd jobs. The trade winds had been light and the temperature as high as ever. *Querencia* lay motionless in the lagoon and the rays of the sun seemed to penetrate through the shelter of the cockpit awning, where I had literally sat gasping in the heat during my extended breaks.

"Far-out!" I grabbed my baseball hat and sun glasses and quickly jumped aboard.

I wished Tiapai spoke English beyond the few words Davey and I taught him in exchange for his Tahitian tutoring. As the number one worker at the yacht club he was strong and dedicated to his every task whether he was doing carpentry, or free-diving to hand-set an anchor, or driving the jet boat to the airport to pick up tourists. He was an incredibly hard worker, as was his wife Tupea, who also worked at the yacht club doing yard work, cleaning, or weaving pandanus for the roofs or special decoration. She was shy and giggled at the slightest embarrassment. They came to the yacht club every day except for Wednesdays and Sundays. They always brought their grandchildren with them to work. Their own children had moved to Papeete in hopes of making more money at less traditional work. This was fairly common for most families in the outer islands. The young adults left and only returned to their parents' island for the holidays. Everyday it seemed harder for younger generation islanders to cling to their ancient way of life. Each new generation seemed more likely to leave for the big city, submitting to a rigid timetable, routine, and supervision in the hustle and bustle of an encroaching modern world.

This stirred me up inside and I found myself often feeling angry about these beautiful islanders having to succumb to the pressures of making a living from a thing called "money", especially when I saw how hard they had to work to make money and how expensive things were. Once I had argued with Noel about the abusive pay scale the French offered Tahitians and he had reminded me that each true Polynesian receives a subsidy check from the government as well. Nevertheless, such subsidies, which probably do keep the Tahitians distracted from the nuclear fallout and sated in their desire for national independence, fall short of the freedom that once must have filled their lives.

But today, Wednesday, was not a day to analyze and solve. Not for Tiapai or for me. Today was a day to go fishing. Four men of three nationalities would accept what pleases and ignore the rest.

I had been eager to take a closer look at Tiapai's boat. He was very proud of it and it provided him with not only recreation but a very real way to provide for his extended family. He had built it himself entirely out of wood and it was of a specific design I have only seen in Polynesia. It looked similar to a typical speedboat except that the forward deck was cut out in the shape of a box just large enough for Tiapai to climb down into and stand up. From here he steered the boat with a joy-stick type of device. To this long stick that came up from the bottom of the boat to his shoulders, cables were attached that were guided aft through pulleys to the outboards. Tiapai just had to lean the stick left or right for steerage. Mounted on the side of this "pilot box" he was standing in was a typical throttle arrangement. The cockpit was entirely empty except for fishing gear; mostly a couple of dozen empty water jugs with line spooled around them, each line ending with a plastic squid lure equipped with a double barbed stainless steel hook. There was a gaff, and then most curious of all to me, a long spear or trident harpoon that extended the length of the twenty foot boat, situated in a crutch ready for quick use.

The overall design of the boat and rig was ingenious. No wonder Tiapai couldn't wait to go fishing! At near full throttle the pilot had a smooth ride on the nose of the boat, almost flying, completely out of the water. From here he could stare down into the clear waves over which he rode and seeing a mahimahi spear it with his harpoon. The boat was obviously incredibly fast as well.

Peu sat aft and Noel and I stood behind Tiapai's box. Then Tiapai hit the throttle. The bow picked up and the force of acceleration nearly knocked me off my feet.

"Can you find your center?" Noel asked with a laugh, demonstrating how it was necessary for one to bend their knees and balance as we skipped over the waves.

"I'd settle for a hand rail, Noel!" I yelled, competing with the noisy, monstrous twin outboards.

In a matter of seconds we were out the pass like a bat from a cave. Out on the deep blue waters. Riding the waves in this unusual boat I may have made an odd picture, clutching as best I could to a small piece of wooden molding, flexing my thighs and keeping my knees bent to prevent them from buckling as we crashed between waves, but Tiapai was in his element. He reminded me of a Polynesian version of Ben Hur racing along in a Roman chariot. Up and down the waves we went with the nose of the boat pointed high, the trusty craft charging along. There was Tiapai with the joystick in his hand, turning the rudder left and then right, steering up one wave and down the next. The throttle lever was mostly left unattended and full forward! Noel and Peu and I clutched as best we could the aft portion of the boat as it crashed between swells. Up and down, forward, port and starboard we went. I wasn't sure exactly where we were going but I was excited. Tiapai's hair was jet black and wavy, his handsome features square and his body fit and brown. He could see no birds on the horizon and they were his indicators for fish. Anxiously he scanned the horizon as we zipped along for the first half-hour, complaining in rapid Tahitian to Peu and in French to Noel that there were no mahimahi to be found. White tropical birds flew above mahi mahi. Without such an indicator, this type of fishing where you chase fish was nearly impossible.

Then finally and quite suddenly Tiapai was steering fantastic figure eights and the rest of us could barely hang on. Through the excitement Noel informed me that Tiapai saw a sailfish and we were chasing it! Peu was helping free up the aft end of the *pātia*, or harpoon. For a split second I too thought I might have seen a glimmer of silver and blue on the side of a wave, but then—nothing. Tiapai suddenly let out a big sigh and pulled the throttle all the way back and shrugged his shoulders.

Tiapai

"Ai yi yi yi yi!" he whooped. The huge sailfish had suddenly disappeared, no longer to be found by Tiapai's piercing eyes.

"Really?" I asked after Noel had translated for me. "Wow."

No sooner had we gotten underway again when Tiapai slowed the boat down again, this time near an apparently lonely piece of drifting wood.

"Tiapai sees a Sea Bass there underneath that piece of wood," Noel once again translated.

"He does?" I asked rather incredulously. I was as fascinated with this type of fishing as I was with Tiapai's excellent eyesight!

Tiapai lifted the long harpoon up from its chocks and then balanced it high above his head. He arched his back into a big bow and then released the *pātia* with all his force, it's sharp points disappearing below the water's surface near the log. Then by pulling on the lanyard it was tethered to, he recovered the end of the spear, grasped it with both hands, and flipped a big fish into the back of the boat.

"*Tano!* [well done]" I exclaimed.

I couldn't believe it. There gasping as it flapped around was this large-mouthed grouper-type fish, reddish brown with dusky bars on each side and a large spiny dorsal fin. It easily weighed twenty pounds. Peu quickly pulled it off the lance and whacked it to silence before throwing it into the iced box.

It was better than nothing but it was not the catch that satisfied. Tiapai slowly motored off again scanning the horizon in frustration. "*I hea manu? I hea manu?* [where are the birds?]" he repeated.

Unexpectedly Tiapai hit the throttle again, pointing at the horizon excitedly saying, "*Manu! 'Auhopu!* [Birds! Tuna!]"

I could see no birds and neither could Noel. After more than five minutes of racing towards the horizon I still couldn't see any birds.

"'*Ua 'ite au ia ratou!* [I saw them!]" Peu suddenly exclaimed.

"Up until now I've always thought I had excellent eyes," I screamed at Noel over the engines. He laughed.

"Yes. Aren't these Tahitian's eyes, especially Tiapai's, amazing?"

After a few more moments I was just starting to see birds on the horizon, brown dots diving and dashing this way and that. In few more minutes we were amongst them and Tiapai cut the throttle, turned around in his pilot box, and ordered us to quickly get the lines out.

"'*Oi'oi, vitiviti! Vitiviti!*"

Peu, Noel, and I tossed the lures over the transom and unraveled the spooled monofilaments from the plastic water bottles. In seconds we had at least three tuna on; we pulled them aboard hand over hand. I wished I had worn gloves, the line nearly cutting through my skin. We all just kept pulling the fish in and flipping the lures out and pulling in more fish, helping each other as much as we could.

Tiapai was laughing not so softly, and I knew he was laughing with us more than at us, although the sight of three men slipping around in a cockpit full of flapping fish must have been a pretty hilarious sight. I was trying not to lose a fish still hooked on a bottle held under one arm while holding down another fish with my left knee and pulling in the line with both hands. In just a minute or so we had eight tuna on the boat and the birds were gone. Tiapai motioned for us to bring all the lines in.

"Tano! Bien!" he yelled out, then hit the throttle full forward again. We were racing off, bouncing around with the fish, trying to straighten out all the lines. We weren't very organized when suddenly we were amidst birds and fast moving tuna once again and Tiapai repeated his command to get the lines out. Now I knew why there were so many hand lines aboard. In just another couple of minutes we had ten more tuna aboard and a slightly bigger tangle of fish and monofilament.

This went on for another hour before Tiapai suggested we quit and head back for the pass. I had been so busy that for the first time I looked back at Bora Bora. We had gone quite a distance from the island in a relatively short time and only the mountain of O'temanu stuck up above the horizon. The sun was starting to fall rather quickly from the lofty sky. I counted twenty-seven tuna, mostly bonito (Skipjack or aku) in the back of the boat. I sat down along with Peu and Noel and started in the long but satisfying process of restoring order to Tiapai's fishing boat.

In a short period of time we were racing back in through the single pass of Bora Bora again and as we planed over the smooth water of the lagoon toward *Querencia* I felt what Tiapai must always feel when he comes back from such fishing expeditions — fired with success as a victorious provider.

Tiapai pulled up alongside *Querencia* to let me off before dropping Noel off at his floating fare and then zipping off to his own family motu a couple of miles away at the northeast end of the reef. Davey was back from town and her eyes were as big as silver dollars. Her face reflected the thrill that was still in mine.

"Now that was a fishing trip I won't soon forget!" I told her.

56.

That following Sunday Tiapai invited all of us, Debi, Noel, Paul and Davey and me to join his family, some of which had arrived from Tahiti, in a large feast, or *tāmā'ara'a*, on his family property on Motu Ha'apititi. Paul elected to go shell diving with Lauren instead on the other side of the island and Noel would catch up with us later, after he delivered some guests by jet boat to Motu Mute where the airstrip was located.

Davey and Debi and I put two cases of Hinano beer and ourselves into our twelve-foot sailing dinghy. It was ten o'clock in the morning when we left the yacht club. Despite our load the main and forward sail, driven by the trade winds, pulled us briskly across the lagoon. We had grown to really love our Metzler sailing dinghy, complete with roller furling and leeboards; it had really been "the ticket" for us on Bora Bora.

Motu Ahuna and the large motu Teviriroa soon passed to port and we threaded our way through narrow channels of coral and sand hollowed by surge flooding over the reef. We continued our northeast course for forty-five minutes, finally able to ease the sails and go downwind towards the reef, coming to a sandy point on Tiapai's family's motu. Tupea and a friend were busy collecting black sea urchins for their eggs. They stopped and sang out a friendly "Ia ora na" greeting to us. We unloaded the dinghy in the shallows and then pulled it up onto the white sand beach of Motu Ha'apititi.

The motu was about the size of a football field and you could hear the surf beating on its other side where the reef lay. In the middle of the motu was the living area which was composed of several structures — one a bath house, very clean with large showers, another a cooking building where all the food was prepared; a third was just a large family room complete with VCR. I presumed the other building to be sleeping quarters or workshops. Electricity, when needed, came from a generator a few hundred feet away. It was easy to see that Tiapai was very pleased with his accomplishments. He had built most all the structures out of concrete with guide wires anchoring the major beams to the ground. The *vero* or cyclones of recent years had impressed upon him the need to build strong foundations. There had been quite a bit of damage in the previous years. Today however, with the exception of a few up-rooted trees, things were in order, even the sand on the paths, and the natural open gathering areas had been carefully swept with reed brooms and rakes. Amidst the shadows cast by the palm fronds patterns ran hiding from the spirit of Mt. O'temanu and the tourist.

Tupea's handicraft was everywhere — the handwoven bowls she had weaved with reva [leaves] sitting in her kitchen, the plaited leaf-mats, and the pandanus thatched roofs atop the fares. She explained to us through Debi that all the leaves were in their natural color, the dark brown being male leaves and the lighter or white leaves being female leaves. For baskets it was necessary that the *reva* be cut green, boiled, and then dried in the sun for a period of three months, or until they dried. Then they were stripped, and woven. This took a period of weeks.

Davey had *that look* in her eyes as we peeked at each other to acknowledge the translation. We both knew that this time consuming skill known as weaving was becoming a lost art form in many parts of Polynesia. We would sadly find it even more so in Hawai'i.

I joined Tiapai and his son-in-law at the side of the cook-fire pit along with Noel who had just arrived. Davey and the other women disappeared down one of the many paths leading to the reef, Tupea leading. I remembered a saying that the real music of the islands is the "giggling of the girls" and chuckled to myself. They had time. For the moment, their work was done. Metata had told us of the respected traditional division of labor between men and women *[tane* and *vahine]* in this culture. Women tended the plots, collected coconuts from the earth, collected mussels and urchins from around the motu, gathered wood, and prepared and served the food after the men had cooked it. They also cared for the animals that were slaughtered for food and wove bark and leaves to provide fabric not purchased.

One of Tiapai and Tupea's daughters, probably in her twenties, remained behind when the rest of the women walked to the reef, almost as if she was shy or "hiding" in the centrally located fare dedicated to meal preparation. There she stood, her silhouette entrancing, quietly preparing fruits and *fei*, the wild pink bananas. I couldn't help but notice that she was very pretty and very pregnant. She lived in Papeete with her French husband; she returned to the motu only to bear her children. Once they were weaned she left them behind with Tiapai and Tupea and the other grandchildren, letting their Polynesian souls cling to their ancient way of life for a short time more. This was certainly a different culture.

Tiapai's daughter

In a few hours Tiapai judged the food in the earth oven, or *hima'a (imu* in Hawaiian), to be done and he shuffled things about, removing the food that had been cooked in large leaves trapping all the natural smoky flavors. His timing was terrific; there had been just enough time for the men to enjoy a few Hinanos and talk of fishing, birds, weather, tools, and politics.

Then we all, men, women, and children, sat down together at picnic tables. Out came suckling pig, mahi mahi, chicken, breadfruit (*'uru*), Tahitian spinach (*fafa*), taro, and yams, much to the exclamation of everyone. Also on the table were popular imported canned goods and imported table wine, despite their expense. Eating and happiness were the essence of this traditional Sunday feast.

"*Tē tāmā'a nei te vahine!*" Tiapai kidded Tupea, noticing that she was enjoying her food as much as he was.

After dinner Tupea lit a few coconut husks so they smoldered just enough to keep the bugs away and we talked until after the stars came out. Then Tiapai and Tupea took Noel and Debi and Davey and me back to the yacht club in their fishing boat, towing our sailing dinghy behind, a waxing moon rising behind the magic mountain.

Back at Noel and Debi's floating fare Davey and I untied our raft to sail for *Querencia* less than 100 yards away.

Almost as if to reward us, Tiapai said unexpectedly in perfect english, "Good night, John. Good night, Davey." Having never heard him speak any English before, we were stunned. It was crystal clear and like a melody.

"*Toto mete* [sweet dreams]," Tupea giggled.

"*Na na* [good night]," Davey answered for both of us. "*Māururu roa!* [Thank-you very much]." Her smile was big and responsive. I felt a special kind of warmth from head to foot.

57.

Today was to be the day that we sailed to Raiatea, about twenty-five miles to the southwest of Bora Bora. We would have been happy to continue our "experiment" in paradise without ever leaving Bora Bora. We were in no hurry to chase anything that we did or didn't already have. We were here to "get into it," and resolved with that attitude we had long stopped the common human activity of trying to find something better. We loved Bora Bora and spent all of our time there. In contrast, the majority of cruisers sailed directly to Papeete where they spent most of their time and money quickly trapped by civilization once again. Then they hurriedly tried to visit the other Tahitian islands, finally stopping only at Bora Bora for a couple of days before heading on to the North Pacific. At this point some were anxious enough about their next ocean crossing that they complained to Davey and me that they found Bora Bora boring!

"Striving to better, oft we mar what's well."
— W. Shakespeare

"Half our life is spent trying to find something to do with the time we've rushed through life trying to save."
— Will Rogers

"There is more to life than increasing its speed."
— Orin L. Crane

"There are two things to aim at in life: first, to get what you want, and after that to enjoy it. Only the wisest of mankind achieve the second."   — L. P. Smith

"Happiness is not having what you want but wanting what you have."   — Anonymous

But there was a need to go to a larger port of call. The time was nearing when our visas would expire and a return trip to Hawai'i would become an inevitability. Major provisioning for the passage was necessary. The town of Utaroa on the island of Raiatea sounded perfect. It was a fairly large town with a variety of stores somewhat comparable to Papeete. Also there was the South Pacific Yacht Charters (SPYC), a French outfit that operated nearby. The manager, Pierre, had assured me that we could probably find a place to tie *Querencia* up in a small boat basin that was about a mile or so from Utaroa. There we would be able to refill our propane tanks, top off my scuba tank, and accomplish boat maintenance somewhat easier than anchored off Bora Bora.

Our early morning departure, however, was delayed. Just at daylight I was awakened by what sounded like water boiling all around the hull. I came up on deck and found that the immediate area in the lagoon all about us was literally packed with small *Papio*, or little Pompano [*Carangidae*]. It wasn't the first time, and we were prepared. The three of us pulled out our bamboo poles and each of us tied on a fishing line and a hook. On the hooks we had tied small white feathers we found along the road. On this morning; however, we discovered that even bare hooks would work. These little fish bit at everything and soon I was cleaning six of them for breakfast! They were delicious and reminded us somewhat of trout in size, taste, and texture.

Other cruising boats in the bay were up and busy collecting their share of this abundant natural resource, with the exception of the yacht, *Irma*, from Stockholm. Aboard were Hanar and Usa and they seemed to be quite comfortable in their cockpit doing nothing else but watching the activity. Hanar rowed over in his dinghy a while later when he saw us unbagging the sails. It was then that I found out why they hadn't joined the other cruisers in fishing the bounty. A huge Jack, madly charging through a school of Pompano, had jumped and landed right into their dinghy attached by its painter to the stern of their boat. Hanar said he had heard all this racket just before sunrise and when he went up on deck he had been shocked to see this huge fish just flapping around in their hard dinghy. Hanar jumped in the dingy and whacked it a couple of times and there it was; ten kilos of excellent fresh food. He passed us a couple of fish steaks for which we were very grateful, along with some cassette tapes to play during our planned week away from "home."

We departed out the Pass Teavanui from Bora Bora with a fresh breeze building and *Querencia* responded beautifully. She impressed us with her speed, taking off like a jack rabbit once we got into the channel between Bora Bora and the islands of Raiatea and Taha'a. Raiatea and Taha'a showed themselves in the distance, two inactive craters of seamounts that broke the surface of the Pacific to form a joined pair of islands lying within the same hourglass-shaped, coral-fringed reef. It was blowing a good twenty knots and under the cheerful sun the sailing turned out to be absolutely terrific. Waves washed the deck now and then as we dipped the starboard rail in the water charging across the channel. Within three hours we were cautiously going along Taha'a's reef.

We found the Pass Rautoanui on Raiatea's West side and easily slipped inside the barrier reef. There we motored up the inside passage until we rounded Point Farepoe where we could then see the small concrete basin located at the end of a small bay. It looked awfully crowded, almost as if boats were stacked on top of each other! But the anchorage, our only other alternative, was very deep (over a hundred feet deep) so we started up the engine and motored into the 'marina', hoping to find a place to tie off.

The wind had picked up and the sky quite unexpectedly was graying over. The concrete basin was only about a hundred square yards in size and as soon as we cleared the entrance our throttle linkage broke. The engine suddenly revved up as I slipped the gear into neutral.

"Oh my God! What's wrong?" Davey asked rather incredulously.

Paul joined her with a blank stare on his face.

I hated situations like this.

"Throttle linkage just broke. Hold on while I slow her down," I answered.

I briefly put the gear lever into reverse until *Querencia* finally came to a near stop in the middle of the basin. People were coming out of their boats and joined others gathering along the quay looking at us. Some were shouting varying forms of advice. Some shook their heads as if we didn't know what we were doing.

"Pay attention you guys. We can take care of this problem ourselves. Don't let the crowd distract you," I advised Paul and Davey. Davey took over the wheel while I scrambled below decks and popped off the engine cover and adjusted the engine throttle linkage manually until it idled. Then I scrambled back on deck.

"Hey, John! Maybe we can get in *there!*" Paul called from the pulpit, pointing to a narrow little slot at the end of the row of boats.

He was right, there was just enough space at the innermost corner of the basin, although we would have to drop a hook off our stern and run a rather weird arrangement of lines off our bow to warp into place if we got lucky enough to get *Querencia* anywhere near position.

"How deep is it there?" I asked the crowd on the quay, pointing to the chosen corner.

At first it seemed that no one understood English, and then a voice rang out, "Must be about six or seven feet."

"Nothing like an American accent at times," I said to myself as I proceeded to maneuver *Querencia* into place by intermittently slipping in and out of gear. Finally in place, Paul jumped ashore to secure a bow line and I winched our stern out hauling-in on the rode from the anchor we had dropped on the way in. We turned off the engine and said hello to the American from Arizona while thanking the others. Davey was fending us off from the cleatless concrete quay on our starboard side. I could see she was scratching her head as to how we were going to tie things off a little better.

Now, quite suddenly, most everyone's attention was turning away from *Querencia* to an unusual black cloud approaching from the southeast. It was weird! It was the type of cloud you'd expect to see in Kansas or in the *Wizard of Oz*, a windstorm with waterspouts. Well aware of the powerful storms that can form over tropical waters and the destructive effects that can come from the whirling winds near their vortex, my interest moved from concern to alarm. In the distance you could see a few sailboats ahead of this diabolic cloud; they were on their sides from the wind before being swallowed up and disappearing. I guessed we had ten minutes at the most before it reached us.

"We're going to have to hustle and get some lines out if we're going to keep *Querencia* off this concrete wall!" Davey pleaded. With the engine throttle broken we weren't going anywhere else.

I quickly jumped into the water with my fins and Paul passed me the ends of two 200-foot lines which I rigged with some purchase across the basin, thanks to the help of a friendly Tahitian. It was just in time. The squall hit and it was blowing fifty mph with near zero visibility before we knew it. We were bouncing on the mud bottom and against the bumpers between us and the quay on the starboard side, but we were okay. Everything that we couldn't tie down we threw below, including ourselves. Peering out the portholes we watched the wind rattle the rigging of all the boats around us like wind chimes. The air was full of debris flying every which direction and some tarps were shredding like lettuce. Then after about thirty minutes, just as suddenly as it had begun, it ended. How strange it was and how glad I was that we weren't caught in the channel between islands when it hit. Later in the day the news reported it as an unseasonal and unusual cyclonic storm that caused minor damage ashore and necessitated the rescue of four boats in the vicinity.

Raiatea was very obliging to our needs. By law we were required to check in at any island we visited and we were disappointed that the gendarmes weren't anywhere as friendly as the gendarmes on Bora Bora. But the people were, despite the fact that their lives were obviously a bit more hectic and business oriented. There were many more stores and hotels and other services, and competition came between people. Still, it was a far cry from the hustle and bustle of Papeete, and we enjoyed the compromise.

Provisioning was easy, with the exception of transporting the goods back to the boat basin which was about five miles from the town of Utaroa. We found everything we needed in the grocery stores, marketplaces, and drug stores. We appreciated the no-questions-asked recognition that was given our checks drawn on a U.S. bank. For a return address, the checks simply had the name of our sailing vessel and the country we hailed from, in the upper left.

Yacht Querencia
United States of America

These checks worked as well at the banks in the Society Islands as they had in the San Juans, Canada, California, or the Marquesas. No problem! We found humor in this, since typically when one would write a check on the mainland, pre-stamped with an abundance of identification and references, including social security number and home-phone, the clerk would always need just one more piece of information. Despite any effort to show responsibility ahead of time by filling all blank space on your checks with long descriptions of fulfilled financial obligation, one nevertheless grew to expect merchants to still ask the name of your first born child. This was not the case with our "Yacht Querencia" checks and I have no explanation why.

Walking about town we were quite surprised to see everywhere posters of the mushroom cloud of an atomic bomb, along with a variety of popular anti-nuclear protest slogans. There definitely was an independent movement here amongst the Tahitians against the constant nuclear testing on the atoll of Mururoa. This protest carried over to further protest against being an autonomous French possession. Maybe *that's* what made the gendarmes uptight; the fact that these beautiful and fabled independent islands, originally blessed with tremendous and incomparable resources, were now destabilizing socially, economically and politically as a French territory. With the ways of old having fallen behind, the remaining Tahitians were searching for a new identity and a new way to develop it. They are not a French or European people.

Pierre at the SPYC recharged my scuba tank for me and refilled our propane tank, too, one of our major concerns. There was no suitable connector to go directly from his large French tank to our American tank (metrics vs. inches) but he knew how to work around that. He took a full 100-liter bottle and hung it in a tree over our little five gallon tank and then proceeded to hook the smaller to the larger using a garden hose and hose clamps. Then by opening both tank valves and letting gravity do its thing he was able to fill our tank mostly full!

"C'est bon!" piped Pierre as he twisted the valves close.

"Hey, that was pretty slick," I acknowledged.

After fixing the throttle linkage and filling the propane tank, my only other major concern was changing the zinc plates on the hull in front of the rudder. This periodic chore is critical to prevent electrolysis and failure of metal hinges, like the ones that hold on the rudder! We had gone through all of our pre-cut and pre-drilled zinc plates and now I needed to find a drill press and make some newly prepared plates from a large zinc slab stored in the bilge. Once again Pierre came to the rescue and took me up to the vocational school in Utaroa. The chore of cutting and drilling new zincs ready to screw on to the hull was accomplished in a matter of moments and I had the pleasure of meeting some very nice young Polynesian students in the process. I was impressed with how seriously they took their studies and how helpful the school was to a foreigner.

Finally, our days on foot scouring the stores and open air mar-
kets of Utaroa for provisions and local treasure were over. The five
miles between town and the yacht basin, our back-packs stuffed and
our aching arms full of heavy packages, had become a bit of
drudgery. We would file our sailing plans with the gendarme, untie
from the yacht basin, and sail back to the tiny crown jewel of Bora
Bora.

There had been many fine moments on Raiatea — the cool
afternoon we spent sitting at the Bali Hai Hotel sipping seductive
Mai Tais while pretending to be your garden variety tourists, and the
evening we had spent aboard one of the charter boats with some
wonderful people from Southern California. We gazed over the
waterfront with sleepy eyes, smelling frangipani, ginger, tuberose,
and tiare blossoms. We had made new acquaintances: American,
French, and Tahitian. We had also continued our pledge to make
friends with flowers and whistle back at birds. We continued to
escape any habit that deprived us of our freedom to choose.

58.

We are sailing stormy waters
Oh my Lord, to be near you
To be free...
— *Sailing*
Gavin Sutherland
Rod Stewart

When we slipped back through the pass into the lagoon of Bora
Bora we were surprised to see that the Bora Bora Yacht Club had five
more sailing vessels about it than when we had left; two red German
hulls complete with youngsters, one American vessel from
Baltimore, Maryland, with Jim and Sara Parker on board (they left
almost immediately for the Cook Islands), one homemade and stout
steel-hulled vessel hailing from Capestown, South Africa with Don
and Jenny on board, and a beautiful fifty-foot wooden ketch bearing

the name *Astral Rose* and flying New Zealand colors. Anchorages on the other side of Pahua point where the *Oa Oa Hotel* [Happy Hotel] and the Club Méditerranée were located were also filling up. A large white 85-foot power boat *Woyaya*, hailing from Newport Beach, California also caught our eye.

"Boats are on the move, man. Must be check-out time in paradise," observed Paul.

We anchored near the B.B.Y.C. and jumped in for a swim. It was great to be back and we were in the mood to meet some of the new boats. So when *Astral Rose* waved us over and asked "us Yanks" aboard for a Kiwi beer we didn't think twice.

We climbed up the boarding ladder and stood on deck gawking a bit. *Astral Rose* was beautiful from stem to stern; her teak, her bright work, even her lines. We turned to meet Tony, his wife Marge, and another couple. They were all in their late thirties and bore big friendly smiles.

"You folks up from down under?" I asked. "We always enjoy meeting people from your part of the world."

"Well, we Kiwis like Yanks too, we do!" Tony asserted. He had sandy blond hair and weathered skin. A blue sailing cap rode on the top of his head perfectly. He was a man's man. I liked that.

"Excepting of course when Yanks mistake us for Aussies," clarified Robert. Robert and his wife had flown in to rendezvous with Tony and Marge.

"Oh, *deah* God, whose taking us for Aussies?" added Marge.

"Not me!" Davey, Paul, and I all said at the same time.

"And it doesn't matter anyway, does it? We're all the same in the end," said Marge.

Marge's girl friend, dark-haired and a bit more shy, shook her head. "Oh, Marge, you can't quite say that. The Aussies are most definitely a bit more crude and common."

"Well, anyway, as I was close to saying," Tony interjected, "There are more similarities between Kiwis and Yanks than Kiwis and Aussies, right? Now I'm right about that, aren't I, Marge, sweetheart?"

"Actually, it is quite true my dear hubbie!" She jumped across the deck and gave Tony a big hug and a kiss. She was ever so slightly plump in her two-piece, but attractive and happy, with a big beamy smile that spanned her face. She struck me as an honest, happy gal that could make a man jubilant or strike him with a rolling pin.

I stood there, chuckling to myself, and listening to this adventure in discourse. I wondered about people. Do we identify with our true self or with the demands of others in our social structures. Or maybe even more confusing, do we identify with the demands put on us by our own self images?

"Seems to me you're ready for another beer, bloke! Care for a tour of the *Rose?*" Tony wasn't going to let me think too long about anything.

The tour showed the boat to be even more wonderful below decks. She was twice as spacious as you would expect and laid out with exquisite attention to function and detail. The diesel engine was positioned between the aft cabin and a companion way that led to the forward salon. It was a real engine room. You could stand-up and actually walk all the way around the engine, which was clean as a whistle.

Tony saw my eyes sparkling. "She's a dream to maintain and work on, John, you can be sure of that."

We wound up spending the rest of the afternoon with our new friends. Tony had been sailing for a long time. Equipped with his experience and skippers license he delivered yachts now and then to various destinations in the Pacific through his boating business in Auckland. Before he had settled down with Marge he had sailed a trimaran fairly regularly up from New Zealand to Fiji, where as a young man he found he could support himself porting bananas and coconuts between ports.

On one passage in which he was single-handedly sailing a particularly top-heavy cargo, he was suddenly grabbed by a storm that turned his trimaran turtle in the middle of the black of night. By sunrise he was in his life raft with five cans of tomatoes and a jug of water, the trimaran long gone to Davey Jones' Locker. On the second day he went to open the tomatoes but noticed that the cans were distended and decided to not eat them. By the fifth day he was nearly starved and barely holding on and thinking about eating the tomatoes anyway, when, as luck had it, a ship saw him and picked him up.

More than hungry, haggard, and dehydrated he had been found. He shared with us this story and his belief that it was totally miraculous that he had made it through the ordeal. The physicians that examined him with quite a bit of curiosity informed him that the tomatoes had been indeed contaminated. Had he eaten them he would have died a certain and horrible death from botulism.

"Seems to me you're ready for another beer, bloke! We can follow our beers with cocktails at the yacht club. We'll pick up our hook and dock the *Rose* over there, we will. Looks all right to me."

"Probably, Tony, but it's not much of a dock, and you'll have to put your beam off the end of the dock and then lead both bow and stern lines amidships to tie them off pilings." I knew it wouldn't set well with Noel to have a large boat blocking traffic at the dock. I was already thinking about how Noel was sore at me for not taking him with us to Raiatea, even though the thought had never even crossed my mind. Like many European men I had met, and unlike most American cowboy types (and even more so with Australians, Canadians, and New Zealanders), he didn't always speak his mind. I found it necessary at times to guess what he might be thinking.

"Well, we'll have a go of it anyway. She'll be right, mate, and I can fill her water tanks in a sensible manner," were Tony's thoughts. After starting the engine we went up on the bow where he stepped on the rubber foot switch of the hydraulic winch. Up came the anchor. Now that was nifty. We were underway and tied off at the yacht club in a few short moments. It seemed like everyone at the bar was staring. The *Astral Rose* drew compliments like bees to honey.

"Mai tais, all around!" Tony proclaimed. It was quickly seconded by Marge and their guests. Then Davey and I cheered in a third motion.

"Oh, my God," I heard Paul mumble to himself.

Tony adjusted the cockpit speakers and then went below to fiddle a bit with the tape deck.

The sun set, throwing extra complexion into our evening drinks and our faces. Then the tape deck kicked into gear. On came Rod Stewart's *Maggie May* album. Rarely did music sound this good.

"Seems to me you're ready for another mai tai! I'd like to insist that you and your family stay for supper — a bit of Marge's kidney pie," Tony added.

We were joining our hosts in getting bombed by now. Tony kept turning up the music which after an hour or so started sounding distorted and scratchy as it made its way out of the tiny speakers. But Marge loved that album as much as Tony and they just kept playing the tape over and over; I do that myself sometimes with a favorite tape.

"Oh, my God," I heard Paul mumble to himself again.

"What?"

"Nothing." But he winked to assure me he was having fun, too. He realized that embarrassing as things might be for us, it would be worse to refuse our new friends that had befriended us so readily. Besides we were having more than a little fun letting it all hang out in the cowboy tradition.

All through supper, and Rod Stewart, Tony kept alive an agreement for four of us to go out to the reef near the pass in our dinghy after dinner and look for lobster. It was a promise we kept; but, we didn't find any lobsters underneath the stars. It was a long row and the by the time we got to the reef off Motu Ahuna, Tony was snoring.

"My dear darling's fallen asleep!" Marge apologized.

"*Aita pea pea.* No problem. Marge, you guys have been great. *Māururu roa!*" I popped back. "I'm ready to saw a few logs myself. Let's head back!" Davey rowed this time, returning us across the bay to the refuge of our Anglo-Saxon yachts.

The next morning we got up a little later than usual, and when we did the *Astral Rose* was gone, on her way to points further east. I wondered if Tony had a headache. I did.

Well, it was probably a good day to move the boat closer to town. We would anchor in the morning shadow of the magic mountain of O'temanu.

Davey on the bow in our new found anchorage

Helping Tiapai anchor floating fares off the reef

Part VIII
The Private Sea

59.

*"Let go of everything you're holding on to.
Now, let go of everything else."*
— Stuart Greene

We liked the hospitality at the charming Oa Oa Hotel, the owners at the time being two Americans. Greg, a retired loan officer in his late thirties, sported a cowboy hat and a big cigar. Elaine did the bookkeeping. Their bartender was a shapely young Tahitian girl named Francine; she spoke Tahitian, French, and English and she made sure nobody lost their sense of humor. The Oa Oa assumed a wonderful California-Tahiti flavoring. We had first discovered it on one of our many trips hiking back to the Yacht Club from town. It was the perfect place for lunch; you could order a "real" cheeseburger in paradise and gaze out the open window at indescribable beauty.

After moving the boat to the small Oa Oa hotel and anchoring in 80 feet of water there was little time left to do much except make ready for our trip north. The anchorage was slightly more exposed and considerably less comfortable, but it we preferred it since it was closer to provisioning in the town of Vaitape. Our trip north to

Hawai'i would be about 2,500 miles as the crow flies and after adding the extra days and miles our sailing would take us, we needed to prepare for a possible three to six weeks at sea. I sat down and made a to-do list.

-keep water tanks full
-keep waterline clean
-keep bilge clean, clean sump traps
-top up diesel, fill spare jugs
-fill one-gallon gasoline jug
-polish all bright work below and above decks
-lubricate windlass and check operation
-organize desk, nav station, books
-oil teak, external and internal
-unfold each and every sail; check stitching, tacks, heads, clews, lugs
-lubricate steering
-complete engine room maintenance
-make oil change, clean water coolant anti-siphon valves, fuel filters
-check batteries, bring up to full charge with generator
-replace chafe tape where needed below decks
-lubricate blocks
-make new silencing mats for staysail blocks
-clean sextant, check operation and battery for light
-check kerosene supply; fill all lamps
-repair fresh water pump in galley
-lubricate wind vane
-clean all fiberglass
-stow shells
-clean under stove and galley
-service salt water sea pump
-layout all the anchor rode and clean, repack in chain locker
-check every screw and bolt aboard and tighten those needing tightening
-check and replace main sail lugs for tracking
-organize and study Pilot Charts and charts for Hawai'i
-service (lubricate) Walker log
-stow 110 lights and all other equipment not used offshore
-check man overboard system
-check operation of all strobes and boat lights
-pack quarter berth with offshore gear
-tape hatches, check above-deck chaffing gear
-check compasses and align as necessary
-check all winches for operation and lubricate as necessary
-re-tie lee clothes
-make float coats, harness, boots, and other offshore gear readily available
-re-stow life raft and do an abandon ship drill
-fire drill

-check all lifelines, stays, shrouds
-check flare organization and emergency
-provision (tape, batteries, food, extra lines for vane, etc.,)
-check out with Gendarme, Bank and Yacht Club
-mail departure notices to parents

We had our work cut out for us! We were either doing our final provisioning or working on the boat constantly for the next couple of weeks. The apprehension about going to sea again for a major passage was added to by the change of weather. The *maramu* or winter wind was upon us. It is similar to a *kona* wind in Hawai'i where the wind blows from a direction opposite than the predominant tradewinds which are from the northeast in the northern Hemisphere and from the southeast in the Southern Hemisphere. Everything seemed strangely different when the temperature dropped ten degrees and the skies turned grey and cloudy. We did have to laugh though when we saw the local Tahitian babies dressed in little sweaters and bonnets. It was still 70°F. Everything is relative. No longer in the lee of the island and unprotected from the weather, one night we even had to stand rotating anchor watches for fear that we might drag ashore. It blew hard and without relief for three days. On the second day a mooring in front of the Oa Oa broke free along with the thirty-five foot French yacht that was tied up to it. We happened to be in the hotel at the time along with the skipper, who was lucky enough for someone to yell out the alarming news to him from the docks and have a waiting raft and outboard ready to race him out to his yacht. He was able to board the drifting boat, start the engine, and power away from danger at the last possible moment.

Most everything we needed to accomplish had to be done while swinging off our anchor once the maramu had passed. It took ten minutes to row to the Oa Oa. When ashore we were twice as close to town, though it still took almost an hour to take the dinghy in to Vaitape to load up on those final necessities that were too big or bulky to walk with. Lucien's store started freezing ham tins of water for us to provide blocks of ice for our galley cooler, helped us pick our fishing lures, and sent us off with a gift of four bottles of wine.

Paul and Lauren were very helpful; they made several trips to town and back filling up the five-gallon plastic fuel jugs we needed to top off *Querencia's* diesel tank. Then they brought four more full jugs to tie down on deck for back-up fuel if we needed it. It was no small feat for sixteen-year-olds, carrying three-hundred pounds of fuel in small containers over half a mile.

But it wasn't all work. We met several more yachts heading all directions of the compass.

We made good friends with the folks onboard *Woyaya*. What a shock to see a single-screw [one propeller] boat so far from the U.S.A. Their only back-up system for propulsion was to use the diesel generator which been rigged with pulleys and belts to enable it to turn the main shaft. Chris, the skipper, was in his twenties and had skippered the boat from Newport, California down and through the Panama Canal and then up to Connecticut and back. Then they had crossed the Pacific to the Society Islands. Their next stops were the Cooks and Fiji. Chris's parents owned *Woyaya* and his best friend Jeff was first mate. Their family business had found immense success in California through plastics manufacturing, producing plastic molds for everything from heart prostheses to the little boxes that hold recording tapes. Lovely people originally from England, their strong background in plastics had enabled them to build *Woyaya* themselves from stem to stern as a family project. She was a truly awesome yacht, obviously built it in the pursuit of perfection. Professionally maintained, she had a spacious interior that opened to wide side decks through weathertight sliding doors. Inside the regal saloon, there was an abundance of windows and ports. The immaculate engine room had more than six feet of headroom. We hadn't been on a ship that big since *Rainbow Warrior* in San Francisco!

"Too bad. We just missed the *BIC* lighter contract," Chris chuckled.

Hanar and Usa of the dutch boat *Irma* came by one day towards the end of our to-do list, and looking for a respite we accepted their offer to join them on an afternoon adventure aboard Bob and Jenny's South African steel sloop. We all spoke English and we had a lot to share. Bob fired up his engine and with the six of us aboard he putted a tortuous route in a very narrow passage between coral heads and the northern tip of the island, until we reached the northeast bight of the lagoon. We had good lighting and used the coconut trees that had been suggested for bearing a course. Eventually, taking it slowly, we reached a beautiful anchorage near Motu Ome and there spent the entire day. It was a large motu on the more weathered side of Bora Bora. During our exploration of Ome we found a small path; I remembered Richard had taken us there years before when we first flew to Bora Bora. The path eventually came to the reef which was teeming with life — none of it human. We were careful not to venture too deep as we waded and looked for shells; several sharks were combing the shallow waters and their dorsal fins stood high out of the water as they zipped along. We eventually hiked back to the boat and went for a snorkel dive inside the more protected lagoon. We found an abundance of mussels in the area which we collected for evening consumption. Then we all kicked back and ate lunch. Hanar told us how he and Usa had sailed into New York Harbor due to a change of sailing plans following their crossing of the Atlantic. They had planned to stay in New York for two weeks but stayed a year. They loved the Americans they had met there.

"The best in the world, man, I tell you," Hanar said. He was round and jolly with red cheeks. Usa, his blond wife, usually very shy, took a long puff on her cigarette and nodded in the affirmative.

"So, John and Davey, I tell you," Hanar continued, "you may be going to Hawai'i, but remember it doesn't have to be forever, man! You can go cruising again someday. This is the real world, man! Not some crap job somewhere with unhappy people fighting over the dollar!"

I promised him we would remember.

"We call him 'Hagar' after the *Hagar the Horrible* cartoon," Bob teased. They had a story, too. They had been attacked by a pod of whales off the Galápagos Islands. They also had been nearly hit by another sailboat in the middle of the night. He found it miraculous that they had survived either incident.

"Do you think there is anything to the belief that some boats *attract* collisions with whales more than others?" I asked.

"I think it's possible, but I don't know why exactly," Bob answered in his unique soft-spoken South African accent.

"Actually, it might be our blue bottom paint, or it might be our steel hull," offered Jenny, now stretched out on deck, the picture of relaxation.

As we were to find out later through correspondence, Bob and Jenny's steel hulled boat was shortly thereafter almost completely destroyed by whales between Fiji and Australia. They limped into Sydney, the hull so bashed in it was nearly a total loss.

Before the afternoon waxed much farther we had to head back before the lighting made it any more difficult to pick our way back through the coral heads. It had been a good R&R for all of us.

That same evening Metata came by our boat in his outrigger. He brought with him still another cousin; we had never met him before. We were thrilled to see Metata, it had been a week or more since we last saw him and we worried we might miss him before we departed the island. He filled our cockpit full of fresh fruits, mostly papaya, and he gave us his *'ukulele* and his favorite paddle or *hoe*. In turn I gave Metata my Fender acoustic guitar. I had loved that guitar for more than a decade. It was the biggest thing I could give to him at the moment, and I still wanted to give him more of me. Davey gave him a big hug and a kiss. It was a very touching moment. Than we all took turns playing the uke and the guitar and singing. They didn't stay long though as it started to rain. I watched Metata and his cousin paddle his outrigger around Pahua Point, and I wondered if we might ever see him again even though he assured us we would. Paul was very disappointed to have not been aboard and to have missed him.

The next three days it blew and rained just as it did with the first maramu. I was beginning to wonder if we had waited too long to leave. *Querencia* pitched about on the mooring we had moved her to; I even felt a little queasy at times.

"Maybe we'll get lucky and have our sea-legs before we even leave port," Davey joked.

We were now just waiting on the weather as was another boat, a beautiful forty-five foot ketch. Aboard were Mark and Jane. Mark was a sailing expert who made a living teaching sailing and delivering yachts. He was active on his single sideband radio on the Pacific Maritime Net and we had listened to him for hours between San Diego and the Marquesas when he reported in each night and described sea conditions and naval tactics. He always sounded confident and self-assured, like an airline pilot.

Mark had met Jane, a flight attendant, in San Francisco. He taught her sailing, they fell in love, and then he had asked her to join him on this adventure delivering a yacht to the Cook Islands. Paul and I were now talking to both of them for the first time in real life. Jane was a very pretty and engaging blonde. Mark had an ego, though, that bothered me.

"Oh, God, you're making a mistake heading for Hawai'i this time of year," he said in his New York accent. "One of those hurricanes is going to blast across the Pacific and pick up your boat and toss it around like it's a toy. Especially those *Hans Christian* boats. Their hardware is always falling apart. Its junk you know."

"It's not a *Hans Christian*; its a *BABA*, Mark," I spoke up. "There is no comparison except maybe that they're both double-enders. They have different designers and are built in different yards."

"Well, whatever it is, a hurricane is going to blow its little ass right off the chart if you get caught out there. And there's a damn good chance of that!" He continued. "You wouldn't catch me making that trip. Unh-uh." Out of the corner of my eye I could see Paul fidgeting.

"Oh, great," I thought to myself.

"Well, Mark, according to the Pilot charts and the *Coastal Pilot* most hurricanes either recurve or dissipate before getting as far west as we'll be. Although they only occur between July and November, August is the most favorable month for a hurricane to reach the area and it's still June. We'll be watching for them and we don't plan on letting one sneak up on us." I managed a smile.

We both knew that '83 had been a quirk of a year. Storms had not followed their traditional routes in almost any ocean of the world. Travelling unusually far West, Hurricane *Iwa* had struck Kaua'i and O'ahu in Hawai'i. Hurricanes rarely strike Hawai'i. The odd storms of 1983, including Iwa, had probably been encouraged by the El Niño. Word had it that the El Niño was over.

"Well, it's your boat, and you probably know what you're doing if you keep up on your weather. Good luck, pal."

"Thanks Mark," I said, winking at Jane.

Paul and I rowed back to *Querencia* where Paul recounted the story to Davey. We pulled out the Pilot Charts, etc. and repeated all our homework. We were right. We should be fine, although we would do good to have left by "yesterday." Regretfully, we would miss the festival atmosphere of Fête, held every year on Bastille Day [July 13th]. The weather was better. It was decided. We would leave the next morning, June 23. We planned to pull up to the little dock in front of the Oa Oa and deflate and stow our raft and top off our water tanks, and then head for the pass.

We got up early the next morning under blue skies only to find that Mark and Jane had pulled up to the small dock with their vessel; there really wasn't enough space for a second boat. We rowed in and asked Mark how long they would be. He said that they were leaving for the Cooks on this same day and that they would be leaving in a few more minutes.

Later when we were in Hawai'i we were surprised yet amused to hear that Mark and Jane had lost the boat they were delivering to the Cooks on the reef at Raratonga. Thankfully, they were not injured.

After waiting a couple of hours we decided it wasn't necessary to go to the dock. Paul made a couple of water runs in the dinghy and then, ready to depart, we wrestled the raft to deflation and stowed it on deck. We were almost ready to go when unexpectedly what should appear coming our way from Vaitape skimming the surface of the lagoon but the French gendarme's speed boat, its blue light flashing and siren wailing as if in a scene from *Miami Vice*.

"Uh-oh... now what?" I asked Paul and Davey. They had nothing to offer. We had filed all our paper work accurately to the best of my knowledge. Obviously they were after someone else.

I was wrong. They police boat came right up to *Querencia*, barely trimming its throttle. Its wake sloshed all the yachts in the anchorage. Hatches were thrown back and heads popped out. At the hotel people gathered at the windows staring. All-right, we were busted. Or was there emergency news?

It wasn't to be either. It was Lauren and his father, and another gendarme who was driving the boat. They had come to wish us luck and give us a nice Bordeaux for our trip.

"Bonne chance! Bonne chance!" Lauren's father said repeatedly. "Au revoir Paul!"

"Good-bye Paul. Good-by Davey. Good-bye Dr. McGrady. I will

miss you very much," said Lauren. It was easy to see he meant it.

"Merci! Merci beaucoup! Au revoir," we responded.

"Pas de quoi. Enchanté de faire votre connaissance," said Lauren's handsome father. Then they left just as abruptly as they had arrived.

"I wonder what everyone staring at us figures?" asked Paul.

"Let them wonder and enjoy it," I chuckled. "They'll never know! Let's untie from our mooring and head for the pass Teavanui."

Somehow, Metata knew when we were leaving. Was it synchronicity or coincidence that once we could see around the point separating the two bays we saw him rowing towards the pass in his outrigger in perfect three-quarter time?

Once we reached the pass Teavanui, *Querencia*, now just under sail power, glided slowly past Metata's idle outrigger. Metata had reached the pass first and sat quietly with his paddle crossed in front of him. His three-year-old granddaughter was in the front of the canoe. We tossed flowers into the swirling waters of the pass when we sailed out, a Polynesian promise that we would return someday. All of us had tears in our eyes. Except for the little girl. She was giggling. None of us said much besides "*Māururu*" and "I love you..."

We said that over and over and over.

60.

"I wondered what it would feel like to be a bird with nothing on my mind but flying and eating. I remembered reading that the smallest bird could travel thousands of miles across the Pacific unencumbered and alone, needing only one piece of baggage: one possession... a twig. He could carry the twig in his beak and when he got tired he simply descended to the sea and floated on it until he was ready to move on again. He fished from the twig, ate from the twig, and slept on the twig. Who needs the QUEEN MARY? He flapped his wings, clamped his life raft in his mouth and set out to see more of the world."

— Shirley Maclaine
Out On a Limb

The first several days out of Bora Bora we were heeled over hard. The wind seemed to never want to drop below thirty knots after the first evening and it seemed to always blow harder at night than in the day. At least the forward motion felt commensurately consistent. We were once again at sea; *Querencia* feeling her way over the watery wilderness that covers the face of our planet Earth. Each of us, full of life, soon looked weathered, flushed, and windblown.

In the last waning minutes of the evening we would drop the jib, and go ahead only under the staysail and a reefed main giving ourselves a bit of a respite. It seemed a good margin of safety as well.

Even still, the rail was often buried beneath the water's surface as *Querencia* charged northeast through wind and choppy six-foot seas blasting us from the east, often mixed with eight-foot swells from the south. After the sun would rise over the horizon in the morning, and we all were up and about, Paul and Davey would raise the jib and trim the forward sails followed by me shaking the reef out of the main sail. I would untie all the shoestring knots that kept the lowered sail in its self-made bag. Then after releasing the down haul at the clew and the webbed tack ring I would haul hard, putting my back into it until the halyard was taut and the sail full.

The days were bright but the sky was full of spray and haze and the sun seemed to hide behind ground glass. It was like a desert prairie swept with gusty winds, except that water instead of dust was thrown into the air all around.

This type of sailing, when you are constantly wedging yourself in and holding on for dear life both in your bunk or in the cockpit is very tiring and somewhat stressful. We heard over the radio that the French government had set off another multi-megaton nuclear blast at their test sight on the tiny island of Mururoa in the southern Societies and I couldn't help but blame this angry weather on that.

None of us felt very well those first few days and to add to our queasiness we had to navigate and drive the boat for as much easting as possible. We calculated that we only needed to maintain a 10° magnetic heading to reach the equator (0°N) at 145°W. Going into the northern hemisphere at a longitude of 145°W was preferred. It was the magical line we had decided on for crossing the equator, being far enough east that we could then accept the northeast trades on our passage without having to be too close hauled. Then we would not have to point so high. Even if we were set off course, the chances would be excellent for hitting the Hawaiian islands which lay between 155°W and 160°W. After several days at sea they were still some two thousand miles away.

We began tracking all the South and North Pacific weather. It was broadcast on shortwave by the United States Coast Guard Service three times a day (17:45, 23:45, and 05:45 GMT) at 13.113.2, 8.765.4, 6.506.4, and 4.428.7 Megahertz. The weather report covered the area from 110°W to 160°E and 50°N and 25°S. Tuning our receiver in with its touchy analog dials as we bounced around was tricky, but we got it down to an art. It was a good habitual skill to develop on our excursion north. Our lives would depend on it in the event of the formation of a threatening tropical storm or hurricane, especially once we crossed the equator.

The bow stem began to leak fairly early in our voyage. As there was no drainage from the forward bulkhead under the v-berth to the bilge, we had a problem. We had to remove our stores, sails, and everything else we had on top of and below the forward berth just to improve our access for inspection. (I cursed this problem and would later, as soon as we reached Hawai'i, put in a drain to the bilge as well as a grate in the floor of the forward hull to insure dryness of our stores in the future). The leak wasn't much, maybe a pint an hour, but soon we were having to remove salt water via hand pumps and a bucket daily. When *Querencia* would shovel seas with her bow she would also ship it in. We moved our stowage in the bow aft, lifting *Querencia's* nose out of the water a bit, and that helped.

We began takings turns going below to the forward "hole" as we called it and bailing. Yuk! Paul, much to my appreciation, wound up taking on the bailing task. He was the lightest of the three of us for crawling up in the bow with *Querencia* on a heel and he minded, but not as much as we did.

He did detest his night watches though, as did each of us. It was black and scary sitting in the cockpit alone at night with *Querencia* racing along like a train. The angle of the boat was such that on some nights the odd wave would smack against the hull and slosh over her rail right into your face. Even below decks lying flat on the cabin sole was the favorite place to be. Nighttime log entries some four days out of Bora Bora give some indication of our discomfort. Once again we were reminded of the old joke that "cruising is the most expensive way to travel third class."

> 0300 I lay, squirmed, stood, and then sat some more in the cockpit for the past three hours. Rough watch, that one was. Wet too. Lots of water coming over the bow and about one and a half cups of it are being shipped in per hour. Just checked "the hole" in the v-berth and saw a bunch of paperback books had somehow managed to fly into it and were floating around. I pumped it out and saved *Desolation Angels*, by Jack Kerouac at the last minute. Now I must read it. The stars are reflective and me too. Barometer 29.86, Course 30° Magnetic.— JFM

> 0714 Extremely rough seas. After continual drenchings, finally I'm OFF! Moon rose around 04:15. My eyes are burning from salt water. Next time I'll wear my snorkeling equipment. — PTW

Unfortunately one of our spare five gallon fuel jugs that was tied to the shrouds on the weather side sprang a leak. Paul and I got up one morning to find Davey, who was already fighting off a bit of a cold, at the end of her watch looking very green. The oily smell of fuel wafting back to the cockpit was all that was necessary to make all of us ill. The teak decks, frequently awash, now had all the rainbow colors of an oil slick. I investigated until I found the guilty jug and then tightened its cap. The fuel was useless, I realized, having now been contaminated by sea water.

Despite my tightening and retightening the cap for the next day and a half, the deck slick persisted as did the nauseous smell. Finally I realized that the neck of the jug had cracked and it was never going to stop leaking. I sealed it best I could with duct tape and then put it over the side. Far from land, in waters miles deep, I said a small prayer that it wouldn't do much harm to the environment, for it was a good riddance, and fresh air was restored. The incident reminded us again, that as welcome as fuel is to mechanical engines and the 20th century, how putrid the stuff is to life itself. The quality of life aboard our thirty foot *Querencia* had been reduced to a sickening existence by one leaking jug of fossil fuel.

Eating wasn't much of a pleasant affair those first few days out of Bora Bora. For breakfast we settled on eating nothing, or at best, splitting one of Metata's papayas. They were very handy, abundant, and tasty. They always seemed to settle our stomachs a bit, too, and I wondered if it was because of the papain enzyme in them. Lunch was simple; we would just eat some bread, cheese, and wine followed by a chunk of coconut meat. Dinner was equally simple — or we would skip it all together. Cooking seemed just too dangerous, and all things considered, our appetites were not much to speak of.

> *The ocean waves beat ceaselessly.*
> *The wind blows from*
> *dawn to dusk.*
> *The passing clouds whisper*
> *Endure! Endure!*

By our second week, the winds had eased a bit and our sea legs had regenerated themselves. Dinner once again became our favorite meal, with Davey usually cooking curry or spaghetti or a fresh caught fish. Still, some dinners were a bit more of a rush than others. One night Davey quickly mixed canned duck, rice, fruit, and spices for what we appropriately named "hurry-duck curry."

As we came into the intertropical convergence zone the winds eased considerably and we were able to relax more. The bow stem stopped leaking almost as if by magic and eventually it dried out altogether, the wood in the stem swelling enough to seal the damned trickle.

61.

The first clue should have been the birds. Petrels suddenly appeared from everywhere, some of them trying in vain to find a place to perch atop the mast which swung in big arcs like an eraser at the end of a restless pencil. We worried that our feathered friends might tangle themselves in the rigging or, worse yet, break off the wind indicator or radio antenna, but such misfortune was not to happen. Instead, by nightfall one of the birds had perched on our life buoy hanging on the taffrail. He was obviously exhausted.

"What a silly bird," I commented as we all stared in fascination at this fluffy little creature hanging on for dear life as *Querencia* bounced around.

"Maybe not so silly," countered Paul, pointing at flashes of lightning just starting to appear over the horizon, "he's probably glad to have a place to *park it* for a while."

"He looks like a 'Willard' to me." Davey said, momentarily drawing our attention back to the petrel.

"We'll call him Willard Port."

The skies were becoming overcast and the wind was now coming from the direction we wanted to go. The best we could do was a heading of 340° on our present tack. We hadn't had a position fix in over a day and with the substantial set from westerly current my confidence in our position was weakening. Encouraged by demons I envisioned the possibility of being way off course and amid mysterious atolls that might reappear for the first time since explorers first reported their existence five hundred years ago. Just to rouse our thinking a little the high seas shortwave broadcast reported a gloomy hurricane by the name of "Douglas" moving west from Mexican waters. It was befriended by another tropical storm "Elita."

As the sun set we tacked *Querencia* so that she headed dead east, shoving her way through stocky little slop. We were not to go far on this night of puffs of undetermined wind and contrary current; we would do well to hold our easting. As the black moonless night descended upon us so did another petrel which sat opposite Willard on the stern rail. We promptly named her "Winnie Starboard". These two birds had either forgotten or lost their twigs! *Querencia* would serve as a good substitute.

We had been averaging about 100 miles a day up to this point and despite our concern for the immediate sullen weather we were satisfied with our performance. I reminded myself that our duty was to only get through the night safely. Winnie and Willard seemed totally unaffected by our presence and the weather. Indeed, as each of us took our watch at the wheel they were agreeable company. Occasionally Willard would fall off his perch, presumably the result of somnolent slackening of his grip. Catching himself before he hit the surface of the water he would then flap ever so hard to catch up to *Querencia* so that he could light once again on his new found ocean sanctuary. It was comical to watch.

Not so comical was the brackish night and falling torrents of rain that fell upon us. Squalls seemed to come from all points of the compass and had so much water in them that each one was like having a monstrous bucket of ocean pour down on *Querencia* from the heavens. Even though it was self-bailing, the steering well where I was standing at the wheel filled with rainwater in a matter of two minutes, right past my favorite leather tennis shoes and clear up to my shins. Meanwhile I suffocated underneath the shallow security of my favorite rain gear. And then the squall would pass and the boat would be left bobbing around in a bewildering sort of silence, void of any fresh air, lurching to the tune of an unsettling odd swell. One such swell filled all the books in the navigation station with so much kinetic energy that they magically jumped from their respective locales and dumped themselves onto Paul just as he was making his way up the companionway.

I felt consumed by vertigo as we twirled around and around, and pounded on the compass globe more than occasionally just to make sure it too wasn't making a fool of me. I stood at the wheel trying to do better than the steering vane, Nelley, and still we did two 360° turns in a matter of minutes.

"There! There! Paul do you hear that? That isn't surf is it?" I asked. When the squalls would come enshrouded in blackness the sound of the rain coming down was like a waterfall and to the imaginative mind it even sounded like there might even be surf breaking in the distance.

"Maybe it's just a squall *out there* dumping its rain on the ocean?"

"That must be what it is. Sure. There are no islands *here*! Those atolls reported by those explorers have never been confirmed. It's believed that they had them confused with current making waves over sea mounts anyway. Caroline Island couldn't be less than 400 miles away."

"I sure hope so," Paul murmured.

Then there was a sudden gust of wind and *Querencia* took off again dashing through the darkness, her rail in the water. I asked Davey to turn on the spreader lights and come up on deck to help us out a bit, if only to help get our bearings and clear the deck.

It was then that a large dolphin suddenly appeared and raced along with us amidships, making a loud "Whoosh" between squeaks. He didn't stay long and it was as if he just came by to see if we were all right.

We tacked often that night, and usually it seemed in vain. Still we did not want to motor until daylight. Then we could see what we might not hear. For tonight our passage would be what it was, and we would listen to the dark and settle for twenty-three miles made good.

The two fluffy petrels sat as they were all night, sleeping and preening — keeping each watch company. Then with the golden glory rays of dawn they fluttered off.

> 0713 Spent 3-7 at the helm going around in circles until 6 when I got the okay from John to start the motor. At sunrise I found us in the strongest current I have ever seen in the ocean, pushing us to the west. Willard preened for half an hour or so and after letting me pet him made an odd little noise and flew off. Winnie left right behind him. They seemed rested and ready for daybreak. I wish we were!. — DT

The next few days we were blessed with an unusual but light and consistent breeze from the southeast. Not beating into the wind, we were able to drop the staysail for the first time in more than a week. We eased the main and jib and enjoyed a broad reach. We observed whales splashing and breathing about us from time to time, and other than the chore of navigating, double checking all our equipment, and dutifully tracking the storm systems, we were having an enjoyable sail. The mast developed an annoying creak, but after close inspection I decided to leave the rigging be. Paul and I played backgammon and Davey and I started what was to become our longest scrabble marathon ever. We liked to play scrabble with an open-dictionary policy and we certainly took our time. I have fond memories of being wedged in the cockpit at a 30° tilt, flipping through *Webster's Collegiate* with the help of the wind, refusing to give up my turn until I had the perfect word. I probably expanded my vocabulary by 200 words just on that one passage alone. Still it was hard work to beat Davey at her game.

We also took turns making up haiku or Zen poetry and during our solitary evening watches we wrote our wits in the log.

> Still calm unity of the sea and sky
> Interrupted only by the cracking of the
> worn white canvas
> The occasional cry of a bird
> passing in the darkness — DT

> Glittering specks of stellar glass litter the
> skies and men write of them as stars. — JFM

> Mom making me coffee before my watch is
> the key to my success. More shooting stars
> now. That's all I want. — PTW

The first sliver of the new moon appeared and with it a nine-pound Yellowfin Tuna on the end of our fishing line. Upbeat moods encouraged us to clean up and organize everything below decks, wash and dry ourselves and our clothes, and have some pretty fancy meals. One breakfast was fresh fish and eggs with biscuits and preserves. What more could one ask for?

On the Fourth of July we all got traditional sunburns as *Querencia* maintained a steady five knots all day. Our American celebration didn't take us much beyond a special bowl of popcorn and an extra game of scrabble, but we didn't mind. Life itself was exciting enough and the last thing one needs on any boat at sea is fireworks. *Querencia* was definitely in the groove and easily doing her 100 miles a day again. One excellent day of sailing followed another. Our three-hour rotating watches worked well for us, there was a waxing moon and lots of good books to read, and plenty of fishing, although we lost more than we caught.

On the sixteenth day I figured we were at least half way; we should be arriving in Hawai'i in twelve to sixteen days. That was very uplifting. On the eighteenth day we sighted our first boat since leaving Bora Bora. It was a sailboat heading south and he passed us between our port side and the horizon. We attempted contact via VHF radio without success.

Being a good blue-water sailor requires a great capacity, something you cannot achieve by merely reading or sailing inland waters. A sailor who achieves this capacity to a greater degree than others does so only by sheer effort and experience. Further, being a good skipper requires that one does not try to criticize other crew members for what he himself fails at, and that he does not put people to shame for what they fail in. On this last major passage picking our way up the globe the three of us became very close and probably the best team of companions ever.

Yet for all the necessary skill suggested, blue water sailing is incredibly simplistic, dependent on everyday decisions that rely on common sense. Those sailors that have only models of the right way to do things are destined for disappointment, for failings are as necessary to genuine human nature as salt is to the sea. The superior sailor or sea captain goes ahead without preconceived courses of action for every occurrence at sea, knowing that at his best he will merely decide for the moment what is the right thing to do, because he must.

Nevertheless there is some sort of madness to being out there in the middle of nowhere in such a little boat. It wasn't the madness of danger you must understand, because relative to the hustle and bustle of automobile traffic and carcinogenic pollutants we were quite safe. It was the madness of what we were doing in comparison to the rest of the world. What different rules, if any, did God have for us? For us everything remained mostly foreign on this rolling heap of water, part of a fluid globe spinning in space. I know we all had our private thoughts and entertained ourselves with fanciful visions of our bodies and souls dancing with gods *and* demons. What was IT all about anyway?

62.

One morning we were motoring with all the sails down along this fat part of the globe. The surface of the ocean was glassy and the only motion was caused by a gentle heaving swell that kept *Querencia* lazily yawing side to side as we continued our journey. Eventually *Querencia* would deliver us north of the equatorial convergence zone and we would find more wind again. The sky was slightly overcast and flotsam bobbed here and there all about us.

Towards the east, just below the rising sun, there appeared quite unexpectedly a large black square. It reminded me of a smokestack off of a cruise liner.

"Or a house!" exclaimed Paul.

We continued to stare at it, speechless, and after passing the binoculars around twice decided that we didn't have the slightest idea what it was. We estimated its distance at two miles, bearing due east from our position of

LAT 08° 08.87' N
LON 146° 05.43' W

Our concern of making a good day's run made us stingy about our time, but we shortly decided that if we didn't make a right turn and go over and checkout what the thing was we would always wonder about it. I rotated the wheel slowly as to not tangle up the fishing line we were trailing behind us and *Querencia* chugged along in a big, broad, sweeping turn. Our fishing line was a large hand line composed of a big nasty hook and several orange and red plastic skirts that Paul and I had crudely tied around it. We were going for a big one.

It seemed like it took forever motoring over to the horizon, but in actuality I'm sure it was only the better part of half an hour. Funny thing, but the closer we got the more confused we felt because we still could not figure out what the heck we were looking at. It was just this big, black, square-shaped box slowly getting bigger and bigger. I felt almost hypnotized standing at the wheel watching the thing.

Somebody mumbled "…eerie…"

How can you decide what size something is if you have nothing to compare it to? "How far away is it now?" I wondered. Was it a football field away or six football fields away? Soon we were really close and then everything happened at once.

We weren't looking at *the thing* anymore. Our eyes were glued to large patches of coral below the surface of the water.

"It's shallow here," Davey signalled instinctively.

"It can't be, Davey! There isn't any land for hundreds of miles. The ocean is almost two miles deep here."

"Oh my God, John! Watch what you're doing!"

I looked up and realized the big black thing was no longer there but *here*, and I was still anxiously motoring towards it, up to that second unaware that it was now only yards away. Swirling currents seemed to be sucking us closer and closer to the mysterious turquoise reef below it.

I could see it; a big, black, rusting heap; it heaved up and down in the swells. Easily two stories high and twenty feet wide, it would surge up and out of the water as much as twelve feet. When it rose, water cascaded down its sides like a stream splashing over a rock ridden glacier. Then after reaching its maximum extension out of the water and looking like a gigantic, rust-encrusted, robotic whale it would fall back into the depths again with a loud groan and whoosh. It was covered with all sorts of marine growth. Goose neck barnacles, seaweed, and splotchy neoplasms covered and disfigured it still beyond any conceivable explanation. All around it the ocean was agitated and the water sputtered.

I turned the wheel hard to port and throttled up for some power. Enough exploring. It was time to move the hell away from whatever it was we had discovered before we were caught in its trap.

"What in the world is it?" asked Davey.

"Pull in the fishing line Paul," I commanded.

No sooner had I spoken when "SNAP!" went the clothes line as it flew across the cockpit. It was too late. Now along with everything else a huge mahi mahi had swallowed the meat hook we had been trailing. The remaining pile of hand-line laying in the scuppers had been scooped up by Paul and it was running away through his fingers. You could hear the line singing as it raced over his skin.

"Ouch! I can't hold it," yelled Paul. The mahi mahi was still making lunge after lunge. It was heading for *the thing*!

"Oh, my God," exclaimed Davey, "*that's fish!*" She pointed at the reef below *the thing*. It wasn't coral or land at all, it was a big ball of fish! Thousands of them were swarming around like a giant ball of termites. Monstrous mahi mahi darted everywhere.Several large sharks also appeared, presumably wanting to see who the new kid in town was.

Querencia's little Volvo diesel pulled us ahead and for the moment we seemed safe. A whole school of fish had broken off and were now following the round hull of *Querencia*. The large sharks and other dorados were visible and excited. In their frenzied state they raced between the thing, the hooked mahi mahi, and the boat. Miraculously Paul still had the fish on, pulling in the hand line best he could. Between the dorado's desperate leaps into the air its long, spiny dorsal fin streamed along the ocean surface like a Mohawk haircut. When the large fish jumped out of the sea its scales would reflect a kaleidoscopic rainbow of blue, purple, green and gold. It was a very impressive fish.

Reasonably confident that we were now putting some distance between us and *the thing*, Davey took over at the wheel and I ran for my spear gun.

"Ease up on the motor, hon, and Paul, try to bring the mahi in close enough so that I can stick it with the spear gun and get it aboard before a shark steals it."

A shark brushed up behind *Querencia* and momentarily got caught between the paddle of the wind vane and the hull. It flapped around noisily splashing water everywhere.

"That damned shark is going to break the wind vane!" I yelled, just as it slithered free.

"Thank goodness..." Davey gasped.

I turned my attention back to the mahi, which was now nearing the boat. Lying on the deck of the boat and leaning over the rail I aimed the point of my spear gun into the blue depths. I pointed it the same direction as the hand line descended and hoped I would get one chance to "gaff it" with the spear gun. I could see sharks and other mahi mahi darting madly around and around and we patiently waited for our catch to appear as Paul played the hand line in and out.

Suddenly the fish was *"there"* and the one opportunity presented itself. I pulled the trigger on the spear gun. *BAM!* Perfect shot. With Paul making sure I didn't fall over board, I pulled the large colorful fish over the rail and out of the jaws of encroaching sharks. There before our eyes in the next few minutes the mahi's golden hue changed to gilded silver and its sheen faded. It was if we could actually see its spirit leave this world.

Using our scales we discovered our fish *du jour* to be thirty-eight pounds! We laboriously and meticulously cleaned it and after some effort Davey managed to get half of it into the oven. When that was through we cooked the rest. For the next two days we ate off the fish almost constantly, for every meal. It was a delicious gift from the sea for which we were most thankful; we kept re-heating and eating it until it was all gone.

Even after we had finally consumed it all some two days later we continued to catch little mahi mahi that followed the boat; part of the school that had broken off from the fish reef. They reminded us of little mountain trout, and they bit at any and every thing including bare hooks. They were a really nice treat and we wasted no time in getting them aboard. For their own reasons, sharks and barracuda were also still following the boat.

Hilo, Hawai'i was about 900 miles away.

63.

After a long discussion we decided that *the thing* was actually a container that had fallen off a cargo ship caught in a storm, maybe a hurricane near Mexico. It had then slowly drifted west in the equatorial currents. Exactly how long it had been out there we weren't sure, maybe a year.

We didn't sleep as well after seeing that large container drifting aimlessly at sea, and the person on watch was more than a little sure that they carefully observed the darkness ahead for anything unusual, ready to make a course change quickly. The weather was cooperative despite a 50% cloud cover. It was typical consistent fifteen-knot trade winds that would occasionally pick up when a shower passed. Even though we were only doing six knots it felt like twenty, and the thought of blindly running into a rusty steel box as big as a house was disconcerting. During daylight hours the sailing continued to be brilliant and we felt comfortable just scanning the horizon irregularly between games of scrabble or Paul's studying or charting our course. At night, however, alone on watch, charging forward in the darkness we had to be as careful as possible; we kept a careful lookout and said more than an occasional prayer.

Passing a freighter to port a few nights later substantiated our feelings that this was a much busier section of ocean than the stretch from San Diego to the Marquesas. It happened on Davey's watch and she woke me to come on deck. We ran the motor and turned on all our lights for the occasion, to insure that we were as visible as possible. Despite repeated radio calls we never could get a response. Nevertheless, once satisfied that the freighter and *Querencia* were each on their separate ways we turned off the engine and lights and returned to only wind power. I went below and collapsed in my sea bunk once again leaving the world of wakefulness and responsibility to Davey.

Later that morning my Casio alarm went off informing me that it was time to relieve Davey of her watch. I could feel that *Querencia* was sailing easily and going ahead gently.

"You doing OK, Davey?"

"I'm fine, take your time," Davey answered.

I accepted the invitation and easily put off rising for another forty-five minutes. When I finally climbed my way out the companionway there I found Davey settled in the cockpit catching forty winks in the early morning light. Nelley was steering effortlessly, the wheel barely turning in the light but consistent air. Davey had her safety-harness on and her journal was in her hands. She had been writing some prose. I grabbed my camera and took a priceless picture before gently plucking the journal from her breast to read her entry.

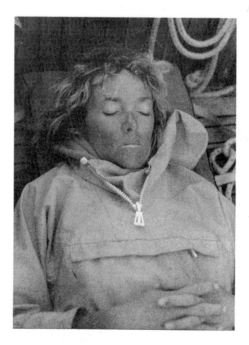

Riding the white capped mottled blue crest
leaving a trail of bubble and foam.
The wind pendulum swings.
The ocean siren still lives out there — I hear
her. The shrill whistle of whales and dolphins. The white puffs on the edge of the
waves scattered into crystal spray by the
pounding hull of our mighty ship. Yesterday's
clouds fade into today's sunshine. The
warmth on my body makes yesterday's torrents of rain and gusts of wind disappear
quickly, as ice in a tropical glass.

"I'm not really asleep, just resting my eyes ten minutes at a time," Davey said softly, opening her eyes as she spoke.

"Meditating too?" I asked. She looked pulchritudinous and was surrounded by a day-glow aura.

"Yes, it's been so peaceful and beautiful this morning. You know John, after experiencing the sunrise watch as many times as I have I'm sure that when I complete this passage my intuitions, my belief system, my *consciousness* will be opened beyond any experience I've ever had before."

I knew exactly what Davey was talking about. I had found my own self quite "high" in such moments of loneness, riding this private sea. It would be more appropriate to call it a state of grace — an incredible feeling of everything being right, everything being "bright and beautiful" — all of existence bathing in a divine love. It was so strong and so powerful a sensation that it totally consumed me while at the same time filling me with an incredible energy.

"Well, I'm off to my bunk. Want me to wake Paul and have him join you?" Davey suddenly spoke.

"No, hon. I'm fine. Let him rest. You go get some real sleep, too," I advised.

I climbed up on the aft rail of *Querencia* while holding on to the the backstay and gazed toward the horizon. I was alone and rested. The sea was consistently beating to the tune of four-foot waves. My whole field of consciousness was bright gold and blue. My thoughts were absolutely wonderful and I was filled with complete happiness as I studied the haloed horizon. *Querencia* charged north, her heel cutting into the fifteen-knot trades, the sun reflecting off her bright work. Her teak, her sails, her red, whites, and blues came alive with color in the new dawn light. My partners Davey and Paul were peaceful and safe below in their sea bunks.

I felt omnipotent. Unlike all my other accomplishments, it was *this incredible voyage* that truly made me feel like I had done something worthwhile with my life. In only a few more hundred miles we would be in Hawai'i, far from this special place at sea, which at the moment felt like the "palm of God's hand." Never would I forget this feeling, I promised myself. Never would I forget meeting in spirit with the great explorers before me. Never would I forget the incredible natural forces that control the Earth. Never in my life have I had a greater fulfillment of *self* than at sea.

"Everything that is made by God is good and holy," I told myself, "from the glory rays of the sun to the joy of man."

The colored brilliance of the rising sun as we reached northward was strong and spectacular. It projected pastels over sky and sea, putting all surrounding objects in a very different light. It was during such incredibly isolated and subtle times that nature reinforced my ability to see the life force that burns within all living things. The life force in the universe has the ultimate sentient ability to make matter alive and let it learn more about itself. Just maybe life is God trying to figure out who He is. It seems like a reasonable enough theory when applied to the natural world. Overall however, this experiment with man must be coming to some sort of a dead end — snarled traffic, overgrown egos and lives revolving around the Almighty Buck instead of the sun, the tides, or the season.

I remember now, how in that shimmering, subdued light of early day the spirit had been very electric, much the same as lightning or static, and it seemed to dance around each of us according to our moods. Each of us had our own corona or aura just as the sun did.

It is hard for many of us to believe that we are more than flesh and bones spinning like rocks and sticks in some inane chronicle of existence. It is also hard to believe that flames protrude millions of miles from the sun since we cannot see its corona except during periods of total eclipse. Yet this corona exists despite any self-centered belief to the contrary. So it is with the spirit, our soul. After all, it wasn't that long ago, really, when we thought that the world was flat!

Learning to better see the life force aura, or radiating glow, around all living creatures excited me. I had always been able to see this phenomenon, only it was now that I really appreciated the ability to be aware of it and its spiritual implications. I remembered vividly how at the moment of my father's death his "light" had faded. It was his spirit leaving his body that I had been witnessing. It had been no different with the large and very beautiful mahi mahi we had taken from the sea the previous week. When it expired its colors faded like disappearing ink. It had been the same with the startled octopi in Bora Bora. When I caught one in my hands it had been amazing to see its exposed and vulnerable skin became a coruscant, psychedelic light show. Life is just that — *alive* — a colorful expression of *the spirit*.

No, this trip was going to do more than just fill us with memories and reflections. If we were fortunate enough to remember what nature had taught us, our lives could continue to be varied, thoughtful, and exemplary. I was convinced. Life for man, as nature intended it, was meant to be a dazzling mosaic of poetry, playfulness, idiosyncrasies and hypothetical philosophies on the origins of our species.

> I saw that the universe is not composed of dead matter, but is, on the contrary, a living Presence; I became conscious in myself of eternal life. It was not a conviction that I would have eternal life, but a consciousness that I possessed eternal life then; I saw that all men are immortal; that the cosmic order is such that without any peradventure all things work together for the good of each and all; that the foundation principle of the world, of all the worlds, is what we call love, and that the happiness of each and all is in the long run absolutely certain. The vision lasted a few seconds and was gone, but the memory of it and the sense of the reality of what it taught has remained during the quarter century which has since elapsed.
>
> —R. M. Bucke
> *Sunbeams, The Sun*

64.

022:50 320° magnetic, 15+ knots, Barometer
29.82, in and out of thunder clouds but no
rain or lightening. Dropped jib on Paul's
watch — discovered that the top hank is broken. Also discovered small hole in main sail
— chafe from reefing line. Must attend to
those in A.M. Had a nice evening with John
— rum and cokes and canned duck on deck
with Querencia charging along. Relieved to
finally get a fix on the Sat Nav that confirms
our arithmetic — surprised how far along we
are. Twenty-eight days seems feasible now.
— DT

The signs of a passage well underway were making themselves visible not only by chafe but by rewards as well. We were nearing Hawai'i, the next port to offer us the opportunity to claim another victorious and successful ocean crossing. We were far enough east that now we could relax the sails and lay off the wind a bit. That was smart thinking. Sailing was much less difficult and more comfortable despite occasional heavy seas, and we worried less and less about reaching our destination. Actually, the three of us became more and more elated.

I came up from below one evening to show my newly drawn plotting sheet to Paul and Davey for approval. Prepared and published by the Defense Mapping Agency Aerospace Center, plotting sheets are for the most part just blank sheets of paper with four equidistant horizontal lines and one vertical line in the center. A longitude scale is provided in the bottom right corner from which you can measure the correct distance between vertical lines of longitude for your given latitude. Using this information and some parallel rulers you turn these pads of plotting sheets into charts on which you draw your course. The vast ocean can be broken down into little squares that you navigate across, a day at a time, bit by bit. Using the compass and a rule and dividers and pen, you then plot your course. It is a little like walking in the dark and counting each footstep.

Only on this afternoon as we crossed 16°N latitude and I filled in the longitude lines of our next plotting sheet I got excited. We were arriving! In the upper left hand corner, near 19°N and 155°W I was inspired to use color water pens to draw in the green SE corner of the Big Island of Hawai'i surrounded with a turquoise reef. We were almost there. Thrilled, soon I had splattered colorful doodles all over the page. I drew a tourist in an aloha shirt with sunglasses and a camera, and then a blue and gold mahi mahi jumping across the sheet, and then the smiling sun. And then there was *Querencia* sailing gallantly with birds and puffy little white clouds all about her.

"Check this out," I said, displaying my work in the cockpit.

"Cool" said Paul.

"That's great! Is that Hilo?" Davey joined in. I had taken the time to draw in Kumukahi Pt., Leleiwi Pt., Pepe'ekeo Pt. and the city of Hilo.

"Yeah! It is!" I said with glee. "With a mountain similar to Mt. Rainier on it we should be able to see the island of Hawai'i from far at sea. It will probably show up as some huge cloud bank just to the port side of our bow."

Being able to navigate has its benefits. There really is no hocus-pocus or midnight wizardry. The only arithmetic required is simple addition and subtraction, and although it may seem tedious at times it definitely becomes easier after you have practiced it for a while. For us, navigating out of sight of land is far more comfortably accomplished than when close to shore. Despite landmarks an error can quickly become more dangerous. Our initial stumbling block to learning ocean navigation was a failure to see the total picture through the dusty and obscure language of the technical books we thought we had to read on the subject. In truth it came easy to us and this was a source of fascination. Coming north I had been careful to compare the three types of offshore navigation.

Just using dead reckoning (a corruption of the old-fashioned term "deduced reckoning") we had never been more than about ten miles from where we thought we were (by comparison to celestial and satellite navigation). Dead reckoning is simple. You keep accurate track of the boat's movement in time and you are able to estimate instantly the ship's position at any given moment. Any changes of course or speed are entered at once in the logbook along with the time and later (if time affords) transferred to the chart, or plotting sheet.

We had used our Walker taffrail log for months before finally giving it up along with the constant chore of clearing its line and propeller of debris or untangling it from the wind vane, rudder, or prop. It wasn't necessary. *Querencia* did four speeds ninety percent of the time. It was always zero, two, four, or six knots. It was easy to guess and be right.

Using a protractor and measuring the actual degree or course made in relation to the compass is also important, as is a careful measurement of time. When the weather is good and consistent and other conditions such as current set or drift are minimal (or absent), entering a recording in the log can be much less frequent than when things are going topsy turvy, fast and slow, this way and that. Because of the importance of knowing your estimated position at all times we customarily calculated the distance traveled and marked it in the log every one to three hours. From it we charted our course one to several times a day. If we were close inshore or in doubtful water we marked our position every half hour. We also marked the course line whenever the speed changed and drew a new course line if we changed our heading.

In deduced reckoning a mariner heads his boat in the direction he wants to go by turning the wheel or tiller and then keeping explicit records of the direction and speed over time so he can calculate his constantly moving position. Naturally, without checks of some sort a boat can get considerably off course after many hours or several days, but sometimes dead reckoning is all a sailor can obtain.

Our second system of navigation, celestial, was also important. Very simply explained we would sight, or "shoot" the elevation of a celestial body (such as the sun) above the horizon using a sextant, a device with which to measure this angle. Its precision is what makes it expensive. You could use a protractor! Once you have the angle, you assume that you are so many degrees latitude and longitude (say, from your dead-reckoning) and then using navigation tables in nautical almanacs you look up constants that allow you to calculate what the elevation or angle of the celestial body at the assumed position would be at the precise time of the sextant shot. If the angle is larg-

er than the angle you measured than you must be toward the celestial body where it sits in the sky. If is smaller than you must be farther away on a circular "line of position" (LOP) drawn around the
celestial object.

You shoot another celestial object and the place where its line of
position crosses or intersects your first LOP is known as a "fix" and
the fix is where you are. My favorite calculations with celestial navigation involved shooting three stars in rapid succession, a three star
fix. You could also shoot the same celestial object over a period of
time. The axis north star Polaris was higher and higher in the sky
each night as we made our way north. From it, an approximation of
latitude was easy.

Of course you must remember that the objects we usually sight
(planets and stars other than Polaris) are in constant motion (east to
west) and a considerable distance away, and that Earth is also curved
and only a small portion can safely be transferred to a flat chart. Also,
there are additional problems such as index error, Dip or Height of
Eye, refraction, semidiameter, and parallax to account for. Therefore
celestial navigation wasn't always as easy as we wished. The key to
success in celestial navigation is checking and rechecking your calculations due to the possibility of mathematical error and then confirming your work with more work. It can take a lot of time. You
keep shooting sights and doing your math. But as I have already said,
there are few people around to argue with you when you point to a
blank chart and say "Here we are!"

Today we also have navigation aided by electronics — handheld
calculators, Loran, radar, standard Satellite Navigation (Sat Nav), or
handheld Global Positioning Systems. Don, the tuna fisherman who
befriended us at the Noyo River once summed it all up for me, "God
gave us electronics because he got tired of seeing us do it the hard
way!"

Radar is seldom found on small boats like *Querencia* because of
its cost, weight, and power needs. As for Loran, popular for coastal
navigation, *Querencia's* transpacific way points went far beyond the
distance where Loran signals start to jump lanes and give erroneous
information. The Global Positioning System, or GPS, was anticipated for several years but space shuttle delays did slow deployment

of satellites. Now, using twenty-four satellites in *fixed* position above the globe, it provides high accuracy and twenty-four-hour fixes worldwide; the ultimate navigation solution.

When we commissioned *Querencia* for blue water sailing in the fall of 1982 GPS was not available yet but Sat Nav was. We put Satellite Navigation aboard even though it cost us $3000. As I've already suggested, it was worth every penny.

Since then we've seen the price of satellite navigation drop drastically. GPS is now available as a handheld device that sells for under $200 and runs on AA batteries! Without a doubt, satellite navigation is one of the most wonderful tools ever to fall into the hands of the adventuring yachtsman. It is truly a blessing that it has gone from governmental to commercial and public usage. It's unique that the yachtsman can get something back out of those tax dollars spent putting those satellites in orbit.

I suppose there will always be those who will label most electronic marvels unnecessary. The only argument against having satellite navigation is if you can't afford it. It can be used anywhere in the world in any weather, without special charts and with an accuracy of at least half a nautical mile.

With the Sat Nav system we used there were five moving navigation satellites in polar orbits about 700 miles high, traveling 15,000 miles per hour and circling the earth every 100 minutes or so. Some of these satellites were launched over a decade ago, but their transmitting signals (about one watt) are still strong and they continue to function flawlessly.

The daily function of the Sat Nav system is maintained by the Navy Astronautics Group of Point Mugu, California as well as tracking stations in Hawai'i, Minnesota, and Maine. The precise orbit of the satellite as a function of time is predetermined, and this and other information is transmitted to the overhead satellite and stored in its memory banks every twelve hours. It is the fact that the satellite "knows" exactly where it is in space that allows Sat Nav receivers to calculate a fix, using a small digital computer to decode and analyze the frequency data a satellite transmits. This opportunity will arise every ninety minutes or so depending on the number of operational satellites crossing at that particular latitude.

Despite being told, "never turn off your Sat Nav," we found there was nothing inherently wrong with doing that, provided we maintained an accurate DR by other means. To save electricity we only used our Sat Nav two hours a day, an hour in the morning and an hour in the evening. We did that for the entire passage from Bora Bora to Hawai'i. By using the "next satellite" feature we knew when the next best satellite was available. The next best satellite was one with a good elevation in the sky and a strong signal. On this passage that happened to be first thing in the morning and at the end of the afternoon. Consistently the Sat Nav began to teach us something; that it could baby-sit us better than we could baby-sit it!

Power was a concern, so we turned off our Sat Nav between fixes and kept an accurate log of our direction and speed over time. Turning off our Sat Nav meant that when we did turn it on again we had to re-initialize it before we could use it, but this wasn't hard and could be accomplished in a minute. To initialize it we had to enter the correct GMT within fifteen minutes and latitude and longitude within three degrees (DR). We also had to enter the date and answer a few minor questions about alarms and antenna height. That was all there was to it! Soon the Sat Nav would start tracking our "bird." Once the data was received and analyzed the Sat Nav would beep and display the fix coordinates. After copying and reviewing the data we needed, taking special care to note when the next good satellite would be coming over the horizon, we would turn the Sat Nav off. It was like having another crew member shoot a fix for us twice a day.

Only when we were within a day or two of landfall would we leave our Sat Nav on and enter our speed and heading manually so that we always had a better consensus on our position immediately; the Sat Nav continuously updating our position based on speed, heading, and time. This is the running DR feature of the Sat Nav.

A few afternoons later our navigation showed us to be only 114 miles from the Kumukahi Pt. light. We had travelled 2,390.5 miles as the crow flies with a mean speed of 91.94256096 miles per day. That evening we all stared silently at the big hazy cloud bank that lay ahead of us on the horizon to the northwest. Behind it the sun was setting and the sky was afire in color. Hawai'i was buried in that cloud bank somewhere. It had to be. Anxiously the next morning we looked for land but we still couldn't see it through the haze. We hanked on our big genoa for our forward sail. Then it was all bright work and sprucing up as we made ready for port and customs.

> 0900 All hands look lively. No luffing or soggering aboard. We're putting our hearts into our elbow grease. — JFM

65.

He pua laha 'ole
[One who is as choice and highly prized as a very rare blossom]
— 'Olelo No'eau
Hawaiian Proverbs
Mary Kawena Pukui

For the past few nights we had been listening to the radio and the driving beat of the number one rock song called *Purple Rain* by a young man named Prince.

Paul was intrigued. "Wow, what was that? Did you hear that? Kind of different, huh?"

"Really! It's sort of like a one-two beat in reverse," I said, not really knowing what I was talking about. This was a new kind of music. We were entering a new time when not only reggae was sweeping the world, but the beat of rap and nonconforming cadenced compositions from musical geniuses like Prince were making their way into the music boxes around the world, particularly in the urban areas where the AM stations throbbed out the heartbeat of young men and women. Paul was getting excited and Davey and I were, too. We realized more than ever that we really had been out of the country for an extended period of time.

"Kind of cool," Paul said. His left leg was jumping up and down. "Wow, hey look, there are lights!"

Sure enough, off the port bow we could see a couple of lights now and then peeping over the horizon between swells. I figured we were thirty-nine miles out so it was probably fishing boats. It was almost eleven at night and we were making our way in. I worried for just for a moment about what sort of civilized muddle might await us.

Unexpectedly two extremely large whales charged alongside us before sounding. It scared the daylights out of me. They had been a bit too close. The starboard kerosene light had gone out and I asked Paul to flip off the radio before I went forward to relight the lantern.

But the whales went on their way and the evening settled down. Things were going fine. The skies were clear and the wind a very obliging steady fifteen knots. We were making it. At two in the morning I was in the sea bunk and Davey made her log entry.

> 290°M 10 knots 30.00 Barometer — Have switched to electric running lights and they are working sell. A few big black clouds. Saw an airplane take off from what must be Hilo! Exciting times!

By the time light started to break the shape of an island slowly revealed itself in the emerging daylight. As the sun rose we found its smoldering volcano, *Kīlauea*, just aft of our port beam. You could smell the sulfur in the air despite its distance. We were at the south-east end of the Hawai'i islands, the Big Island of Hawai'i.

The Big Island's area is twice that of all the other islands in the State of Hawai'i combined. Also known as the "Volcano Island," it has five volcanoes, two still active — Mauna Loa and Kīlauea. Mauna Kea and Mauna Loa, the two volcanoes that dominate the island, rise to heights of nearly 14,000 feet and are the highest in the state. In actuality these Hawaiian islands were formed by several volcanoes rising above the surface of the sea. On the Big Island this volcanic eruption and island building is still continuing.

If the mountains of Mauna Kea and Mauna Loa are measured from the ocean floor where they originate they are amongst the tallest mountains in the world, over 30,000 feet high, a distance of more than five miles — several hundred feet higher than Mt. Everest in the Himalayas! The whole Hawaiian archipelago actually did emerge from the deep-profound-darkness of the ocean about twenty-five million years ago, the result of eruptions caused by mantles of the earth's crust colliding on the floor of the Pacific Basin. Geologically, the Hawaiian Islands represent some of the most massive works ever created by mother nature.

The early Hawaiian people believed that these volcanoes represented the power of *Pele*, a beautiful blond fiery goddess with the complexion of moonlight. She produced the eruptions and thus controlled the land that was given and taken away by the awesome eruptions. Pele represented not only the force of nature, but also the balance of it. Born as a tongue of flame from the mouth of *Haumea*, the mother of all living creatures, she journeyed through most of the nations of Polynesia before finally arriving by canoe at Nihoa, an uninhabited island north of the Hawaiian islands. Finding no fire she paddled on to Kaua'i, then O'ahu where she dug Diamond Head crater. From Diamond Head she moved on again, this time to Maui where she resided several centuries in Haleakalā crater until its last eruption in 1790. Finally she came to rest in the Halema'uma'u pit of Kīlauea on the Big Island of Hawai'i. Many people have a firm conviction that she still lives there to this day; in the sulphurous mists, the pāhoehoe [smooth lava], and in the flames that burst from the earth.

It is generally believed by the scientific community that the early Hawaiian people themselves were Polynesians who migrated over two thousand miles from the Marquesas to the Big Island in giant double-hulled canoes between 500 and 1100 A.D. Recently this belief has been supported by the successful voyage of the *Hōkūleʻa*, a large sailing outrigger in which modern Hawaiians repeated the skills of their seafaring ancestors by roaming the Polynesian Triangle navigating only by the stars (and other signs of nature).

When they first arrived in Hawaiʻi these ancient Polynesians found a different and specialized flora and fauna. These life species had crossed the wide ocean barrier from all directions, mostly by chance. The relatively few species that had successfully established themselves were ones that were the most adapted for the long journey, as were the Polynesians themselves with their uncanny ability to live and sail upon the ocean's surface and navigate by the stars. So these first human visitors found Hawaiʻi a pristine place, an undisturbed sanctuary with over 2,000 plants that grew nowhere else in the world and with abundant and rich marine life. Here also were some seventy species of spectacular birds, including the Hawaiian duck and goose, but surprisingly there were none of the aggravating insects, reptiles, or amphibians. On shore the only mammals found were the Hawaiian hoary bat and the monk seal. It was a fragile system of plant and animal life living in a near perfect climate.

The early Polynesian colonist radically modified this habitat in the Hawaiian Islands through their primitive agricultural development and the introduction of pigs, dogs, and rats. Nearly a thousand years later mariners began arriving from the East and West introducing goats, European pigs, sheep, cattle, horses, cats, other species of rodents, insects, and along with social diseases, some of the world's most debilitating and lethal germs. Once again another naive Polynesian paradise had been introduced to infestation and disease. Today it is possible that as few as five original species of birds remain, the rest extinct, although over 150 species of exotic birds have been introduced to the islands, and dozens of mammals and reptiles. Some mammals which were introduced with good intention such as the mongoose, a natural predator of the rat, became a devastating predator for ground-nesting birds as well, and these new predators grew like wildfire.

There are but few "pure-blooded" Hawaiians left. When

Captain Cook first arrived, there were approximately 250,000 pure Hawaiians in the Islands. Now perhaps there are only 6,000 although over a million human beings call the islands home. Paul and Davey and I already knew this. But what we didn't know until we had spent our time in the South Pacific and Metata had taught us, is that Polynesians have always been a melting-pot race proud of their heritage. Hawai'i may be a far cry from its Polynesian origin but it is still populated by a remarkable mixture of races with the same goal of living together in harmony, in a nearly perfect environment of stunning beauty and balmy year round weather.

Querencia shuddered as we fired up her engine and began to motor sail along the coast, headed for Hilo Harbor, anxious to put in early in the afternoon. We were finding the winds somewhat lighter and the seas smaller. It was time to get in to port while the getting was good. We would not risk a night entry.

Soon we were approaching the breakwater on Blonde Reef that protects Hilo Harbor. The lush green growth of the uplands around what appeared to be a charming rural city was more and more visible.

Davey was on the VHF radio, which we hadn't used really since San Diego. (It seemed all the local boats that used radio used CB in Tahiti). She was getting a patch through by the telephone company to her parents home in Utah. Suddenly she was speaking to her mom Ginny.

"Hello, Mom?"

"Hi, honey! How are you guys? Where are you?"

"We're great. We made it! We're getting ready to pull into Hilo on the Big Island of Hawai'i. It took us 27 days! Over."

All of us on board *Querencia* were beaming ear to ear. It had been our first real transmission to the outside world in weeks. The radio was magic, as was the sound of Ginny's voice. We were elated and triumphant. We all leaned toward the VHF radio to hear Ginny's response.

"Good. Well, Caroline arrived yesterday. I just got back from taking her to the beauty shop. She had her hair cut. It is cute. At least I think so. Caroline's not too sure about it though. But it's nothing to worry about. She'll get used to it in a couple of days or so, uh, over."

"Well, we're safe and sound and we just wanted you to know,

Mom. And we had a terrific passage. Over," Davey said sort of blandly into the microphone.

"We're going to go to your sister's for dinner tonight. Should be fun. I'm getting ready to fix some lunch now, although I haven't quite figured out what we're going to have yet, uh, over."

"Sounds great, Mom. Well... we'll call from a phone in Hilo. Bye mom, over and out."

"Bye, honey, and take care. We love you and give our love to Paul and John. CLICK"

The three of us looked at each other sort of dumbfounded. And then we laughed really hard.

"What are we laughing at?" asked Davey, sincerely, smiling.

Paul asked, "*Nobody gets it*, do they?"

"Gets what, Paul?" I asked, chuckling.

"Cruising! I mean we just sailed across this huge ocean in a tiny boat and we're all excited to share our experience with someone and the first person we talk to finds Caroline's hair-do the hottest topic of the day!"

"Now wait a minute, Paul, what is Ginny supposed to say? It's just that she isn't comfortable speaking on the radio," Davey said, mildly defensive.

"Your mother is right, Paul," I said, "...but you're right too. *Nobody really gets it.*"

Part IX
Hawai'i

66.

"Experience is not what happens to a man.
It is what a man does with what happens to him."
— Aldous Huxley

"There are only two lasting bequests we can hope to give our
children. One of these is roots; the other wings." — Anonymous

Fluorescent buoys marked the harbor passage past the breakwater into a dredged channel that had been created long ago so that larger ships could put in. We would not be the first *haole* [Caucasian] boat to anchor in Hilo. For two hundred years farmers, jewelers, tailors, teachers, doctors and missionaries had started new lives here in this simple and old-fashioned town. It was in Hilo that the ships which brought them across the wide ocean dropped anchor after first navigating through the coral heads of the wide bay.

Inside the harbor we made our way past Kaula'inā'iwi and Coconut Island, into Kūhiō Bay, and from there into the tiny concrete boat harbor of Radio Bay, which was beyond the main piers and facilities reserved for shipping. Once inside this small basin we found a string of other yachts all tied up Tahiti-style to a ten-foot south wall which was had a few large cleats here and there. There was only one spot left, and with reverse gear, a two hundred foot line, and the help of the friendly Hawaiian Harbormaster, we were able to back in to it, dropping our hook off the bow on the way in. It was two o'clock in the afternoon.

As this was our port of entry, *Querencia* had been flying her yellow "Q" flag. As skipper I was prepared to go ashore and report to U.S. Customs which I understood to be located in a building just outside the port gates. As it turned out it wasn't necessary for me to go ashore. Before I had the chance we were greeted by agent Jack Cooper of U.S. Customs, a grand Humphrey Bogart sort of senior who came aboard, scanned below decks, asked us the required questions of declaration, and filled out the necessary paper work. He then accepted our invitation to sit down and have a chat with us. He had many questions about cruising. We must have spoken for a half-hour and he might have stayed longer but for the arrival of a dark-skinned young man by the name of Mel from the Department of Agriculture. We had managed to eat our last grapefruits, brought up from Bora Bora, but we still had some potatoes, onions, and green beans which we surrendered almost with glee, looking forward to a short walk to a real store with fresh food, or better yet, to a restaurant!

Most of the ten other boats tied to the quay in Radio Bay were empty, with the exception of beautiful *Lion Wing* out of San Francisco with Bo and Annie Hudson aboard. They were our neighbors on our starboard side. Avid sailors, Bo and Annie were finishing up an Hawaiian cruise as a shakedown prior to an extended cruise through the South Pacific. We were surprised to see that Annie remembered us. We had frequented a marine supply store she helped manage when we were in San Francisco the year before, picking everyone's brain in search of a solution for the case of our mysteriously dying engine!

"Oh, yea, I remember you!"

"It turned out to be a pin hole air leak in the fuel line. Finally fixed it in San Diego," said Davey.

We took pleasure in their warm welcome and their help in getting secured and organized. Bo, a retired airplane pilot, showed me a new trick to loosen up *Querencia's* now turquoise deck plates which had seized during the course of the passage. In return for "loosening up" our deck plates I "tightened up" [recemented] a gold crown that had lifted off one of his molars the previous day. I had been carrying my dental emergency kit for thousands of miles without ever having a need for it, so it felt "about time" to use it. I had given penicillin injections to our South African friend Bob in Bora Bora [at the request and according to the prescription of a local physician for staph] but that was not a dental application. Although *Querencia* could be nearly a floating emergency room, I can't complain that we didn't need to use it. Our sailing life was basically a healthy one.

Stern to the quay in Radio Bay.

With *Querencia* finally safeguarded, the three of us took showers at the facilities near the docks and then began the walk south along the road towards town. We drifted along the road feeling displaced, cars and trucks zipping by at what seemed like incredible speeds, people racing to and from God knows what. We came across to an abandoned lot where a small grove of Banyan trees stood. Philodendron vines crawled in spiral paths up their trunks, conjuring up memories of old Tarzan movies. We took a moment's refuge in the shaded tall grass of the plat to center ourselves and admire the greenery before continuing our walk.

Once we made it into town we drifted from what was to us one extravagance after another: pizza, arcade games, ice cream and the movie, *Indiana Jones and the Temple of Doom*.

Coming out of the theater, darkness met us and we walked back along the shoulder of the road, against the traffic and the headlights, returning to *Querencia*. We slipped aboard quietly, Davey and I crawling into our v-berth to sleep together for the first time in nearly a month, Paul taking the larger berth in the salon. No need for a lee cloth tonight. *Querencia* floated flat, despite breakers crashing against the sea wall protecting Radio Bay from the open ocean.

The following morning we awoke early and took another walk. We were fascinated to find abandoned avocado and papaya trees and pepper bushes all bearing an abundance of fruit. When we returned to the harbor Davey made avocado sandwiches. We ate them and munched on fresh American potato chips while we lazily watched local men and women fishing for 'ama'ama, casting-out a type of seaweed they used as bait. They were having great success and out of the small crowd of people fishing in the bay there were one or two catches a minute. 'Ama'ama are thick-bodied mullet, torpedo-shaped fish, silvery with faint stripes along their sides. Found in all tropical and temperate seas these medium to large size fish were in season. They had come to feed on algae taken up in mouthfuls from the bottom of brackish waters. One Hawaiian lady angler told me that the place where she collected her seaweed was a secret only known by her.

By late afternoon we had met most of the other cruisers aboard their boats including a handsome couple, John and Debbie Dye on *Sea Gull*. *Sea Gull* had arrived from the Society Islands just days before us. We faintly remembered their green-hulled boat sailing by *Querencia's* anchorage one day and them waving on their way out the Pass Teavanui. They had a visitor aboard, Steve Neumann, who had flown over from Honolulu where his yacht, *Athena*, was tied off in the Ala Wai Yacht Harbor. Steve was a fascinating, magnanimous character that later became an important friend.

We also met Willie on *Charity*, our neighbor on our port side. An American originally from Austria, Willie still harbored a bit of an accent. You half expected him to yodel when he got excited. He had been an educational toy engineer for Mattel in Los Angeles before escaping to sea. He was on his way to Tahiti and one evening later we would share our "local" Tahitian knowledge with him as he prepared what he called the "only meal I cook worth serving — chicken and dumplings." The following summer when Willie met up with us on his return to Honolulu, following nearly a year's absence, one of the first things he wanted to do was go see the fantasy movie *The Never Ending Story*. He even offered to pay our admission if we would accompany him and his girl friend to the showing, so enthused he was to share the animation technology with us. Thank goodness not only for Santa Claus and coo-coo clocks, but engineers that make toys instead of stealth bombers. Maybe one day we will be lucky enough to live in a peaceful world where schools will have all the money they need to buy educational toys and governments will have to have bake sales to gather funds to build weapons of war.

We also came to know Captain David Anderson and first mate Gus Konchar aboard the 60-foot steel-hulled ketch *Deo Gratias*. The *Deo* had just made a nineteen-day crossing from Marina Del Ray, Los Angeles, and carried seven passengers. Seeing that she had just arrived, sitting there in the golden sun of late afternoon, we walked over to where she was awkwardly tied up against pilings at the entrance to Radio Bay (the space along the quay already having been taken). We were invited aboard for cocktails and *pūpū* (hors d'oeuvres), complete with entertainment provided by a yellow-breasted Amazon talking parrot named Delila. The luxuriousness of the *Deo Gratias* was accented by her 18" portholes, a fo'c'sle, and a woodburning fireplace. This was the first of many visits to the *Deo* while she was in the Hawaiian islands and the beginning of a lifelong friendship with David, twenty years my senior and just possibly a day or two younger in disposition.

The next few days we rented an automobile. After re-acquainting myself with the gas and brake pedals we were off to explore the rest of the Big Island. There was so much ground to be covered it was easy to see why they called it the "Big Island." With a length of ninety-three miles and a width of seventy-six miles it is over two-and-a-half million acres in size, a whole lot bigger than the islands we had been used to! The island of Hawai'i has everything: the rain forests of Florida, the deserts of Arizona, the coastlines, grassland, foothills and mountains of California, and its own unique subtropical signature. It is also here that the legendary volcano goddess Pele had made her home in the Kīlauea caldera, dazzling us with her fiery display at night, shooting fiery fountains of lava hundreds of feet into the air.

When we weren't sightseeing we were sipping cool drinks in Kona or enjoying a picnic amidst the green grasses of South Point. It was fun being tourists. Not completely the tourist, we always had *Querencia* in Radio Bay to go home to. By comparison to the other towns of the Big Island we found Hilo to be a friendly fishing and agricultural community with modern stores and quite reasonable prices. We were particularly thrilled with the off-loading of tuna each morning from the sampan fishing fleets onto Suisan Dock. Fierce bidding occurred in the wholesale auction of some very large and magnificent fish.

Sometimes it feels as if life should only be composed of prolonged and leisurely travels, seeing the sights, void of any mundane concerns beyond those of food and shelter. But it can't always be that way. Paul called his other father in Washington state in consideration of returning there to complete his high school studies in the fall. After placing the call he came back to the boat looking a bit ashen with the news that his paternal grandmother in Spokane had died and it was necessary that he fly back to the mainland immediately for the funeral. Davey and I were deeply saddened by his departure.

Paul had been an integral part of our adventure and its success, much more than I would have ever guessed. It wasn't just that he became part of our winning team, equal to Davey and me in crewing and handling the boat, but that he had enriched the trip and our lives with his presence. Watching him grow to be a man with our full uninterrupted attention had been as fascinating a thing as anything else we had experienced.

Paul had learned a few things about life he wouldn't have learned in school. I had learned a few things myself, such as being a loving father at the same time as being a responsible skipper. There had been times when we both had lost our tempers. There had been times when we had all sat around feeling awful. But there had been many more times spent not only as a fully functional crew, but also as a functioning and happy family that taught itself how to make the best of life, without the distractions found on shore.

"Hey, John," Paul said. His leg was jumping up and down again, like it did when he was relaxed and excited at the same time. This was his last night on *Querencia* before flying out.

"What, Buzzer?"

"I just want you to know that this trip has taught me that I can always get where I want to go providing I'm willing to start from where I am. I'm going to go finish high school in Washington, and then I'm coming back to Hawai'i. I hope you and Mom decide to stay in Hawai'i too."

"I think we just might stay in Hawai'i, Paul, we love Polynesia as much as you do. Are you sure you want to come back to Hawai'i next year if we're still here?"

"Definitely!" answered Paul enthusiastically.

Davey and I both knew that Paul could accomplish whatever he set his mind to. He had discovered two new tools on our cruise that would help him achieve his goals; motivation and a capacity for endurance.

That night, before he left, Paul copied something called *Ten Wishes*, a little piece I found in Jamaica when I had been there in 1979, consulting with the Peace Corps. I always kept it handily available in *Querencia's* library and re-read it from time to time.

Ten Wishes

1. A few friends who understand me — and yet remain my friends.

2. Work of real value, without which the world would feel poorer.

3. An understanding heart.

4. Moments of leisure.

5. A mind unafraid to travel an unblazed trail.

6. The power to laugh.

7. Nothing at the expense of others.

8. A view of eternal hills and unresting sea, and of something beautiful made by the hand of man.

9. The sense of the presence of God.

10. And the patience to wait for the coming of things and the wisdom to know when they come.

Paul flew out of Hilo, going to weather in a jetliner for a change. He would make the 2,000-mile-plus trip in less than five hours and receive a hero's welcome. That year his grade average jumped two full points and the following summer he *did* return to Hawai'i.

67.

"My life is a vast and insane legend reaching everywhere without beginning or ending, like the Void—like Samsara — A thousand memories come like tics all day perturbing my vital mind with almost muscular spasms of clarity and recall..."

— Jack Kerouac
Desolation Angels

We were off again, this time to Honolulu, a distance of about two-hundred miles. We were anxious to get to sea; we had been forced to postpone our trip by gusty thirty-five-knot trades and eighteen-foot seas in the channels of the Hawaiian Islands. We had been warned by Bo to take small craft warnings in Hawaiian waters seriously and we did.

"When the flow doesn't go, don't go," Davey sang, cheerfully reminding me that there wasn't a need to bet against the house. For the first time in thousands of miles it was back again to just the two of us. We missed Paul.

Eventually the weather eased and we motored out of Hilo one morning at 0730, eager to get around the eastern point of the Big Island before the afternoon trades picked up. We cooked some turkey legs to stash away for later in the day in case cooking became too difficult. Noon was upon us and the trades, a great twenty-knot breeze, carried us north past Pepe'ekeo Point and up the Hāmākua coast. Huge vistas opened up with magnificent green valleys folding along the side of the island. Puffy, mystical clouds lingered on the slopes up the mountains and numerous waterfalls could be seen hiding in steep uninhabited jungle behind the curtain of mist created by the pounding surf. High above, frigate birds flew along the edge of these spectacular cliffs drenched in the sunshine that beamed down on them. It was a clear afternoon and the sky was a deep sapphire blue. Once again, we found ourselves mixing our feelings of bliss with a feeling of longing — longing to share each and every second of the cruising experience with the people we love, with all of mankind.

The wind kept building and in no time we were passing the Waipi'o Valley flanked with the 2,000-foot cliffs of the Kohala Mountains. This valley had once been a favorite spot of the *ali'i* or Hawaiian royalty who had given it the nickname of *Valley of the Kings*. The terrain was irregular and the lush neighboring valleys remained uninhabited along this section of coast. We wondered about our own loneness this coming night and how hard the wind would be blowing when we got into the channel between Hawai'i and Maui. We decided before sunset to reheat our turkey legs and accompanied them with corn on the cob and slices of big, red, juicy tomatoes. Davey brought our plates out into the cockpit just as the sun was setting so we might enjoy our meal during the waning daylight hours, the sky aglow with the same colors of our prepared food; oranges and yellows and reds. My peripheral vision caught flying fish darting between the waves, gliding and flitting between the crest and trough. All about us was white foam and blue water.

Shortly after dark we saw the 'Upolu Light at the north tip of the Big Island and we knew that we had completed our reach up the east coast and nothing but the 'Alenuihāhā Channel lay between us and Maui, now looming ahead of us, a faint, jagged outline above the dim horizon. The 'Alenuihāhā [great billows smashing] Channel, notorious for its accelerated winds and high seas, is twenty-six miles wide. The trade winds become quite strong, bottle-necking in from the East Pacific and, combined with a current of two knots setting to the west, the channel is usually very rough. Sailors have joked that the last two syllables in the name of the channel, "haha," are a reminder the channel always gets the last laugh. At 2000 hours under a nearly full waxing moon we found ourselves in a sea of ten-foot waves and strong tide rips. There was a good twenty-five knots of wind and shortening sail was in order. We already had a reef in the main and decided to drop one of our forward sails as well.

Dropping the jib was a challenge. With the seas so turbulent, I wasn't happy about leaving the helm entirely to the automatic wind steering. A wave would break occasionally just short of violence and I wanted to be near the helm in case of a broach. At the same time I wanted to give Davey a hand on the foredeck. What I did was make two short sprints to the mast to lower the halyard and adjust this and that. I thought of Jerry Lewis in an old movie. Davey was her usual self, seemingly focused on her task at hand, swinging around on the wire jib stay like a toy chimpanzee. Thank God for our safety harnesses and jack lines. Nevertheless, once we were both safe back in the cockpit we agreed that we were back to having another difficult, dark night ahead of us. But for now, *Querencia* was comfortable and going ahead.

We had wondered what the middle of the channel was going to be like. We had guessed bigger waves, and we were right! We flipped on the Sat-Nav just after 2300 hours to start getting fixes to confirm our position; all lights behind us from the Big Island were now well over the horizon. "Wow!" we kept saying to each other as awesome, frightening, rollers would come sweeping through. You could hear the really enormous waves fifteen seconds before they reached the boat, a thunder bowling along with the wave like a passing train. Then they would break, and after the smash they hissed and bubbled, glistening moonlight reflecting in the surrounding foam all about us.

With all the motion and apprehension, merrily going below and plopping down in the sea-bunk for a good night's rest wasn't an easy thing to do. It had been a while since we had been under way in such conditions and our anxiety was heightened by our expectation of being at Maui before the light of day. Alertness is necessary for good judgment, and it being best that one of the two of us be at least somewhat rested, I lay down in the cockpit while Davey stood diligently at the wheel. It was warm, yet some kind of chill had me in my float coat, curled up, huddled, and wedged in, my ankles bare, my cheek against the cool teak deck. *Querencia* seemed like a large surfboard, charging along in front of a wave until it finally overtook her, then the stern whipping this way, then that way. Davey struggled at the helm, water occasionally jumping over the rail and into the cockpit in little jeweled droplets. The motion reminded me of "The Octopus" I used to ride at the circus and fairgrounds when I was a kid.

When I closed my eyes I fell into suspended consciousness; a kaleidoscope of colors danced on my eyelids, along with designs, geometric shapes, and then true dreaming movies. I became totally involved in my dreaming; it overwhelmed me. And yet as a result of my efforts to remain prepared if called, I was totally aware of the motion, of the sound of the waves, of Davey's presence. I felt queerly safe, a sentient being on a journey through a small part of the cosmos, my body wracked with fatigue, and yet my mind so stimulated, so free, associations flooded my thoughts and ran like a river cascading through my levels of awareness. What I was experiencing was a phenomenon that accompanies unusual circumstances like stress, exhaustion, disorientation, and shock. It happens to people in isolation and people subjected to unfamiliar realities. The Yogis of India sleep on nails to get the effect — the effect of lingering between the two realities of being awake and being asleep to the point where you are watching yourself dreaming.

CRASH!

An odd wave had caught us on the beam and thrown us on our side. I sat up quickly only to feel still another wave pick up our stern from the aft starboard quarter and throw us sideways so far that this time our port rail stayed buried in the wave trough for what seemed an eternity. I grabbed the pedestal and stood on the cockpit coaming as Davey spun the wheel hard over to right the boat. Seawater was streaming back over the deck and into the cockpit. Thanks to the scuppers and the self-bailing cockpit, things were soon back to "normal." It had been an hour since I first closed my eyes. It felt like it had only been five minutes.

"Short rests are in order for both of us, hon... here, let me take the helm for a while..."

Davey, relieved, took her turn lying down in the cockpit. Sleeping, yet far from a deep sleep, she also watched herself dreaming in a state of semi-consciousness. We didn't talk about this "dreaming" until the next day when we were fascinated to discover that we each had been enchanted with such similar experiences right in the middle of the 'Alenuihāhā!

"Has to be something to do with alpha or theta waves," I insisted.

"*Lucid dreaming*" was Davey's description.

By 0200 we were fairly well across the channel and were making our approach into the six-mile-wide 'Alalākeiki Channel, reaching northwest between Maui and Kaho'olawe islands. The seas were now divided between the aft quarter and the beam on the starboard side. For the most part we were out of the monstrous seas, yet there was still the occasional roller coming slightly north of east that was bigger than the rest and would surprise us by knocking us on our ear. When this happened we cracked off and tried to run with it. Once the rogue passed we resumed our northerly westerly tack, inching our way into the channel. Even though we were now more off the wind, we kept the boom hauled in just over the rail. In the event of a broach we didn't want to bury the end of the boom in the sea.

Less sure in uncertain conditions, it became more necessary than ever to steer entirely by hand. One wave roared through — an eighteen-footer taking all awards. Luckily it had been preceded by a twelve-footer, and with that notice I was alarmed enough to look upon the rough waters behind us. This gave me just enough time to line up *Querencia's* stern perpendicular to the next wave's approach. The stern lifted high to meet it, then settled as the wave rolled under amidships. The bow followed suit, picking up its sprit and pointing it towards the heavens. Past the bow the wave broke in a luminescent froth accompanied by an ominous roar. Gently *Querencia* resumed a more normal attitude and settled down, giving up what had looked like an excellent angle for launching into space.

"I'm glad I was ready for that one!"

Davey, now wide awake, put her watchful eye behind us for any more surprises as I turned the boat once again into the weather, resuming our reach into the 'Alalākeiki Channel.

The southwest tip of Maui became visible with the flashing Hanamanioa Point light, and the outline of the uninhabited island Kaho'olawe, was visible on our port side in the waning moonlight. Eventually the seas lessened and the wind eased. We were getting into the lee of Maui and into the channel. Passing the Hanamanioa Point light on our beam, we both felt a tremendous relaxation flood our limbs. I set the automatic steering with a course straight up the middle of the channel and we slumped back in the cockpit enjoying the effect. We knew we were free of danger, with the exception of the commercial traffic and little Molokini Islet, whose marker light was now becoming visible. Molokini Islet is one-third of a mile long and only 150 feet high. In shape it actually resembles a croissant, being the bare rim of an ancient volcano crater in which the northern part of the rim has submerged. We calculated that we would be at Molokini at sunrise. A cruising guide we had on board recommended the crater for temporary anchorage, and we were looking forward to stopping and doing some serious catnapping. Passing tugs towing barely-lit barges an eighth of a mile behind them kept us wary and we would diligently flash our "D" signal on the sail with our hand torch. Hopefully other traffic would recognize our most endeared safety signal, "Keep clear of me — I am maneuvering with difficulty." We continued to take turns at the wheel, only occasionally asking each other for an opinion.

When day finally did break it was spectacular and we found ourselves surrounded by some of Hawai'i's finest scenery. The ten-mile-long island of Kaho'olawe, at the time a restricted military bombing target, was isolated and quiet, its high black cliffs accented with iron-rich red slopes. On our other side the mountains of Maui were starting to unfold around us. The wind died almost completely and we dropped all our sails and motored towards the ancient caldera of the Molokini crater. Designated a Marine Life Conservation District in 1977, today Molokini remains mostly a controlled diving area where tour boats from Maui bring avid tourists to day trip and enjoy the endless varieties of fish, seaweed, and coral in its crystal blue waters. Today it was still early and there were no other boats. The only sign of civilization on the island was the light beacon. This didn't surprise us as the *Pilot* warned that Molokini had an almost solid coral bottom, not particularly blessed with good holding for overnight anchoring. It was also exposed to the trades when they built up in the afternoon.

"Maybe we could anchor for the day anyway," I suggested as I turned the wheel and slowly started bringing *Querencia* around and into the crater. Davey casually turned on the depth sounder, and it immediately started complaining in aggravating beeps that the depth was only eight feet.

"Eight feet!" Davey shouted. *Querencia* loaded has a draft of about five feet.

Our lack of local knowledge and skimpy sailing directions had almost put us aground. There is serious shoaling on Molokini's northwestern tip. The water was clear and beautiful coral figures displayed themselves all around us while skittering schools of fish that looked like animated creations from the movie *The Yellow Submarine* swam up to *Querencia's* hull looking for handouts. Not knowing exactly which way to turn we held our breath while I threw the gear shift into reverse stopping *Querencia*. Then I slowly backed her out and beyond danger, amazed by how close we had come to running aground despite our cautious approach.

There is a saying that every sailor runs aground sooner or later. But it's never fun and can be quite dangerous, particularly in bad weather. We had run aground once in the southern Puget Sound. With a tide change of ten feet we were left high and dry, luckily in sand, and had to spend the better part of the day with our guest, Ken Osborne, sitting on the side of the hull drinking rum while we awaited the flood to return, right the boat, and float us off.

We decided instead to abandon the idea of anchoring in Molokini crater and continued on as effortlessly as possible. We raised but a minimum of "canvas" and enjoyed the calm seas and wind in the 'Au'au Channel between the islands of Maui and Lāna'i, meanwhile inching ourselves North. I volunteered to make a whopping breakfast, letting our Aries guide us along. We enjoyed T-bone steaks, eggs, and fried potatoes and tall glasses of ice cold milk — a nice formal meal served at the salon table. After dishes, Davey popped into the sea bunk for some shut-eye while I took Robert Anton Wilson's book *Right Where You Are Sitting Now* up on the foredeck and enjoyed having a lazy watch for a change. The sun was climbing up the sky rapidly and I kept moving more into what little shade I could find to deal with the microwave effect. In the next two hours only a couple of chartered fishing boats passed in the distance, giving me ample opportunity to enjoy relaxed muscles and a full belly. Indeed, the sea was like a bathtub, and I was amazed how Nelley was steering us toward our uncertain destination despite only a knot of forward motion.

68.

"The loveliest fleet of islands that lies anchored in any ocean."
— Mark Twain

Davey came up deck after an hour or so and we switched places. This was as good as anchoring and a whole lot less work. Davey laid out on the deck to enjoy some serious all-over sun bathing while reading Robin Graham's *Home is the Sailor* while I took my turn in the sea bunk. I longed to return to my travels from the night before when I had caught my twenty winks in the middle of the 'Alenuihāhā.

"Well, I'm off to explore a new dream-scape," I told Davey. I was determined to enjoy *this dreaming* and *remember* it.

Two hours later I awoke and could remember nothing specifically, but instead I had a profound sense of closeness with my deceased father. It was as if I had been a child only yesterday, and I had sat on his lap, feeling the security of his muscular body, his gentle voice, the smell of his shirt and his skin. The hull was gurgling and I rested and relaxed, taking my time before slowly regaining full consciousness. Eventually I crawled out the hatch to see that the wind had picked up to a very light twelve knots.

We reset the sails for maximum performance and pushed on for Lahaina along the west side of Maui. The coast was backdropped by mountains having every imaginable shade of green. These greens bunched up higher and higher until they finally tangled with the puffy white of clouds hanging in the sky. Lush deep cut gorges and gulches opened up showing pathways into lofty, somnolent jungles. Along the shore, Lahaina became more and more prominent. Lahaina was the colorful resort town that had once been the whaling capital of the Pacific and the capital of Hawai'i. Here as many as 500 whaling ships a year helped to put Hawai'i on the map. Hawaiians, sailors, and missionaries helped to create an unchecked, boom-town situation that ran away with itself like a dog chasing its tail. Some of America's greatest books, such as *Moby Dick* by Herman Melville, were inspired here. Then in 1871 an early Arctic storm destroyed nearly the entire Pacific Whaling fleet and closed an era. Possibly it is because of this storm that the Hawaiian waters still manage to survive as a winter resort for the *koholā* (Humpback whale) despite continued blunderings like the *Valdez* disaster in other parts of the world. Today the grog shops of old Lahaina are gone. They have been replaced with touristy restaurants, art galleries, and trendy boutiques that sell everything from helicopter rides to T-shirts gilded with golden geckos. Nevertheless, the wooden storefronts along the waterfront still hint at Lahaina's bawdy past.

"Wow! Look at all the colors," I said, dumbfounded by what appeared to be a colorful gondola passing from Pu'u Kukui point in the West Maui Mountains to the 'Au'au Channel and back. How could that be? We were now in fifteen knots of wind and Davey studied the area carefully through our trusty binoculars. We had been sitting on the rail in the shade of the main sail, trailing our feet in the water eating shrimp salads and drinking beer and watching the wondrous sights go by. The gondola proved to be people paragliding behind a ski boat!

Next I was starting to see sailboats anchored in the open roadstead off Lahaina, rolling and heaving in the swells. "What do you think, Davey, should we try dropping a hook and call it a day?"

"No thanks," Davey murmured. "Looks too rolly — reminds me of Monterey. I couldn't relax."

The wind was freshening, and we decided once again to forego anchoring and keep going towards O'ahu.

"Well, maybe we'll find something on Moloka'i."

Cracking off first towards the island of Lāna'i and then tacking across the Kalohi Channel we approached the south side of Moloka'i, distinguished by its fantastic, precipitous summits displaying their profiles in the late afternoon sun. I spent the better part of this journey reading the Hawai'i section of the *Pacific Pilot* madly searching for a place to put in out of the wind. Learning to navigate through the Hawaiian islands proved no easier than pronouncing the landmarks.

> 1700 Our sightseeing has been abruptly interrupted by a confusing sea; the result of the intersection of the three channels — the Kalohi, the 'Au'au, and the Pailolo. Quite suddenly twenty-five knots of wind has filled in, hand in hand with a strong incoming tide. We quickly slipped a single reef in the main and are still charged along near seven knots down what they call "the slot" between Moloka'i and Lāna'i. We are kicking ourselves for not anchoring in the swells of Lahaina, but now they're well astern of us and barely visible. Some relief may lie ahead along the straight shore of Moloka'i behind a breakwater at Kaunakakai. We'll be there about dark if we are lucky. Even still we should expect forceful winds and tricky anchoring.— JFM

It wasn't easy going and we felt confused, heading west between two unfamiliar coasts. The day was ending and the sun dropped lower and lower in the sky until its reflection shone directly in our faces. About a mile off the southern coast of Moloka'i, Davey flipped on the depth sounder as a precautionary measure since we were on an onshore tack and our vision was handicapped. As it had earlier in the day at Molokini, the depth sounder immediately started beeping intermittently, but this time we were going six knots, not one. We were only in twelve feet of water.

"Not again! What is going on?" we frantically asked each other. I felt as if *Maui*, the mystical Hawaiian god of a thousand tricks, had been leading our attention astray with some sort of tomfoolery. Legend has it that Maui used his cleverness and his superhuman powers to lasso the sun long ago, thereby slowing the passage of the sun and time permanently over these islands.

A glance by Davey over the side was all we needed for a quick visual confirmation of the sounding. It put her into gasping antics.

"Jibe! Jibe!" she yelled pointing away from Moloka'i, normally known as The Friendly Isle.

Suddenly I was very tired of coastal navigation. My mind was reeling, my brain grilled from yet another full day under the sun.

"Jibing! Watch your head!" I yelled, turning the wheel instantly in a quick and dirty fashion. We didn't have the time to release the starboard running back, and when the boom came across the support battens in the main sail whacked over it furiously like baseball cards flapping against the spokes of a bicycle wheel. While I pondered the next move, the jib and its sheets, let free in the emergency, proceeded to wrap themselves in a knot around the forestay. Gusts were coming down the channel now over twenty-five knots, the seas four to five feet. To untangle everything without cutting it free we had to jibe again as soon as we were able, going towards shore only long enough to take pressure off the main and release the starboard running back. Davey ran forward to drop the tangled jib.

Next we were on an offshore tack again, the whole ordeal only taking seconds. Nevertheless, if we had been any closer to shore, we may have run aground in the worst of conditions. With only one chart at 1:250,000 scale and a skimpily read *Coastal Pilot*, we weren't aware that the coastal reef can extend more than a mile from Moloka'i's south shore. Alarmed and aware that twilight was beginning, we did as we had done so many times before, we abandoned any proximity with land. We headed west southwest and out of Kalohi Channel, away from any strange landfalls after dark. A tug towing a monstrous barge passed us on our port side going in the opposite direction. With the hues cast from the setting sun it was a fantastic sight; the barge pounding its way against the seas, sending spray twenty feet into the air. We turned on our running lights and settled in for a long night.

Davey had made some of her famous spaghetti earlier in the day. She brought it out into the cockpit still in the pot, and armed with spoons we managed to devour huge mouthfuls before sending it back to the range to be lashed down with bungies. We snacked on it off and on all night. The western-most point of Moloka'i became faintly visible on our starboard quarter and the last of the island of Lāna'i passed our port beam and slowly faded from sight. The wind had eased twenty knots but the seas were four to eight feet. After a few calculations and careful analysis of our past evening performance we decided to slow *Querencia* down and make O'ahu landfall well after daybreak the following morning. We dropped the main altogether and set the staysail to be self-tending. After carefully adjusting the self-steering we swept the decks, organized all our sheets, and clicked in both running backs. We were ready for anything. The person on watch would have few worries other than traffic.

I had been in the sea bunk about an hour when Davey asked me to witness our first threatening vessel and help her determine its intentions. I stuck my head out the hatch to see a huge cruise ship, the *Constellation*, steaming up the channel bearing down on us. Three attempts at radio contact failed, both on VHF channel sixteen and the commercial channel. I abandoned fiddling with 'the wireless' and began more overt measures. Soon *Querencia* was all lit up again, and in addition we flashed our "D" signal on the staysail. It worked, and none too soon. Just as I was ready to fire up the engine and begin more evasive action the *Constellation* seemed to stop and then belch huge clouds of black smoke out of her stacks as she reversed engines and changed directions. For a brief moment she sat there rolling in the shinning sea under the full moon like a floating city. Slowly she turned, showing her starboard lights, assuring us that she would pass us well off to port on a southerly heading. I pondered what it would be like to be a passenger on the *Constellation* that night. We could almost hear the laughter of people on the dance floor and the clinking of champagne glasses spilling over the stern. We both drooled at the idea of such luxury and comfort.

Davey tossed up her thoughts. "I could get into that; a hot tiled shower, full-service galley complete with cook, sit-down table service. Follow that with dancing and champagne — *oh boy*, could I get into that…"

"*Stop. Stop!* I can't stand it! We'll be okay. Just one more night at sea and then tomorrow — Honolulu," I promised.

After a few quiet moments to herself Davey went below to try and sleep. I sat in the cockpit watching this floating "Las Vegas," now powering well away from us, passing over the horizon, throwing its glow into the celestial sphere above her. Little puffs of smoke continued to come out of the *Constellation's* shrinking smokestack like a scene from a dream. The heavens above were beautiful! I turned around to see the constellations Cygnus and Orion lying on their sides in the northeastern sky. It was the first time we had seen Orion since the previous Spring on our passage from San Diego to the Marquesas.

For the next two hours I continued to watch the panorama around *Querencia* as she surfed down waves in the settling weather. The ocean heap shimmered like mercury floating in a deep blue-black bowl. The moon wore studded stars on his lapel. Little flashes on the horizon blinked at me now and then — brave little fishing boats off Penguin Bank.

Penguin Bank is a 100 to 200-foot shelf that extends off the West extremity of Moloka'i for a distance of twenty-eight miles. Then the bottom drops off sharply, giving birth to a strong and erratic northerly current. Luckily, the current was setting us in the right direction. I could see the brightness in my peripheral vision between sea and sky gather more and more definition. The dithered glow was the lights of O'ahu! High feelings of confidence and joy started within me. My two-hour watch seemed short and easy. We were getting across the twenty-two-mile stretch from Moloka'i to O'ahu quite well under just a minimum of sail.

Later on Davey's watch, she saw a fishing boat approach us after moving parallel with us for an hour or so. The night was darker now. Davey flipped on some more lights and monitored VHF channel sixteen as the boat, with its single white light above the wheelhouse, kept coming closer.

She woke me up with a start, "John, I think there is something sinister about that boat."

I wiped the sand from my eyes and crawled out in the waning moonlight and stared at this black hull rolling along in pace with us. Slowly my eyes became accustomed to the darkness and I could see the figure of a man standing on the boat deck about 50 yards away. It was eerie. He reminded me of myself, just standing there, grasping a rail, his eyes staring out into the blackness. A wave would meet the strange boat on its beam now and then, and it would roll like a knotty log. Slowly *Querencia* pulled away. Half an hour later the encounter was over. We were back to thinking about sunrise and Honolulu and alternating our naps again.

With the rising of the sun, the sea became a friendly and cheery clear indigo blue. Diamond Head, possibly one of the most photographed landmarks in the world, was just becoming visible. We turned on the diesel and putt-putted, letting out the fishing line in hopes of snagging a fish. The VHF came alive with transmissions from racing boats, commercial traffic, and phone patches. This was going to be the biggest port of call since we left San Diego seven months before. Although I had been to the Hawaiian Islands twice before in my life, I had never been to Waikīkī and Davey thought it was about time. We were so excited we weren't really hungry. Nevertheless we talked ourselves into an egg sandwich, remembering our rule to never enter port on an empty stomach.

The sun rose and it got hotter and hotter, and then wonderfully a breeze filled in and we soon resumed full sail. Eighty-foot *Maxi* racing yachts sailed past Diamond Head and out to the Pan American Clipper Cup triangle series. We beared off and ran more parallel with shore as we closed with Black Point. Dolphins made a miraculous and surprising appearance, jumping in big arcs ahead of the bow sprit. Huge beings these mature dolphins; they had pulled alongside us, water streaming and gushing over their sleek bodies.

"What a greeting party!" exclaimed Davey as I ran below to fetch my camera.

We crawled up on the bow and watched a group of five riding the bow wake, their dorsal fins touching the bobstay from time to time. Other groups of this intelligent species were racing to and fro around *Querencia*, jumping in unison. Squeaking unceasingly and in synchronization, it was obvious that they were communicating explicitly. My struggles with the camera proved fruitful. I was able to catch the jumping dolphins, the Clipper Cup boats, the wind-swept sea, the cratered slopes of the extinct volcano Diamond Head, the skyscrapers beyond and... whew! It was too much!

As we rounded the red Diamond Head buoy in gusty winds, the dolphins disappeared and figures began to take shape along the shore. We were sailing along the famous beaches of Waikīkī. Helicopters and tour boats bubbled around us. As we jibed and lowered the forward sail my prized "Fort Bragg Police" baseball cap blew off. We jibed again and started the engine and negotiated the rescue of my hat with the gaff. After that we ran our dock lines, set our bumpers, and prepared for docking as we entered the channel of the Ala Wai Yacht Harbor. In a matter of moments I was standing on the Texaco fuel dock getting directions to the harbormaster's office. We were instantly bombarded by dozens of questions from tourists and sailors and we quite suddenly realized how exhausted we were. Our trip from Hilo had been fifty-two hours of nonstop coastal navigation. We felt that certain familiar numbness you feel when returning to land from the sea. I excused us; and we fled, continuing to motor *Querencia* into the mouth of the harbor to a little dock in front of the harbormaster's office.

My vision was blurred with the distractions of civilization. In the air-conditioned office my body felt large and vibrant. Everything was so slow and dreamlike. Finally we were assigned a slip and I moved *Querencia* again through the busy harbor, at last securing her between a concrete dock and a piling. We jubilantly tied her off and took hot showers. Then we walked the beach, mesmerized just by the event of *walking* first of all, and then by seeing the hotels, the white sand, the surfers, the tourists. There were so many people. We lost ourselves in the crowd, giggling like two children enjoying a carefree stroll. Quite accidentally we found ourselves under the careful scrutiny of two security guards. We looked around us at chairs and movie lights and a platform beneath our feet. Actors and actresses, directors and make-up people surrounded us, several smiling at us. Somehow we had walked onto a movie set.

We quickly apologized and exited stage left. From there we stumbled into a terrible little tourist trap where we each had four ice-waters before escaping. Then continuing our sally we chanced upon Chuck's Steakhouse for dinner. Davey's dad Bob had brought Ginny, Davey, and her two sisters here to the very same restaurant nineteen years ago! Dinner was not only great, it was romantic. In the background we listened to Hawaiian music, so very much more melodic than Tahitian.

After dinner we felt immensely positive — there wasn't a thing wrong with the world. We moved our coffee to the bar where we swapped ocean tales with the young Hawaiian bartender. He was a surfer with a keen interest in how we found the midnight waves of the 'Alenuihāhā. In turn I asked him to teach me a few key phrases in Hawaiian and we discussed the many similarities between Hawaiian and Tahitian.

I couldn't think of a word that sounded similar to *aloha*, certainly not *ia ora na*. "What does aloha mean exactly?"

"*Aloha* is a word that you can say to mean hello or goodbye. Its translation isn't exact; it's kind of special, yea? *Eye to eye, face to face, I greet you and give to you my peace and my breath of life,*" he told us.

I was thinking of how this meaning of aloha hinted at the beauty and complexity not only of the Hawaiian language but all of Polynesia. I was thinking of Metata.

"*'okole maluna...*" our kanaka bartender interrupted with a laugh, passing us each an after-dinner drink on the house. "That means 'bottoms up!'"

Totally sated, we found our way home through the exciting city lights. It was the ageless scene of two merry sailors making their way back to the ship from shore leave. We climbed into the v-berth and, undisturbed by any dreams we might have had at sea, we slept soundly with yet one more passage under our belts.

69.

"Yesterday is history
Tomorrow is a mystery
Today is a gift
That is why we call it
The Present"
— Anonymous

After spending our maximum length of stay as a guest in our state-assigned berth, we tied *Querencia* up bow to the quay and stern to the horizon at the Texaco dock adjacent the channel in the Ala Wai harbor. There was a bit of surge, but, nonetheless, it has to be one of the most scenic tie-ups in all of the world. After a major haul-out for repairs and maintenance we kept the Ala Wai as our home port while we spent our final months of living aboard and further explored the Hawaiian neighbor islands. Our favorite sails were to Moloka'i, either its north shore or Lono Harbor on the south shore, Mānele Bay on Lāna'i, or Honolua Bay on Maui. But we also enjoyed spending our days in Waikīkī with all its excitement. An afternoon sail in the lee of Diamond Head with friends became a frequent happening. There are few harbors in the world where you can find warm blue water sailing as easily and as quickly as the Ala Wai. Often we would follow a sail up by dropping the anchor in front of the Royal Hawaiian Hotel for a swim and lunch.

I have met many people who could not imagine living in Waikīkī. But for us, secure in the adjacent Ala Wai harbor on our family yacht, it was a fun experience. Maybe it would have been different for us if we had arrived from another major city like Los Angeles instead of coming in from living off our hook for two years. We loved it.

Harbors are most always magical places. For us the magic of the Ala Wai was that you could be so close to such a wacky, wild tourist area with so many bells and whistles and still be able to escape it completely by a short walk back to *Querencia* in the harbor. That made Waikīkī a totally different experience. We loved the stimulation we got from people watching, professional entertainment, and I must confess, even the shopping. Davey often jokes that the main reason we came to live in Hawai'i (since it was never in our original sailing plans) was because of my determination to sail to Honolulu to pick up a new portable typewriter with bubble memory that Noel had demonstrated for me in Bora Bora. I had to have one, and it was a motivating force in making our sail to O'ahu. Honolulu is after all a major city and you can get almost *anything* you want the same day you want it.

While the dominant population center of Hawai'i is O'ahu, it has grown less than 10 percent in the past decade compared to the astronomical growth rates of Maui, Kaua'i and Hawai'i. Over six million visitors come to the islands every year and sometimes Davey and I had the feeling they were all in Waikīkī! But tourists don't comprise the permanent population. You don't have to go far, even nearby Magic Island or Ala Moana, and the less obvious truth becomes clear — that Hawai'i's population is indeed a composite of many ethnic groups and that *none of them constitutes a majority*. Of the population 32% is of totally mixed ancestry, Caucasians and Japanese each account for 23%, Filipinos comprise 11%, Chinese comprise 5%, and the remaining 6% is made up of Hawaiians, Koreans, Blacks, Puerto Ricans, and Samoans. Every group is a minority and any day you are likely to meet a man or woman of Chinese-Hawaiian-Irish-Portugese-German-Spanish-Japanese ancestry. No kidding! To me this is one of Hawai'i's many fascinations and a preview of our future world.

Meanwhile, for us two *haole malihini* (Caucasian newcomers) *Querencia* was a very private place to be. It is a fact that two boats can be moored right next to each other and have more privacy between them than any two apartments or residential dwellings on "the hard." The quiet and serenity of the Ala Wai was wonderful, and the sunsets often flavored with spectacular rainbows are some of the most beautiful in the world. Every evening we would sit in the cockpit with our cocktails and watch the paddlers stroking their way out the harbor channel to practice in the swells outside. For an extra treat, on Friday nights there were the sailboat races from the Hawai'i and Waikīkī Yacht Clubs. The race boats were mostly light *J-24s* and we got a big kick out of watching them manage their huge colorful spinnakers with the occasional gusts that whipped down from the *pali* [cliff] and drove them right by our tie-up and out to sea.

Later in the evening, a rap on the hull and an "Ahoy, *Querencia!*" usually brought the face of one of our new or old sailing friends encouraging us to join them in a walk down Lewers street for a night on the town. Often we went, dancing until the wee hours of the morning to rock music or pop hits. Our favorite hang-out was the *Green Rose Saloon* where the *Eddy Zany Band* cranked out some real "kick-butt" rock'n'roll and Davey and I twisted and jumped around in our flip-flops to the sound of the beat. Cruisers were soon known as regulars and not only did the bouncer start smiling at our arrival, but Corbin, the tall Polynesian bass player, would always stop everything and announce the entrance of the "prestigious harbor yacht club society." We usually felt spent shortly after midnight and after saying good night to the band would take the shortest path to the beach where we would make the fifteen-minute walk back to the harbor along the uncrowded shoreline in the temperate night air. Laughter and comedy ricocheted amongst us along the way. Once in the harbor we would disband and each make way to our respective vessels.

It was getting later in the year now and even though Hawai'i did not have a definite fall season, it was getting cooler. Sleep was never better as we edged our way into November.

It was three in the morning and the sound of the driving rain and howling wind woke me up. I lay there still half-asleep enjoying *Querencia's* gentle rocking and listening to all the mooring lines creak and the gang planks grate on the concrete quay. Then I heard it — the sound of a large power boat with a single screw coming into the Ala Wai channel.

"Davey! Davey! That's *Woyaya* coming in," I announced, shaking her shoulder relentlessly. I popped open the forward hatch to see if my hearing was serving me correctly.

"What, John? I'm asleep."

"That's *Woyaya* coming in," I repeated.

Who? What? How can you know that?"

"I'd recognize the sound of that screw turning anywhere, and... I'm right!" I proclaimed once I had a sight of Woyaya motoring in. I threw on my shorts and ran out into the rain and made my way onto the vacant space at the dock. I waved enthusiastically to Chris and Jeff, calling them over and pointing out the dock cleats. I stood by to take a line.

"Hey, Chrisso! Look whose here," Jeff yelled up to the bridge.

"Hey! Hi, John! How you doing, guy? All right!"

Once we had *Woyaya* tied off we stayed up most of the night talking story — filling each other in on what had happened since we had last seen one another. They had had a wonderful time in the Cooks, with the exception of the news about Mark and Jane's boat. From the Cook Islands *Woyaya* had gone on to Fiji.

"Jeff found himself a bachelor's paradise down there. Every night he was bringing a new island lady back to the boat," teased Chris.

"Well, maybe not every night," countered Jeff, grinning sheepishly. His blond hair and fair complexion made him blush rather easily.

Unfortunately, in Fiji, Chris's dad had contracted meningitis and he and "Mum" had to take an emergency flight back to the mainland for hospitalization. His dad survived; however, a full recovery took months. Chris and Jeff and a third mate had brought *Woyaya* back up to Hawai'i for the winter. It being a bit late in the year for the North Pacific, they had to drive *Woyaya* dead against severe wind and waves most of the way. The passage had been less than pleasant at times.

"Yeah, like the night we were out in the middle of nowhere in rough weather and the anchor chain came off its chocks and somehow all 500 feet of chain paid out as it made its descent from the bow. We didn't know what all the noise was at first, and getting it all back aboard while the bow pitched up and down was kind of a hassle," Chris said. Chris never exaggerated about anything, and like most good skippers always played down any challenge the sea threw at him.

"Yea, *kind of a hassle*," mimicked Jeff facetiously. "Hey… not to change the subject, but we brought back a freezer full of lobster. You're going to have to help us eat it all starting tomorrow."

"Refrigeration conked out on us about a day ago," Chris added, "yea, I can broil the lobster and Davey can just keep making those great salads she made down in Bora."

"And we'll have it with baguettes. We can get them at *Shirokiya's*" said I.

"And beer — I've been dying for a beer. We drank all we had two days out of Fiji," said Jeff, laughing.

So the next night was the first night of many we spent enjoying Chris and Jeff and *Woyaya*. *Woyaya* spent the next few months in the Ala Wai and we had more than a little fun together. Both about ten years younger than I, they always had enough energy to make up for what I seemed to be lacking. We were always going on a new mini-adventure. Since *Woyaya* was equipped with a Boston Whaler and scuba gear, Gus from *Deo Gratias* and I joined Chris and Jeff for frequent dives off Diamond Head where we went spearfishing, gathered octopus and spiny lobster, or just swam with the dolphins taking underwater pictures.

It was a grand life, *still*. When we weren't sailing or buddy-boating we were enjoying our renewed relationship with America and Americans, especially cruisers. For the holiday season our daughters,

Rain and Caroline, flew out to join us, followed by a visit from Joe and Anita. It seemed like something was always happening — something fun. On New Year's Eve we helped Jeff and Captain Chrisso string *Woyaya* with tiny white lights from stem to stern and go out the harbor for a cruise along Waikīkī. It was beautiful.

70.

"Life is what you make it."
— Anonymous

"Man shall not join together what God has torn asunder."
— Wolfgang Pauli

It was at the Texaco dock that we became friends with one of life's more fascinating individuals, Steve Neumann, and it would be a mistake to not share what little I know of Steve's adventure in life as it has for the most part escaped print.

"You know, Steve, when I write the *Querencia* chronicles someday I think it would be neat to drop in a few lines about what happened to you in Fiji," I said one evening as we played cribbage.

"Bitchin," he agreed, "fifteen-two, four, six, eight and twelve is twenty and I'll take the two you missed for twenty-two." He chuckled and grinned ear to ear behind his jet black sunglasses well secured against the bridge of his nose with surfer "froggies." It was almost a regular thing, Steve and I playing crib on either his boat or ours while watching the prettiest sunset on Earth.

I came from a lineage of good cribbage players and I was amazed at his prowess with the game. I tried not to let it bother me too much. Nobody had beat me consistently at cribbage like Steve did since I played my father. It obviously had something to do with luck. Steve wasn't always so lucky, though.

Suddenly I had an air-lock in my chest and my face turned bright red as I gasped for my breath, as if I were trying to work past what felt like a baked potato stuck in my throat. "Just heartburn," I reassured Steve.

"Oh, yea? That's what I said to my dad. Next thing I knew I was, at the age of ten, the second person in California to have open-heart surgery, plastic valves and the whole bit." Steve wore a scar the shape and size of the Southern Cross on his thorax. It extended down to his abdomen, and was cross-hatched shoulder to shoulder.

"Scared my father half to death," he continued. "He was a pretty proficient politician and realtor in Orange [county]. Believe it or not his full name was Alfred E. Neumann, so I grew up answering a lot of prank phone calls. These were my first hints that I wasn't destined for a *normal* life," Steve half-chuckled.

Steve isn't a large man, but he is a big person, genuinely giving and sensitive to the needs of others.

His mom and dad became sick from separate illnesses and by the age of sixteen both Steve and his older sister Roxanne were orphaned. It was his sister, Rox, and he against the trust officers. Thanks in a large part to his sister sticking up for him, Steve was able to get the college education he wanted aboard a tall ship in a "Credits at Sea" program. From there as soon as he had legal access to his inheritance he bought a wooden "Mason 38" ketch, *Athena*, that he and his girl friend sailed down through Mexico, through the Marquesas, Tahiti, and on to Fiji. Somewhere shortly after cocktails at the Suva Yacht Club on Viti Levu Island one evening, his girl friend and his crew jumped ship, leaving him alone to face a hurricane a few days later with winds of up to 200 mph.

Steve decided to stay aboard *Athena* through the ordeal that fateful day, sitting at his mahogany roll-top navigation station talking on single-sideband radio to friends. He had five anchors out and kept replacing chafe gear and snubber lines at regular intervals. Eventually he could no longer go on deck without the risk of getting blown over the side. Everything else on deck had parted, including *Athena's* dinghy. It was getting dark and the other yachts in the bay had disappeared. Visibility was rapidly approaching zero.

Suddenly the storm really started to crank and everything went at once, as if in an explosion. *Athena* lurched up and down and then over onto her side, crashing loudly, the sound of wood splintering all about.

"Hey, John, you know what it takes to be a cruiser?" Steve asked, coolly shuffling the deck of cards.

"What's that, Steve?" I catechized.

"You've got to have nerves of steel and shit for brains." After a short pause he added "Arrr... me buckos!" A patch over one eye wouldn't have been out of place with Steve. He already had an ear ring, a classy one at that — diamond studded.

Steve had told his friends ashore in Fiji that when and if *Athena* was to be lost he would shoot off flares. In that scary moment below decks when Steve was bouncing between bulkheads like a hacky sack between kneecaps, he knew he had to make it to the hatch and shoot off a flare. He wanted to live.

With the tremendous list of *Athena*, it took all of Steve's effort just to climb the few stairs of the companionway and pull back the hatch, stand up, wedge himself in with his shoulders, and aim his twelve-gauge flare gun into the howling blackness over his head and pull the trigger.

The gun blasted off and much to Steve's amazement the flare hit a ceiling a few feet above his head and bounced back, narrowly missing him. Steve climbed up and peered over the side. There he saw the red flare spinning wildly in circles of debris strewn all over the dance floor of the Suva hotel discotheque! The flare had ricocheted off the ceiling where the boat had come to rest after arriving through the front wall of the hotel! *Athena* did not wash any farther inland, and this is where she sat for the remainder of the storm.

It took months, but Steve managed to repair and refloat *Athena*, which actually suffered only moderate damage considering what happened to the hotel. The native Fijians helped immensely, even cutting coconut trees to construct a roller system to get *Athena* down the beach and into the water once again.

Athena's dingy was returned by a Fijian. Steve tried to thank him but the Fijian insisted that Steve was the one to be thanked. As a matter of fact he couldn't thank Steve enough. The Fiji native had climbed a tree over a mile inland to escape flooding waters at the height of the storm. The tree hadn't been high enough and the Fijian was preparing himself to swim for it when the dingy floated by for the taking, saving his life.

There were other complications. Steve contracted a severe staph infection from injuries sustained in the grounding. This worsened his compromised cardiac condition. Nevertheless, eventually *Athena* was back on the rolling heap, beating up to Hawai'i, and tying off at the Texaco dock in the Ala Wai. When *Querencia* had come to Hawai'i she had become *Athena's* new port side neighbor.

"Fifteen-two, four, six, eight, and eight is sixteen and the right jack for seventeen," Steve interrupted my drifting mind as he pegged off his points. "Hell, even though I wish I wasn't, today I'm inoperable. The doctors tell me I'm a walking miracle; thirty years with the same old plumbing from the original time they cut me, " Steve added,"…and I'll take two more for the fifteen you missed on your last peg."

Steve Neumann

Part X
Letting Go

71.

I'm not afraid to die.
I just don't want to be there when it happens.
— Woody Allen

Tacking continuously back and forth in an effort to approach the rocks on the west coast of Lānaʻi was very difficult. Back and forth *Querencia* and the forty-five-foot Tasmanian ketch *Kalua*, with her new owners Tom and Nancy aboard, beat through the stiff wind and white water spray. Eventually we motor sailed into the area known as "Five Needles" to anchor somewhat protected from the wind, on the southern side of the rocks.

In the Ala Wai, *Kalua* recently had become our new neighbor, tied to the quay on the port side of *Querencia*. Tom was an intense individual, and he and I had discovered our age and pursuit of adventure in common. We had planned this inter-island sailing trip, buddy-boating.

We lowered our anchors just past the wind line in the deep blue anchorage and swam ashore using masks to check our "lunch hooks" on the way. Even from the surface thirty feet above, the anchors were clearly visible in the crystalline water. Chain led down from *Querencia* twice the depth to the hook, its flukes digging well into the sand bottom of this bight fringed with black rocks.

The rocks were a splendor to look at once ashore. Lava had come down from the island on its journey and fallen into deep swirling waters. Tall, monolithic black chunks of rocks, five to be exact, were strewn among pools I imagined to have been built by an Elysian god. The water came in and filled the caverns and then drained once again into the sea; the motion was powerful and Sisyphean, a cyclonic coming and going of the surge and surf.

Gus from *Deo Gratias* had told me that when he had come here aboard *Woyaya* with Chris and Jeff the conditions had been perfect; the ocean had been totally flat. They dove the pools and picked spiny lobsters by the dozen.

For us the conditions were far from perfect and we settled on gathering 'opihi [*Cellana talcosa*], precious, delicious little limpets with the shells reminiscent of Chinamen's hats and flesh like that of miniature abalone. We all had our wet suit tops on and booties and fins when we came ashore with our goody bags. Tom and I had each brought a knife for plucking any resistant 'opihi from the rocks.

They were in abundance. We put our masks and fins aside and started collecting them easily. Tom and I had somewhat cautiously wandered way out on the end of the rock point. The tide was just changing to a flood encouraging the odd set of large waves to roll in now and then.

"Good God, look at the size of that tiger cowry in front of you, John!" Tom said gleefully.

I looked up and there it was, a *leho* shell, a good three inches in length, almost within grasp. It was only one more step away. It was between waves and I didn't have time to think about it; I had to go for it then if I wanted it.

"Can you make that, John?" Tom asked.

I went for it. But just before I reached it, I was met by a huge wave that hit me right in the face and knocked me off my slippery feet. I was aghast to feel my body being pulled off the cliff and over the rock and coral face by the sheer power of a "larger than large" wave. I felt like an ant caught in an abyss. I clutched madly at the ragged rocks and coral, but still I could not stop myself. The skin was scraped off my fingers and then *I was gone.*

I made a last look for Tom and saw that he had retreated to higher ground and was now watching me from above, his face expressing anxiety.

"Help me, Tom, help me!" I yelled. And I meant it. Soon I had been swept into a deep whirlpool and when the next wave crashed overhead it pushed me down, down, down... under the surf where it was pounding against the cliff. A calm response overtook me.

"I can not, repeat, can not panic. Ride this thing out momentarily and think it out." I thought to myself. "You are alive and you have a wet suit jacket on and booties, and you have a chest full of air and this wave is just pushing you down temporarily."

Slowly I began to rise. Thank God for the buoyancy that the wet suit top provided me.

I kept talking to myself. "You may have cut up your legs and hands, but mostly you're scared from being sucked off a ten foot high rock precipice."

Another wave came in and I covered my head with my arms to keep my skull from being bounced off a rock. I was thinking how incredibly stupid this accident had been and how here I was about to die this silly death after sailing all those thousands of miles and diving so many waters. I was going to be another one of those ocean statistics where enough caution hadn't been heeded. What was my family going to think? Why did I take my eyes off the ocean and go for the cowry shell? Opening my eyes all I could see were bubbles.

I came to the surface.

"John. John! Listen to me man! *Listen to me.*" Tom had worked down to as close as he could get on the cliff above.

"John, throw the knife... throw the knife, man," Tom was telling me.

I was frightened. I wasn't even thinking. In my left hand was the cherished hunting knife my Dad had given me. I didn't even realize I was still clutching onto it. I was shaking from head to foot, half swimming, half bouncing off rocks, but somehow I managed to throw the knife towards shore as hard as I could.

Two more waves came in, the first sending me down again like the previous one. Before I could really catch my breath the next wave had also caught me. A second phase of panic came over me as I realized this could be a protracted and painful death! I was clutching at coral once again with my bleeding hands, frantically gasping for air by the time the last wave had released me.

Tom had been yelling at the girls to bring a pair of fins but he now turned to me.

"John. John! Listen to me! *Listen to me. You are going to have to swim out. Swim out!*" He was yelling at me.

I was desperately grasping a head of coral.

"Hell, I *know that* but do I have to *do it*, too? This isn't supposed to be happening to me," I remember thinking. I was fortunate to have Tom to help me remember what to do. Your body reacts differently when you lose your cool. Call it shock.

"Swim out through the next set [of waves]. *Give it all you've got man!*" Tom instructed.

Luckily I had enough time to grab some air. I was totally spent. I was sputtering and coughing and shaking and aching, but when that next wave came in I jumped through it toward the blue horizon with everything I had. Tom and Nancy and Davey told me later I looked like I had been shot out of a cannon and was almost swimming in air along the surface of the water. I swam with all my might, bumping over coral heads here and there on my way out, white water all around me. But I made it. I was free. I looked back at Tom who was directing me to swim back along the north side of Five Needles to a sandy spot in the bight where I could come ashore.

My cuts needed immediate attention. Tom said he was glad to have me back in one piece; he had just been getting ready to put the fins on and come in and try to get me if he had to. He returned the hunting knife I had thrown ashore and produced the cowry shell too! He suggested that we all swim back to *Kalua*.

"I wasn't sure you were coming up after that last set of waves," he remarked.

"Me neither," I gulped.

Together all of us quickly swam back to *Kalua*. I remember holding hands with Davey as we swam back to *Kalua*. Her hand felt so good. How wonderful life and love is. I wondered if Davey knew just how close I'd come to "buying the farm." I knew. My thoughts turned to the two large sacks of 'opihi we were carrying back to the boat. Together we would have a wonderful feast and everything would be okay with my world once again.

On the deck of *Kalua* I was removing my face mask and Nancy and Davey were nursing my wounds when Tom, with a big smile on his face, passed me a straight shot of scotch.

"Take this John. You'll feel better." Tom turned his head in a quick three-sixty, inspecting the anchorage.

Suddenly Tom's brow became wrinkled and his smile turned sour. This was a sign of new trouble. "Hell, *Kalua* is slipping her hook." Tom complained. The wind had picked up and was whistling in the rigging.

"Oh my God, John, look at *Querencia*," Davey gasped.

I turned around and saw that *Querencia* had pointed her nose downwind and was pulling away. Her anchor chain hung straight down.

"Let's go, John, if we're going to catch her," Davey reminded me.

I set the scotch down, and Davey and I jumped back in the water putting our fins on in mid-air. Tom yelled that he would watch for us and pick us up if needed. He was already bringing up his anchor.

Querencia, once fifty feet from *Kalua*, was now fifty yards away. We realized we had to swim with all our might to catch her before she got out of the lee and into accelerated winds and rough seas. Even though she was bare poled she was moving away nearly as fast as we could swim. It was a long, tough swim, and I'm not sure we would have caught up with *Querencia* without fins.

Davey reached *Querencia* before I did and climbed up the ladder. I climbed up the steering wind vane. *Querencia* was now past the wind line and twenty-five-knot gusts were sweeping over her. Looking back we could see *Kalua* well behind us with her hook finally up; she was turning out towards us.

Once on deck we felt safe, and felt *Querencia* was safe, too. The wind was blowing the direction of Fiji, over 3000 miles away, and there wasn't much between us and Fiji. We could relax for a moment or two. I looked down and saw I was dripping blood from my knees on to the teak deck and went below for a towel while Davey started winching up the anchor. It felt great to be on board again and there was no rush to do anything. Back on deck I relieved Davey at the anchor windlass. And while the wind continued to intensify and howl, she went below and poured me the stiff scotch I hadn't had time for.

As we raised the staysail and began steering the boat for a passage to Molokaʻi, we looked back at "Five Needles." Now almost invisible in the morning shadow of Lānaʻi, the mysterious place seemed more than a little sinister to us; it was if we had violated some ancient Hawaiian spirit.

Even though the wind continued to build, with some gusts at 30 knots, we were at ease. Nothing seemed that hard anymore and we had lots of time to bring up and adjust all our sails, reefed as they were. Couldn't be a better time to fish, I thought.

"Certainly not a bad time to break our luck," Davey said.

A change of luck!

We zipped across the channel in the heavy seas between Lānaʻi and Molokaʻi covering the distance in one of our quickest sails ever. Half way across, the clothespin holding the hand-line to a shroud "popped," and we hauled in a twelve pound yellow-fin tuna, or *ahi*, as it is called in the Hawaiian language. The wind vane steered making it quite a bit easier to land and manage the fish among all the sailing sheets. We didn't even have to unhook our life harnesses.

Late that afternoon when we reached Moloka'i we followed *Kalua* into Hale o Lono Harbor, a man-made cove left over from an abandoned quarry venture. It offered at least partial refuge on this isolated lee side of Moloka'i. There wasn't much room inside Lono this late in the day; a lot of summer cruising boats and fishing sampans were also seeking shelter. But there was one spot.

We anchored there and rafted up. Tom and Nancy's eyes got as big as silver dollars when they saw the wonderful ahi we had hooked. Davey and Nancy planned a salad and together we prepared and ate all we could of that wonderful fish and the 'opihi. We even barbecued the tuna on the stern rail grill of *Kalua*.

"So what the hell did we do wrong besides not let out enough scope, John?" Tom asked.

"Well, it was an incoming tide, the wind picked up, and that sand we saw our hooks digging into when we swam into shore obviously was only a couple of feet deep with a sloping rock slate bottom beneath," I answered, having figured it out for myself.

As the sun set in all its magnificence we passed around the cowry shell and laughed about the things we could afford to. Life was strong and rich. Soon the stories came out with the stars, pinholes of light twinkling through a *temporary*, black velvet blanket.

"Hard to believe there are one hundred billion galaxies up there each with one hundred billion stars, isn't it Johnny?" Tom asked.

72.

"In a world full of fugitives, the person taking the opposite direction will appear to be running away."
— T. S. Eliot

With the coming of spring, both *Woyaya* and the *Deo* left for the mainland. Steve made plans to spend summer on the mainland and invited Paul to stay aboard *Athena* until he returned in fall much to Paul's and our delight. As for Davey and me, we knew that our time living aboard *Querencia* was soon coming to a close, at least temporarily. Rus and Kathy sailed *Lila Marguerite* over from Monterey and we enjoyed an inter-island sail with them before they headed on to the Panama Canal and the Atlantic. Their visit reminded us that our perspective of the size of the world had been enhanced. It really isn't that big. But for the most part Davey and I had temporarily finished our sailing explorations of Hawai'i and the Pacific, and knew that just as *Querencia* was the kind of boat meant to be exercised at sea, our educated minds were meant to be more regularly stimulated. Living aboard a small boat and being underway is quite different than living aboard a small boat not going anywhere.

It was an appropriate time to re-examine and reaffirm our lives. Quietly we planned to safely tuck *Querencia* away in a cool lagoon somewhere by fall and move ashore, hoping we could find a small, affordable cottage to rent near the beach. There we could start a new life. It would not be easy. Our three-year cruise had exhausted our bank accounts more than we expected. The dentist that bought my practice ultimately went bankrupt leaving me holding the bag. New acquaintances had as difficult a time trying to comprehend what we had done with our lives as past friends had had in supporting us at the beginning of our trip. And we had a new resolve about how we would choose our daily work, because we knew that how we would spend our days is, of course, how we would spend our lives. We would have to endure hardship associated by not compromising our future; living for the day and waiting for the best. We looked beyond what we considered the fortuitous circumstances created by our past choices, our families, our society, our government. Somehow we would have to fit in. No, it would not be easy, but we had almost completed our cruising days and we knew it was time to "drop in" before we could "drop out" again.

Kalua was rammed quite unexpectedly one midnight in June by the *Queen Victoria*, a 100 foot, 130 ton power yacht hailing from Argentina. It was a crash one doesn't soon forget. Davey and I were asleep at the time of impact, a deafening explosion. I expected to see our hull crushed. I clambered out the companionway and saw the huge boat stuck into *Kalua's* beam. *Kalua* was lying over on her side listing and leaning hard against *Querencia* which in turn was climbing up on *Athena* which in turn pushed against the boat on its starboard, etc., like a row of dominoes.

Tom and Nancy had happened to be in the cockpit, saw the *Queen Victoria* having engine trouble in the basin and then saw it turn suddenly and head directly on a collision course with *Kalua* at a speed of five knots. At the last possible moment Nancy jumped off the bow sprit and onto the dock. Tom stood fast on *Kalua's* deck yelling at the top of his lungs, but it was to no avail; the skipper had left the bridge and gone to the engine room to fix a sticky linkage. While below he inadvertently engaged forward gear.

I was fearful that *Querencia* had also been holed and yelled a warning to Davey who was already out of the bunk. *Kalua*, in addition to being holed on her port side, had been pushed partially up onto the cement dock, her bob stay and jack stays broken, her whole rig threatening to come down. One-inch chunks of concrete from the dock lay all about. Tom had been knocked entirely out of *Kalua's* cockpit and was climbing back aboard her via the wind vane. Bruised and battered, his left leg cut and bleeding, once aboard he grabbed the barbecue off *Kalua's* stern rail and started beating it in frustration against the hull of the *Queen Victoria*, all the while screaming bloody murder. The killer ghost ship remained in forward gear for three or four minutes pressing against *Kalua*. Finally a dark figure appeared on the deck of the *Queen Victoria* and we started to sort things out.

Kalua almost sank and we were all busy with emergency procedures, calming ourselves in the chaos so that we might best assess the damage and solve the problems at hand. Ultimately the Coast Guard, Honolulu Police Department, Marine Police, Federal U.S. Marshal's office, attorneys, and marine surveyors became involved in the assessment. Although eventually making a complete recovery, *Kalua* sustained severe damages and had to be hauled out on the hard for months. *Athena* needed her aft port quarter replanked. While *Querencia* appeared to have virtually no damage we totally stripped her of all stowage and had her professionally surveyed stem to stern. Although jostled around, *Querencia* suffered only cosmetic damage of a few hundred dollars. Our tough boat had pulled us through again.

But there were additional concerns and Davey and I had to file a claim to help satisfy fees totaling over two thousand dollars from the surveyors, the U.S. Marshals, and our attorney.

By the time we had *Querencia* back together again Davey and I recognized that the whole ordeal had been more than an interruption for us, it was the hottest time of the year and we had been stuck at the dock. With our fall plans in the back of our minds and the intention of salvaging the remainder of our summer we opted on an extended sail.

So it came to be that Paul, Davey, and I, were sailing again to another island for the first time in a year, spending the better part of the first day underway for Hale o Lono Harbor on Moloka'i. The sailing for the most part was perfect, fifteen knots of wind and the water a perfect blue. Two Transpac boats racing from San Francisco passed us going the opposite direction towards their gathering place on O'ahu, their colorful spinnakers puffed out ahead of them, pulling them downwind. When sailing from O'ahu we usually arrived on Moloka'i shortly after noon, but the wind was so light that at 1300 we found ourselves in the "washing machine" off Lā'au Point, the west end of Moloka'i. Here where the water shoals quickly to thirty fathoms we seemed to be stuck on a treadmill with no forward progress. With the wind near nothing we tried motoring. *Querencia* drove up the front side of a wave until reaching the top. Here the prop would clear the water's surface and the engine revved wildly. I would then cut the throttle and let *Querencia* slide down the backside of the wave. There her bow dug into the next choppy roller, stopping us until I powered up again. This went on for two hours until, with the help of a fresh breeze, we escaped the worst of the tide rip. Nevertheless we still had to tack nine times to make it the last four miles up Kalohi Channel to Lono.

Lono Harbor, named after the *Kahiki* god, Lono, for whom The Hawaiian people initially mistook Captain Cook, is one of our very favorite places. Except during Aloha Week in October when it is the site of big doings for the annual Moloka'i to O'ahu outrigger canoe races, it is almost always nearly abandoned. Although large and uncomfortable swells sometimes occur in the harbor, it affords safe anchorage in nearly all weather, being protected by two breakwaters.

The facility, originally privately owned, was for the bulk handling of sand and it is rumored that much of the sand on Waikīkī came from here. On this evening the harbor was empty except for the skeletons of some abandoned quarry machinery. During the last moments of daylight a fishing sampan came in and anchored behind us. Paul could see that only one young local was aboard so when he rowed ashore in the dinghy he went by the sampan to see if he wanted a lift. He did and they went ashore together, Davey and I electing to stay aboard *Querencia*. On the return Paul dropped the skipper off at the sampan where he gave Paul three *ula'ula* [red snapper].

When we awoke the next morning the sampan had already departed. It was a beautiful day and we spent it beachcombing east and west along Moloka'i's south shore and free diving just outside the mouth of the harbor. We thoroughly enjoyed not seeing any other people — this area remaining smugly undiscovered even more than the rest of Moloka'i which is famous for *not* being developed. We also collected an abundance of 'opihi. Even though recently I'd nearly drowned gathering the tasty little critters, nothing could keep us from enjoying them either raw or dropping them in hot water for a minute or two, till they popped out of their shell to be dipped in melted butter.

In the evening some local folks drove down the dusty dirt road from above the ridge and fished for *ulua* [Giant Trevally] from shore along the entrance channel of Lono. We rowed ashore to chat with them. Nobody said much, but it was very relaxing to be with nature again, far from the frenzied crowd; the moon just coming up, the waves rolling in — each one with its own special sound; Coleman lanterns hissed and cast shadows in the night. We made our way back to *Querencia* after about an hour. It felt so good for the three of us to be on board again together, and as relaxed as we were we couldn't help but feel excited about continuing our current adventure. We set our alarm for 04:45 so that we could get an early start and head across the channel to Lāna'i before the wind picked up.

> 0645 After having breakfast and stowing our gear we departed Lono at 0545. The surf had come up over night, and we watched the channel carefully for about 15 minutes before

> making a run for it between sets; we had our
> sails up and the engine on. A few boats have
> been caught in Lono's channel with conked
> out engines and no wind, thrown on their
> side and either trashed or wrecked. The
> splintered hull of a yacht lies in pieces on the
> breakwater as a grim reminder. —DT

We were off for another day sail, this time to Lāna'i island trans-versing the usually fierce Kalohi Channel. Today "the slot" did not sleep late and the wind funneled down between Moloka'i and Lāna'i and gusted ten knots over what it was doing elsewhere. As soon as we had pulled away from the bight, it blew a solid twenty-five knots and the seas were their customary eight feet. After reefing I gave the helm to Paul who took it eagerly. He was having a blast, totally elated to be at sea again.

"One nice thing is that the water is pretty warm compared to Washington state. Here you don't mind getting sloshed. One laugh and you're back to normal!" Then he let out a loud whoop like a lucky rodeo cowboy.

"Arr... me buckos. She be right!" I encouraged the happy helmsman while Davey and I lay down in the cockpit passing fizz water back and forth, ducking the odd wave that splashed over the rail. We were giggling. It was a luxury to have Paul piloting the boat for us between channels.

Paul steers Querencia for Lāna'i

By nine we were across the channel and in the lee of the west side of Lānaʻi. The wind almost went to nothing and we fired up the motor past Honopū Bay where Five Needles stood. We then went past Kaumalapau Harbor, a commercial barge landing dedicated to the pineapple industry, and finally Pali Kaholo, where a deep sense of stillness filled us as we sailed along deserted, sheer rock bluffs rising straight up from the ocean's edge to a height of over a thousand feet. Then we went around the southwest tip of Lānaʻi, past the location of Kaūnōlū, an ancient Hawaiian village with a paved trail. It had once been the favorite summer fishing spot of Kamehameha the Great (1756 - 1819), the first chief to conquer and rule the Hawaiian islands, uniting them and establishing them into the next century as the Kingdom of Hawaiʻi.

We tacked up the seventeen-mile-wide Kealaikahiki Channel between Lānaʻi and Kahoʻolawe until we cleared Hulopoʻe Bay (White Mānele Bay) and Puʻu Pehe [Sweetheart Rock]. Puʻu Pehe is commonly called "Cathedral Rock" since it looks like that from above and below the water. The famous underwater caverns here are known by scuba divers as Lānaʻi's "cathedrals." Jutting out from the southern coast it is a clear landmark. We pulled into Black Mānele Bay flanked with its high inky cliffs, past the buoy and into the small boat harbor. Navigating around a breakwater that runs parallel with shore we made our way down through the ten-foot dredged channel and into the boat basin. Normally there is space for only two dozen small boats and all of the slips are taken, but today there was one slip available and we took it with the harbormaster's blessing. The owner of the slip was gone for a few weeks. Having a dock for your boat in Mānele on the enchanting island of Lānaʻi is very, very special.

73.

Lānaʻi is 140 square miles in area, or slightly over 90,000 acres. According to Hawaiian legend, it was originally occupied only by evil spirits, and it was the last island to be settled. For more than 500 years after the other islands had been inhabited by the Polynesians, Lānaʻi remained alone — a "ghost island," even though it lies only nine miles across the 'Au'au channel from the west coast of Maui.

According to legend a Maui chief, King Ka'alaneo, had a strapping, prankish son named Kaululā'au. Kaulula'au was always getting into trouble by pulling up breadfruit trees in the village of Lahaina (then known as Lele). The fruit of the tree was a food necessity to his people and Ka'alaneo was more than embarrassed. In his anger he exiled his son to Lāna'i with instructions to rid it of the evil spirits and "get a life." If his son Kaululā'au was successful he would announce his regrets and his new maturity by burning a fire that could be seen across the 'Au'au Channel.

The king's son, a skillful hunter, hid in one of Lāna'i's many caves during the nights and chased the spirits in the day. Ultimately he was successful in banishing the spirits one by one. He then built his signal fire on the beach of Lāna'i and was welcomed back as a hero by his people on Maui. With the evil spirits removed, Hawaiians from the neighboring islands started migrating to Lāna'i. At that time, about 1400 AD, they lived for the most part on the northeast, windward coast, raising taro and fishing. They found little vegetation on the southern interior of the island. Some high-minded settlers attributed the curious desolation of the island to Kaululā'au's migratory bad habit of pulling up plants.

Lāna'i remained a popular location for chieftains to exile criminals and social outcasts well into the nineteenth century. The remnants of the Hawaiian Exile Colony still exist on the northwest coast near Ka'ena Point. Some believe that a Spanish galleon was wrecked off Lāna'i in the 1500s, bringing Europeans to Hawai'i long before Captain Cook's voyage in 1778. This explains some mysteries; the Spanish-looking feathered helmet of the Hawaiian warrior and a pre-Cook history of light-skinned people, some with cloaks and iron daggers. Afterall, the Spanish were making commercial voyages from Acapulco, Mexico to the Philippines more than 200 years before Cook even ventured into the Central and North Pacific.

In 1898 a young graduate of Harvard University, James Dole, came to O'ahu and started a commercial venture, planting pineapples. No one knows exactly when the pineapple (*halakahiki*, [*Ananas comosus*])arrived in Hawai'i. The pineapple probably originated in Brazil and hitched a ride to the South Pacific with explorers of the day, just as did the woody, flowered bougainvillea vine. Eventually, it was most likely carried to Hawai'i by early voyagers from Tahiti. By 1922 Dole was able to buy the entire island of Lāna'i with the proceeds of his pineapple enterprise. The price was slightly more than one million dollars. At the time it was one of the biggest real estate transactions in the world. Jim Dole's ambition was fueled by his own belief that the island was worth twenty times as much and he turned Lāna'i into the world's largest pineapple plantation, building Kaumalapau Harbor and Lāna'i City in the process. He paid a fair wage and attracted Chinese, Japanese and Filipino workers to his model town from which most of today's residents, about three thousand, are descendents.

We found *the Pineapple Isle* in a period of transition. Today, its days as an isolated, undeveloped plantation of halakahiki are over. The dirt roads have been paved and two new hotels have recently been built to tap into the lucrative tourism industry which dwarfs not only the income from Hawai'i's sugar crop, but also from its pineapples. Nevertheless, Lāna'i is one of the last islands to succumb to tourism and here you can still discover the hidden, timeless nature of Hawai'i.

Joan McKintyre, with her long, wild, flowing red hair, spectacled, and wearing earth sandals when she was not barefoot, was the current harbormaster. We found her fascinating. Joan spent the first evening sitting with us in *Querencia's* cockpit exchanging stories about Polynesia — we told her Tahitian tales and she talked Hawaiian story to us; all the while in the background we played cassette tapes from both cultures and took turns strumming Metata's 'ukulele. She had come to Lāna'i nearly a decade before and had for the first year camped on the point above the Mānele-Hulopo'e Marine Life Conservation Area living in solitude — observing dolphins, counting humpbacks, writing, and slowly learning enough of the island and the local language and customs to be accepted as a Lāna'i *kama'āina* [native to the land].

"Lāna'i in the old Hawaiian language meant a *hump*, or *swell*," and that's how it got its name," Joan told us, "because, as you probably noticed, that's exactly what it looks like from sea."

She kept a fascinating journal of her observations during her hermitage and received international acclaim as Sierra Club author of *The Art of Whale Watching* and *Mind in the Sea*. Free as the wind, she was preparing to leave the following day on a "scouting" trip to Samoa where she would pursue more about the Polynesian culture. While she was gone we were welcome to use her VW *Thing*. She would leave it for us at her *hale* [house] in Lānai City.

The next morning after Davey and I returned from an hour's hike to catch the sunrise on the top of *Pali Lei no Haunui* above the east cliffs of Mānele, Paul joined us in hitching a ride with one of the many friendly residents up the winding road, 18 miles to Lāna'i City. Up on the plateau the road was flanked with miles of silvery pineapple fields. Lāna'i City was getting its roads paved just this year. It was ambitiously called a city; it was really much more of a quaint, well-kept, little plantation town. The temperature dropped from 90° F at Mānele to a cool 70° F at Lāna'i City. We found a few stores, a laundromat, a library, a post office, two gas stations, the original Lāna'i Hotel, and brightly painted houses with big colorful gardens. All of this was nestled amidst an abundance of cool Norfolk pines. For a moment, we forgot we were in Hawai'i and felt rather that we were in a little town in Idaho. The Norfolks, now an island trademark, were actually planted by a New Zealander, George C. Munro, about 1910. He had been hired by the Lāna'i Ranch and enjoyed sowing seeds from his saddlebags wherever he went.

Lāna'i for us was the closest one could get to being out of the country on a remote island in the Pacific Ocean and still be in the United States of America. Cruisers must go to each of the four stores in Lāna'i City to get their provisions; batteries in the hardware and potatoes store, chicken in the one with the best poultry, wine in another, fresh bread in still another. Tourists were carted over from Maui for a couple of hours here and there, but it was mostly local residents. We did well on Lāna'i making friends and people remembered us from when we were there in May. Tiny little ladies with straw hats and red kerchiefs waved renewed welcomes to us.

Once provisioned it was back to the harbor in Joan's *Thing* where a short 10 minute walk along a dusty road led to us to the eastern side of the peninsula and one of the most beautiful beaches in the world — White Mānele, or Hulopo'e Beach Park, film location for *From*

Here to Eternity. A more perfect beach there never was — a white, fine sand beach fringed with palm trees, outlining a crystal clear bay full of interesting and extensive coral foundations.

We snorkeled surrounded by purple finger coral, lobe coral, cauliflower coral and orange tube coral, all the while colorful reef fishes fearlessly surrounding us. There were all kinds; Moorish idol fish, blennies, wrasse, damsel fish, tangs, puffers, lionfish, red and blue parrot fish, and Hawai'i's state fish — the little one with the long name — *humuhumunukunukuāpua'a* [Lagoon triggerfish or *Rhinecanthus aculeatus*].

When we weren't snorkeling or up in Lāna'i City, we basked in the sun like seals, played paddle-ball or frisbee, or body surfed for hours on end. With hurricane *Ignatio* far to our south the swell was up and the surf ran high for several days. Young boys, experienced board surfers, came down from the city and caught the near perfect curls on the rocky south edge of the bay. We also explored the tide pools along the shore between Black and White Mānele. There we found a large cave on the water's edge which we came to know later as *Keana'ō'io*. We were so intrigued exploring the cave that the tide nearly caught us daydreaming. But after my experience at Five Needles I thought I knew better and decided we would do well to make a rapid, however hazardous, scramble up a sheer rock face to safety above us.

We also decided to discover some of Lāna'i's miles of red dirt trails, so the following day we returned Joan's buggy and rented a four-wheel-drive jeep from Nishimura's Chevron Service for the steep up-and-down grades that are all over the island. On the top of our list was the Munro Trail, a winding three mile dirt road that extends the length of Lāna'ihale mountain rising behind Lāna'i City to a height of 3,370 feet. We wound up the mountain, skirting yawning ravines and eventually dipping into a shadowed, dense forest, a mixture of evergreen and tropical. Sometimes from up here you can see Maui, Moloka'i, Hawai'i, and even O'ahu. But on this day it was more usual; the mist came ghosting through the ferns and pines and engulfed us. We drove the length of the trail through the unspoiled highlands very slowly and carefully, engrossed with all the green growth; morning glories, wild orchids, *'Ōhi'a* trees with their magnificent *lehua* blossoms, wild herbs and berries, and mountain *naupa-ka* and guava. *Kukui* or candlenut trees outlined the valleys below us. At one time their white, oily kernels had been used for lights, hence the tree is a symbol of enlightenment.

Soon we were at the summit, then heading down the trail. Bright sunshine was just minutes below along with the subtle scent of eucalyptus carried on the tradewinds. We surrendered our rain ponchos to tank tops and at the bottom turned right down Keōmuku road to Shipwreck Beach on the northeast side of the island. The eight-mile stretch is a beachcomber's paradise, named because the trade winds roaring between Moloka'i and Maui often get powerful enough to drive boats up on the reef of Lāna'i, especially in inclement weather with poor visibility. Although most of the wreckage occurred when the wooden sailing ships and steamers anchored off Lahaina regularly, one rusty hulk offshore is a relic of World War II.

But having chosen not to spend this day beachcombing, we were off again in no time, back along the deserted sand beach roads, back up Keōmuku road, and toward the northwest part of the island to find "Garden of the Gods," a scattered assembly of colossal rocks and atypical lava architecture. We found it about seven miles from Lāna'i City in the middle of a brush-choked wilderness. Deserted, it looked liked a moon surface covered with weird rock formations and wind strewn sands. Here the average annual rainfall in inches is zero! Rocks or meteors appeared to have dropped from the sky just yesterday and lay all about. Every time we drive through the Garden of the Gods it looks different; the cactus and succulents cast different shadows, the sun dramatically shifting the colors of the rock pinnacles in the different canyons depending on its elevation in the sky and the time of year.

Not afraid to eat more dust, we forged on, continuing our great 4-wheel-drive adventure. Here and there we saw yellow and orange *kauna'oa*, an air plant that grows wild on barren soil and is the official lei flower of Lāna'i. The farther we went the slower our exploration became until eventually there was only a suggestion of a road left. Some trails extended down the ridges, toward the water's edge on Kalohi Channel. But each one seemed very treacherous and there was no guarantee we could make it to the bottom. And what if we couldn't? How might we turn around? Our mission was to find remnants of the Hawaiian Exile Colony. Which trail should we take?

Just then a herd of Mouflon sheep, a wild sheep with large curling horns, reddish brown coats with gray buff patches on their sides and white buttocks, popped over the ridge, startling themselves as much as us. The Mouflon had been established early on Lānaʻi in the 1950s as a trophy animal. We already had seen wild goats, and Axis deer, a native of the park land forest of central and southern India and Ceylon, and a few Pronghorn Antelope imported from Montana. Indeed Lānaʻi had become a haven for game animals, including quail, chukars, pheasant, and wild turkeys. We took the Mouflon as a sign, and hung a right. The jeep immediately was on a steep grade.

"Oh my God!" was Paul's reaction from the rear seat.

In the rear view mirror I could see Paul… all caulked in a chalky rust, his face stained with red dirt. He was perspiring, and the caked dirt was dripping off the creases of his forehead.

"Hey Paul!" I bantered.

"What?"

"Your mascara's running, *ha ha ha!*"

"Hey John, you should see yourself, *ha ha ha!*"

I looked in the mirror at myself, and then at Davey. Indeed we all looked like contestants from a Tammy Bakker look alike contest.

But in reality it was the first time I'd ever taken "four-wheeling" so seriously. I didn't want the jeep to slide off or, worse yet, roll off the trail. Neither did I want the jeep to "high-center"; we didn't want to spend the night out here.

It took us nearly an hour going only a couple of miles per hour to reach the end of the road. At the "end of the road," the wind howled over long forgotten rock walls, some that were *heiau* — remnants of worship temples much like the Tahitian *marae*. Scattered along the rocky coast were old abandoned shacks and debris; beds, wood stoves, and the like. We couldn't see anyone, but we agreed that it felt as if people were watching us. We had no way of knowing for sure if it was the old exile colony on Lānaʻi, but it was definitely spooky.

We split a coke, gulped half a sandwich and then spoke in unison. "Let's get out of here!"

We jumped back in the jeep and picked our way out, dust billowing in the hazy sun setting behind us. Slowly up the trail we went, the jeep stopping and starting, turning this way then that on the bumpy, red-rocky road. Seven-foot cactus and *kiawe* bushes flanked the trail. In a second a bramble reached in the open vehicle and grabbed Davey's arm, leaving it with a deep, bleeding scratch.

"Make it bleed some more, hon, we don't want it to get infected. Kiawe wounds are known for getting infected. Hey, would you like to know where kiawe comes from?"

"No, not really," she said, milking more blood from her scratch as she spoke. "Just watch where you're going."

"It is an Algaroba tree, a *Prosopis pallida*, from Peru, first planted in Hawai'i over a hundred years ago..." I yelled over the motor.

"Fascinating... your distractions."

Creatures scattered away from our grunting motor and hid under the rough underbrush. Finally, after what seemed a rosary of prayers, we were back on the ridge. We left the haunting atmosphere behind us and headed directly for Lāna'i City and then on to Mānele.

74.

Holupo'e Beach, White Mānele, faces west, and the shoreside park with its picnic tables and barbecues offers facilities that are hard to pass up at sunset. Every night we carried our cooler with drinks and dinner, a lantern, the necessary utensils, and shuffled our way in our flip-flops from *Querencia's* moorage back to this white sand beach to eat, drink, and be merry.

It was here that we became friends with the road crew, who came down to the beach every evening to enjoy the ocean and barbecue their dinner and talk story. They asked us to join them one evening; David, Sid, William, Kenneth, Gaylen, Billy, Henry, Freddie... they were all from the Maui County road crew. Just as much as we enjoyed them they seemed equally fascinated with us, *Querencia*, and her stories. These were *real* people, good-hearted and full of common sense. They reminded us of our friends from Bora Bora, especially Metata and Tiapai. As soon as they noticed that your bottle of Heineken was getting the slightest bit warm, they would insist on replacing it with a fresh one from the cooler. This month their job would be complete and the city roads of Lāna'i City would be paved. Then they would return to Maui and their wives and children.

Freddie was the foreman. We had met before when we came to Lāna'i earlier in the year and they were just starting the roads. A deep-sea sports fisherman, he had given me explicit advice on catching tuna in local waters using a hand line — something we had not been very successful at once *Querencia* had arrived in Hawaiian waters. Freddie had given us specific instructions for everything — the length of leader, the speed of the boat, and the type of lure.

"But, more than anything, you must believe in your lure," he had emphasized, "because if you do not *believe* in your lure you will not catch any fish. The fish knows these feelings, but he is also curious and will come to your boat even without a lure. So if you are ready with the right gear and *believe* in your lure you will catch a fish. This I promise you."

He was right. Our very next channel crossing we caught a large ahi.

When we saw the road crew in town they always waved, and at the day's end we played with them in the splashy colors of White Mānele beach. One night a colony of spinner dolphins joined our BBQ party frolicking on the horizon doing playful vaults.

"So, you don't want to go back to the mainland. You've been in Hawai'i one year already and now you're going to stay?" asked Freddie.

Freddie, about forty-five-years of age, wore a dark moustache on his handsome face and looked to be of Hawaiian extraction. He had dark, roguish eyes and a terrific smile. As a matter of fact he seemed to be wearing the same smirk that Metata wore.

"Yea, I think so," I answered, "we're going to work real hard and make Hawai'i our new home."

Davey smiled at me, looked at Freddie, then nodded in agreement.

"Ah, that's the problem," Freddie said half-joking. "You haoles come over here and work so hard that now we too must also work hard just to keep up!"

Freddie and his friends and Davey and I all laughed at the same time. There is an old Polynesian belief that wherever there is laughter there is also the supreme being. Every time God sees himself he laughs.

"So you're kama'āina already! Then I must invite you. At the end of the week, on Saturday, we will be throwing a *lū'au* for the town to celebrate and bless the new road and to show our appreciation to the people of Lāna'i for their patience. We would like you to come," said Freddie.

"We'd love too. We've been to a Tahitian "lū'au," but Paul hasn't ever been to one. He missed it."

"Well, we're digging the *imu* with a front loader [laughter]! We'll come pick Paul up early Saturday morning so he can help with all the preparations. This time, Paul, you won't miss a thing. You're going to be busy all day. This is how it is with a lū'au, the men do the cooking."

This filled Paul with anticipation. He could barely wait for the end of the week. Neither could we.

In the meantime Davey, Paul, and I also became friends with Bob Moon, a contemporary all-American fellow about my age who had come to Lāna'i a decade or so ago and had married a very pretty Polynesian woman, Rita. When he wasn't home helping Rita raise their two children he was skippering guests aboard a Columbia 38 named *Stacked Deck*. It sailed out of Lāna'i to the other islands. We told Bob about our 4-wheel-drive adventure and how we had managed to see everything we wanted except for some petroglyphs.

"Petroglyphs? Well, if Pat and Harvey don't mind, you can join us. We're going to go down to Point Palaoa on *Stacked Deck* tomorrow morning," offered Bob. "We can anchor, land the dinghy, hike into Kaūnōlū and see petroglyphs there." He had sandy blond hair, and he flashed me a very relaxed Robert Redford grin. "I can show them to you. Amazingly enough, they are just lying there."

Bob's clients this week were Harvey, a retired and remarkably fit sixty-five-year-old executive from Macy's, and his girl friend Pat. They insisted we do the day with them. So Paul, Davey, and I jumped aboard *Stacked Deck* and the six of us were off for Palaoa

Point to rediscover history.

We anchored around the point near *Kāneʻāpua Rock*," more commonly known as "Shark Rock." Here we nestled into a small bight. It had a rocky shoreline, but there were scattered patches of sand. It was the same below the water's surface just offshore, and we kept motoring in a circle until Bob was convinced we had found the patch of sand he wanted to drop *Stacked Deck's* anchor on.

"Is it called Shark Rock for the obvious reason?" asked Harvey.

"Yes, it is," Bob smiled. "There are a lot of sharks here on the south side of Lānaʻi. Last summer four of us came here to go diving and we had to get out of the water because of sharks. We weren't too leisurely about getting out either — there were about six of them, tiger sharks, and they got really excited over us." Bob smiled again.

Paul and I knew. We had been snorkeling just outside Black Mānele two days previous and a large shark had made a pass at us before deciding to move on. There is something about having a large, heavy-bodied shark next to you, looking you dead in the eye with a coal black pupil.

We paddled ashore in the dinghy and hiked up the jagged shoreline to *Kahekili's Leap*. Here King Kamehameha in the early nineteenth century had watched his warriors prove their courage and allegiance by leaping six stories into the ocean from the top of the cliff. At the base of the cliff where it met the ocean was a 15-foot ledge that the jumper had to clear to survive.

Davey, Paul, and I joined Harvey and Pat, crouching down, clinging on to each other peering over the sheer drop off.

"Not all of them made it," said Bob, "but it must have helped Kamehameha weed out one heck of an army since his warriors managed to whip all the other Hawaiians on all the other islands, except for Kauaʻi and Niʻihau. There the other Hawaiian chiefs yielded through diplomacy rather than war."

We walked a bit farther and then on the other side of the precipice Bob stopped our descent to point out an image of a man holding a paddle, carved into the rock.

"You wouldn't think so because of the lack of tourists, thank-God, and park rangers, but this petroglyph is considered one of the best preserved early Hawaiian markings. Just below us here, in the ravine, are the ruins of Kamehameha's village, Kaūnōlū, along that dried-up stream bed. It was used as a summer residence up until about 1870."

We carefully climbed down the short face into the ravine. It was obviously once quite a different place, even though now it was near-ly overgrown. Bob showed us one wall and a partially hidden stone foundation. Once we knew what we were looking for, a bunch more stone foundations jumped out of the overgrowth all around us.

"The first one is always the hardest to find, then they're every-where," Bob said. "The Bishop Museum did an archaeological study here and found the remnants of eighty-six hales and thirty-five stone shelters. Kamehameha used to bring his whole extended family here every year. It was his favorite fishing spot."

Then Bob pointed behind us on the bank where we had walked down. Now we could see it, the *Halulu Heiau*. It was a rudimentary terrace made of large stones, but it had been a pre-Christian place of worship and here, once upon a time, sacrifices had been made to any of hundreds of Hawaiian-Polynesian deities. After seeing the Kahekili Leap I couldn't help but wonder if any of the sacrifices might have been human.

It had been a wonderful day and it wouldn't of happened with-out Bob. Later that night later we all joined for a farewell dinner as Harvey's and Pat's guest at the Hotel Lānaʻi. We all ordered the catch of the day, *ono*, and talked story until the restaurant closed. Harvey kept insisting I write a book.

75.

The sun wasn't even up yet when we heard a truck pull up to the docks Saturday morning. Paul was already to go and I stuck my head out the hatch only in time to see him jump in the front seat with Billy and Gayle from the road crew. They waved the *shaka* sign at me qui-etly.

Davey and I caught our ride up the hill to Lānaʻi City much later, near noon as had been suggested. We had been told that it wasn't necessary to bring anything, but we went by a grocery store and picked up a couple of cases of beer. The Social Hall, where the lūʻau was happening, was actually in an old lodge where the road crew had been living over the summer. It was way up the hill and my arms felt like noodles by the time we arrived.

We were warmly greeted by the rest of the crew. They were right, I had no need to bring anything. Stacked next to the ice chests were at least thirty cases of beer and soda of every possible label.

The lodge was quite spectacular, having previously been the country estate of the island plantation's "boss man" and his family, sitting on the hill behind the city nestled in tall pines at the edge of a forest. Inside the lodge there were log walls, big pine beams and hardwood floors. A trophy Mouflon hung over a big fireplace. The lodge must of had twenty rooms, most of them empty except for a few pieces of furniture or the temporary occupation of the road crew.

We found Paul out back, near the kitchen yard door. He had been working all morning and he was still working. Next to him was an immense amount of *kālua* pork piled in a large vat. He was helping Gayle pound the meat after Freddie pulled it off the bones.

"You should've seen it, you guys," Paul excitedly said to Davey and me, "we opened up the imu about an hour ago and removed the pig. Everybody waited to put it in the pit until I arrived this morning. The pig was all wrapped up in banana leaves and laid on a bed of kiawe coals and lava rocks. Then we covered it up with this large mound of stuff: a layer of leaves, then burlap, then canvas, then dirt. It steamed away for hours, and we just pulled it out about 45 minutes ago. It doesn't look to me like we're going to waste very much — we're preparing everything."

Sid was in one section of the huge ranch style kitchen making *laulau*, a Hawaiian concoction of pork, beef, salted fish and taro tops. He was steaming them in *ti* leaves, a woody plant of the agave family, genus *Cordyline*.

Kenneth, wiping his brow, called from another stove in the kitchen for me to come help stir the *naʻau loko*. A big pot was bubbling slowly away with mysterious dark contents. It was the intestines and organs of the pig.

"Kind of like what you folks might call chitlins," said Kenneth.

"Oh, yea?" Actually, later I found it to be quite tasty.

Paul had also helped William pound the taro root which had also been in the imu. *Taro* (also known as *kalo*) is a large, tropical Asiatic plant [*Colocasia esculenta*] with shield-shaped leaves. After pounding the root it had turned into a concentrate that Paul at first mistook for chocolate pudding, following a joking suggestion. Then when William added the water to give it a consistency of thick purple paste they told him the truth. It was *poi*, a starch staple still popular in Hawai'i after hundreds of years.

"'Two-finger poi." clarified William, "That means it's kind of thick. We also have three-finger poi, which is thinner."

More and more people began arriving. As the cooking preparations neared completion the men started breaking free from the chores to down a few cool ones. We took up an offer from David to meet Loli, a local boy dressed in black jeans with a black T-shirt and a tattoo on his left arm. He had a long braid of hair hanging down the back of his head.

Loli gave me a big Hawaiian handshake, throwing in a free lesson on how "the brothers" do it.

"Hey, *brah*! How's it?" Loli asked.

"Great... great imu, great people, great lodge."

"Yea, I remember this lodge when the boss-man worked here. The big haole boss would sit up here on his horse in the front yard, *right there*, and stare down on the pineapple fields all day long," told Loli. "When I was a little boy I would watch him. He would just sit there with his big boots resting in the stirrups watching us through his binoculars. I remember his boots. Everybody was afraid of him. You could see him sitting up here on his horse all the way down in the fields, and if you didn't see him you knew he was riding down to punish a pineapple worker for not working hard enough! He would wack'em with his switch."

"Oh, that's horrible," said Davey. "Do you still work in the pineapple fields?"

"Oh, yea! But now our bosses are local and we have machines, too. I make most of my money betting on cockfighting. I just won $200 this morning at the cock fight. Chicken fighting used to be big time in Hawai'i but *bum-bye* [by-and-by] now only in the rural areas. It's illegal, yea?" He told of the specially groomed gamecocks with razor-sharp blades attached to their ankles and how his special cock would either win or die in the central fighting pit. "Aiyeee, better cool it, brah, there is the sheriff."

I turned around, and there indeed was the sheriff. Arriving in his squad car and emerging complete with badge, gun and squelching radio attached to his belt, he looked a bit out of place, like Barney Fife. Lāna'i has one small jail and about as much crime as Bora Bora. But I could appreciate people wanting it to stay that way. The sheriff really was humorous in a genuine way. We huddled closer to hear him talk about his itinerary for the week. As he drank his soda, he told us about all the jeeps that had gotten stuck that week. The big incident was the tourist who tore the front fender off a rental car by accident.

Many of the families from town were beginning to arrive, each bringing additional offerings, most of them ethnic additions. There was sushi, sashimi, tako, saimin, rice, fish cakes, rice cakes, lomi salmon (salmon marinated with onions and tomatoes), potato salad, macaroni salad, bean salad, and *haupia* [coconut pudding]. All of this to add to kālua pig and extras.

The pastor arrived and men, women, and children went inside to the Social Hall where tables and chairs had been arranged for eating. Everyone followed the pastor's direction, joining hands in a large ceremonious circle. It was then that I noticed that in the group of about 200 people there were only three haoles present; Davey, Paul, and myself! Thanks was given to the food preparation of Freddie's gang and all the offerings from the aunties in Lāna'i. Then after a blessing of the new road, and a Christian prayer, everyone sat down and ate for hours.

It's hard to say what our highlight on Lāna'i was, but since I love to eat, I'll have to say this lū'au was one of those special experiences I will never forget. In addition to the food being delicious, the lū'au was surprisingly enchanting. It's easy to see how the Polynesian lū'au continues to enjoy a reputation around the world.

After their meals, people sat around talking while they finished with coconut pudding and fresh lychees.

A few teenagers danced hula demonstrating their ability and special awareness for their elders. In ancient times, being chosen as an *'ōlapa* [hula dancer] was a great honor. Months were spent memorizing the chants and the movements of the dance as well as the history and tradition of every lei, skirt, and instrument used to complement the hula. Even today to be a good dancer is to be gifted — to know how to move like the wind or demonstrate the force of the ocean or a volcano.

At the end of the afternoon we were given a ride back down to Mānele Bay. Sitting in the back of a pickup, we descended from the cool plateau through the pineapple fields down to the hot beach. I was thinking of all the interesting contrasts we had found in Lāna'i in the past month. It felt like only two weeks had gone by. It was time to head back to O'ahu.

Just before first light the next day Paul stood bleary-eyed on the dock waiting for my signal to shove off. This was just another ending, another beginning to an end of a cruise which landed in Hawai'i.

From Lāna'i we set sail across the 'Au'au channel under full sail, past Lahaina and anchoring just up the coast off of Kā'anapali, Maui. The wind howled and picked up and blew all night. By the next morning they were reporting thirty knots of wind and eighteen foot seas. We had only seven miles to go, a planned motor sail along the northwest coast of Maui to Honolua Bay. We found the seas were twelve feet high and twelve feet apart. The wind was right on our nose.

We started out lazily, half hesitating, until a big wave reminded us to get our act together. We turned our motor off and cracked off the wind a bit. Then, using every finger like a marlinespike, we bent our sails up the Pailolo channel between Moloka'i and Maui. *Querencia* picked up her cue and delivered us to peaceful Honolua Bay. Lying barely in the lee, Honolua is an incredible coral and sea life preserve, protected like a fish pond. The bay looks to the west and the green mountains of Moloka'i.

We spent a week in Honolua, resisting any urge to go anywhere else. Swimming in the rich clear water, we snorkeled with fish four feet long! The tide came in and the tide went out while we rested and relaxed and explored. One night the three of us talked over our future sailing plans in the islands. Suddenly the candles flickered and the skies broke and it poured buckets upon buckets of perfumed tropical rain. It made us laugh. After working feverishly to shut all the portholes we put the charts away and continued our talk, but not just about sailing — about *life*.

Paul, Davey, and I loved life to the very core and rind. It seemed to us that many people are disappointed or discontent in life to some extent. They complain of their luck and lament over what they did, or did not do. People complain of being trapped in a life they shouldn't have chosen — leading lives of "quiet desperation."

Sailing our dream had given us the opportunity to cut off our fears and expectations and just experience life. Crossing oceans reminded us that we all need do is simplify; simplify the outward circumstances of our lives; simplify our needs and ambitions; delight in the simple pleasures which the world of nature affords us.

No longer did we accept the common definitions of success, and no longer were we as easily moved by the judgment of others. Our idealistic goals of the sixties and seventies had also changed. We looked to ourselves rather than a political movement for inner guidance. Maybe the primary importance in life is to live in a communion with the nature of things as an uncompromising individual.

Our decision was final. Moving back to the mainland would be like wearing a broken watch. We were committed to staying in Hawai'i. Here, in comparison to most places, there really is no appreciable pollution, the air and the sea remain clear, and the people friendly. And living in a world as small as ours, it is good to be a minority. It teaches you to accept others as your would accept yourself.

We left Honolua early the next morning. We sailed across the Pailolo Channel to the east end of Moloka'i and the Hālawa Valley. The wind had eased and it was perfect sailing. A reach, then a run, down the north coast of Moloka'i past cliffs thousands of feet high covered with moss and streaming with waterfalls. Puffy, steamy clouds hung where they could and *Querencia* screamed down the coast at over six knots wing on wing with our genoa full and Nelley the wind vane doing all the steering. That evening we anchored in a bight on the west end of the island.

The next day we sailed our final leg, across the channel to O'ahu and "our little grass shack" wherever it might be.

76.

*"The minute you begin to do what you want to do,
it's really a different kind of life."*
— Buckminster Fuller

I sat there on the water's edge and wondered about all the beaches around the world like this one, so much like Bora Bora and yet someplace else, those beaches with clean white sand and a curling surf thumping a roar against a barrier reef, those exposed to fresh tradewinds that blow popcorn clouds across a royal blue sky which zip by overhead, passing like friends on the other side of a plate glass window.

Lanikai beach has such a pretty lagoon, protected by two islands and a barrier reef, filled with bright turquoise water. The rippled surface of the lagoon transcribes the effect of breeze and current. Looking across the lagoon there are dark shapes on the surface here and there. At first they look like shadows from the clouds until you notice that they, unlike the puffy clouds, are not moving. They are patches of coral and fish, little colonies, scattered just underneath the surface of the lagoon.

The sun blinked off and on, intermittently hidden by the clouds. The sky was full of bright light, and beaming down it brought a throbbing heat that warmed my aching bones of winter. One moment there was all white light, the next, cross-hatched shadows and glory rays.

I relaxed my eyes and concentrated on the surf in the distance. Some waves were bigger than others. You could hear each unique contribution to their distant thunder. Others crashed against the islands and then sprayed upward. For a few seconds these white foamy creations seemed to escape the loneliness of gravity and lift towards the heavens.

Closing my eyes in reverie, my mind played this movie-reel again. Flooded retinas carried these images into new memories. Some day these memories would return as inspirations for dreams. Dreams of the beach at Bora Bora or the Marquesas, or California, or Lanikai, or…

"Nothing like this on the mainland. Uh-Uh! No-way!", a crisp young man's voice suddenly popped the little fantasy bubble that I was floating in.

It was my nephew, Scott, who had come to spend a couple of weeks with us. A whipper-snapper of a young man at age eleven, he shot at life from the hip without the need, ever, to stop and reload. Two buddies, we had a lot to catch up on, and we took our time, just two guys hanging out.

This was Scott's second day of his first trip to Hawai'i and we were both temporarily spent after body-surfing for three hours. Even still his eyes were big and full of adventure and he just kept talking about how beautiful and exciting everything was.

Jokingly, I tossed my head up at the sky (as if to ask God) and said "I wonder what the poor people are doing today?" It was an old line, but it was still fun.

Scott really liked that one. He picked up on it right away. From then on, every day when we were really having fun together in some special way he would say "Gee, Uncle John, I wonder what the poor people are doing today?"

And we came up with a whole list of what *they* were doing. Some people *really were poor* and stuck in some horrible situation somewhere, and then some were *just poorly stuck* in their BMW in rush hour traffic on some freeway, maybe in Kansas City or Pittsburgh. But we weren't poor by any common measurement. No sirree! We had our teeth and our hair and our tans and the sun and good-looking girls and palm trees and Coca-Cola and an emerald lagoon with a gentle breeze and ocean waves. Life was great.

When he did pause from time to time and day to day, Scott always came to reflect upon his situation with the words "I'm having a GREAT vacation here", or "I love Hawai'i", and *"I wonder what the poor people are doing today."*

"Uh-oh," I wondered, hoping he understood the intent of my original humor and would somehow in the future gracefully negotiate the life choices that would soon besiege him on his journey into adulthood.

"Always choose time over money"
— Robert Fulghum

One day toward the end of Scott's visit the three of us were having lunch in our humble little cottage in Lanikai. After a meal of homemade chili (Scott was learning the recipe from me) I suggested to Davey that she finish her work back in the office, and Scott and I do the dishes. Besides teaching Scott jungle-hiking and paddle-ball and surfing and learning the fine art of the Macintosh, I was trying to get in a quick course on the independent skills necessary to take care of oneself in today's world. After all, I explained, one day he would be a bachelor and would need to know how to survive.

Scott

"You mean how to be a man's man! Right Uncle John?," Scott guessed correctly, full of enthusiasm.

A deal was struck. I would clear and he would rinse. He would wash and I would dry. We would be done in no time. Then Scott discovered we didn't have an automatic dish washer.

"Where's the dishwasher?" Scott asked.

"Don't have one," I replied.

"Did you ever have one?"

"Sure, Davey and I each have had more than one in our lives, but we don't have one now."

"What did you do with them?" Scott asked, suddenly trying to think this mystery all the way through. He had never done dishes without an electric dishwasher in his entire life and he had done the dishes lots of times for his mom and dad.

"We either sold them or gave them away." I answered.

"Why?" He was asking an honest question.

I explained that selling them may have been part of selling our homes, and, that if we'd given them away it was no big deal since giving things away sometimes allows you to keep what you lose. At any rate all of it was part of a big decision that enabled us to sail the Pacific Ocean for three years and it was indeed, without a shadow of a doubt, the best three years of our lives. We had made real choices, some not so easy, about what we wanted out of life. Although we would love to have a dishwasher, and even missed one, we didn't have one.

"Besides," I blurted out with a hint of anxiety creeping into my voice, *"it's good for you to see how the other half lives!"*

Scott pensively passed the white porcelain plate back and forth underneath the steady stream of warm water pouring from our plumbed faucet, washing the soap suds off. He was unruffled by my somewhat complicated answer, yet thinking so hard I could hear the gears turning in his head. Then he looked up at me and cracked the biggest grin I've ever seen on an eleven-year-old.

"And *what half is that* Uncle John? *The rich half or the poor half?*" The kid even winked.

There was a short pause of about half a second and then we both exploded in spontaneous laughter, in total harmony with each other.

I guess I'm reminded once again that most of the friends we make along the way, regardless of their age, are our teachers, or gurus, in one way or the other.

"You and I,
we were captured.
We took our souls and we flew away.
We were right, we were giving.
That's how we kept what we gave away."

— Neil Young, *Comes a Time*

Davey and I wanted to get away from the "nature of the beast," away from a world where the most important thing is money and desires are fueled by greed. We did get away from *that* in the state of grace that comes from being in the middle of the ocean in a small boat. We also came to realize during *Querencia's* travels that it *was true*. Wherever there are men and women doing business in the world there is also going to be *the beast* at some level or another. Unless we chose not to live among men, like hermits, this reality had to be accepted. But having lived the dream as well as the reality strengthened us, and we felt fortunate and even blessed to have had such a wonderful voyage on *Querencia*. Now, even as we live closer to society again, we keep that courage to continue to dream. We know how important it is to value our beliefs and respect each other.

Our cruising years had a lasting, positive effect on our couple, molding us into a tandem force to face the future together. We have crossed so many waters to get where we are, shared so many experiences, drank from the same cup of happiness and sadness repeatedly, once again, without the normal distractions. This life let us realize the depth of our love for each other in a way that one never forgets. I had been searching a long time for someone exactly like Davey and when I found her she made *it* all worthwhile. Together we saw the light, we sailed the dream, we looked upon the world anew. Real love is more than a relationship, it is an *understanding*.

Each and everyone of us is truly "sailing his dream" in a journey called *life*. Our actions follow our thoughts and our thoughts are like the weather. They come and go. They can be sunny and happy, or they can be stormy and worrisome. In the end, what we do with our glorious once-in-a-lifetime opportunity boils down to freewill and choice. Certainly to say anything else is for most of us an excuse.

> *"Let go into the mystery*
> *Let yourself go"*
> -Van Morrison, *the mystery*

Every time we say we *"have* to do" something we'd better mean what we say rather than just saying what we mean. When we say "have" that should mean everything we have — all our resources, each and everyone of them, including freewill and choice. From my adventure I know that each person at sometime in his life would do well to be left to his own devices, cradled in nature's arms, far from the beaten path. Everyone's life could be changed by being more daring and willing to let go of old ways and old insecurities. Many people have wishbones where their backbone ought to be. If an opportunity presents itself to you for an adventure take the calculated risk. You may very well return knowing that being alive in the mystery is reason alone for song and dance.

Querencia remains for us a place to go home to all of these feelings. It continues for us to be a shelter, a refuge, a centering experience.

Sometimes we go out and anchor overnight. Filling a kerosene lantern can bring back a flood of memories. We can gaze at the heavens and remind ourselves of the infinite beauty of the stars that are always with us, or go to sleep in our v-berth and retire just a moment from the busy world. In the morning, if we really wanted to, we could weigh anchor and sail away to another paradise across the big blue sea.

Glossary

abaft the beam — behind a perpendicular line extending out from the middle of the boat

abeam — off the beam or on the side of the boat

aft — towards the stern of the boat; to move aft is to move back

ahi — yellowfin, ahi; a type of tuna

Aladdin cleat — a cleat that attaches to the backstay over the cockpit, usually used for hanging a lantern

anchorage — a place for anchoring

astern — in the direction of, or behind, the stern

backstay — a wire mast support leading aft to the deck or another mast

backwinded — when the wind hits the leeward side of the sails

bar — a shoal

batten — a short piece of wood or plastic inserted in a sail to keep it taut

beam — the greatest width of the boat, usually in the middle

bearing — direction according to compass

berth — sleeping bunk aboard the boat

bight — a bend in the shoreline

binnacle — compass stand

bitter end — the final inboard end of chain or line

block — pulley

bluewater sailing — open ocean sailing, as opposed to being in a lake or sound

bone in her teeth — sailing well underway such that spray is thrown out at the stem of the boat

boot stripe — a different color strip of paint at the waterline

bow — forward end of a boat

bright work — varnished woodwork or polished metal

broach — a turning or swinging of the boat that puts the beam of the boat against the waves, creating a danger of swamping or capsizing

bulkhead — a partition below decks that separates one part of the vessel from another

bulwarks — rail around the deck

buoy — floating marker used for navigation

cabin sole — the bottom surface of the enclosed space under the deck of a boat *canvas* — slang for sail. Originally sails were made of canvas.

catamaran — twin hulled boat

celestial navigation — to calculate your position using time, the position of celestial bodies, and mathematical tables

chafe gear — gear used to prevent damage by rubbing

Chichester — Sir Francis Chichester, the great English sailor who authored the terrific books *Alone Across the Atlantic* and *Gypsy Moth Circles the Globe*

chocks — a heavy metal fitting fixed to the deck of a ship through which a line for mooring, towing, or anchor rode is passed

ciguatera — a severe type of food poisoning caused by eating contaminated fish

cleat — a two-horned fitting for securing a line

clear the decks — remove unnecessary things from the decks

clew — the lower aft corner of the fore and aft sails

close hauled — sails and boom pulled in tight, enabling the boat to point as high as possible to the direction the wind is coming from

clove hitch — two half hitches

coaming — the raised border around the cockpit, or a hatch to keep out water

companionway — staircase that leads to the cabin

course — compass heading or the angle of the boat in sailing against the wind

crabbing — going sideways due to set (also catching crabs!)

D signal — safety signal, "Keep clear of me. I am maneuvering with difficulty."

deadhead — a floating log

deck plate — a metal plate fitting on the deck that can be opened to take on fuel or water

DR — dead reckoning, deduced reckoning; your position based on speed, direction, and time

dorado — a dolphinfish (misnomer), same as mahi mahi

double ender — boat with a pointed bow and stern

dinghy — a small open boat, usually carried aboard a yacht for going ashore

draft — water depth required to float the boat

ebb — tide passing from high to low, with the current going out to sea

El Niño — a warm inshore current annually flowing south along the coast of Ecuador. About every seven to ten years it extends down the coast of Peru, where it has a devastating effect.

fall off — to pay off to leeward or away from the wind

fathom — nautical measurement equivalent to a depth of six feet

fiddle — strip around a table to prevent items from falling off when the boat is at a heel

fishhook — slang sailing expression for a piece of metal or shroud that cuts or stabs you, the injury usually not discovered until later

fix — the determined boat's position

fluke — the digging end of the anchor; also wind irregularity

flood — incoming tidal current

flotsam — floating items of a ship or its cargo at sea, floating debris

fo'c'sle — separate crew quarters before the mast

Force 8 — gale force wind on the Beaufort Wind Scale

foredeck — the forward part of a boat's main deck

foresail — forward sail

fouled — caught or twisted up

futzing — meddling or fooling around

genoa — also known as genny, usually the biggest jib on the boat

GMT — Greenwich Meridian Time, also known as Universal Time

GPS — global positioning system; uses satellites in fixed orbits

going to weather — to sail against the prevailing wind and seas

gooseneck — fitting that secures the boom to the mast

Great Circle — a course plotted on the surface of the globe that is the shortest distance between two points

ground tackle — anchor and anchor gear

gunnels — also gunwhale; the boat railing

halyard — also halliard; the cordage used to haul the head of a sail up the mast

hanks — metal hooks used to secure a sail to a stay; to hank on a sail is to hook it on a stay using the hanks

hard over — turning the wheel as far as possible

harden up — to steer closer to the wind, usually by pulling in on the sheets

hatch — opening on deck with a cover

haul around — change from a run to a reach

head — currently the bathroom aboard a boat

head (of a sail) — upper corner of a sail

headsail — a sail forward of the mast

heave to — to stop forward movement by bringing the vessel's bow into the wind and keeping it there

heaves — upward displacing swells

heel — the lean of a sailboat when sailing; the extent of the tilt of the boat

helm — the wheel

hike out — climb to windward

hook — anchor

hove to — see heave to

hull speed — the fastest a sailboat will go, usually dependent on
      length of the hull at the waterline

inverter — electrical power converter; converts square-wave DC current
      to sine-wave AC current

iron spinnaker — auxiliary engine

jack line — a line run for safety purposes from the cockpit forward to the
      bow of the boat, inside the rail. Clipping on to the jack line
      with the lanyard of our safety harnesses we were able to mini-
      mize being lost overboard when going forward to crew in
      severe conditions

Jack-Tar — a sailor from the clipper ship days, so named because they
      would tar their hair to prevent infection and make it easy to cut

jetsam — debris, jettisoned items, floating at sea

jib — a foresail. On a cutter this is the forward most sail, as opposed to
      staysail located between the jib and the main

jibe — also gybe; to turn the boat downwind from one side of the wind to
      the other

jig — fishing technique of lowering a weighted lure until just above the
      bottom, then alternately jerking the rod upwards and lowering it
      to give action to the lure

kapu — also tapu (Tahitian); to be taboo. In Polynesian society, in
      addition to forbidden locations there were also various culture
      taboos

ketch — two masted sailboat that has an after mast forward of the rudder

knot — a nautical mile (equivalent to 1.15 miles or 1.852km). Also, any
      of various tangles of line formed by methodically passing the
      free end through loops and drawing it tight.

landfall — first sight of land

lanyard — a short rope or cord that attaches to an item onboard a boat,
      usually for keeping it attached to the boat

latitude — an angular measurement or distance measured in degrees,
      north or south from the equator which is 0°.

lazaret — a storage space below the deck in the cockpit

lee — the side away from the direction of the wind, also used in context
      to refer to a sheltered place out of the wind, as in the lee of the
      island

lee cloth — a cloth hung on the lee side of a berth (the down side when
      the boat has heel to it) to keep one from rolling out of their bunk

lee shore — a shore that wind blows onto; it is best to stay well off a lee
      shore in a storm

leeward — downwind

Lin Pardie — contemporary sailor and author (70s and 80s) recognized
      for her accomplishments

lifeline — stout line around the deck of the boat to keep crew from
     falling overboard

list — inclination of a boat due to excess weight on one side or the other

longitude — distance in degrees east or west of Greenwich, England,
     meridian which is 0°

mahimahi — a powerful fish with a large head, found in tropical and
     subtropical waters

mainsail — the main sail of the sail boat set off the mast and main boom

marlinespike — a pointed metal tool for separating the strands of a rope
     in splicing

meat hook — slang expression for a large fishing hook

midships — the middle of the boat

mooring — a float providing a tie off for a boat, usually set to a
     permanent anchor

Mother Carey's Chickens — storm petrels

motor-sailing — sailing with the motor on and in gear

motu — moku (Hawaiian); small island usually at the reef

offing — seaward, a safe distance from shore

old salt — a very experienced and/or old sailor

onboard — on the boat

orcas — killer whales

P flag — signal flag known as the "Blue Peter" [blue square in a white]
     that indicates the vessel is about to proceed to sea."

pāhua — giant clam found in tropical waters

painter — a line used for securing or towing a boat

pareau — (traditional Polynesian one-piece wrap); also lavalava

part — fray or break

Paul Gaugin — French painter known for his Marquesan and Tahitian
     works after 1891

pay out — to slacken on a line

pedestal — columnar support for the wheel in the cockpit

phosphorescence — luminescence

plumeria — a fragrant blossoming tree found in the tropics and subtropics

pooped — having a wave wash over the stern of the boat

port — the left side of the boat; also a harbor

pull — in rowing, to row an oar, putting your back into it

put in — to enter a port or harbor

pitch — plunging of a vessel fore and aft

Polaris — the North Star, the star that is located over the north pole
     and is the center of revolution for the Earth

pulpit — platform over the sprit of the boat enclosed in a metal
     framework

preventer — line and tackle which limits the movement of the boom, usually for the purpose of preventing accidents

quarter — the side of a boat aft of beam and forward of the stern

Q flag — all yellow signal flag meaning "My vessel is healthy and I request free pratique."

quay — wharf used to discharge cargo

rail — top of the bulwarks on the edge of the deck

reaching — sailing a course that is neither close hauled or downwind

reef — to shorten sail, usually by partially lowering it and tying it off with reefing lines

rigging — standing rigging refers to shrouds and stays, while running rigging refers to halyards and sheets that control the sails

rode - the line or chain attached to the anchor

roller - a wave

rolling heap — slang expression meaning ocean

rudder — plate hinged to the stern of the vessel used to steer the boat by turning the wheel or tiller

running — going with the wind, downwind sailing (to run downwind)

running backs — running backstays; temporary backstays used to stabilize the mast and prevent undue flexing in the pumping action of the sea over an extended voyage. Usually attached by tangs to the mast opposite to where the staysail stay is attached.

rip current — as in tide rip; water disturbance created by conflicting current and wind

safety harness — a harness, usually made of webbing, worn over the shoulders and around the chest equipped with a lanyard for preventing being swept overboard in severe conditions

sampan — a small boat with a narrow design, originally found in Japan and China

samson post — also sampson post;

salon — also saloon; main social cabin of a boat

SAT NAV — satellite navigation unit; uses satellites in moving orbits

scope — the length or extent of anchor rode

scopolamine — a drug prescribed for motion sickness

sculling oar — a large oar used for propelling a boat by moving from side to side; also used for an emergency rudder

scuppers — overboard drain holes on deck

seized - bound together

self-tending — tacks itself

set — the direction of the tide or current, the leeway course of the boat

shackle — a metal link which can be open and closed for joining chain to anchor, etc.

sheet — the lines leading from the clew of a sail with which you pull in or let it out *ship in seas* — take in seas

shroud — a wire used to stay or hold a mast in position to which the sails may also be hanked

single sideband — a radio frequency used by boats equipped with shortwave radio

skipjack — bonito, aku; a type of tuna

slats — battens

slatting — flapping

snubber — a spring line tied from the boat to chain rode, usually near the water's surface. It helps disperse tension forces. It also prevents damage to the boat by ground tackle and can help in the retrieval of the ground tackle in heavy weather. (to reduce the snap of the rode when it stretched out)

soggering — being lazy and unassuming of responsibility

sou'wester — a wind coming from the southwest

sounding — diving

spreaders — small spars between the mast and shrouds

spring line — a line tied between two opposing forces that has a neutralizing effect on the force vectors, such as those creating by surge. At the dock with a bow line and stern line tied off, a spring line is often added to limit the working movements of a floating vessel even more.

sprit — a spar that extends the bow of the boat

starboard — right; on the right side of the boat

staysail — On a cutter this is the sail located between the jib and the main sail

stern — the rear of the boat

stow — to store onboard

stores — provisions stored onboard

studding out a sail — extending a sail using a whisker pole

sump pump — small pump for shower drainage

surge — rising and falling of the sea, usually due to wave action

tack — change the sail course by bringing its bow across the wind, moving the boom to the other side of the boat when beating

tack (of a sail) — forward lower corner of a sail

taffrail log — Walker log; a propeller drawn through the water that operates an odometer on the boat registering the distance sailed

tang — a fitting on the mast for securing rigging

tender — dinghy

the hard — land

tonnage — the weight, in tons, of a boat. Querencia weighs 7 tons net.

topping lift — a line or wire for lifting the boom that runs from the top of the mast *torch* — old sailing term for lantern that throws out a beam of light. Now it also can refer to a flashlight.

trailing — dragging, as in "dragging a line"

trimaran — a boat with three hulls

underway — moving under power of sail or motor

victuals — food

vittles — victuals

v-berth — usually the forward berth of the boat, located in the bow

VHF — very high frequency radio

watch - working shift

warp — move a boat by hauling on lines attached to docks or anchors

whip — rope rove

whisker pole — a spar used to hold out the clew of the jib when running

winch — mechanical device for hauling in a line

windlass — winch for hauling in the anchor chain or line

wind rose — a diagram usually shown on pilot charts that indicates the frequency and intensity of wind from different directions for a particular place

windward — upwind

wing on wing — running before the wind with sails on opposite sides such as the main on one side of the boat and the genny on the other

yar — fit and beautiful (boat)

yaw, yawing — to turn from side to side in an uneven course

zincs — zinc plates attached to the hull to minimize electrolysis (and ultimate failure) of the metal in the rudder and other areas

Index

Acumen, 40
Ahuna Motu, 230
'Alalākeiki Channel, 298
Ala Moana, 310
Ala Wai Yacht Harbor, 291, 308-17, 319
Alcratraz Island, 67
Aldebaran, 119
'Alenuihāhā Channel, 295-98, 301, 309
Alford, Vern and Jo, 26, 123
Algol, 119
Allen, Woody, 319
Alone Across the Atlantic (Chichester), 51
Anacapa Island, 95
Anacortes, 26
Anderson, Captain David, 291
Apple Tree Cove, 12,
Arena, Pt., 62, 64
Arguello, Pt., 83
Astral Rose, 241, 244
Athena, 290, 316-17, 326-27
Atlantic High (Buckley), 6
'Au'au Channel, 300, 303, 332, 346
Auckland Harbour, 73, 242
Auriga, 119
Avalon Bay, 100
Baja, 107, 116
Bare Island, 18
Battleship Island, 23
Beagle, 186
Betelgeuse, 119
Bidet, Lauren, 189-191, 201-203, 209, 249, 254-55
Big Island: *See* Hawai'i Island
Black Pt., Catalina, 96
Black Pt., O'ahu, 307
Bligh, Captain, 126
Blonde Reef, 284
Blue Banks Anchorage, 95
Bodega Bay, 65
Bogart, Humphrey, 121, 159, 288
Bora Bora Yacht Club, 182, 189-90, 206, 240-41, 249
Bora Bora, 104, 105, 129-30, 137, 150, 168, 171, 176-256, 264, 273, 288-89, 310, 338, 345, 348
Borgnine, Ernest, 62
Boundary Bay, 21
Brendon Voyage, The (Severin), 107
British Columbia, 16, 26
Brown's Point, 9
Buchon, Pt., 81
Bucke, R. M., 273
Buckley, William F., 6, 7
Buffet, Jimmy, 184
Burguyne Bay, 27
Burroughs, John, 191
Cabo San Lucas, 101
California, 1, 2, 5, 10, 22, 43-106, 147, 152, 183, 238, 240-41, 250, 278, 315, 348
Canada del Refugio, 88
Canada, xii, 11, 16, 176, 238
Canis Major, Canis Minor, 119
Cape Cod, 9
Cape Flattery, 9, 36
Cape Horn, 83, 115
Cape Mendocino, 50, 54
Cape San Martin, 80
Cape Tikapo, 144
Capella, 119

Carbrillo, Juan Rodriguez, 98
Carina, xii, 78, 101
Carmel, 77-79
Carney, Art, 23
Caroline Island, 262
Carr Inlet, 9
Carter, Jo and Eli, 14, 17
Cascades, 10, 13, 19
Cassiopeia, 119
Castor, 119
Chai Ling, 92
Channel Islands, 79-100
Charity, 291
Chart Guide for Southern California, 94
Chichester, Sir Francis, xiv, 51, 107, 114, 121
Christy Anchorage, 91-93
City of Eureka, 47
Claytor, Greg and Elaine, 247
Clouds of Magellan, 132
Coconut Island, 287
Columbia River, 41, 46
Comes a Time (Young), 351
Commencement Bay, 8, 9
Conception, Pt., 82-85
Constellation, 305
Cook Islands, 187, 208, 240, 250, 253-54, 312
Cook, Captain James, 157, 187, 284, 328, 332
Cooper, Jack, 288
Coronado Islands, 106, 107, 240
Coronado, 2, 102
Cousteau Society, 149
Coy, John 133
Crane, Orin L., 234
Crescent City, 46-49, 51
Cross, Chrisopher, 94
Cygnus, 306
Dalai Lama, the, 206-07
Dana, Richard, 32, 76
Danelsson, Bengt, 154
Dante Alighieri, 111
Darwin, Charles, 186
Deception Pass, 12
Deo Gratias, 291, 313, 320, 325
Desolation Angels (Kerouac), 259, 294
Diamond Head, 282, 307, 310, 313
Diver's Cove, 27
Dole, James, 332-33
Don't Push the River (Stevens), 156
Drake, Sir Francis, 66
Dutch Harbor, 69
Dye, John and Debbie, 290
Eagle Point, 18
Easter Island (Rapa Nui), 18, 155-56
Echo Bay, 18, 19
Eel Canyon, 50
El Niño, 39, 253
Eliot, T. S., 325
Emerald Cove, 97
Emerson, Ralph Waldo, 209
Emm Too, 49, 56, 78
Empress Hotel, 16
Erickson, Harold and Edie, 78
Farepiti, Pt., 193
Farepoe, Pt., 236
Favorite, 21
Fiji, 242, 250, 312, 314-16, 324

Five Needles, 319-24, 331
Florence, iii
Fort Bragg, 52, 53, 307
Fox Cove, 20, 21, 24
Franklin, Benjamin, 64
Freud, Sigmund, 7
Friday Harbor, 14, 17, 25, 28, 29, 149, 175
From Here to Eternity (movie) 334-35
Fulghum, Robert, 349
Fuller, Buckminster, 348
Galápagos Islands, 251
Ganges, 27
Garden of the Gods, 336
Garrison Bay, 23
Gaugin, Paul, 148
Gemini, 119
Gencauskas, Joe and Anita, 9, 23, 314
Gipsy Moth Circles the Globe (Chichester), 51, 107
Glorietta Bay, 102-106
Golden Gate Bridge, xii, 66
Golden Guide of Weather, 123
Goodman, Benny 100
Graham, Robin, 301
Greene, Stuart, 247
Greenpeace, 69-75
Griffin Bay, 25
Guadalupe Island, 80, 107, 108
Gulf Islands, 26
Gulf of Santa Catalina, 101
Gulf of the Farallones, 65
Gull Island, 95
Gypsy Spirit, 92
H.M.S. Raglund, 11
Haleakalā, 282
Half Moon Bay, 76
Halulu Heiau, 342
Hamilton, George, 161
Hammarskjold, Doug, 143
Hanamanioa Point, 298-99
Haro Strait, 17, 23, 27
Harris, Chris, 250, 312-14, 320
Hawai'i Island, 155, 275, 279, 281-96, 310, 335
Hawai'i, 51, 73, 90, 155, 181, 197, 231, 248, 251,
              254, 257, 264, 269, 272, 274, 281-353
Ha'apitipiti Motu, 230
Hāmākua Coast, 294
Henry Island, 23
Heyerdahl, Thor, 154
Higman, R. James, vii
Hilo, 269, 275, 281, 284-94, 308
Hiscock, Eric, xiv
Hōkūle'a, 283
Holmes, Olvier Wendell, 66
Home is the Sailor (Graham), 301
Honolua Bay, 310, 346-47
Honolulu, 294, 290, 294, 305-06, 311
Honopū Bay, 331
Hope Island, 12
Horn, Paul, 133, 134
Hot Water (Buffet), 184
Huahine Island, 178
Hudson, Bo and Annie, 288
Hulopo'e Bay (White Mānele Bay): *See* Mānele Bay
Hurricane Douglas, 260
Hurricane Ignatio, 335
Hurricane Iwa, 253

Huxley, Aldous, 287
Hālawa Valley, 347
Indian Rock, 97
Inside (Paul Horn), 133
Irma, 235, 250
Island Sea Shell, 90
Isthmus Cove, 98
Jack Nicholson, 34
Java, 26, 123
Jung, Carl, 7, 31
Jupiter, 126
Ka'alaneo, 332
Kā'anapali, 346
Ka'ena Point, 332
Kamehameha, 331, 341-42
Kahekili's Leap, 341-42
Kaho'olawe Island, 298, 331
Kalohi Channel, 302-04, 328, 330, 336
Kalua, 319, 322-27
Kāne'āpua Rock, 341
Kaua'i Island, 156, 282, 310, 341
Kaula'inā'iwi Island, 287
Kaululā'au, 332
Kaumalapau Harbor, 331, 333
Kaunakakai, 303
Kaūnōlū, 331, 340, 342
Kealaikahiki Channel, 331
Keana'ō'io Cave, 335
Kerouac, Jack, 259, 294
Kesey, Ken, 54
Kīlauea Volcano, 281-82
Kingston, 12
Kohala Mountains, 295
Kon Tiki (Heyerdahl), 154, 253
Kona, 292
Konchar, Gus, ii, 291, 313, 320
Kūhiō Bay, 287
Kumukahi, Pt., 275, 279
La Conner, 14
La Jolla, 1, 2, 77, 101
Lā'au Point, 328
Lahaina, 301-02, 346
Lake Union, 5
Lāna'i Island, 300, 303, 319, 329-36, 346
Lange, David, 73-75
Lāna'ihale, 335
Lanikai, 348-350
Le Blanc, Russ and Kathy, 77, 326
Leleiwi, Pt., 275
Leo, 119
Lewis, Jerry, 296
Lila Marguerite, 77, 326
Lion Wing, 288
Little Fisherman Cove, 98
Loma, Pt., 101, 106
Long Island, 24, 24
Lono (Hawaiian god), 328
Lono Harbor, 310, 325, 328-30
Los Angeles, 100, 310
Love Boat, 104
Maclaine, Shirley, 255
Magellan, Ferdinand, 132
Maggie May (Stewart), 243
Magic Island, 310
Magu, Pt., 278
Malibu, 2

Mānele Bay, 310, 331,334-35, 338-341, 346
Maple Bay, 27
Marcele, 26
Marin Peninsula, 66
Marina Del Ray, 291
Marquesas, 101, 104, 105, 126, 138, 141, 143-169, 171,
        187, 238, 269, 283, 306, 315, 348
Matai Bar (Marquesas), 161-165
Mataiva, 176
Matia Island, 18, 24
Maui (Hawaiian god), 303
Maui Island, 155, 295-96, 310, 332, 335-36,
        338-39, 346
Mauna Kea, Mauna Loa, 282
Maupiti Island, 201
Max, Peter, 9
McGrady, Gale C. (Mac), vii, 3, 4, 273, 314
McGrady, Kyle, iii
McGrady, Rain Juli, vii, 26-29, 68, 195
McKintyre, Joan, 333-34
Mead, Margaret, 154
Memories, Dreams, Relfections (Jung), 31
Mendocino Bay, 52, 53, 56
Metata: *See* Viritua
Mexico, 26, 80, 103-04, 107, 115, 117, 269, 315
Michener, James, 179
Milky Way, 91, 130-31
Mission Bay, 2
Moby Dick (Melville), 302
Moloka'i Island, 302-06, 310, 325, 328-30, 335-36,
        346-347
Molokini Islet, 299-300, 303
Monterey, 7, 76-80, 101, 302
Moon, Bob and Rita, 340-42
Morley, Christopher, 87, 197
Morrison, Van, 352
Mosquito Pass, 23
Mt. Rainier, 10, 19, 275
Mummy Rock, 25
Munro, George C., Munro Trail, 335
Mururoa Atoll, 239, 256
Mussel Rock, 46
Neah Bay, 35, 36
Neumann, Steve, 290, 314-17, 325
New Caledonia, 208
New Zealand, 73, 155, 197, 208, 215, 241-42
Newman, Paul, 192
Newport Beach, 241, 250
Newton, Sir Isaac, 106
Nihoa Island, 282
Ni'ihau Island, 341
Noyo River, 53-58, 61
Nuka Hiva, 105, 138, 141-69, 183
Oa Oa Hotel, 241, 247, 249, 254
'Olelo No'eau, (Pukui), 280
Olympic Mountains, 9. 10, 13
Ome Motu, 251
Orcas Island, 18, 28
Oregon State, 13, 15, 26
Orion, 96, 119, 306
Osborne, Ken, vii, 100, 122, 300
Out on a Limb (Maclaine), 255
O'ahu Island, 155, 253, 282, 302, 306, 328, 335, 346
O'temanu, Mt., 182, 198, 213-217, 229, 231, 244
Pacific Island Pilot, 169
Pacific Maritime Net, 118

Pahua, Pt., 182, 241
Palaoa, Pt., 340
Pailolo Channel, 303, 346-47
Pali Kaholo, 331
Pali Lei no Haunui, 334
Pan, Peter, 210
Panama Canal, 215, 250, 326
Papeete, 149, 178, 188-89, 225, 232, 234, 238
Pardie, Lin, 34
Parker, Jim and Sara, 240
Patos Island, 18, 21
Pauli, Wolfgang, 314
Pele (Hawaiian goddess), 282
Pender Island, 20, 27
Penguin Bank, 306
Penn Cove, 13
Pepe'ekeo, Pt., 275, 294
Pereiera, Fernando, 73, 75
Perseus, 119
Philippines, 215, 332
Pinos, Pt., 76, 79
Pleiades, 119
Pollus, 119
Port Angeles, 34, 35
Possession Sound, 13
Postma, Richard, Martine and Maui, 179, 181-82, 251
Povai Bay, 214
Previos Island 27
Prevost Bay, 18
Procyon, 119
Pu'u Kukui Pt., 302
Purple Rain (Prince), 280
Pukui, Mary Kawena, 280
Puget Sound, 1, 5, 6, 8-10, 12, 41, 221, 300
Pu'u Pehe, 331
Queen Victoria, 326-27
Radio Bay, 287-92
Raiatea Island, 198, 200, 233-240, 243
Rainbow Warrior, 69-75, 250
Raratonga, 254
Rautoanui Pass, 236
Rawn, Bob and Beverly, 53-58
Red Isles Reef, 27
Redford, Robert, 340
Refugio Beach, 87
Regulus, 119
Resonde II, 78, 101, 112
Reyes, Pt., 65
Reynolds, Burt, 208
Rigel, 119
Right Where Your Are Sitting Now (Wilson), 300
Robbins, Tom, 13, 121
Roche Harbor, 17, 18, 22, 24, 27, 28
Rocos Alijos, 109
Rogers, Will, 234
Roosevelt, Teddy, 22
Rosario Strait, 14
Roth, Hal, 148
Sagan, Carl, 186
Sailing (Cross), 94
Sailing (Sutherland, Stewart), 240
Sailing Through Paradise (Buckley), 4
Salstpring Island, 27
San Diego, 78, 95, 101-108, 143, 146, 269, 284,
        288, 306-07
San Francisco, xii, 6, 29, 33, 46, 48, 52, 62, 66-76,

112, 165, 206, 250, 253, 288, 328
San Juan, 53, 54
San Juan Channel, 34
San Juan Island, 17, 22-25, 27
San Juan Islands, 5, 6, 11, 13-29, 212, 238
San Louis Obispo, 81
San Louis, Pt., 81
San Miguel Island, 93, 94
San Sebastian, 95
Sanata Barbara Channel, 83, 84, 89
Sansum Narrows, 27
Santa Ana, 92, 104
Santa Barbara Island, 95, 96
Santa Catalina Island, 96-98
Santa Claus, 291
Santa Cruz Island, 89, 91-95
Santa Nicholas Island, 95
Santa Rosa Island, 91, 93, 94
Saratoga Passage, 13
Satellite Channel, 27
Sausalito, 67-75
Sea Gull, 290
Sea of Cortez, 101
Seashell, 15, 17
Seattle, 3, 5, 7, 9, 10, 14, 18, 26, 29, 33, 80, 113,
        172, 186, 195
Shakespeare, William, 61, 234
Shark Rock, 341
Shelter Island, 2, 102
Shilshole, 10, 11, 33
Shipwreck Beach, 336
Silver Strand Beach, 102
Sirius, 119, 221
Skagit Valley, 13, 14
Skipjack Island, 18
Slocum, Joshua, xiv
Smith, L. P., 234
Snoring Bay, 29
Snyder, Ed and Dale, 27, 29, 33-48, 59, 308
Socrates, 130
Solomon Islands, 157
South Point, 292
Southern Cross, 119, 184, 315
Stacked Deck, 340-41
Steilacoom, 9
Stevens, Barry, 156
Stewart, Rod, 240, 244
Still Life With Woodpecker (Robbins), 121
Strait of Juan de Fuca, 12, 14, 34
Strawberry Point, 13
Stuart island, 15, 18
Sucia Island, 18-21
Sumba, 49
Sunbeams, The Sun, 273
Sur, Pt., 79
Sutherland, Gavin, 240
Suva, Suva Yacht Club, 315-16
Swanson Channel, 27
Tacoma Narrows, 9
Tacoma, 8, 9, 82
Taha'a Island, 235, 236
Tahiti, 155, 168, 178, 208, 238, 256, 284, 288,
        291, 315, 333, 337
Taiohae Bay, 145
Tatoosh Island, 36
Taurus, 119

Teahuatea, Pt., 218
Teavanui Pass, 179, 209, 223, 235, 255, 290
Telegraph Harbour, 27
Temple, Bob and Ginny, 22-24, 159, 284-85, 308
Ten Wishes, 293
Teviriroa Motu, 230
The Mystery (Morrison), 352
Thetis island, 27
Thoreau, Henry David, 7, 213
Topua Motu, 203
Travolta, John, 208
Trinidad Head, 49
Tuamotus, 74, 168, 176, 187, 208
Turn Point, 18
Twain, Mark, 301
Two Years Before The Mast (Dana), 32
Two on a Big Ocean (Roth), 148
U.S. Coastal Pilot, 77, 83, 253, 299, 302, 304
Ua Huka Island, 141, 144
Ua Pu, 169
Ulysses, 134
Upolu Island, 156
'Upolu Light, 295
Utaroa, 234, 238-240
Vaitape, 187, 188, 190, 206, 209, 215, 220, 247, 249, 254
Valdez, 302
Van Buskirk, Al and Ginny, 8, 15, 16, 21, 28
Vancouver Island, 16, 27
Vanity, 151, 158, 166, 168
Vashon Island, 1, 133
Vavau, 187
Vehia, 179, 181, 182
Venus, 126
Victoria, B.C., 16
Viritua, Metata, 191-201, 214-15, 217-222, 231,
        255, 259, 284, 309, 339
Viti Levu Island, 315
Waikiki, 307-317, 329
Waipi'o Valley, 293
Waldron Island, 18
Washington State, 9, 10, 13-39, 79, 114, 119, 149,
        150, 293. 330
Washington, George, 115
Watts, Alan, 6
Wa'adah Island, 36
Webster's Collegiate Dictionary, 221, 263
Well, Simone, 39
Whale Rock, 25
Whidbey Island, 13
Willows, Dr. Dennis, 149
Wilson, Anton, 300
Witherspoon, Caroline vii, 11, 12, 14, 29, 68,
        102, 195, 284-85, 314
Witherspoon, Paul vii, 11, 12, 29, 102-294, 326,
        328-47
World to The West, A (Cloughley), 197
Woyaya, 241, 250, 312-14, 320, 325
Young, Neil, 11, 351